Great Sto
Kafka and Rilke

Meistererzählungen von
Kafka und Rilke

FRANZ KAFKA
RAINER MARIA RILKE

A Dual-Language Book

Edited and Translated by
STANLEY APPELBAUM

DOVER PUBLICATIONS, INC.
Mineola, New York

Bibliographical Note

This Dover edition, first published in 2003, is a new selection of stories by Kafka and Rilke, presented in the original German text, reprinted from standard editions (the dates of first publication range from 1902 to 1922; see the Introduction for detailed bibliography), together with new English translations by Stanley Appelbaum, who also furnished the Introduction and footnotes.

Library of Congress Cataloging-in-Publication Data

Kafka, Franz, 1883–1924.
  [Short stories. English & German. Selections]
  Great stories by Kafka and Rilke = Meistererzählungen von Kafka und Rilke : a dual-language book / Franz Kafka, Rainer Maria Rilke ; edited and translated by Stanley Appelbaum.
       p. cm.
  ISBN 0-486-43197-5 (pbk.)
  I. Title: Meistererzählungen von Kafka und Rilke. II. Rilke, Rainer Maria, 1875–1926. Short stories. English & German. Selections. III. Appelbaum, Stanley. IV. Title.

PT2621.A26A225 2003
833'.912—dc21

2003053286

Manufactured in the United States of America
Dover Publications, Inc., 31 East 2nd Street, Mineola, N.Y. 11501

Contents

iii

INTRODUCTION

Kafka and Rilke, two titans of early twentieth-century German literature, one Jewish, the other Catholic, were both born in Prague when
Bohemia was still a part of the Austro-Hungarian Monarchy, ruled
from Vienna. The city was characterized by a social dichotomy after
the pan-European revolution year of 1848: the Germans and Jews
concentrated on industry and trade, while the Czechs were principally
farmers and laborers. But by 1880, in an irreversible trend, the
Czechs had captured the majority in the local government, and the
Germans were increasingly marginalized. In this twilight just before
and after 1900, however, the German writing in the city experienced
a kind of golden age, being represented not only by the two authors in
this volume, but also by such others as Franz Werfel, Max Brod, and
Gustav Meyrink. Prague was extremely cosmopolitan, drawing talent
from all around. Much of the writing was experimental, and Kafka and
Rilke were by no means the only purveyors of fantasy and the supernatural.

Kafka

Life. Franz Kafka was born in 1883. His father was a merchant whose
object lessons in arbitrary tyranny shaped his son's psyche and literary
production. After a good secondary education Kafka entered the local
German university, the Karl-Ferdinand, in 1901. There in 1902 he
met Max Brod (1884–1968), who was to be his lifelong friend and ad-
viser, then his literary executor. After receiving a law degree in 1906,
Kafka became a clerk in an insurance firm, while trying his hand at
writing (he had begun by at least 1904). The year 1908 was not only
that of his first small publication, but also that of his joining a semi-
governmental insurance company that handled workmen's accident
claims. He remained with the firm for the next fourteen years, and,
apart from a few journeys abroad (the first in 1909), his biography

consists chiefly of his authorial activities. He never married (he broke off all three of his engagements, two of them to the same woman), and he lived with his parents until he was over thirty.

The year 1912 was crucial for him; he considered one of the stories he wrote that year, "Das Urteil" (usually rendered as "The Judgment," though "The Sentence," or even "The Verdict," would be a better translation), as his breakthrough, the proof that he was justified in seeking fame as an author; in the same year he also began the never-finished novel that would eventually be published as *Amerika* (he continued working on it into 1914), and wrote what is probably his most famous story, "Die Verwandlung" ("The Metamorphosis"; "The Transformation" would be a closer translation, because German possesses the word *Metamorphose,* which he could easily have used, had he so chosen). "Das Urteil" was published in 1913 (periodical) and 1916 (volume), "Die Verwandlung" in 1915 (both forms).

In 1914 he wrote the story "In der Strafkolonie" ("In the Penal Colony"; published 1919) and began his novel *Der Prozeß* (*The Trial,* on which he worked into 1916). In 1916 and 1917 he wrote most of the stories that were to be included in the 1919 volume *Ein Landarzt* (*A Country Doctor*), twelve of which are included in this Dover edition. In 1917 he was diagnosed with tuberculosis, and began taking medical leaves from his job; he was to visit a number of clinics and sanatoriums. By 1920 he was no longer working regularly as a claims investigator, and in 1922 he took early retirement with a pension.

By 1921 he had begun writing his novel *Das Schloß* (*The Castle*). In 1923 he moved to Berlin to work as a free-lance author; in that year he prepared a new volume of short stories, *Ein Hungerkünstler* (*A Hunger Artist*) for publication (two stories from that collection, already published in magazines in 1922, complete the Kafka selections in the present volume). He died in 1924 while still reading proof of that volume, which appeared shortly after his death.

Brod, his literary executor, apparently disobeyed Kafka's last wishes by saving, and eventually publishing, the papers he had left behind. Thus, most of Kafka's work was published posthumously: all three novels, about two thirds of his stories and small prose pieces, extensive diaries, and a large number of letters.

In German-speaking lands, Kafka was a seldom-read cult figure before 1933, when his work was suppressed. Extensive fame first came to him in France and in the United States during the Second World War. Since that war, he has been acclaimed as an international figure of the first rank, a master of fantasy and a major spokesman for twen-

tieth-century man, his terror, confusion, and anguish under the pressure of the world's intrusiveness and his own consciousness.

The Stories Included Here. Of the fourteen stories in this Dover volume, twelve (in their original sequence) are from the volume *Ein Landarzt. Kleine Erzählungen* (*A Country Doctor. Brief Stories*), first published in 1919 by the Kurt Wolff Verlag, Munich and Leipzig. The original volume also contained the title story, "Ein Landarzt," as its second item and, as its last, the story "Ein Bericht für eine Akademie" ("A Report to an Academy").[1] Though Kafka himself referred to these pieces, written from 1915 to 1917, as *Geschichten,* as well as *Erzählungen,* not all of them are what we would normally call "stories," some could be designated as sketches, parables, or character studies.

Several of Kafka's letters to the publisher throw light on the genesis of the volume:

In a letter of July 7, 1917, Kafka states that he is sending thirteen items written during the preceding winter, adding, in one of his frequent fits of self-doubt, "They're far from being what I really intended."

A letter of July 27, 1917, reveals that the publisher was pleased; now Kafka is sending him "Ein Traum," and he suggests including "Vor dem Gesetz," which had already appeared in an *Almanach* (annual sampler volume) of the Kurt Wolff Verlag.

On August 20, 1917, Kafka supplies a list of contents, which includes all fourteen items eventually published in the volume, in their final sequence, but also another story, as third on the list: "Ein Kübelreiter" (later translated as "The Bucket Rider"). This piece was first published in the December 25, 1921 issue of *Die Prager Presse,* and was included, with "Der" replacing "Ein," in posthumous collections, 1931 and 1936.

In his letter of September 4, 1917, Kafka thanks Wolff for a pleasing sample of the forthcoming typography.

On January 27, 1918, he states that the volume is to include fifteen stories; he insists on the sequence of stories he had already furnished, he determines the eventual title, and he supplies the eventual dedication: to his father.

---

1. Those two stories are not here because they already appear in a Dover dual-language Kafka volume, *Best Short Stories / Die schönsten Erzählungen* (1997; same translator; ISBN 0-486-29561-3), along with "Das Urteil," "Die Verwandlung," and "In der Strafkolonie."

A letter dated October 1, 1918, is slightly confusing: Kafka asks the publisher to omit a story called "Ein Mord" ("A Murder"; never mentioned previously) because it is too similar to the story "Ein Brudermord,"[2] and he is apparently just now submitting a manuscript of "Ein Traum"; in addition, he agrees that he won't be sent proofs to read.

Most of the pieces in *Ein Landarzt* had appeared in periodicals (and even books) before the 1919 volume publication:

"Der neue Advokat," "Ein altes Blatt," and "Ein Brudermord" were first published in the July & August 1917 issue of the bimonthly *Marsyas* (edited by Theodor Tagger; published by Heinrich Hochsinn, Berlin).

"Vor dem Gesetz" was first published in the Prague Jewish weekly *Selbstwehr* (*Self-Defense*), September 7, 1915. Then it appeared in 1916 in the Kurt Wolff (Leipzig) yearbook *Vom jüngsten Tag. Ein Almanach neuer Dichtung* (*From the Most Recent Day* [or: *Concerning Judgment Day* (!)]. *An Annual of New Writing*).

"Schakale und Araber" was first published in the great Jewish philosopher Martin Buber's monthly *Der Jude* (*The Jew*; Berlin and Vienna), in the October 1917 issue, together with "Ein Bericht für eine Akademie," with the collective title "Zwei Tiergeschichten" ("Two Animal Stories"). Then it appeared in the anthology volume *Neue deutsche Erzähler* (*New German Story Writers*), edited by J. Sandmeier, Furche Verlag, Berlin, 1918.

"Eine kaiserliche Botschaft" was first published in the September 24, 1919 issue of *Selbstwehr* (see "Vor dem Gesetz," above).

"Die Sorge des Hausvaters" was first published in the December 19, 1919 issue of *Selbstwehr.*

"Ein Traum" was first published in *Das jüdische Prag* (*Jewish Prague*), an anthology published by the editors of *Selbstwehr* in 1916 (dated 1917). Then it appeared again in 1916 in *Der Almanach der neuen Jugend auf das Jahr 1917* (*Annual of New Young Writers for 1917*), edited by Heinz Barger and published by the Verlag Neue Jugend, Berlin. Next, it appeared in the January 6, 1917 issue of the *Prager Tagblatt* (*Prague Daily*).

("Auf der Galerie," "Ein Besuch im Bergwerk," "Das nächste Dorf," and "Elf Söhne" were apparently not published before the 1919 *Landarzt* volume.)

The story "Auf der Galerie," with its circus setting, is representative

---

2. This, apparently an early version of "Ein Brudermord," was indeed dropped from the volume and published separately by Kurt Wolff (Leipzig, 1918) in his annual *Die neue Dichtung* (*New Writing*).

of Kafka's fascination with popular performing arts (see also the last
two Kafka items in this Dover volume).

Though no setting is given for "Ein altes Blatt" and "Eine kaiserliche Botschaft," both the nomadic-invasion situation, in the former,
and the palace that is a city within a city, in the latter, immediately
bring China to mind (and Kafka specifically designated China as his
locale elsewhere).

"Vor dem Gesetz," a very Talmudic parable, appears almost verba-
tim in the key chapter, "Im Dom" ("In the Cathedral"), of *Der Prozeß*.
In the novel the tale is told to the protagonist, Josef K., by a priest, and
they analyze it at length afterward.

The main character in "Ein Traum" has the same name as the one
in *Der Prozeß*.

The last two Kafka stories in this Dover anthology were written in
1922. "Erstes Leid" was first published in 1922 (dated 1921) in the periodical *Genius* (edited by Carl Georg Heide and Hans Mardersteig),
published by Kurt Wolff (Munich). (In a postcard to Brod, dated June
26, 1922, Kafka says he sent it to Wolff the month before, but is thinking of retracting that "repulsive little story.") "Ein Hungerkünstler"
was first published in *Die Neue Rundschau* (*The New Survey*; edited
by Oskar Bie, S. Fischer, and S. Saenger), (October) 1922 issue, published by S. Fischer, Berlin and Leipzig. Both stories later appeared,
along with two others, in the 1924 volume *Ein Hungerkünstler. Vier
Geschichten* (*A Hunger Artist. Four Stories*), published by the Verlag
"Die Schmiede" ("The Smithy"), Berlin, in the series *Die Romane des
XX. Jahrhunderts* (*The Novels of the Twentieth Century*).

"Erstes Leid" is a less fully developed variant of "Ein Hungerkünstler." In both stories an eccentric performer allegorically repre-
sents the creative artist (if not suffering mankind in general). The
practice of presenting trapeze acts in large vaudeville houses is unfor-
gettably depicted in the German silent film *Varieté* (*Variety;
Vaudeville*; 1925; directed by E. A. Dupont).

"Ein Hungerkünstler" is probably the most celebrated Kafka story
in this Dover volume, and it is indeed one of his most intriguing and
most completely worked-out, with his trademark combination of close
reasoning and ultimate enigma. The title is impossible to translate; for
recognition value the old rendering "A Hunger Artist" is retained
here, though it simply isn't English. Unfortunately no standard
English term for a showman who fasts for long periods on public display seems to exist; one dictionary's suggestion, "professional starver,"
is even worse.

In the Kafka items, as well as the Rilke, the present translation, which strives to be very complete and accurate, retains the paragraphing of the original German texts, even though some of the paragraphs are inordinately long for modern American tastes, and some don't come to an end when one speaker of direct dialogue ceases and another takes over.

Rilke

Life. Unlike Kafka, who spent most of his life in Prague, Rilke as an adult had a distaste for the city, probably because of unhappy childhood associations. He was born in 1875 and christened René Maria Rilke, changing his first name to Rainer only in 1897. His father, who had been in the army, was a railroad official. The poet's parents separated when he was nine and, after having been pampered by his mother, he felt abandoned by her as he remained with his father.[3] Between 1886 and 1891 he boarded at two military schools; his father hoped he would become an army officer, but it was a period of great misery for the introspective, unathletic boy. During the next five years he attended a business school and studied with private tutors, while testing his powers as a writer; his first published work was a volume of poetry in 1894.

From 1896 to 1899 Rilke studied in Prague, Munich, and Berlin, while becoming immersed in the world of literature and art. In Munich in 1897 he met Lou Andreas-Salomé (1861–1937); daughter of a Russian general and wife of a university professor, this fascinating writer of stories and literary history had been a friend of Nietzsche. They became lovers and made two journeys to Russia together, from April to June of 1899 and from May to August of 1900; this travel experience was like a mystic revelation to Rilke, who memorialized it in his story cycle *Geschichten vom lieben Gott* (in this Dover volume) and in poetry. (Already deeply committed to art studies, he visited painters as well as writers in Russia.)

From 1900 to 1902 Rilke lived in the artists' colony on the heaths in and near Worpswede (northern Germany, not far from Bremen), where he wooed two artists. On April 28, 1901 he married the sculptor Clara Westhoff (1878–1954), and their daughter Ruth, his only child, was born on December 12 of that year. They treated their mar-

---

3. Eventually, his mother outlived him.

riage very casually, like artistic "bohemians," and for the rest of the poet's life saw each other only occasionally, while remaining friends. From 1902 on, Rilke's life was largely nomadic. In that year he moved to Paris to write a monograph on Rodin, with whom his wife studied; subsequently he used Paris as a jumping-off place for his extensive European travels up to the First World War. Devoted exclusively to his writing, he did hardly any other work, but was charismatically dependent (after his father's death in 1906 deprived him of income from that quarter) on publishers, friends, lady admirers, and other generous patrons. (True, in 1905 and 1906 he served Rodin as a sort of private secretary.) In 1911 and 1912 he was the guest of a princess in her castle at Duino, near Trieste; there he began work on the famous *Duineser Elegien* (*Duino Elegies*), which weren't completed for another eleven years.

During the war he was drafted into the Austrian home reserves and worked in the military records office. After the war, technicalities of his political situation and citizenship made him seek Switzerland as a refuge, and he lived there from 1919 on. In 1921 a member of the Reinhart family of Winterthur (in the German part of Switzerland), outstanding art collectors and peerless Maecenases, presented him with a small château at Muzot, in the mountains of Suisse Romande. But Rilke suffered from leukemia, and from 1923 to his death in 1926 was frequently in clinics and sanatoriums.

Oddly, Rilke had published hardly anything of importance, except for the poem cycle *Das Marienleben* (*The Life of the Blessed Virgin;* 1913), between his superb novel *Die Aufzeichnungen des Malte Laurids Brigge* (*The Notebook of Malte Laurids Brigge;* 1910) and his late masterpieces, the above-mentioned *Duineser Elegien* and the *Sonette an Orpheus* (*Sonnets to Orpheus*), both 1923. His poetry was the most important and most influential part of his oeuvre, other volumes being *Das Stundenbuch* (*The Book of Hours*), 1905, and especially the *Neue Gedichte* (*New Poems*) of 1907 and 1908, in which he introduced his highly admired "objective" (descriptive, imagistic) poems. His prose work included stories and plays (both of these genres only very early in his career), as well as monographs on art and literature.

The Stories Included Here. Rilke's stories and prose sketches, some seventy in all, precede his 1902 move to Paris; the ones selected here are perhaps the best. By far his most popular work in his own lifetime, and beyond, was a poetically tinged (or "verse-infected")

story based on a document he had found while doing genealogical research (he hoped to find an ancestral history of military glory, but the Rilkes of the story were probably not related to him): "Die Weise von Liebe und Tod des Cornets Christoph Rilke."[4] It was written on one stormy night in the fall of 1899; as Rilke later reported, he had been incited to set the story down "by the clouds, which, in a strange flight, were scudding past the moon high in the sky." He reworked the piece in August 1904, and it was first published two months later in the Prague periodical *Deutsche Arbeit* (*German Work*). In the first half of 1906 (ending June 12) he made further alterations (producing the definitive text that appears in this Dover anthology) for the edition in volume form, which was published at the end of that year by the Axel Juncker Verlag in Berlin. (Before the 1906 edition, the hero's first name had been Otto, not Christoph; his rank, cornet, indicated a cavalry standard-bearer.) The little book has always been an enormous success in the German-speaking lands. In 1912 it was made Number 1 of the Insel Verlag's popular "library" series *Die Insel-Bücherei*, and sold over a million copies in the next fifty years.

The action takes place during an Imperial (Austrian; Holy Roman Empire) campaign in Hungary in 1663 against the Turks, who, after conquering the Balkans, were still making serious incursions into central Europe. The commanding general, who figures briefly in the story with his name misspelled, was Count Johann von Sporck (1601–1679); born near Paderborn in northern Germany, he had already distinguished himself during the Thirty Years' War; there was a picture of him prominently displayed in one of Rilke's military schools.

Actually printed along with the poems in at least one complete-works edition, this story is indeed very poetic, and the passage about the ball in the mansion is even riddled with internal rhymes. In a letter to André Gide, 1914, Rilke mentions the possibility that Gide might translate the story into French. (Another letter, in 1915, testifies to the patriotic appeal that the piece had during the First World War: it was performed in Leipzig to a musical setting.)[5]

The story "Die Turnstunde" is a self-standing fragment of a "military novel" that Rilke often considered but never wrote. It recalls the hated regimentation, and the callousness of both staff and student body, in Rilke's military schools, where he had been an indifferent

---

4. *Weise*, translated as "Ballad" in this Dover volume, has been rendered as "Lay" or "Song" previously. The rendering "Manner" ("Manner of Loving and Dying . . .") by one translator is simply ludicrous.   5. In 1942–43, the Swiss composer Frank Martin (1890–1974) set the text for alto and small orchestra.

gymnast. He wrote down the first version in his private journal on November 5, 1899. The second, definitive version (reprinted here), which scarcely differs, was first published in Berlin, in the February 1, 1902 issue of *Die Zukunft* (*The Future*), the celebrated liberal weekly that Maximilian Harden (1861–1927) had founded in 1892. The alterations, such as they were, were probably made late in 1901. This may have been Rilke's favorite among his own individual (that is, non-cycle) stories; it was the only such (fully prose) piece he chose at the end of his life for inclusion in the collected-works edition then being prepared (published 1927).

The story cycle *Geschichten vom lieben Gott,* partly a record of the mystical experience of the trips to Russia, was written at a time when Rilke was producing instinctive, emotional poetry, like that in the *Stundenbuch* (written 1899–1903). The only story volume of his that sold well (twelve editions during his lifetime), it was also chosen by him for inclusion in the (1927) collected-works edition. It was written on seven nights in November 1899, between the tenth day of the month and the twenty-first. No part of it was "prepublished" in periodicals before it appeared at the very end of 1900 (letters pinpoint stages in the process) with the title *Vom lieben Gott und Anderes* (*Concerning the Good Lord, and Other Matters*) and the subtitle *An Große für Kinder erzählt* (*Told to Adults for Children to Hear*); the publisher was the Insel-Verlag, at the time in the hands of Schuster & Loeffler, Berlin and Leipzig. (An Insel reprinting one year later drops the names of Schuster & Loeffler, and of the city Berlin.) The publishers themselves subsequently requested a revision, which Rilke undertook in February and March of 1904; the second, definitive edition (our Dover text) appeared in June 1904 with the title we now know, with a table of contents indicating that the first section ("Das Märchen von den Händen Gottes") is the introduction, and with a new dedication reading (in translation) as follows:

"My friend, at one time I placed this book in your hands, and you cherished it as no one had done before. And so I have grown accustomed to think of it as belonging to you. Therefore permit me to inscribe your name not merely in your own copy, but in every copy of this new edition; let me write: 'The *Stories About the Good Lord* belong to Ellen Key.' Rainer Maria Rilke. Rome, April 1904." (Ellen Key, 1849–1926, was a Swedish feminist writer [her still modest wishes were for women to be properly educated for motherhood; she did not yet picture them in the job market] with whom Rilke had

begun to correspond in 1902; from June to December 1904 she was
his hostess in Sweden.)

Though some of the stories in the *Lieber Gott* collection have appeared as individual excerpts in some anthologies, the cycle is tightly
unified in all kinds of specific and thematic ways (with recurring in-
terlocutors and leitmotifs, such as "heights and abysses" [which a previous translation blindly blurs]), and it cries out to be read as a whole.

Childlikely imaginative and reverent, as well as sharply satirical, the
cycle is a kind of rebellion against established religion and the mental
stagnation of the middle class; it also romanticizes childhood, in a sort
of compensation for the author's perturbed young years. In a beautiful letter of 1921, Rilke states that he can no longer reconstruct the
evolution of the cycle because he was writing instinctively in those
days; he suggests that his own lonely childhood, in which inanimate
objects meant a great deal to him, had given him the idea that children wanted the company of God; thus, he had wished to bring God
into the realm of immediate everyday experience, instead of having
Him remain a remote, transcendental concept.

Rilke probably reworked several Russian (more specifically,
Ukrainian) sources for some of the stories; the heroine of the final
piece seems to be based on a famous real-life resident of Munich's
artist quarter, Schwabing: Franziska, Gräfin zu (Countess of)
Reventlow (1871–1918), a story writer with an emancipated life style
and subject matter.

NOTE: The lower-case initials of pronouns referring to God are in
compliance with the most recent *Chicago Manual of Style,* and not
with the wishes of the translator!

Great Stories by
Kafka and Rilke

Meistererzählungen von
Kafka und Rilke

KAFKA: ERZÄHLUNGEN

Der neue Advokat

Wir haben einen neuen Advokaten, den Dr. Bucephalus. In seinem Äußern erinnert wenig an die Zeit, da er noch Streitroß Alexanders von Mazedonien war. Wer allerdings mit den Umständen vertraut ist, bemerkt einiges. Doch sah ich letzthin auf der Freitreppe selbst einen ganz einfältigen Gerichtsdiener mit dem Fachblick des kleinen Stammgastes der Wettrennen den Advokaten bestaunen, als dieser, hoch die Schenkel hebend, mit auf dem Marmor aufklingendem Schritt von Stufe zu Stufe stieg.

Im allgemeinen billigt das Barreau die Aufnahme des Bucephalus. Mit erstaunlicher Einsicht sagt man sich, daß Bucephalus bei der heutigen Gesellschaftsordnung in einer schwierigen Lage ist und daß er deshalb, sowie auch wegen seiner weltgeschichtlichen Bedeutung, jedenfalls Entgegenkommen verdient. Heute – das kann niemand leugnen – gibt es keinen großen Alexander. Zu morden verstehen zwar manche; auch an der Geschicklichkeit, mit der Lanze über den Bankettisch hinweg den Freund zu treffen, fehlt es nicht; und vielen ist Mazedonien zu eng, so daß sie Philipp, den Vater, verfluchen – aber niemand, niemand kann nach Indien führen. Schon damals waren Indiens Tore unerreichbar, aber ihre Richtung war durch das Königsschwert bezeichnet. Heute sind die Tore ganz anderswohin und weiter und höher vertragen; niemand zeigt die Richtung; viele halten Schwerter, aber nur, um mit ihnen zu fuchteln, und der Blick, der ihnen folgen will, verwirrt sich.

Vielleicht ist es deshalb wirklich das beste, sich, wie es Bucephalus getan hat, in die Gesetzbücher zu versenken. Frei, unbedrückt die Seiten von den Lenden des Reiters, bei stiller Lampe, fern dem Getöse der Alexanderschlacht, liest und wendet er die Blätter unserer alten Bücher.

KAFKA: STORIES

The New Lawyer

We have a new lawyer, Dr. Bucephalus. Little in his outward appearance recalls the days when he was still the warhorse of Alexander of Macedonia. But anyone familiar with the circumstances notices a few things. All the same, on the courthouse steps I recently saw a quite simpleminded court usher gazing in wonderment at the lawyer with the professional glance of a petty habitué of the racetrack when the lawyer, raising his thighs high in the air, climbed step by step, his shoes resounding on the marble.

In general the bar approves the reception of Bucephalus. With amazing insight they tell themselves that, as the social order is constituted today, Bucephalus is in a difficult position and that, for that reason as well as for the sake of his significance in world history, he deserves to be met halfway in any case. Today—and nobody can deny this—there is no Alexander the Great. To be sure, many people know how to kill; nor is there any lack of skill in stabbing one's friend with a lance across a banquet table; and many people find Macedonia too cramped, so that they curse Philip, their father—but nobody, nobody can lead an army to India. Even then the gates of India were unattainable, but their direction was indicated by the royal sword. Today the gates are altogether elsewhere, removed to a more distant and loftier place; nobody points in their direction; many people carry swords, but merely to gesticulate with them, and the eyes that wish to follow them become confused.

Therefore it's perhaps really for the best to immerse oneself in lawbooks, as Bucephalus has done. Free, his flanks not pressed by a rider's loins, by quiet lamplight, far from the hubbub of Alexander's battles, he reads and turns the pages of our old books.

Auf der Galerie

Wenn irgendeine hinfällige, lungensüchtige Kunstreiterin in der Manege auf schwankendem Pferd vor einem unermüdlichen Publikum vom peitschenschwingenden erbarmungslosen Chef monatelang ohne Unterbrechung im Kreise rundum getrieben würde, auf dem Pferde schwirrend, Küsse werfend, in der Taille sich wiegend, und wenn dieses Spiel unter dem nichtaussetzenden Brausen des Orchesters und der Ventilatoren in die immerfort weiter sich öffnende graue Zukunft sich fortsetzte, begleitet vom vergehenden und neu anschwellenden Beifallsklatschen der Hände, die eigentlich Dampfhämmer sind – vielleicht eilte dann ein junger Galeriebesucher die lange Treppe durch alle Ränge hinab, stürzte in die Manege, rief das: Halt! durch die Fanfaren des immer sich anpassenden Orchesters.

Da es aber nicht so ist; eine schöne Dame, weiß und rot, hereinfliegt, zwischen den Vorhängen, welche die stolzen Livrierten vor ihr öffnen; der Direktor, hingebungsvoll ihre Augen suchend, in Tierhaltung ihr entgegenatmet; vorsorglich sie auf den Apfelschimmel hebt, als wäre sie seine über alles geliebte Enkelin, die sich auf gefährliche Fahrt begibt; sich nicht entschließen kann, das Peitschenzeichen zu geben; schließlich in Selbstüberwindung es knallend gibt; neben dem Pferde mit offenem Munde einherläuft; die Sprünge der Reiterin scharfen Blickes verfolgt; ihre Kunstfertigkeit kaum begreifen kann; mit englischen Ausrufen zu warnen versucht; die reifenhaltenden Reitknechte wütend zu peinlichster Achtsamkeit ermahnt; vor dem großen Salto mortale das Orchester mit aufgehobenen Händen beschwört, es möge schweigen; schließlich die Kleine vom zitternden Pferde hebt, auf beide Backen küßt und keine Huldigung des Publikums für genügend erachtet; während sie selbst, von ihm gestützt, hoch auf den Fußspitzen, vom Staub umweht, mit ausgebreiteten Armen, zurückgelehntem Köpfchen ihr Glück mit dem ganzen Zirkus teilen will – da dies so ist, legt der Galeriebesucher das Gesicht auf die Brüstung und, im Schlußmarsch wie in einem schweren Traum versinkend, weint er, ohne es zu wissen.

Ein altes Blatt

Es ist, als wäre viel vernachlässigt worden in der Verteidigung unseres Vaterlandes. Wir haben uns bisher nicht darum gekümmert und sind

In the Upper Balcony

If some frail, tubercular bareback rider, in the ring, on a swaying horse, before an untiring audience, were driven around in a circle uninterruptedly for months on end by a merciless, whip-brandishing ringmaster, whirring on her horse, throwing kisses, swiveling her waist; and if this performance, to the unceasing roar of the band and the air blowers, continued into the perpetually expanding gray future, accompanied by the dying and freshly swelling claps of those applauding hands which are actually steam hammers—then, perhaps, a young upper-balcony ticketholder might hasten down the long staircase through every tier, might dash into the ring, and might shout "Stop!" through the fanfares of the band that suits its music to every occasion.

But since this is not the case; since a beautiful lady, all in white and red, flies in, between the curtains that the proud men in uniform open in front of her; since the ringmaster, devotedly seeking her gaze, pants at her in an animal-like pose, carefully lifts her onto her dapple gray as if she were the granddaughter he loved best in the world, who was setting out on a perilous journey, and he can't make up his mind to give the signal with his whip, but finally, mastering himself, gives it with a crack; then runs alongside the horse with his mouth open, following the rider's leaps with a steady gaze, scarcely comprehending her skill, trying to warn her with exclamations in English, furiously enjoining the hoop-carrying grooms to be most strictly attentive, imploring the band with his hands raised to cease playing just before the great breakneck leap, and finally lifting the little lady off her trembling horse, kissing her on both cheeks, and considering no appreciation by the audience worthy of her; while she herself, supported by him, standing high on tiptoe, dust blowing around her, her arms outstretched and her little head laid back, desires to share her happiness with the entire circus—this being the case, the balcony spectator puts his face on the railing and, submerging in the concluding march as if in a deep dream, he weeps without knowing it.

Page from an Old Text

It's as if a great deal had been neglected in the defense of our country. Until now we haven't been concerned about it and

unserer Arbeit nachgegangen; die Ereignisse der letzten Zeit machen uns aber Sorgen.

Ich habe eine Schusterwerkstatt auf dem Platz vor dem kaiserlichen Palast. Kaum öffne ich in der Morgendämmerung meinen Laden, sehe ich schon die Eingänge aller hier einlaufenden Gassen von Bewaffneten besetzt. Es sind aber nicht unsere Soldaten, sondern offenbar Nomaden aus dem Norden. Auf eine mir unbegreifliche Weise sind sie bis in die Hauptstadt gedrungen, die doch sehr weit von der Grenze entfernt ist. Jedenfalls sind sie also da; es scheint, daß jeden Morgen mehr werden.

Ihrer Natur entsprechend lagern sie unter freiem Himmel, denn Wohnhäuser verabscheuen sie. Sie beschäftigen sich mit dem Schärfen der Schwerter, dem Zuspitzen der Pfeile, mit Übungen zu Pferde. Aus diesem stillen, immer ängstlich rein gehaltenen Platz haben sie einen wahren Stall gemacht. Wir versuchen zwar manchmal aus unseren Geschäften hervorzulaufen und wenigstens den ärgsten Unrat wegzuschaffen, aber es geschieht immer seltener, denn die Anstrengung ist nutzlos und bringt uns überdies in die Gefahr, unter die wilden Pferde zu kommen oder von den Peitschen verletzt zu werden.

Sprechen kann man mit den Nomaden nicht. Unsere Sprache kennen sie nicht, ja sie haben kaum eine eigene. Untereinander verständigen sie sich ähnlich wie Dohlen. Immer wieder hört man diesen Schrei der Dohlen. Unsere Lebensweise, unsere Einrichtungen sind ihnen ebenso unbegreiflich wie gleichgültig. Infolgedessen zeigen sie sich auch gegen jede Zeichensprache ablehnend. Du magst dir die Kiefer verrenken und die Hände aus den Gelenken winden, sie haben dich doch nicht verstanden und werden dich nie verstehen. Oft machen sie Grimassen; dann dreht sich das Weiß ihrer Augen und Schaum schwillt aus ihrem Munde, doch wollen sie damit weder etwas sagen noch auch erschrecken; sie tun es, weil es so ihre Art ist. Was sie brauchen, nehmen sie. Man kann nicht sagen, daß sie Gewalt anwenden. Vor ihrem Zugriff tritt man beiseite und überläßt ihnen alles.

Auch von meinen Vorräten haben sie manches gute Stück genommen. Ich kann aber darüber nicht klagen, wenn ich zum Beispiel zusehe, wie es dem Fleischer gegenüber geht. Kaum bringt er seine Waren ein, ist ihm schon alles entrissen und wird von den Nomaden

have gone about our business; but the events of recent days worry us.

I have a shoemaker's establishment on the square in front of the imperial palace. Scarcely do I open my shop in the morning half-light when I already see the entrances to all the streets that empty into the square occupied by armed men. They aren't our soldiers, however, but obviously nomads from the north. In a manner I can't comprehend they have infiltrated all the way to the capital, which after all is quite distant from the border. At any rate, they're here; there seem to be more of them every morning.

In accordance with their nature, they camp in the open air, because they loathe houses. They occupy themselves with whetting their swords, putting points on their arrows, and performing equestrian exercises. They've turned this quiet square, which was always kept scrupulously clean, into a real stable. To be sure, we sometimes try to run out of our shops and clear away at least the worst garbage, but we've been doing so less and less often, because it's a useless exertion and, what's more, it makes us risk getting trampled by the wild horses or wounded by the whips.

It's impossible to converse with the nomads. They don't know our language, and, in fact, they scarcely have one of their own. They communicate with one another in the manner of jackdaws.[1] Time and again we hear those jackdaw calls. To them our way of life and our institutions are just as incomprehensible as they are matters of indifference. Therefore they're even averse to using any sign language. You can dislocate your jaw and twist your hands out of joint, they haven't understood you and they never will understand you. They often grimace; at such times their eyes roll up and foam pours from their mouths, but by doing so they neither wish to tell you something nor even to frighten you; they do it because that's their way. They simply take whatever they need. You can't say they use force. When they reach for something, we step aside and abandon everything to them.

They've taken plenty of good items from my supplies, too. But I can't lament over it when, for example, I watch how things are with the butcher across the way. Scarcely does he bring in his merchandise when it's already entirely snatched away from him

---

1. Is it a coincidence that, of all birds, Kafka chooses the jackdaw, his own namesake? ("Jackdaw" is *kavka* in Czech.)

verschlungen. Auch ihre Pferde fressen Fleisch; oft liegt ein Reiter neben seinem Pferd und beide nähren sich vom gleichen Fleischstück, jeder an einem Ende. Der Fleischhauer ist ängstlich und wagt es nicht, mit den Fleischlieferungen aufzuhören. Wir verstehen das aber, schießen Geld zusammen und unterstützen ihn. Bekämen die Nomaden kein Fleisch, wer weiß, was ihnen zu tun einfiele; wer weiß allerdings, was ihnen einfallen wird, selbst wenn sie täglich Fleisch bekommen.

Letzthin dachte der Fleischer, er könne sich wenigstens die Mühe des Schlachtens sparen, und brachte am Morgen einen lebendigen Ochsen. Das darf er nicht mehr wiederholen. Ich lag wohl eine Stunde ganz hinten in meiner Werkstatt platt auf dem Boden und alle meine Kleider, Decken und Poster hatte ich über mir aufgehäuft, nur um das Gebrüll des Ochsen nicht zu hören, den von allen Seiten die Nomaden ansprangen, um mit den Zähnen Stücke aus seinem warmen Fleisch zu reißen. Schon lange war es still, ehe ich mich auszugehen getraute; wie Trinker um ein Weinfaß lagen sie müde um die Reste des Ochsen.

Gerade damals glaubte ich den Kaiser selbst in einem Fenster des Palastes gesehen zu haben; niemals sonst kommt er in diese äußeren Gemächer, immer nur lebt er in dem innersten Garten; diesmal aber stand er, so schien es mir wenigstens, an einem der Fenster und blickte mit gesenktem Kopf auf das Treiben vor seinem Schloß.

»Wie wird es werden?« fragen wir uns alle. »Wie lange werden wir diese Last und Qual ertragen? Der kaiserliche Palast hat die Nomaden angelockt, versteht es aber nicht, sie wieder zu vertreiben. Das Tor bleibt verschlossen; die Wache, früher immer festlich ein- und ausmarschierend, hält sich hinter vergitterten Fenstern. Uns Handwerkern und Geschäftsleuten ist die Rettung des Vaterlandes anvertraut; wir sind aber einer solchen Aufgabe nicht gewachsen; haben uns doch auch nie gerühmt, dessen fähig zu sein. Ein Mißverständnis ist es; und wir gehen daran zugrunde.«

Vor dem Gesetz

Vor dem Gesetz steht ein Türhüter. Zu diesem Türhüter kommt ein Mann vom Lande und bittet um Eintritt in das Gesetz. Aber der Türhüter sagt, daß er ihm jetzt den Eintritt nicht gewähren könne. Der Mann überlegt und fragt dann, ob er also später werde eintreten dürfen. »Es ist möglich«, sagt der Türhüter, »jetzt aber nicht.« Da das

and gulped down by the nomads. Even their horses eat meat; often a horseman will lie down next to his mount and both of them will feed off the same piece of meat, each one at one end of it. The butcher is nervous and doesn't dare stop delivering meat. But we understand this, take up a collection for him, and support him. If the nomads didn't get meat, who knows what they'd take it into their heads to do? But who knows what they'll think of doing even if they get meat daily?

Recently the butcher thought he might at least spare himself the trouble of slaughtering the animals, and one morning he brought a live ox. He mustn't ever do that again. I lay for about an hour at the very back of my shop, flat on the floor, with all my clothes, blankets, and cushions heaped on top of me, merely to keep from hearing the bellowing of the ox, which the nomads were leaping on from all sides in order to tear pieces out of its warm flesh with their teeth. Things had already been quiet for a long time before I ventured outside; like winebibbers around a cask, they were lying wearily around the remains of the ox.

At that very moment I thought I saw the emperor himself at a window of the palace; he usually never comes to these outer rooms, but always resides in the innermost garden; but this time he was standing (or so it seemed to me at least) at one of the windows, his head bowed, watching the goings-on in front of his palace.

"What's going to happen?" we all wonder. "How long will we endure this burden and torment? The imperial palace has attracted the nomads but it's incapable of chasing them away again. The gate remains locked; the guards, who always used to march in and out festively, remain behind barred windows. The salvation of our country is entrusted to us, the artisans and shopkeepers, but we aren't up to such a task; nor did we ever boast of being able to do it. It's a misunderstanding, and it will be the death of us."

On the Threshold of the Law

Outside the abode of the law there stands a doorkeeper. To this doorkeeper there comes a man from the country who requests admittance to the law. But the doorkeeper says that, right now, he can't grant him admittance. The man thinks it over, then asks whether he'll be able to go in later. "It's possible," says the doorkeeper, "but

Tor zum Gesetz offensteht wie immer und der Türhüter beiseite tritt, bückt sich der Mann, um durch das Tor in das Innere zu sehn. Als der Türhüter das merkt, lacht er und sagt: »Wenn es dich so lockt, versuche es doch, trotz meines Verbotes hineinzugehn. Merke aber: Ich bin mächtig. Und ich bin nur der unterste Türhüter. Von Saal zu Saal stehn aber Türhüter, einer mächtiger als der andere. Schon den Anblick des dritten kann nicht einmal ich mehr ertragen.« Solche Schwierigkeiten hat der Mann vom Lande nicht erwartet; das Gesetz soll doch jedem und immer zugänglich sein, denkt er, aber als er jetzt den Türhüter in seinem Pelzmantel genauer ansieht, seine große Spitznase, den langen, dünnen, schwarzen tatarischen Bart, entschließt er sich, doch lieber zu warten, bis er die Erlaubnis zum Eintritt bekommt. Der Türhüter gibt ihm einen Schemel und läßt ihn seitwärts von der Tür sich niedersetzen. Dort sitzt er Tage und Jahre. Er macht viele Versuche, eingelassen zu werden, und ermüdet den Türhüter durch seine Bitten. Der Türhüter stellt öfters kleine Verhöre mit ihm an, fragt ihn über seine Heimat aus und nach vielem andern, es sind aber teilnahmslose Fragen, wie sie große Herren stellen, und zum Schlusse sagt er ihm immer wieder, daß er ihn noch nicht einlassen könne. Der Mann, der sich für seine Reise mit vielem ausgerüstet hat, verwendet alles, und sei es noch so wertvoll, um den Türhüter zu bestechen. Dieser nimmt zwar alles an, aber sagt dabei: »Ich nehme es nur an, damit du nicht glaubst, etwas versäumt zu haben.« Während der vielen Jahre beobachtet der Mann den Türhüter fast ununterbrochen. Er vergißt die andern Türhüter, und dieser erste scheint ihm das einzige Hindernis für den Eintritt in das Gesetz. Er verflucht den unglücklichen Zufall, in den ersten Jahren rücksichtslos und laut, später, als er alt wird, brummt er nur noch vor sich hin. Er wird kindisch, und, da er in dem jahrelangen Studium des Türhüters auch die Flöhe in seinem Pelzkragen erkannt hat, bittet er auch die Flöhe, ihm zu helfen und den Türhüter umzustimmen. Schließlich wird sein Augenlicht schwach, und er weiß nicht, ob es um ihn wirklich dunkler wird, oder ob ihn nur seine Augen täuschen. Wohl aber erkennt er jetzt im Dunkel einen Glanz, der unverlöschlich aus der Türe des Gesetzes bricht. Nun lebt er nicht mehr lange. Vor seinem Tode sammeln sich in seinem Kopfe alle Erfahrungen der ganzen Zeit zu einer Frage, die er bisher an den Türhüter noch nicht gestellt hat. Er winkt ihm zu, da er seinen erstarrenden Körper nicht mehr aufrichten kann. Der Türhüter muß sich tief zu ihm hinunterneigen, denn der Größenunterschied hat sich sehr zuungunsten des Mannes verändert. »Was willst du denn jetzt noch wissen?« fragt

not now." Since the portal to the law is open, as before, and the door-keeper steps aside, the man stoops to look inside through the portal. When the doorkeeper notices this, he laughs and says: "If it tempts you so, why not try to go in despite my prohibition? But keep in mind: I am powerful. And I am merely the lowest-ranking door-keeper. From room to room, however, there are other doorkeepers, each more powerful than the last. Not even I can bear the very sight of the third one." The man from the country didn't expect such dif-ficulties; after all, the law should be accessible to everyone at all times, he thinks to himself, but when he now inspects more closely the doorkeeper in his fur coat, his big pointy nose, and his long, sparse, black Tartar's beard, he decides it's better to wait until he re-ceives permission to go in. The doorkeeper gives him a stool and lets him sit down at one side of the door. There he sits for days and years. He makes many attempts to be admitted, and wearies the door-keeper with his requests. The doorkeeper frequently puts him through brief interrogations, asking him about his home district and much else, but they are unconcerned questions like those posed by great lords, and at the end he tells him time after time that he can't let him in yet. The man, who has taken along many provisions for his journey, uses everything, no matter how valuable, to bribe the door-keeper with. The doorkeeper accepts it all, to be sure, but then says: "I'm accepting this merely so that you don't think you've neglected anything." During the many years the man observes the doorkeeper almost uninterruptedly. He forgets about the other doorkeepers, and this first one appears to him as the sole obstacle to admittance to the law. He curses the unhappy chance, in the first years recklessly and loudly, later on, as he grows older, merely grumbling to himself. He becomes senile and, since in his years-long study of the door-keeper he has also recognized the fleas in his fur collar, he asks the fleas, too, to help him and to change the doorkeeper's mind. Finally his sight becomes bad and he doesn't know whether it's really getting darker all around him or it's only his eyes deceiving him. But now in the darkness he does discern a glow that breaks unextinguishably from the door to the law. Now he doesn't live much longer. Before his death all his experiences during that entire time collect in his head to form one question which he has hitherto never yet asked the doorkeeper. He beckons him over, since he can no longer raise his stiffening body. The doorkeeper is compelled to bend a long way down to him, because the difference in their size has altered, much to the man's disadvantage. "What do you still want to know now?"

der Türhüter, »du bist unersättlich.« »Alle streben doch nach dem
Gesetz«, sagt der Mann, »wieso kommt es, daß in den vielen Jahren
niemand außer mir Einlaß verlangt hat?« Der Türhüter erkennt, daß
der Mann schon an seinem Ende ist, und, um sein vergehendes
Gehör noch zu erreichen, brüllt er ihn an: »Hier konnte niemand
sonst Einlaß erhalten, denn dieser Eingang war nur für dich bestimmt. Ich gehe jetzt und schließe ihn.«

Schakale und Araber

Wir lagerten in der Oase. Die Gefährten schliefen. Ein Araber, hoch
und weiß, kam an mir vorüber; er hatte die Kamele versorgt und ging
zum Schlafplatz.

Ich warf mich rücklings ins Gras; ich wollte schlafen; ich konnte
nicht; das Klagegeheul eines Schakals in der Ferne; ich saß wieder
aufrecht. Und was so weit gewesen war, war plötzlich nah. Ein
Gewimmel von Schakalen um mich her; in mattem Gold erglänzende,
verlöschende Augen; schlanke Leiber, wie unter einer Peitsche ge-
setzmäßig und flink bewegt.

Einer kam von rückwärts, drängte sich, unter meinem Arm durch,
eng an mich, als brauche er meine Wärme, trat dann vor mich und
sprach, fast Aug in Aug mit mir:

»Ich bin der älteste Schakal, weit und breit. Ich bin glücklich, dich
noch hier begrüßen zu können. Ich hatte schon die Hoffnung fast
aufgegeben, denn wir warten unendlich lange auf dich; meine Mutter
hat gewartet und ihre Mutter und weiter alle ihre Mütter bis hinauf
zur Mutter aller Schakale. Glaube es!«

»Das wundert mich«, sagte ich und vergaß, den Holzstoß anzuzün-
den, der bereitlag, um mit seinem Rauch die Schakale abzuhalten,
»das wundert mich sehr zu hören. Nur zufällig komme ich aus dem
hohen Norden und bin auf einer kurzen Reise begriffen. Was wollt ihr
denn, Schakale?«

Und wie ermutigt durch diesen vielleicht allzu freundlichen
Zuspruch zogen sie ihren Kreis enger um mich; alle atmeten kurz und
fauchend.

»Wir wissen«, begann der Älteste, »daß du vom Norden kommst,
darauf eben baut sich unsere Hoffnung. Dort ist der Verstand, der
hier unter den Arabern nicht zu finden ist. Aus diesem kalten
Hochmut, weißt du, ist kein Funken Verstand zu schlagen. Sie töten
Tiere, um sie zu fressen, und Aas mißachten sie.«

the doorkeeper asks; "you're insatiable." "After all, everyone strives for the law," the man says, "so how is it that in all these years no one but me has requested admittance?" The doorkeeper realizes that the man is now breathing his last, and, in order to make himself heard to the dying man, he roars at him: "No one else was able to be admitted here, because this entrance was set aside for you alone. Now I'm going over to close it."

Jackals and Bedouins

We were camping in the oasis. My comrades were sleeping. A Bedouin, tall and dressed in white, passed by me; he had tended to the camels and was going to his sleeping place.

I threw myself onto the grass on my back; I wanted to sleep; I couldn't; the mournful howl of a jackal in the distance; I sat up again. And what had been so far was suddenly near. A throng of jackals all around me; eyes flashing with dull gold and fading again; slender bodies, moving regularly and nimbly as if commanded by a whip.

One came from behind, thrust himself close to me, passing under my arm, as if he needed my warmth, then stepped in front of me and spoke, nearly eye to eye with me:

"I am the oldest jackal far and wide. I'm glad that I can still greet you here. By now I had almost given up hope, because we've been awaiting you for an infinitely long time; my mother waited, and her mother, and all her mothers in turn, all the way back to the mother of all jackals. Believe me!"

"It surprises me," I said, forgetting to ignite the wooden stake which lay in readiness to ward off the jackals with its smoke, "it surprises me a great deal to hear that. It's only by chance that I've come from the far north on a brief journey. What do you want, jackals?"

And, as if encouraged by those perhaps overly friendly words, they drew their circle more closely around me; they were all breathing in short puffs.

"We know," the eldest began, "that you come from the north; it's on that very fact that we base our hopes. That is where intelligence dwells, which can't be found amid the Bedouins here. You see, from that cold arrogance not one spark of intelligence can be struck. They kill animals to eat them, and they have contempt for carrion."

»Rede nicht so laut«, sagte ich, »es schlafen Araber in der Nähe.«

»Du bist wirklich ein Fremder«, sagte der Schakal, »sonst wüßtest du, daß noch niemals in der Weltgeschichte ein Schakal einen Araber gefürchtet hat. Fürchten sollten wir sie? Ist es nicht Unglück genug, daß wir unter solches Volk verstoßen sind?«

»Mag sein, mag sein«, sagte ich, »ich maße mir kein Urteil an in Dingen, die mir so fern liegen; es scheint ein sehr alter Streit; liegt also wohl im Blut; wird also vielleicht erst mit dem Blute enden.«

»Du bist sehr klug«, sagte der alte Schakal; und alle atmeten noch schneller; mit gehetzten Lungen, trotzdem sie doch stillestanden; ein bitterer, zeitweilig nur mit zusammengeklemmten Zähnen erträglicher Geruch entströmte den offenen Mäulern, »du bist sehr klug; das, was du sagst, entspricht unserer alten Lehre. Wir nehmen ihnen also ihr Blut und der Streit ist zu Ende.«

»Oh!« sagte ich wilder, als ich wollte, »sie werden sich wehren; sie werden mit ihren Flinten euch rudelweise niederschießen.«

»Du mißverstehst uns«, sagte er, »nach Menschenart, die sich also auch im hohen Norden nicht verliert. Wir werden sie doch nicht töten. So viel Wasser hätte der Nil nicht, um uns rein zu waschen. Wir laufen doch schon vor dem bloßen Anblick ihres lebenden Leibes weg, in reinere Luft, in die Wüste, die deshalb unsere Heimat ist.«

Und alle Schakale ringsum, zu denen inzwischen noch viele von fern her gekommen waren, senkten die Köpfe zwischen die Vorderbeine und putzten sie mit den Pfoten; es war, als wollten sie einen Widerwillen verbergen, der so schrecklich war, daß ich am liebsten mit einem hohen Sprung aus ihrem Kreis entflohen wäre.

»Was beabsichtigt ihr also zu tun?« fragte ich und wollte aufstehn; aber ich konnte nicht; zwei junge Tiere hatten sich mir hinten in Rock und Hemd festgebissen; ich mußte sitzenbleiben. »Sie halten deine Schleppe«, sagte der alte Schakal erklärend und ernsthaft, »eine Ehrbezeigung.« »Sie sollen mich loslassen!« rief ich, bald zum Alten, bald zu den Jungen gewendet. »Sie werden es natürlich«, sagte der Alte, »wenn du es verlangst. Es dauert aber ein Weilchen, denn sie haben nach der Sitte tief sich eingebissen und müssen erst langsam die Gebisse voneinander lösen. Inzwischen höre unsere Bitte.« »Euer Verhalten hat mich dafür nicht sehr empfänglich gemacht«, sagte ich. »Laß uns unser Ungeschick nicht entgelten«, sagte er und nahm jetzt zum erstenmal den Klageton seiner natürlichen Stimme zu Hilfe, »wir sind arme Tiere, wir haben nur das Gebiß; für alles, was wir tun wollen, das Gute und das Schlechte, bleibt uns einzig das Gebiß.« »Was willst du also?« fragte ich, nur wenig besänftigt.

"Don't talk so loud," I said; "Bedouins are sleeping nearby."

"You're really a foreigner," said the jackal, "or else you'd know that never yet in the history of the world has a jackal been afraid of a Bedouin. We should fear them? Isn't it sufficient misfortune to be exiled among such people?"

"Maybe, maybe," I said; "I don't presume to judge of such matters, which are so far from my ken; the quarrel seems to be a very old one; it probably is inherited with one's blood, and so it will perhaps end only in bloodshed."

"You're very clever," the old jackal said; and they all breathed even faster, with hyperactive lungs, even though they were in repose; an acrid smell, which at moments I could only bear by clenching my teeth, emanated from their open maws. "You're very clever; what you say is in accordance with our old teachings. And so we'll take their blood and the quarrel will be over."

"Oh!" I said, more violently than I intended; "they'll defend themselves; they'll shoot you down by the pack with their rifles."

"You misunderstand us," he said, "in your human way, which I see is no different even in the far north. We're not going to kill them, you see. The Nile wouldn't have enough water to wash us clean. As it is, we run away at the very sight of their living bodies, into cleaner air, into the desert, which is our home for that very reason."

And all the jackals around, which had meanwhile been joined by many more which had come from a distance, put their heads down between their forelegs, and rubbed them with their paws, as if wishing to conceal a repugnance so horrible that I would have liked most to jump up high in the air and flee from their circle.

"So what do you intend to do?" I asked, and I wanted to stand up; but I couldn't; two young animals behind me had taken a firm bite into my jacket and shirt; I had to sit there. "They're carrying your train," the old jackal said in explanation, gravely, "their way of honoring you." "Make them let me go!" I cried, turning now to the elder, now to the young ones. "Of course they will," the old one said, "if you so desire. But it will take a little while, because, as is customary, they've bitten in deeply and must separate their upper and lower jaws only slowly. Meanwhile hear our request." "Your behavior hasn't made me very receptive to it," I said. "Don't hold our clumsiness against us," he said, and now he summoned to his aid for the first time the mournful tone of his natural voice; "we're poor animals, and all we have is our teeth; for everything we want to too, good or bad, only our teeth are available to us." "What do you want, then?" I asked, not much soothed.

»Herr« rief er, und alle Schakale heulten auf; in fernster Ferne
schien es mir eine Melodie zu sein. »Herr, du sollst den Streit beenden, der die Welt entzweit. So wie du bist, haben unsere Alten den
beschrieben, der es tun wird. Frieden müssen wir haben von den
Arabern; atembare Luft; gereinigt von ihnen den Ausblick rund am
Horizont; kein Klagegeschrei eines Hammels, den der Araber absticht; ruhig soll alles Getier krepieren; ungestört soll es von uns leergetrunken und bis auf die Knochen gereinigt werden. Reinheit,
nichts als Reinheit wollen wir«, – und nun weinten, schluchzten alle
– »wie erträgst nur du es in dieser Welt, du edles Herz und süßes
Eingeweide? Schmutz ist ihr Weiß; Schmutz ist ihr Schwarz; ein
Grauen ist ihr Bart; speien muß man beim Anblick ihrer
Augenwinkel; und heben sie den Arm, tut sich in der Achselhöhle die
Hölle auf. Darum, o Herr, darum, o teuerer Herr, mit Hilfe deiner
alles vermögenden Hände, mit Hilfe deiner alles vermögenden
Hände schneide ihnen mit dieser Schere die Hälse durch!« Und
einem Ruck seines Kopfes folgend kam ein Schakal herbei, der an
einem Eckzahn eine kleine, mit altem Rost bedeckte Nähschere
trug.

»Also endlich die Schere und damit Schluß!« rief der Araberführer
unserer Karawane, der sich gegen den Wind an uns herangeschlichen
hatte und nun seine riesige Peitsche schwang.

Alles verlief sich eiligst, aber in einiger Entfernung blieben sie
doch, eng zusammengekauert, die vielen Tiere so eng und starr, daß
es aussah wie eine schmale Hürde, von Irrlichtern umflogen.

»So hast du, Herr, auch dieses Schauspiel gesehen und gehört«,
sagte der Araber und lachte so fröhlich, als es die Zurückhaltung
seines Stammes erlaubte. »Du weißt also, was die Tiere wollen?«
fragte ich. »Natürlich, Herr«, sagte er, »das ist doch allbekannt;
solange es Araber gibt, wandert diese Schere durch die Wüste und
wird mit uns wandern bis ans Ende der Tage. Jedem Europäer wird
sie angeboten zu dem großen Werk; jeder Europäer ist gerade derjenige, welcher ihnen berufen scheint. Eine unsinnige Hoffnung
haben diese Tiere; Narren, wahre Narren sind sie. Wir lieben sie
deshalb; es sind unsere Hunde; schöner als die eurigen. Sieh nur,
ein Kamel ist in der Nacht verendet, ich habe es herschaffen
lassen.«

Vier Träger kamen und warfen den schweren Kadaver vor uns hin.
Kaum lag er da, erhoben die Schakale ihre Stimmen. Wie von
Stricken unwiderstehlich jeder einzelne gezogen, kamen sie, stokkend, mit dem Leib den Boden streifend, heran. Sie hatten die

"Sir," he cried, and all the jackals began to howl; in the remote distance it sounded like a melody to me. "Sir, you must end the quarrel that is setting the world at loggerheads. Our elders described the man who is to do so as resembling you exactly. We must make the Bedouins leave us in peace; we must have breathable air, the view of the horizon roundabout cleansed of them; no lamenting cry of a sheep being slaughtered by a Bedouin; all animals must die in peace; without disturbance they must be drained of their blood and picked clean to the very bones by us. Purity, we want nothing but purity" (at this point they were all weeping and sobbing); "how can you bear it in this world, you noble heart and sweet bowels? Their whiteness is filth, their blackness is filth; their beards are repellent; when you look at the corners of their eyes, you've got to spit; and when they raise their arms all hell opens up in their armpits. Therefore, good sir, therefore, dear sir, with the help of your all-capable hands, with the help of your all-capable hands cut their throats with these shears!" And in obedience to a jerk of his head a jackal came over carrying a small pair of sewing shears covered with old rust dangling from one of his canine teeth.

"So, the shears at last, and that's an end of it!" shouted the Bedouin leader of our caravan, who had stolen up to us against the wind and was now swinging his gigantic whip.

All the jackals dispersed in the greatest of haste, but at some distance they nevertheless halted, cowering close together, all those animals so tightly packed and rigid that it looked like a narrow sheepfold with will-o'-the-wisps flying around it.

"And so, sir, you too have seen and heard this performance," the Bedouin said, and he laughed as merrily as the natural reserve of his tribe permitted. "So you know what the animals want?" I asked. "Of course, sir," he said; "after all, it's known far and wide; as long as Bedouins exist, those shears will travel through the desert and will wander with us to the end of time. They're offered to every European for the mighty task; every European is precisely the one designated, as it seems to them. These animals possess an absurd hope; fools, they're really fools. We love them for that reason; they're our dogs, better-looking than yours. See here, a camel died during the night, and I've had it brought here."

Four bearers came and threw the heavy cadaver down in front of us. Scarcely was it lying there before the jackals raised their voices. As if each individual were being drawn irresistibly by ropes, they came up hesitantly, their bellies grazing the ground.

Araber vergessen, den Haß vergessen, die alles auslöschende Gegenwart des stark ausdunstenden Leichnams bezauberte sie. Schon hing einer am Hals und fand mit dem ersten Biß die Schlagader. Wie eine kleine rasende Pumpe, die ebenso unbedingt wie aussichtslos einen übermächtigen Brand löschen will, zerrte und zuckte jede Muskel seines Körpers an ihrem Platz. Und schon lagen in gleicher Arbeit alle auf dem Leichnam hoch zu Berg.

Da strich der Führer kräftig mit der scharfen Peitsche kreuz und quer über sie. Sie hoben die Köpfe; halb in Rausch und Ohnmacht; sahen die Araber vor sich stehen; bekamen jetzt die Peitsche mit den Schnauzen zu fühlen; zogen sich im Sprung zurück und liefen eine Strecke rückwärts. Aber das Blut des Kamels lag schon in Lachen da, rauchte empor, der Körper war an mehreren Stellen weit aufgerissen. Sie konnten nicht widerstehen; wieder waren sie da; wieder hob der Führer die Peitsche; ich faßte seinen Arm.

»Du hast recht, Herr«, sagte er, »wir lassen sie bei ihrem Beruf; auch ist es Zeit aufzubrechen. Gesehen hast du sie. Wunderbare Tiere, nacht wahr? Und wie sie uns hassen!«

Ein Besuch im Bergwerk

Heute waren die obersten Ingenieure bei uns unten. Es ist irgendein Auftrag der Direktion ergangen, neue Stollen zu legen, und da kamen die Ingenieure, um die allerersten Ausmessungen vorzunehmen. Wie jung diese Leute sind und dabei schon so verschiedenartig! Sie haben sich alle frei entwickelt, und ungebunden zeigt sich ihr klar bestimmtes Wesen schon in jungen Jahren.

Einer, schwarzhaarig, lebhaft, läßt seine Augen überallhin laufen.

Ein Zweiter mit einem Notizblock, macht im Gehen Aufzeichnungen, sieht umher, vergleicht, notiert.

Ein Dritter, die Hände in den Rocktaschen, so daß sich alles an ihm spannt, geht aufrecht; wahrt die Würde; nur im fortwährenden Beißen seiner Lippen zeigt sich die ungeduldige, nicht zu unterdrückende Jugend.

Ein Vierter gibt dem Dritten Erklärungen, die dieser nicht verlangt; kleiner als er, wie ein Versucher neben ihm herlaufend, scheint er, den Zeigefinger immer in der Luft, eine Litanei über alles, was hier zu sehen ist, ihm vorzutragen.

They had forgotten about the Bedouins, forgotten about their hatred; the presence of the strong-smelling corpse blotted out everything else and cast a spell over them. One was already hanging on the neck and located the artery at his first bite. Like a small, furious pump attempting just as unquestioningly as hopelessly to put out a fire too strong for it, each muscle in his body was tugging and twitching in its given place. And by now all of them were heaped up high on the corpse, occupied the same way.

Then the caravan leader lashed them hard with his biting whip from all sides. They raised their heads, half drunk and swooning; they saw the Bedouins standing in front of them; they now felt the whip on their muzzles; they recoiled with a leap and ran some distance to the rear. But the camel's blood was already lying in puddles, with vapor rising from it, and its body was torn wide open in several places. They couldn't resist; they were back again; again the caravan leader raised his whip; I gripped his arm.

"You're right, sir," he said, "we'll leave them to their trade; besides, it's time to break camp. You've seen them. Peculiar beasts, aren't they? And how they hate us!"

Visitors to the Mine

Today the chief engineers were down among us. Some order of the management was issued to drive new tunnels, and so the engineers came to take the very first measurements. How young those people are, and at the same time so different from one another! They've all developed without constraints, and their clearly distinguished natures manifest themselves untrammeled, even in their youthful years.

One of them, with black hair, lively, lets his eyes race everywhere.

A second, with a notepad, takes notes while he walks, looks around, makes comparisons, writes things down.

A third, his hands in his jacket pockets, making all his clothing taut, walks erect; preserves his dignity; only the constant biting of his lips indicates his impatient, irrepressible youth.

A fourth gives explanations to the third, who doesn't ask for them; shorter than the third man, trotting alongside him like a tempter, his index finger always in the air, he seems to be reciting a litany to him about everything to be seen here.

Ein Fünfter, vielleicht der oberste im Rang, duldet keine
Begleitung; ist bald vorn, bald hinten; die Gesellschaft richtet ihren
Schritt nach ihm; er ist bleich und schwach; die Verantwortung hat
seine Augen ausgehöhlt; oft drückt er im Nachdenken die Hand an
die Stirn.

Der Sechste und Siebente gehen ein wenig gebückt, Kopf nah an
Kopf, Arm in Arm, in vertrautem Gespräch; wäre hier nicht offenbar
unser Kohlenbergwerk und unser Arbeitsplatz im tiefsten Stollen,
könnte man glauben, diese knochigen, bartlosen, knollennasigen
Herren seien junge Geistliche. Der eine lacht meistens mit katzenar-
tigem Schnurren in sich hinein; der andere, gleichfalls lächelnd,
führt das Wort und gibt mit der freien Hand irgendeinen Takt dazu.
Wie sicher müssen diese zwei Herren ihrer Stellung sein, ja welche
Verdienste müssen sie sich trotz ihrer Jugend um unser Bergwerk
schon erworben haben, daß sie hier, bei einer so wichtigen
Begehung, unter den Augen ihres Chefs, nur mit eigenen oder
wenigstens mit solchen Angelegenheiten, die nicht mit der augen-
blicklichen Aufgabe zusammenhängen, so unbeirrbar sich beschäftigen dürfen. Oder sollte es möglich sein, daß sie, trotz alles Lachens
und aller Unaufmerksamkeit, das, was nötig ist, sehr wohl bemerken?
Man wagt über solche Herren kaum ein bestimmtes Urteil abzu-
geben.

Andererseits ist es aber doch wieder zweifellos, daß zum Beispiel
der Achte unvergleichlich mehr als diese, ja mehr als alle anderen
Herren bei der Sache ist. Er muß alles anfassen und mit einem
kleinen Hammer, den er immer wieder aus der Tasche zieht und
immer wieder dort verwahrt, beklopfen. Manchmal kniet er trotz
seiner eleganten Kleidung in den Schmutz nieder und beklopft den
Boden, dann wieder nur im Gehen die Wände oder die Decke über
seinem Kopf. Einmal hat er sich lang hingelegt und lag dort still; wir
dachten schon, es sei ein Unglück geschehen; aber dann sprang er mit
einem kleinen Zusammenzucken seines schlanken Körpers auf. Er
hatte also wieder nur eine Untersuchung gemacht. Wir glauben unser
Bergwerk und seine Steine zu kennen, aber was dieser Ingenieur auf
diese Weise hier immerfort untersucht, ist uns unverständlich.

Ein Neunter schiebt vor sich eine Art Kinderwagen, in welchem
die Meßapparate liegen. Äußerst kostbare Apparate, tief in zarteste
Watte eingelegt. Diesen Wagen sollte ja eigentlich der Diener
schieben, aber es wird ihm nicht anvertraut; ein Ingenieur mußte
heran, und er tut es gern, wie man sieht. Er ist wohl der Jüngste,
vielleicht versteht er noch gar nicht alle Apparate, aber sein Blick ruht

A fifth, perhaps the highest-ranking, won't abide any company; now he's in front, now in the rear; the group paces itself by him; he's pale and feeble; responsibility has hollowed his eyes; often, as he thinks about things, he presses his hand to his forehead.

The sixth and seventh are a little stooped as they walk, their heads close together, their arms linked, in a confidential conversation; if this weren't obviously our coal mine and our working area in the deepest tunnel, you might think that these bony, beardless, bulbous-nosed gentlemen were young clergymen. One of them laughs to himself most of the time with a catlike purr; the other, also smiling, is the spokesman, occasionally beating time to his words with his free hand. How sure these two gentlemen must be of their jobs; indeed, what good service they must have already rendered to our mine despite their youthfulness, if down here, during such an important inspection, within their superior's view, they are allowed to occupy themselves so unswervingly with nothing but their own business, or at least with matters unconnected with their momentary task! Or can it be possible that, despite all their laughter and inattention, they are observing quite clearly everything that is needful? One scarcely dares come to a definite verdict concerning gentlemen of this type.

On the other hand, however, it's beyond doubt that the eighth man, for instance, is incomparably more on top of things than they are; in fact, more than all the other gentlemen. He's got to touch everything and tap it with a small hammer, which time after time he takes out of his pocket and replaces there again. Sometimes, despite his elegant clothing, he kneels down in the dirt and taps the ground, then again, only while walking, the walls or the ceiling over his head. Once he stretched out at full length and lay still there; we thought at first that he had had an accident; but then he jumped up with a slight twitch of his slender body. So, he had only been making an examination again. We think we know our mine and the stones in it, but we can't understand what this engineer is constantly examining here in this way.

A ninth man pushes a sort of baby carriage in front of him, in which the measuring instruments lie. Extremely expensive instruments, swathed in a thick layer of the softest absorbent cotton. This cart should really be pushed by the attendant, but it isn't entrusted to him; an engineer had to do it and, as we can see, he enjoys doing it. He's probably the youngest; perhaps he doesn't yet understand every instrument, but his eyes rest on

immerfort auf ihnen, fast kommt er dadurch manchmal in Gefahr, mit
dem Wagen an eine Wand zu stoßen.

Aber da ist ein anderer Ingenieur, der neben dem Wagen hergeht
und es verhindert. Dieser versteht offenbar die Apparate von Grund
aus und scheint ihr eigentlicher Verwahrer zu sein. Von Zeit zu Zeit
nimmt er, ohne den Wagen anzuhalten, einen Bestandteil der
Apparate heraus, blickt hindurch, schraubt auf oder zu, schüttelt und
beklopft, hält ans Ohr und horcht; und legt schließlich, während der
Wagenführer meist stillsteht, das kleine, von der Ferne kaum sichtbare Ding mit aller Vorsicht wieder in den Wagen. Ein wenig
herrschsüchtig ist dieser Ingenieur, aber doch nur im Namen der
Apparate. Zehn Schritte vor dem Wagen sollen wir schon, auf ein
wortloses Fingerzeichen hin, zur Seite weichen, selbst dort, wo kein
Platz zum Ausweichen ist.

Hinter diesen zwei Herren geht der unbeschäftigte Diener. Die
Herren haben, wie es bei ihrem großen Wissen selbstverständlich ist,
längst jeden Hochmut abgelegt, der Diener dagegen scheint ihn in
sich aufgesammelt zu haben. Die eine Hand im Rücken, mit der anderen vorn über seine vergoldeten Knöpfe oder das feine Tuch
seines Livreerockes streichend, nickt er öfters nach rechts und links,
so als ob wir gegrüßt hätten und er antwortete, oder so, als nehme er
an, daß wir gegrüßt hätten, könne es aber von seine Höhe aus nicht
nachprüfen. Natürlich grüßen wir ihn nicht, aber doch möchte man
bei seinem Anblick fast glauben, es sei etwas Ungeheures,
Kanzleidiener der Bergdirektion zu sein. Hinter ihm lachen wir
allerdings, aber da auch ein Donnerschlag ihn nicht veranlassen
könnte, sich umzudrehen, bleibt er doch als etwas Unverständliches
in unserer Achtung.

Heute wird wenig mehr gearbeitet; die Unterbrechung war zu aus-
giebig; ein solcher Besuch nimmt alle Gedanken an Arbeit mit sich
fort. Allzu verlockend ist es, den Herren in das Dunkel des
Probestollens nachzublicken, in dem sie alle verschwunden sind.
Auch geht unsere Arbeitsschicht bald zu Ende; wir werden die
Rückkehr der Herren nicht mehr mit ansehen.

Das nächste Dorf

Mein Großvater pflegte zu sagen: »Das Leben ist erstaunlich kurz.
Jetzt in Erinnerung drängt es sich mir so zusammen, daß ich zum
Beispiel kaum begreife, wie ein junger Mensch sich entschließen

them constantly; in that way, at times he almost runs the risk of banging the cart into a wall.

But another engineer is there, walking alongside the cart and preventing this. This man obviously understands the instruments thoroughly, and seems to be their real curator. From time to time, without stopping the cart, he takes out one component of the apparatus, looks through it, unscrews or screws it back, shakes it and taps it, holds it to his ear and listens; finally, while the cart-pusher generally comes to a halt, he places the little thing, which can scarcely be seen from a distance, back in the cart with the greatest of care. This engineer is a little imperious, but only for the sake of the apparatus. Ten paces in front of the cart, we must already step aside at a silent signal of his finger, even when there's no place to step aside to.

Behind these two gentlemen the unoccupied attendant walks. As is natural, in view of their great learning, the gentlemen have long since set aside all arrogance, whereas their attendant seems to have accumulated it all within his own person. One hand held behind him, the other in front stroking his gilt buttons or the fine cloth of his uniform, he frequently nods to the right and left, as if we had greeted him and he were responding, or as if he assumed we had greeted him but couldn't verify it from his exalted heights. Of course, we don't greet him, but at the sight of him, one might almost believe that it's a tremendous thing to be an attendant in the main office of the mine management. Naturally, we laugh behind his back, but, since even a thunderclap couldn't make him turn around, he nevertheless remains as something inexplicable in our estimation.

Today not much more work is accomplished; the interruption lasted too long; visitors like those take away with them all thoughts of work. It's much too tempting to gaze after the gentlemen into the darkness of the trial tunnel into which they all disappeared. Besides, our shift is nearly over; we won't get to see the gentlemen on their way back.

The Next Village

My grandfather used to say: "Life is amazingly short. Now, in memory, I find it so compressed that I can barely comprehend, for example, how a young person can determine to take

kann, ins nächste Dorf zu reiten, ohne zu fürchten, daß – von unglücklichen Zufällen ganz abgesehen – schon die Zeit des gewöhnlichen, glücklich ablaufenden Lebens für einen solchen Ritt bei weitem nicht hinreicht.«

Eine kaiserliche Botschaft

Der Kaiser – so heißt es – hat dir, dem Einzelnen, dem jämmerlichen Untertanen, dem winzig vor der kaiserlichen Sonne in die fernste Ferne geflüchteten Schatten, gerade dir hat der Kaiser von seinem Sterbebett aus eine Botschaft gesendet. Den Boten hat er beim Bett niederknien lassen und ihm die Botschaft ins Ohr geflüstert; so sehr war ihm an ihr gelegen, daß er sich sie noch ins Ohr wiedersagen ließ. Durch Kopfnicken hat er die Richtigkeit des Gesagten bestätigt. Und vor der ganzen Zuschauerschaft seines Todes – alle hindernden Wände werden niedergebrochen und auf den weit und hoch sich schwingenden Freitreppen stehen im Ring die Großen des Reichs – vor allen diesen hat er den Boten abgefertigt. Der Bote hat sich gleich auf den Weg gemacht; ein kräftiger, ein unermüdlicher Mann; einmal diesen, einmal den andern Arm vorstreckend schafft er sich Bahn durch die Menge; findet er Widerstand, zeigt er auf die Brust, wo das Zeichen der Sonne ist; er kommt auch leicht vorwärts, wie kein anderer. Aber die Menge ist so groß; ihre Wohnstätten nehmen kein Ende. Öffnete sich freies Feld, wie würde er fliegen und bald wohl hörtest du das herrliche Schlagen seiner Fäuste an deiner Tür. Aber statt dessen, wie nutzlos müht er sich ab; immer noch zwängt er sich durch die Gemächer des innersten Palastes; niemals wird er sie überwinden; und gelänge ihm dies, nichts wäre gewonnen; die Treppen hinab müßte er sich kämpfen; und gelänge ihm dies, nichts wäre gewonnen; die Höfe wären zu durchmessen; und nach den Höfen der zweite umschließende Palast; und wieder Treppen und Höfe; und wieder ein Palast; und so weiter durch Jahrtausende; und stürzte er endlich aus dem äußersten Tor – aber niemals, niemals kann es geschehen –, liegt erst die Residenzstadt vor ihm, die Mitte der Welt, hochgeschüttet voll ihres Bodensatzes. Niemand dringt hier durch und gar mit der Botschaft eines Toten. – Du aber sitzt an deinem Fenster und erträumst sie dir, wenn der Abend kommt.

a horse ride to the next village without fearing that—quite apart from unfortunate accidents—the span of a normal life with a fortunate course will be basically far from sufficient for such a ride."

A Message from the Emperor

The emperor—it is said—has sent to you, to you the private person, the pathetic subject, the tiny shadow that has fled from the imperial sunlight into the remotest distance, to you of all people the emperor on his deathbed has sent a message. He had the messenger kneel by his bed and whispered the message in his ear; it meant so much to him that he even had it repeated in his own ear. By a nod of his head he confirmed the correctness of the utterance. And in front of all the spectators of his death—all obstructing walls are torn down and the grandees of the realm are standing in a circle on the high outer steps, which form a broad arc—in front of them all he dispatched the messenger. The messenger set out immediately; a powerful, tireless man; thrusting forward one arm after another, he cuts his way through the throng; if he meets with resistance, he points to his chest, on which he wears the sun badge; and he moves forward easily, like no other. But the throng is so great; there's no end to their residences. If a clear space opened before him, how he'd fly, and you'd probably soon hear the splendid pounding of his fists on your door. But instead, how futilely he exerts himself! He's still squeezing through the rooms in the inner palace; he'll never get through them; and should he succeed in this, nothing would be gained; he'd have to fight his way down the steps; and should he succeed in this, nothing would be gained; he'd have to cover the distance of the courtyards; and after the courtyards there's the second palace, encircling the first; and once again stairways and courtyards; and once again a palace; and so on for millennia; and should he finally plunge out of the outermost gate—but that can never, never happen—he'd still find the capital city before him, the hub of the world, heaped full with its sediment. No one cuts his way through here, least of all with a message from a dead man.—But you sit at your window and formulate it in dreams when evening comes.

Die Sorge des Hausvaters

Die einen sagen, das Wort Odradek stamme aus dem Slawischen und sie suchen auf Grund dessen die Bildung des Wortes nachzuweisen. Andere wieder meinen, es stamme aus dem Deutschen, vom Slawischen sei es nur beeinflußt. Die Unsicherheit beider Deutungen aber läßt wohl mit Recht darauf schließen, daß keine zutrifft, zumal man auch mit keiner von ihnen einen Sinn des Wortes finden kann.

Natürlich würde sich niemand mit solchen Studien beschäftigen, wenn es nicht wirklich ein Wesen gäbe, das Odradek heißt. Es sieht zunächst aus wie eine flache sternartige Zwirnspule, und tatsächlich scheint es auch mit Zwirn bezogen; allerdings dürften es nur abgerissene, alte, aneinandergeknotete, aber auch ineinanderverfitzte Zwirnstücke von verschiedenster Art und Farbe sein. Es ist aber nicht nur eine Spule, sondern aus der Mitte des Sternes kommt ein kleines Querstäbchen hervor und an dieses Stäbchen fügt sich dann im rechten Winkel noch eines. Mit Hilfe dieses letzteren Stäbchens auf der einen Seite, und einer der Ausstrahlungen des Sternes auf der anderen Seite, kann das Ganze wie auf zwei Beinen aufrecht stehen.

Man wäre versucht zu glauben, dieses Gebilde hätte früher irgendeine zweckmäßige Form gehabt und jetzt sei es nur zerbrochen. Dies scheint aber nicht der Fall zu sein; wenigstens findet sich kein Anzeichen dafür; nirgends sind Ansätze oder Bruchstellen zu sehen, die auf etwas Derartiges hinweisen würden; das Ganze erscheint zwar sinnlos, aber in seiner Art abgeschlossen. Näheres läßt sich übrigens nicht darüber sagen, da Odradek außerordentlich beweglich und nicht zu fangen ist.

Er hält sich abwechselnd auf dem Dachboden, im Treppenhaus, auf den Gängen, im Flur auf. Manchmal ist er monatelang nicht zu sehen; da ist er wohl in andere Häuser übersiedelt; doch kehrt er dann unweigerlich wieder in unser Haus zurück. Manchmal, wenn man aus der Tür tritt und er lehnt gerade unten am Treppengeländer, hat man Lust, ihn anzusprechen. Natürlich stellt man an ihn keine schwierigen Fragen, sondern behandelt ihn – schon seine Winzigkeit verführt dazu – wie ein Kind. »Wie heißt du denn?« fragt man ihn. »Odradek«, sagt er. »Und wo wohnst du?« »Unbestimmter Wohnsitz«, sagt er und lacht; es ist aber nur ein Lachen, wie man es ohne Lungen hervorbringen kann. Es klingt etwa so, wie das Rascheln in gefallenen Blättern. Damit ist die Unterhaltung meist zu Ende. Übrigens sind

The Father's Worry

Some say the word Odradek comes from the Slavic, and try to prove the formation of the word on that basis. Whereas others believe it comes from the German and is merely influenced by the Slavic. But the unsureness of both interpretations probably points to the correct conclusion that neither one hits the mark, especially since neither of them allows one to find a meaning for the word.

Of course, no one would occupy himself with such studies if there weren't really a being called Odradek. At first it looks like a flat, star-shaped bobbin for twisting yarn, and moreover it actually seems to be covered with yarn; but it would have to be merely torn-off, old, knotted-together, but also snarled bits of yarn of the most varied types and colors. But it isn't merely a bobbin: a small transverse rod protrudes from the center of the star, and another rod is attached to that one at a right angle. With the aid of that second rod on one side, and one of the rays of the star on the other side, the whole creature can stand erect as if on two legs.

You'd be tempted to believe that this configuration once had some useful form, and is now merely out of shape. But this doesn't seem to be the case; at least there's no visible hint of it; incomplete members or places showing breakage, which would point to such a history, are nowhere to be seen; to be sure, the creature as a whole appears to make no sense, but it's complete in its own way. Anyway, no further details can be supplied, because Odradek is extraordinarily quick-moving and can't be caught.

At various times he stays in the attic, in the stairwell, in the corridors, in the vestibule. Sometimes he can't be seen for months on end; at such times he has probably moved to other houses; but then he inevitably returns to our house. Sometimes, when you're walking out the door and he happens to be leaning against the banisters at the foot of the stairs, you get the urge to talk to him. Of course, you don't ask him any difficult questions, but you treat him like a child—his very tininess induces you to do so. "What's your name?" you ask him. "Odradek," he says. "And where do you live?" "No settled address," he says with a laugh; but it's only a laugh that can be produced if you have no lungs. It sounds more or less like the rustling of fallen leaves. Most of the time the conversation ends there. Besides, even

selbst diese Antworten nicht immer zu erhalten; oft ist er lange
stumm, wie das Holz, das er zu sein scheint.

Vergeblich frage ich mich, was mit ihm geschehen wird. Kann er
denn sterben? Alles, was stirbt, hat vorher eine Art Ziel, eine Art
Tätigkeit gehabt und daran hat es sich zerrieben; das trifft bei
Odradek nicht zu. Sollte er also einstmals etwa noch vor den Füßen
meiner Kinder und Kindeskinder mit nachschleifendem Zwirnsfaden
die Treppe hinunterkollern? Er schadet ja offenbar niemandem; aber
die Vorstellung, daß er mich auch noch überleben sollte, ist mir eine
fast schmerzliche.

Elf Söhne

Ich habe elf Söhne.

Der erste ist äußerlich sehr unansehnlich, aber ernsthaft und klug;
trotzdem schätze ich ihn, wiewohl ich ihn als Kind wie alle andern
liebe, nicht sehr hoch ein. Sein Denken scheint mir zu einfach. Er
sieht nicht rechts noch links und nicht in die Weite; in seinem
kleinen Gedankenkreis läuft er immerfort rundum oder dreht sich
vielmehr.

Der zweite ist schön, schlank, wohlgebaut; es entzückt, ihn in
Fechterstellung zu sehen. Auch er ist klug, aber überdies welter-
fahren; er hat viel gesehen, und deshalb scheint selbst die heimische
Natur vertrauter mit ihm zu sprechen als mit den Daheimgeblie-
benen. Doch ist gewiß dieser Vorzug nicht nur und nicht einmal
wesentlich dem Reisen zu verdanken, er gehört vielmehr zu dem
Unnachahmlichen dieses Kindes, das zum Beispiel vom jedem an-
erkannt wird, der etwa seinen vielfach sich überschlagenden und
doch geradezu wild beherrschten Kunstsprung ins Wasser ihm nach-
machen will. Bis zum Ende des Sprungbrettes reicht der Mut und die
Lust, dort aber statt zu springen, setzt sich plötzlich der Nachahmer
und hebt entschuldigend die Arme. – Und trotz dem allen (ich sollte
doch eigentlich glücklich sein über ein solches Kind) ist mein Verhältnis zu ihm nicht ungetrübt. Sein linkes Auge ist ein wenig kleiner als
das rechte und zwinkert viel; ein kleiner Fehler nur, gewiß, der sein
Gesicht sogar noch verwegener macht als es sonst gewesen wäre, und
niemand wird gegenüber der unnahbaren Abgeschlossenheit seines
Wesens dieses kleinere zwinkernde Auge tadelnd bemerken. Ich, der
Vater, tue es. Es ist natürlich nicht dieser körperliche Fehler, der mir
weh tut, sondern eine ihm irgendwie entsprechende kleine

these replies can't always be obtained; often he's mute for a long time, like the piece of wood that he seems to be.

In vain I wonder what will become of him. Can he die? Everything that dies has had some sort of goal, some sort of activity previously, in the course of which it has consumed itself; but that's not the case with Odradek. Will he then perhaps at some time still roll down the steps, with a length of yarn dragging behind, landing at the feet of my children and my children's children? Indeed, he obviously does no harm to anyone; but the notion that he is to outlive me as well is almost painful to me.

Eleven Sons

I have eleven sons.

The first one is outwardly very plain-looking, but serious and clever; in spite of that I have no very high estimate of him, though I love him as a child like all the rest. His way of thinking seems too simple to me. He looks neither to the right nor to the left, nor into the distance; he constantly runs about—or, rather, turns in a circle—in his limited pattern of ideas.

The second one is handsome, slim, well built; it's delightful to see him in a fencing stance. He's clever, too, but, beyond that, worldly-wise; he's seen a lot, and therefore even our local nature seems to speak to him more intimately than to the stay-at-homes. But surely this advantage is not merely, and not even basically, a result of his travels; rather, it's part of this child's inimitable qualities, which, for example, are acknowledged by anyone who wants to imitate, let's say, his dive, which includes several somersaults and is yet kept under a control that borders on violence. Courage and desire last until the tip of the diving board, but there, instead of jumping, the imitator suddenly sits down and raises his arms apologetically.—And, despite all this (after all, I should really be glad to have such a child), my relationship with him is not unclouded. His left eye is a little smaller than the right, and blinks a lot; only a small defect, certainly, which makes his face even more daring than it would have been, and no one would single out that smaller, blinking eye in view of the unapproachable perfection of his nature. I, his father, do so. Of course, it's not that physical defect which pains me, but a slight irregularity of his mind which somehow corresponds to it,

Unregelmäßigkeit seines Geistes, irgendein in seinem Blut irrendes Gift, irgendeine Unfähigkeit, die mir allein sichtbare Anlage seines Lebens rund zu vollenden. Gerade dies macht ihn allerdings anderseits wieder zu meinem wahren Sohn, denn dieser sein Fehler ist gleichzeitig der Fehler unserer ganzen Familie und an diesem Sohn nur überdeutlich.

Der dritte Sohn ist gleichfalls schön, aber es ist nicht die Schönheit, die mir gefällt. Es ist die Schönheit des Sängers: der geschwungene Mund; das träumerische Auge; der Kopf, der eine Draperie hinter sich benötigt, um zu wirken; die unmäßig sich wölbende Brust; die leicht auffahrenden und viel zu leicht sinkenden Hände; die Beine, die sich zieren, weil sie nicht tragen können. Und überdies: der Ton seiner Stimme ist nicht voll; trügt einen Augenblick; läßt den Kenner aufhorchen; veratmet aber kurz darauf. – Trotzdem im allgemeinen alles verlockt, diesen Sohn zur Schau zu stellen, halte ich ihn doch am liebsten im Verborgenen; er selbst drängt sich nicht auf, aber nicht etwa deshalb, weil er seine Mängel kennt, sondern aus Unschuld. Auch fühlt er sich fremd in unserer Zeit; als gehöre er zwar zu meiner Familie, aber überdies noch zu einer andern, ihm für immer verlorenen, ist er oft unlustig und nichts kann ihn aufheitern.

Mein vierter Sohn ist vielleicht der umgänglichste von allen. Ein wahres Kind seiner Zeit, ist er jedermann verständlich, er steht auf dem allen gemeinsamen Boden und jeder ist versucht, ihm zuzunicken. Vielleicht durch diese allgemeine Anerkennung gewinnt sein Wesen etwas Leichtes, seine Bewegungen etwas Freies, seine Urteile etwas Unbekümmertes. Manche seiner Aussprüche möchte man oft wiederholen, allerdings nur manche, denn in seiner Gesamtheit krankt er doch wieder an allzu großer Leichtigkeit. Er ist wie einer, der bewundernswert abspringt, schwalbengleich die Luft teilt, dann aber doch trostlos im öden Staube endet, ein Nichts. Solche Gedanken vergällen mir den Anblick dieses Kindes.

Der fünfte Sohn ist lieb und gut; versprach viel weniger, als er hielt; war so unbedeutend, daß man sich förmlich in seiner Gegenwart allein fühlte; hat es aber doch zu einigem Ansehen gebracht. Fragte man mich, wie das geschehen ist, so könnte ich kaum antworten. Unschuld dringt vielleicht doch noch am leichtesten durch das Toben der Elemente in dieser Welt, und unschuldig ist er. Vielleicht allzu unschuldig. Freundlich zu jedermann. Vielleicht allzu freundlich. Ich gestehe: mir wird nicht wohl, wenn man ihn mir gegenüber lobt. Es heißt doch, sich das Loben etwas zu leicht zu

some poison wandering through his bloodstream, some incapability of rounding out to perfection the predisposition of his life which is visible to me alone. It's just this, though, which, on the other hand, makes him my true son, because this defect of his is at the same time the defect of our whole family, and is merely too noticeable in this son.

My third son is also handsome, but it's not the kind of good looks that I like. His good looks are those of a singer: the cupid's-bow mouth; the dreamy eyes; the head that needs drapery behind it to be effective; the disproportionately bulging chest; the hands that readily fly into the air and sink back again much too readily; the legs that walk affectedly because they're incapable of giving support. And besides: the tone of his voice isn't full; it's deceptive for a moment; it makes the connoisseur prick up his ears; but runs out of breath shortly afterward.—Despite the fact that in general all factors induce me to display this son prominently, I nevertheless prefer to keep him hidden; he himself isn't pushy, but not because he recognizes his shortcomings: rather, out of innocence. Also, he feels like a stranger in our day and age; as if he did indeed belong to my family, but, in addition, to another one, forever lost to him, he's often melancholy, and nothing can cheer him up.

My fourth son is perhaps the most sociable of them all. A true child of his era, he's comprehensible to everyone, he stands on the same ground everyone else does, and everyone is tempted to give him a friendly nod. Perhaps it's this universal recognition that gives his nature an element of lightness, his movements an element of freedom, his judgments an element of unconcern. You'd like to repeat some of his statements often, but only some, because, taken as a whole, he suffers from really excessive frivolity. He's like a man who takes off admirably, cuts through the air like a swallow, but then ends up in the dreary dust hopelessly, a zero. Thoughts like these make the sight of this child bitter to me.

My fifth son is lovable and kind; he promised much less than he delivered; he was so insignificant that in his presence you literally felt alone; but all the same he has won some prestige. If I were asked how it happened, I could scarcely reply. Perhaps after all, innocence makes its way most easily through the raging of the elements in this world, and an innocent he is. Perhaps too innocent. Friendly to everyone. Perhaps too friendly. I confess: I feel queasy when someone praises him to me. After all, praise

machen, wenn man einen so offensichtlich Lobenswürdigen lobt, wie
es mein Sohn ist.

Mein sechster Sohn scheint, wenigstens auf den ersten Blick, der
tiefsinnigste von allen. Ein Kopfhänger und doch ein Schwätzer.
Deshalb kommt man ihm nicht leicht bei. Ist er am Unterliegen, so
verfällt er in unbesiegbare Traurigkeit; erlangt er das Übergewicht, so
wahrt er es durch Schwätzen. Doch spreche ich ihm eine gewisse
selbstvergessene Leidenschaft nicht ab; bei hellem Tag kämpft er sich
oft durch das Denken wie im Traum. Ohne krank zu sein – vielmehr
hat er eine sehr gute Gesundheit – taumelt er manchmal, besonders
in der Dämmerung, braucht aber keine Hilfe, fällt nicht. Vielleicht
hat an dieser Erscheinung seine körperliche Entwicklung schuld, er
ist viel zu groß für sein Alter. Das macht ihn unschön im Ganzen, trotz
auffallend schöner Einzelheiten, zum Beispiel der Hände und Füße.
Unschön ist übrigens auch seine Stirn; sowohl in der Haut als in der
Knochenbildung irgendwie verschrumpft.

Der siebente Sohn gehört mir vielleicht mehr als alle andern. Die
Welt versteht ihn nicht zu würdigen; seine besondere Art von Witz
versteht sie nicht. Ich überschätze ihn nicht; ich weiß, er ist gering-
fügig genug; hätte die Welt keinen anderen Fehler als den, daß sie
ihn nicht zu würdigen weiß, sie wäre noch immer makellos. Aber in-
nerhalb der Familie wollte ich diesen Sohn nicht missen. Sowohl
Unruhe bringt er, als auch Ehrfurcht vor der Überlieferung, und bei-
des fügt er, wenigstens für mein Gefühl, zu einem unanfechtbaren
Ganzen. Mit diesem Ganzen weiß er allerdings selbst am wenigsten,
etwas anzufangen; das Rad der Zukunft wird er nicht ins Rollen bringen, aber diese seine Anlage ist so aufmunternd, so hoffnungsreich;
ich wollte, er hätte Kinder und diese wieder Kinder. Leider scheint
sich dieser Wunsch nicht erfüllen zu wollen. In einer mir zwar be-
greiflichen, aber ebenso unerwünschten Selbstzufriedenheit, die
allerdings in großartigem Gegensatz zum Urteil seiner Umgebung
steht, treibt er sich allein umher, kümmert sich nicht um Mädchen
und wird trotzdem niemals seine gute Laune verlieren.

Mein achter Sohn ist mein Schmerzenskind, und ich weiß
eigentlich keinen Grund dafür. Er sieht mich fremd an, und ich fühle
mich doch väterlich eng mit ihm verbunden. Die Zeit hat vieles gut
gemacht; früher aber befiel mich manchmal ein Zittern, wenn ich nur
an ihn dachte. Er geht seinen eigenen Weg; hat alle Verbindungen mit
mir abgebrochen; und wird gewiß mit seinem harten Schädel, seinem
kleinen athletischen Körper – nur die Beine hatte er als Junge recht
schwach, aber das mag sich inzwischen schon ausgeglichen haben –

comes somewhat too easily when you praise someone who's as obviously praiseworthy as my son is.

My sixth son, at least at first glance, seems like the deepest thinker of them all. A moper, and yet a babbler. Therefore it isn't easy to get to him. When he's on the losing side, he falls prey to unconquerable sadness; if he gains the upper hand, he maintains it by babbling. But I don't deny he has a certain selfless passion; in broad daylight he often fights his way through thoughts as if in a dream. Without being ill—on the contrary, his health is very good—he sometimes staggers, especially at dusk, but he needs no help, he doesn't fall. Perhaps his physical development is to blame for that phenomenon, he's much too tall for his age. That makes his overall appearance unlovely, despite conspicuously good-looking details, his hands and feet, for example. In addition his forehead, too, is ugly; somehow shrunken in the skin as well as in the bone structure.

My seventh son belongs to me more than all the rest, perhaps. The world is incapable of appreciating him; it doesn't understand his special brand of humor. I don't overestimate him; I know he's pretty insignificant; if the world had no other fault than its inability to appreciate him, it would still be flawless. But within the family I wouldn't want to do without this son. He contributes not only unrest, but also respect for tradition, and, at least to my way of thinking, he combines the two into an unassailable totality. But he himself is the man least capable of making something out of that totality; he'll never start the wheel of the future turning, but this predisposition of his is so encouraging, so promising; I wish he had children and *they* had children. Unfortunately it looks as if this wish will never come true. In a state of self-satisfaction which I, to be sure, can understand, but which I find nevertheless undesirable, and which is moreover in enormous contrast to the opinion of those around him, he goes around alone, pays no attention to girls, but in spite of that will never lose his good mood.

My eighth son is my child of sorrows, and I don't really know any reason for it. He looks at me like a stranger, and yet I feel close paternal ties to him. Time has improved many things, but in the past I was sometimes seized with trembling when I merely thought about him. He goes his own way; he has severed all ties to me; and surely with his hard skull and his short, athletic body—only his legs were really weak when he was a boy,

überall durchkommen, wo es ihm beliebt. Öfters hatte ich Lust, ihn zurückzurufen, ihn zu fragen, wie es eigentlich um ihn steht, warum er sich vom Vater so abschließt und was er im Grunde beabsichtigt, aber nun ist er so weit und so viel Zeit ist schon vergangen, nun mag es so bleiben wie es ist. Ich höre, daß er als der einzige meiner Söhne einen Vollbart trägt; schön ist das bei einem so kleinen Mann natürlich nicht.

Mein neunter Sohn ist sehr elegant und hat den für Frauen bestimmten süßen Blick. So süß, daß er bei Gelegenheit sogar mich verführen kann, der ich doch weiß, daß förmlich ein nasser Schwamm genügt, um allen diesen überirdischen Glanz wegzuwischen. Das Besondere an diesem Jungen aber ist, daß er gar nicht auf Verführung ausgeht; ihm würde es genügen, sein Leben lang auf dem Kanapee zu liegen und seinen Blick an die Zimmerdecke zu verschwenden oder noch viel lieber ihn unter den Augenlidern ruhen zu lassen. Ist er in dieser von ihm bevorzugten Lage, dann spricht er gern und nicht übel; gedrängt und anschaulich; aber doch nur in engen Grenzen; geht er über sie hinaus, was sich bei ihrer Enge nicht vermeiden läßt, wird sein Reden ganz leer. Man würde ihm abwinken, wenn man Hoffnung hätte, daß dieser mit Schlaf gefüllte Blick es bemerken könnte.

Mein zehnter Sohn gilt als unaufrichtiger Charakter. Ich will diesen Fehler nicht ganz in Abrede stellen, nicht ganz bestätigen. Sicher ist, daß, wer ihn in der weit über sein Alter hinausgehenden Feierlichkeit herankommen sieht, im immer festgeschlossenen Gehrock, im alten, aber übersorgfältig geputzten schwarzen Hut, mit dem unbewegten Gesicht, dem etwas vorragenden Kinn, den schwer über die Augen sich wölbenden Lidern, den manchmal an den Mund geführten zwei Fingern – wer ihn so sieht, denkt: das ist ein grenzenloser Heuchler. Aber, nun höre man ihn reden! Verständig; mit Bedacht; kurz angebunden; mit boshafter Lebendigkeit Fragen durchkreuzend; in erstaunlicher, selbstverständlicher und froher Übereinstimmung mit dem Weltganzen; eine Übereinstimmung, die notwendigerweise den Hals strafft und den Körper erheben läßt. Viele, die sich sehr klug dünken und die sich, aus diesem Grunde wie sie meinten, von seinem Äußern abgestoßen fühlten, hat er durch sein Wort stark angezogen. Nun gibt es aber wieder Leute, die sein Äußeres gleichgültig läßt, denen aber sein Wort heuchlerisch erscheint. Ich, als Vater, will hier nicht entscheiden, doch muß ich eingestehen, daß die letzteren Beurteiler jedenfalls beachtenswerter sind als die ersteren.

but that may have already become adjusted in the interim—he'll get along wherever he wishes. Frequently I have felt the urge to call him back, to ask him how things really are with him, why he cuts himself off from his father that way, and what his basic goal is, but now he's so far away and so much time has passed that things may as well remain as they are. I hear that, unlike all my other sons, he has a full beard; naturally that doesn't look good on such a short man.

My ninth son is very elegant and has that sweet look which men use on women. So sweet that occasionally it can even seduce me, though I know that literally all it takes is a damp sponge to wash away all that supernatural glow. The special thing about this boy is that he's not at all out to seduce; he'd be satisfied to spend his life lying on the couch and wasting his sweet look on the ceiling or, even better, letting it rest behind his closed eyes. When he's in this position that he prefers, he likes to talk, and not badly; concisely and graphically; but only within narrow limits; if he goes beyond them, which is unavoidable because they're so narrow, his speech becomes quite empty. People would show their displeasure if they had any hope of being noticed by those sleep-filled eyes.

My tenth son has the reputation of a dishonest character. I won't completely deny that failing or completely confirm it. What is a certainty is that, when people see him coming with his solemnity that is much too great for his age, in his always tightly buttoned frock coat, in his old but too carefully brushed black hat, with his immobile face, his somewhat prominent chin, his eyelids that bulge heavily over his eyes, the two fingers he sometimes puts up to his mouth—whoever sees him that way thinks: what an infinite hypocrite! But now listen to him speak! Intelligently; thoughtfully; in curt fashion; evading questions with malicious agility; in amazing, natural, and happy harmony with the universe; a harmony that forces one to stiffen one's neck and hold one's body up straight. Many who consider themselves very clever and have felt repelled by his appearance for that reason, as they thought, have been powerfully allured by his words. But there are other people who remain indifferent to his appearance, but find his words hypocritical. I, as his father, don't want to decide the matter here, but I must confess that at any rate the latter group are worthy of more consideration as judges than the former.

Mein elfter Sohn ist zart, wohl der schwächste unter meinen Söhnen; aber täuschend in seiner Schwäche; er kann nämlich zu Zeiten kräftig und bestimmt sein, doch ist allerdings selbst dann die Schwäche irgendwie grundlegend. Es ist aber keine beschämende Schwäche, sondern etwas, das nur auf diesem unsern Erdboden als Schwäche erscheint. Ist nicht zum Beispiel auch Flugbereitschaft Schwäche, da sie doch Schwanken und Unbestimmtheit und Flattern ist? Etwas Derartiges zeigt mein Sohn. Den Vater freuen natürlich solche Eigenschaften nicht; sie gehen ja offenbar auf Zerstörung der Familie aus. Manchmal blickt er mich an, als wollte er mir sagen: ›Ich werde dich mitnehmen, Vater.‹ Dann denke ich: ›Du wärst der Letzte, dem ich mich vertraue.‹ Und sein Blick scheint wieder zu sagen: ›Mag ich also wenigstens der Letzte sein.‹

Das sind die elf Söhne.

Ein Brudermord

Es ist erwiesen, daß der Mord auf folgende Weise erfolgte:

Schmar, der Mörder, stellte sich gegen neun Uhr abends in der mondklaren Nacht an jener Straßenecke auf, wo Wese, das Opfer, aus der Gasse, in welcher sein Büro lag, in jene Gasse einbiegen mußte, in der er wohnte.

Kalte, jeden durchschauernde Nachtluft. Aber Schmar hatte nur ein dünnes blaues Kleid angezogen; das Röckchen war überdies aufgeknöpft. Er fühlte keine Kälte; auch war er immerfort in Bewegung. Seine Mordwaffe, halb Bajonett, halb Küchenmesser, hielt er ganz bloßgelegt immer fest im Griff. Betrachtete das Messer gegen das Mondlicht; die Schneide blitzte auf; nicht genug für Schmar; er hieb mit ihr gegen die Backsteine des Pflasters, daß es Funken gab; bereute es vielleicht; und um den Schaden gutzumachen, strich er mit ihr violinbogenartig über seine Stiefelsohle, während er, auf einem Bein stehend, vorgebeugt, gleichzeitig dem Klang des Messers an seinem Stiefel, gleichzeitig in die schicksalsvolle Seitengasse lauschte.

Warum duldete das alles der Private Pallas, der in der Nähe aus seinem Fenster im zweiten Stockwerk alles beobachtete? Ergründe die Menschennatur! Mit hochgeschlagenem Kragen, den Schlafrock um den weiten Leib gegürtet, kopfschüttelnd, blickte er hinab.

Und fünf Häuser weiter, ihm schräg gegenüber, sah Frau Wese, den Fuchspelz über ihrem Nachthemd, nach ihrem Manne aus, der heute ungewöhnlich lange zögerte.

My eleventh son is gentle, probably the weakest of my sons, but deceptive in his weakness; you see, at times he can be forceful and determined, but even then his weakness remains fundamental somehow. But it's not a disgraceful weakness; rather, something that appears as weakness only on this earth of ours. For example, isn't readiness for flight also a kind of weakness, since it involves wavering and uncertainty and fluttering? My son manifests something of that sort. A father is naturally not delighted by such qualities; indeed, they obviously tend toward the dissolution of the family. At times he looks at me as if he wanted to say: "I'll take you along, father." Then I think: "You'd be the last man I'd entrust myself to." And his eyes seem to reply: "So, may I at least be the last."

Those are my eleven sons.

A Fratricide

It has been proved that the murder took place as follows:

Schmar, the killer, took up his stand about nine o'clock in the moonlit night at the street corner where Wese, the victim, had to turn from the street on which his office was located onto that street, where he lived.

Cold night air, piercing everyone. But Schmar had put on only a thin blue suit; moreover, the jacket was unbuttoned. He felt no cold; besides, he was constantly in motion. He held his deadly weapon, half bayonet, half kitchen knife, completely unsheathed and always firmly in his grasp. He observed the knife in the moonlight; the blade flashed; not enough for Schmar; he struck it against the bricks in the pavement until sparks flew; he regretted this, perhaps, and in order to repair any damage, he rubbed it over the sole of his boot like a violin bow while, standing on one leg, leaning forward, he listened simultaneously to the ringing of the knife on his boot and the sounds in the fateful side street.

Why was all this patiently endured by the retiree Pallas, who was observing it all nearby from his second-story window? Go and fathom human nature! With his collar standing up, his bathrobe tied around his ample body, shaking his head, he looked down.

And five houses farther along, diagonally opposite him, Mrs. Wese, her fox fur over her nightgown, was looking out for her husband, who was unusually late coming home that evening.

Endlich ertönt die Türglocke vor Weses Büro, zu laut für eine Türglocke, über die Stadt hin, zum Himmel auf, und Wese, der fleißige Nachtarbeiter, tritt dort, in dieser Gasse noch unsichtbar, nur durch das Glockenzeichen angekündigt, aus dem Haus; gleich zählt das Pflaster seine ruhigen Schritte.

Pallas beugt sich weit hervor; er darf nichts versäumen. Frau Wese schließt, beruhigt durch die Glocke, klirrend ihr Fenster. Schmar aber kniet nieder; da er augenblicklich keine anderen Blößen hat, drückt er nur Gesicht und Hände gegen die Steine; wo alles friert, glüht Schmar.

Gerade an der Grenze, welche die Gassen scheidet, bleibt Wese stehen, nur mit dem Stock stützt er sich in die jenseitige Gasse. Eine Laune. Der Nachthimmel hat ihn angelockt, das Dunkelblaue und das Goldene. Unwissend blickt er es an, unwissend streicht er das Haar unter dem gelüpften Hut; nichts rückt dort oben zusammen, um ihm die allernächste Zukunft anzuzeigen; alles bleibt an seinem unsinnigen, unerforschlichen Platz. An und für sich sehr vernünftig, daß Wese weitergeht, aber er geht ins Messer des Schmar.

»Wese!« schreit Schmar, auf den Fußspitzen stehend, den Arm aufgereckt, das Messer scharf gesenkt. »Wese! Vergebens wartet Julia!« Und rechts in den Hals und links in den Hals und drittens tief in den Bauch sticht Schmar. Wasserratten, aufgeschlitzt, geben einen ähnlichen Laut von sich wie Wese.

»Getan«, sagt Schmar und wirft das Messer, den überflüssigen blutigen Ballast, gegen die nächste Hausfront. »Seligkeit des Mordes! Erleichterung, Beflügelung durch das Fließen des fremden Blutes! Wese, alter Nachtschatten, Freund, Bierbankgenosse, versickerst im dunklen Straßengrund. Warum bist du nicht einfach eine mit Blut gefüllte Blase, daß ich mich auf dich setzte und du verschwändest ganz und gar. Nicht alles wird erfüllt, nicht alle Blütenträume reiften; dein schwerer Rest liegt hier, schon unzugänglich jedem Tritt. Was soll die stumme Frage, die du damit stellst?«

Pallas, alles Gift durcheinanderwürgend in seinem Leib, steht in seiner zweiflügelig aufspringenden Haustür. »Schmar! Schmar! Alles bemerkt, nichts übersehen.« Pallas und Schmar prüfen einander. Pallas befriedigt's, Schmar kommt zu keinem Ende.

Frau Wese mit einer Volksmenge zu ihren beiden Seiten eilt mit

Finally the doorbell outside Wese's office, too loud for a doorbell, resounds across town, and into the sky, and Wese, the diligent night worker, steps out of the building there, still invisible in this street and announced only by the indication of the bell; at once the pavement counts his tranquil steps.

Pallas leans far out; he doesn't want to miss a thing. Mrs. Wese, calmed by the bell, closes her window with a rattle. But Schmar kneels down; since for the moment he has no other bare parts, he presses only his face and hands against the stones; where everyone is cold, Schmar is on fire.

Precisely at the borderline between the two streets Wese comes to a halt; only leaning on his walking stick does he probe the street opposite him. A caprice. The night sky has attracted him, the dark blue and the gold. Unconsciously he looks at it, unconsciously he strokes the hair under his raised hat; nothing up there moves closer together, to inform him of the immediate future; everything remains in its absurd, unfathomable place. It's basically very sensible for Wese to continue walking, but he's walking into Schmar's knife.

"Wese!" Schmar cries, standing on tiptoe, his arm extended upward, the knife lowered at a sharp angle. "Wese! Julia is awaiting you in vain!" And Schmar stabs him on the right side of his neck and on the left side of his neck, and, the third time, deep in his stomach. Water voles, when cut open, utter a cry similar to Wese's.

"Done!" says Schmar and throws the knife, that superfluous bloodstained ballast, against the nearest facade. "The bliss of murder! The relief, the rapture caused by shedding someone else's blood! Wese, you old night shadow, friend, beerhall companion, you're trickling away on the dark pavement of the street. Why aren't you simply a blood-filled bladder, so I could sit on you and make you disappear completely? Not every wish comes true, 'not all my blossoming dreams came to maturity,'[2] your heavy remains lie here, already unable to feel any kick. What does the stupid question mean that you're asking that way?"

Pallas, choking down all the poison confusedly in his body, stands in his housedoor, which bursts open in two panels. "Schmar! Schmar! Observed everything, overlooked nothing!" Pallas and Schmar examine each other. Pallas is satisfied, Schmar can't stop.

Mrs. Wese, with a throng of people on either side of her, has-

---

2. An ironic quotation from Goethe's poem "Prometheus."

vor Schrecken ganz gealtertem Gesicht herbei. Der Pelz öffnet sich, sie stürzt über Wese, der nachthemdbekleidete Körper gehört ihm, der über dem Ehepaar sich wie der Rasen eines Grabes schließende Pelz gehört der Menge.

Schmar, mit Mühe die letzte Übelkeit verbeißend, den Mund an die Schulter des Schutzmannes gedrückt, der leichtfüßig ihn davonführt.

Ein Traum

Josef K. träumte:

Es war ein schöner Tag und K. wollte spazierengehen. Kaum aber hatte er zwei Schritte gemacht, war er schon auf dem Friedhof. Es waren dort sehr künstliche, unpraktisch gewundene Wege, aber er glitt über einen solchen Weg wie auf einem reißenden Wasser in unerschütterlich schwebender Haltung. Schon von der Ferne faßte er einen frisch aufgeworfenen Grabhügel ins Auge, bei dem er haltmachen wollte. Dieser Grabhügel übte fast eine Verlockung auf ihn aus und er glaubte, gar nicht eilig genug hinkommen zu können. Manchmal aber sah er den Grabhügel kaum, er wurde ihm verdeckt durch Fahnen, deren Tücher sich wanden und mit großer Kraft aneinanderschlugen; man sah die Fahnenträger nicht, aber es war, als herrsche dort viel Jubel.

Während er den Blick noch in die Ferne gerichtet hatte, sah er plötzlich den gleichen Grabhügel neben sich am Weg, ja fast schon hinter sich. Er sprang eilig ins Gras. Da der Weg unter seinem abspringenden Fuß weiter raste, schwankte er und fiel gerade vor dem Grabhügel ins Knie. Zwei Männer standen hinter dem Grab und hielten zwischen sich einen Grabstein in der Luft; kaum war K. erschienen, stießen sie den Stein in die Erde und er stand wie festgemauert. Sofort trat aus einem Gebüsch ein dritter Mann hervor, den K. gleich als einen Künstler erkannte. Er war nur mit Hosen und einem schlecht zugeknöpften Hemd bekleidet; auf dem Kopf hatte er eine Samtkappe; in der Hand hielt er einen gewöhnlichen Bleistift, mit dem er schon beim Näherkommen Figuren in der Luft beschrieb.

Mit diesem Bleistift setzte er nun oben auf dem Stein an; der Stein war sehr hoch, er mußte sich gar nicht bücken, wohl aber mußte er sich vorbeugen, denn der Grabhügel, auf den er nicht treten wollte, trennte ihn von dem Stein. Er stand also auf den

tens over, her face completely aged by fright. Her fur opens, she dashes onto Wese; her nightgown-clad body belongs to him, the fur, which closes over the husband and wife like turf over a grave, belongs to the crowd.

Schmar, overcoming his last bout of nausea with difficulty, his mouth pressed against the shoulder of the policeman, who fleet-footedly leads him away.

A Dream

Josef K. dreamed:

It was a fine day and K. wanted to go for a walk. But he had scarcely taken two steps before he was already in the cemetery. The paths there were very complicated, winding in an unpractical way, but he glided over one such path, as if on a raging river, in an immovably hovering attitude. Even at a distance he caught sight of a recently raised grave mound, at which he wanted to stop. This grave mound exerted what was almost an allurement for him, and he thought he could never reach it speedily enough. But at times he hardly saw the grave mound; his view of it was obstructed by flags, their cloth twisting and beating together with great force; the flagbearers couldn't be seen, but it looked as if great jubilation prevailed there.

While his eyes were still staring into the distance, he suddenly saw that same grave mound next to him on his path, in fact nearly behind him already. He jumped quickly onto the grass. Since the path continued to dash onward beneath his feet as he leapt off, he swayed and fell on his knees right in front of the grave mound. Two men were standing behind the grave, holding a tombstone in the air between them; scarcely had K. arrived when they thrust the stone into the earth, where it stood as if it were firmly anchored. Immediately a third man came out of the shrubbery, a man whom K. recognized at once as an artist. He was wearing only trousers and an improperly buttoned shirt; on his head he had a velvet cap; in his hand he held an ordinary pencil, with which he was already drawing figures in the air as he came nearer.

With this pencil he now started working at the top of the stone; the stone was very tall, so he didn't have to stoop at all, but he had to lean forward because the grave mound, which he

Fußspitzen und stützte sich mit der linken Hand auf die Fläche des Steines. Durch eine besonders geschickte Hantierung gelang es ihm, mit dem gewöhnlichen Bleistift Goldbuchstaben zu erzielen; er schrieb: ›Hier ruht —‹ Jeder Buchstabe erschien rein und schön, tief geritzt und in vollkommenem Gold. Als er die zwei Worte geschrieben hatte, sah er nach K. zurück; K., der sehr begierig auf das Fortschreiten der Inschrift war, kümmerte sich kaum um den Mann, sondern blickte nur auf den Stein. Tatsächlich setzte der Mann wieder zum Weiterschreiben an, aber er konnte nicht, es bestand irgendein Hindernis, er ließ den Bleistift sinken und drehte sich wieder nach K. um. Nun sah auch K. den Künstler an und merkte, daß dieser in großer Verlegenheit war, aber die Ursache dessen nicht sagen konnte. Alle seine frühere Lebhaftigkeit war verschwunden. Auch K. geriet dadurch in Verlegenheit; sie wechselten hilflose Blicke; es lag ein häßliches Mißverständnis vor, das keiner auflösen konnte. Zur Unzeit begann nun auch eine kleine Glocke von der Grabkapelle zu läuten, aber der Künstler fuchtelte mit der erhobenen Hand und sie hörte auf. Nach einem Weilchen begann sie wieder; diesmal ganz leise und, ohne besondere Aufforderung, gleich abbrechend; es war, als wolle sie nur ihren Klang prüfen. K. war untröstlich über die Lage des Künstlers, er begann zu weinen und schluchzte lange in die vorgehaltenen Hände. Der Künstler wartete, bis K. sich beruhigt hatte, und entschloß sich dann, da er keinen andern Ausweg fand, dennoch zum Weiterschreiben. Der erste kleine Strich, den er machte, war für K. eine Erlösung, der Künstler brachte ihn aber offenbar nur mit dem äußersten Widerstreben zustande; die Schrift war auch nicht mehr so schön, vor allem schien es an Gold zu fehlen, blaß und unsicher zog sich der Strich hin, nur sehr groß wurde der Buchstabe. Es war ein J, fast war es schon beendet, da stampfte der Künstler wütend mit einem Fuß in den Grabhügel hinein, daß die Erde ringsum in die Höhe flog. Endlich verstand ihn K.; ihn abzubitten war keine Zeit mehr; mit allen Fingern grub er in die Erde, die fast keinen Widerstand leistete; alles schien vorbereitet; nur zum Schein war eine dünne Erdkruste aufgerichtet; gleich hinter ihr öffnete sich mit abschüssigen Wänden ein großes Loch, in das K., von einer sanften Strömung auf den Rücken gedreht, versank. Während er aber unten, den Kopf im Genick noch aufgerichtet, schon von der undurchdringlichen Tiefe aufgenommen wurde, jagte oben sein Name mit mächtigen Zieraten über den Stein.

Entzückt von diesem Anblick erwachte er.

didn't want to step on, separated him from the stone. So he stood on tiptoe, supporting himself with his left hand on the surface of the stone. By means of an especially skillful manipulation he succeeded in producing gold letters with the plain pencil; he wrote: "Here lies. . . ." Each letter turned out clean and beautiful, deeply engraved and in perfect gold. After writing those two words, he looked back at K.; K., who was very eager for the continuation of the inscription, paid hardly any attention to the man, but looked only at the stone. Indeed, the man prepared to continue writing, but he couldn't; something interfered, he let the pencil sink, and turned back toward K. again. Now K. looked at the artist, too, and noticed that he was in great confusion, but he couldn't give a reason for it. All his previous liveliness had vanished. This brought K. into confusion as well; they exchanged helpless glances; there was some ugly misunderstanding which neither one could resolve. Now, inopportunely, a little bell started to ring, too, from the funeral chapel, but the artist gesticulated with his raised hand and it stopped. After a little while it began again, this time very softly and, at no special command, breaking off at once; it was as if it merely wanted to test its sound. K. was inconsolable over the artist's situation; he started to weep, and he sobbed for some time into his hands, which he held in front of his face. The artist waited for K. to calm down, and then he decided to go on writing after all, since he found no other solution. The first small stroke he drew was a redemption for K., but the artist obviously accomplished it only with extreme reluctance; besides, the writing was no longer as beautiful; above all, the gold seemed to be lacking; the writing was pale and unsteady, but the letter became very large. It was a J; when it was nearly completed, the artist furiously stamped into the grave mound with one foot, making the earth fly into the air all around. Finally K. understood him; there was no longer any time to ask his pardon; with all his fingers he dug into the earth, which made almost no resistance; everything seemed prepared in advance; only as an illusion had a thin coating of earth been raised; right behind it a great steep-sided pit opened, into which K., turned onto his back by a gentle current, submerged. But while he was already being received below by the impenetrable depths, his head still erect on his neck, up there his name raced across the stone with mighty flourishes.

Delighted at that sight, he awoke.

Erstes Leid

Ein Trapezkünstler – bekanntlich ist diese hoch in den Kuppeln der großen Varietébühnen ausgeübte Kunst eine der schwierigsten unter allen, Menschen erreichbaren – hatte, zuerst nur aus dem Streben nach Vervollkommnung, später auch aus tyrannisch gewordener Gewohnheit sein Leben derart eingerichtet, daß er, solange er im gleichen Unternehmen arbeitete, Tag und Nacht auf dem Trapez blieb. Allen seinen, übrigens sehr geringen Bedürfnissen wurde durch einander ablösende Diener entsprochen, welche unten wachten und alles, was oben benötigt wurde, in eigens konstruierten Gefäßen hinauf- und hinabzogen. Besondere Schwierigkeiten für die Umwelt ergaben sich aus dieser Lebensweise nicht; nur während der sonstigen Programm-Nummern war es ein wenig störend, daß er, wie sich nicht verbergen ließ, oben geblieben war und daß, trotzdem er sich in solchen Zeiten meist ruhig verhielt, hie und da ein Blick aus dem Publikum zu ihm abirrte. Doch verziehen ihm dies die Direktionen, weil er ein außerordentlicher, unersetzlicher Künstler war. Auch sah man natürlich ein, daß er nicht aus Mutwillen so lebte, und eigentlich nur so sich in dauernder Übung erhalten, nur so seine Kunst in ihrer Vollkommenheit bewahren konnte.

Doch war es oben auch sonst gesund, und wenn in der wärmeren Jahreszeit in der ganzen Runde der Wölbung die Seitenfenster aufgeklappt wurden und mit der frischen Luft die Sonne mächtig in den dämmernden Raum eindrang, dann war es dort sogar schön. Freilich, sein menschlicher Verkehr war eingeschränkt, nur manchmal kletterte auf der Strickleiter ein Turnerkollege zu ihm hinauf, dann saßen sie beide auf dem Trapez, lehnten rechts und links an den Haltestricken und plauderten, oder es verbesserten Bauarbeiter das Dach und wechselten einige Worte mit ihm durch ein offenes Fenster, oder es überprüfte der Feuerwehrmann die Notbeleuchtung auf der obersten Galerie und rief ihm etwas Respektvolles, aber wenig Verständliches zu. Sonst blieb es um ihn still; nachdenklich sah nur manchmal irgendein Angestellter, der sich etwa am Nachmittag in das leere Theater verirrte, in die dem Blick sich fast entziehende Höhe empor, wo der Trapezkünstler, ohne wissen zu können, daß jemand ihn beobachtete, seine Künste trieb oder ruhte.

So hätte der Trapezkünstler ungestört leben können, wären nicht

First Sorrow

A trapeze artist—as everyone knows, this art, performed high up beneath the domes of the great vaudeville theaters, is one of the most difficult of any attainable by man—had, initially only from a striving for perfection, but later also from a habit that had become tyrannical, so organized his life that, for all the time he was working in the same house, he would remain on his trapeze day and night. All his needs, which were very modest anyway, were met by servants who worked in shifts; they'd stand guard below and they'd haul up and down anything that was needed above in specially constructed containers. No particular difficulties were created for other people by this way of life; only during the rest of the numbers on the program it was a little disturbing to have him remaining up there (which couldn't be concealed), because even though at such times he generally kept still, here and there some of the spectators' eyes strayed in his direction. But the various managers forgave him for that because he was an extraordinary, irreplaceable artist. Besides, people naturally realized that he didn't live that way out of mischief, and that in fact only in that way could he maintain himself in constant practice and keep his art at its peak.

But life up there was healthful, besides, and when, in the warmer season, the side windows were thrown open all the way around the vaulting, and the sun entered forcefully into the twilit space along with the fresh air, it was even beautiful there. To be sure, his intercourse with other people was limited; only from time to time did a fellow gymnast climb up the rope ladder to him—then the two would sit on the trapeze, one leaning on the right-hand supporting rope, the other on the left-hand one, and they'd converse—or else construction workers would repair the roof and exchange a few words with him through an open window; or else the house fireman would examine the emergency lighting on the highest balcony and call out some remark to him which was respectful, but not very audible. Otherwise there was silence around him; only some employee, who might have strayed into the empty theater in the afternoon, would occasionally gaze contemplatively up into the heights, which were almost too remote to be seen, where the trapeze artist, unable to tell that anyone was observing him, practiced his stunts or rested.

The trapeze artist could have lived that way undisturbed were

die unvermeidlichen Reisen von Ort zu Ort gewesen, die ihm äußerst lästig waren. Zwar sorgte der Impresario dafür, daß der Trapezkünstler von jeder unnötigen Verlängerung seiner Leiden verschont blieb: für die Fahrten in den Städten benützte man Rennautomobile, mit denen man, womöglich in der Nacht oder in den frühesten Morgenstunden, durch die menschenleeren Straßen mit letzter Geschwindigkeit jagte, aber freilich zu langsam für des Trapezkünstlers Sehnsucht; im Eisenbahnzug war ein ganzes Kupee bestellt, in welchem der Trapezkünstler, zwar in kläglichem, aber doch irgendeinem Ersatz seiner sonstigen Lebensweise die Fahrt oben im Gepäcknetz zubrachte; im nächsten Gastspielort war im Theater lange vor der Ankunft des Trapezkünstlers das Trapez schon an seiner Stelle, auch waren alle zum Theaterraum führenden Türen weit geöffnet, alle Gänge frei gehalten – aber es waren doch immer die schönsten Augenblicke im Leben des Impresario, wenn der Trapezkünstler dann den Fuß auf die Strickleiter setzte und im Nu, endlich, wieder oben an seinem Trapez hing.

So viele Reisen nun auch schon dem Impresario geglückt waren, jede neue war ihm doch wieder peinlich, denn die Reisen waren, von allem anderen abgesehen, für die Nerven des Trapezkünstlers jedenfalls zerstörend.

So fuhren sie wieder einmal miteinander, der Trapezkünstler lag im Gepäcknetz und träumte, der Impresario lehnte in der Fensterecke gegenüber und las ein Buch, da redete ihn der Trapezkünstler leise an. Der Impresario war gleich zu seinen Diensten. Der Trapezkünstler sagte, die Lippen beißend, er müsse jetzt für sein Turnen, statt des bisherigen einen, immer zwei Trapeze haben, zwei Trapeze einander gegenüber. Der Impresario war damit sofort einverstanden. Der Trapezkünstler aber, so als wolle er es zeigen, daß hier die Zustimmung des Impresario ebenso bedeutungslos sei, wie es etwa sein Widerspruch wäre, sagte, daß er nun niemals mehr und unter keinen Umständen nur auf einem Trapez turnen werde. Unter der Vorstellung, daß es vielleicht doch einmal geschehen könnte, schien er zu schaudern. Der Impresario erklärte, zögernd und beobachtend, nochmals sein volles Einverständnis, zwei Trapeze seien besser als eines, auch sonst sei diese neue Einrichtung vorteilhaft, sie mache die Produktion abwechslungsreicher. Da fing der Trapezkünstler plötzlich zu weinen an. Tief erschrocken sprang der Impresario auf und fragte, was denn geschehen sei, und da er keine Antwort bekam, stieg er auf die Bank, streichelte ihn und drückte sein Gesicht an das eigene, so daß er auch von des Trapezkünstlers Tränen überflossen

it not for the unavoidable trips from place to place, which were extremely burdensome to him. Of course, his impresario took care that the trapeze artist was spared any unnecessary prolongation of his suffering: for trips within cities they used racing cars, with which they dashed at top speed through the unpeopled streets, whenever possible at night or the earliest morning, though even this was too slow for the trapeze artist's longing; on trains, an entire compartment was reserved, in which the trapeze artist, in a surely lamentable but at least partial substitute for his regular way of life, spent the journey up in the luggage net; in the next venue where he was to perform, the trapeze was already in place in the theater long before the trapeze artist's arrival, and all doors leading to the stage were wide open and every corridor kept free—but it was always the happiest time in the impresario's life when the trapeze artist then set foot on the rope ladder and in a flash was finally back up again, hanging from his trapeze.

No matter how many trips the impresario had successfully completed, each new one was still painful to him all over again, because, aside from everything else, trips were in any case jangling to the trapeze artist's nerves.

They were riding together again that way, the trapeze artist lying in the luggage net and dreaming, the impresario leaning in the window corner opposite, reading a book, when the trapeze artist spoke to him softly. The impresario was at his service at once. The trapeze artist said, biting his lips, that for his performance he now would always need two trapezes, two trapezes facing each other, instead of the previous single one. The impresario consented to this immediately. But, as if the trapeze artist wanted to show that in this matter the impresario's agreement was just as insignificant as his refusal might have been, he said that never again, under no circumstances, would he perform on just one trapeze. At the very idea that this could ever happen he seemed to shudder. The impresario, hesitantly and observing him, explained once again that he altogether approved: two trapezes were better than one, and this new arrangement was beneficial in other ways, too; it made the act more varied. Then the trapeze artist suddenly began to cry. The impresario jumped up, very frightened, and asked what had happened. Receiving no answer, he climbed onto the seat, patted him, and pressed his face to his own, so that he was also soaked by the trapeze artist's tears. But it

wurde. Aber erst nach vielen Fragen und Schmeichelworten sagte der
Trapezkünstler schluchzend:»Nur diese eine Stange in den Händen
– wie kann ich denn leben!« Nun war es dem Impresario schon
leichter, den Trapezkünstler zu trösten; er versprach, gleich aus der
nächsten Station an den nächsten Gastspielort wegen des zweiten
Trapezes zu telegraphieren; machte sich Vorwürfe, daß er den
Trapezkünstler so lange Zeit nur auf einem Trapez hatte arbeiten
lassen, und dankte ihm und lobte ihn sehr, daß er endlich auf den
Fehler aufmerksam gemacht hatte. So gelang es dem Impresario, den
Trapezkünstler langsam zu beruhigen, und er konnte wieder zurück in
seine Ecke gehen. Er selbst aber war nicht beruhigt, mit schwerer
Sorge betrachtete er heimlich über das Buch hinweg den
Trapezkünstler. Wenn ihn einmal solche Gedanken zu quälen begannen, konnten sie je gänzlich aufhören? Mußten sie sich nicht immerfort steigern? Waren sie nicht existenzbedrohend? Und wirklich
glaubte der Impresario zu sehn, wie jetzt im scheinbar ruhigen Schlaf,
in welchen das Weinen geendet hatte, die ersten Falten auf des
Trapezkünstlers glatter Kinderstirn sich einzuzeichnen begannen.

Ein Hungerkünstler

In den letzten Jahrzehnten ist das Interesse an Hungerkünstlern sehr
zurückgegangen. Während es sich früher gut lohnte, große derartige
Vorführungen in eigener Regie zu veranstalten, ist dies heute völlig
unmöglich. Es waren andere Zeiten. Damals beschäftigte sich die
ganze Stadt mit dem Hungerkünstler; von Hungertag zu Hungertag
stieg die Teilnahme; jeder wollte den Hungerkünstler zumindest einmal täglich sehn; an den spätern Tagen gab es Abonnenten, welche
tagelang vor dem kleinen Gitterkäfig saßen; auch in der Nacht fanden Besichtigungen statt, zur Erhöhung der Wirkung bei
Fackelschein; an schönen Tagen wurde der Käfig ins Freie getragen,
und nun waren es besonders die Kinder, denen der Hungerkünstler
gezeigt wurde; während er für die Erwachsenen oft nur ein Spaß war,
an dem sie der Mode halber teilnahmen, sahen die Kinder staunend,
mit offenem Mund, der Sicherheit halber einander bei der Hand haltend, zu, wie er bleich, im schwarzen Trikot, mit mächtig vortre-
tenden Rippen, sogar einen Sessel verschmähend, auf hingestreutem
Stroh saß, einmal höflich nickend, angestrengt lächelnd Fragen
beantwortete, auch durch das Gitter den Arm streckte, um seine
Magerkeit befühlen zu lassen, dann aber wieder ganz in sich selbst

was only after many questions and flattering words that the trapeze artist said with a sob: "Only this one bar in my hands—how can I live?!" By now it was easier for the impresario to console the trapeze artist; he promised that from the very next station he would telegraph the next venue concerning the second trapeze; he reproached himself aloud for having allowed the trapeze artist to work so long on a single trapeze, and thanked him and praised him highly for having finally called his attention to that mistake. In that way the impresario managed to calm the trapeze artist down gradually, and he was able to return to his corner. But he himself was not calm; seriously worried, he secretly studied the trapeze artist, glancing over the top of his book. If such thoughts once began to torment him, could they ever cease altogether? Wouldn't they necessarily increase constantly? Didn't they threaten his existence? And, in fact, the impresario thought he saw that now, in the apparently calm slumber in which the weeping had ended, the first wrinkles had begun to etch themselves on the trapeze artist's smooth, childlike forehead.

A Hunger Artist

During the most recent decades interest in showmen who fast in public has greatly waned. Whereas it was formerly very profitable to produce and manage large-scale performances of that sort, it's totally impossible today. The times were different. Back then the whole town was occupied with the "hunger artist"; from one day of fasting to the next, people's interest increased; everyone wanted to see the hunger artist at least once a day; on the later days of the performance, there were season ticketholders who sat in front of the little barred cage for days on end; viewings took place even at night, to heighten the effect with torchlight; on fine days the cage was brought outside, and then it was especially the children to whom the hunger artist was exhibited; whereas for grownups he was frequently only a joke, in which they showed interest only because it was fashionable, the children watched in amazement, open-mouthed, holding hands to feel safer, as the pale man, in a black body stocking, with extremely prominent ribs, even scorning a stool, sat on the strewn straw, now, nodding politely, answered questions with a strained smile, and also extended his arm through the bars to let people feel how thin he

versank, um niemanden sich kümmerte, nicht einmal um den für ihn
so wichtigen Schlag der Uhr, die das einzige Möbelstück des Käfigs
war, sondern nur vor sich hinsah mit fast geschlossenen Augen und
hie und da aus einem winzigen Gläschen Wasser nippte, um sich die
Lippen zu feuchten.

   Außer den wechselnden Zuschauern waren auch ständige, vom
Publikum gewählte Wächter da, merkwürdigerweise gewöhnlich
Fleischhauer, welche, immer drei gleichzeitig, die Aufgabe hatten,
Tag und Nacht den Hungerkünstler zu beobachten, damit er nicht
etwa auf irgendeine heimliche Weise doch Nahrung zu sich nehme.
Es war das aber lediglich eine Formalität, eingeführt zur Beruhigung
der Massen, denn die Eingeweihten wußten wohl, daß der Hungerkünstler während der Hungerzeit niemals, unter keinen Umständen,
selbst unter Zwang nicht, auch das geringste nur gegessen hätte; die
Ehre seiner Kunst verbot dies. Freilich, nicht jeder Wächter konnte
das begreifen, es fanden sich manchmal nächtliche Wachgruppen,
welche die Bewachung sehr lax durchführten, absichtlich in eine
ferne Ecke sich zusammensetzten und dort sich ins Kartenspiel vertieften, in der offenbaren Absicht, dem Hungerkünstler eine kleine
Erfrischung zu gönnen, die er ihrer Meinung nach aus irgendwelchen
geheimen Vorräten hervorholen konnte. Nichts war dem Hungerkünstler quälender als solche Wächter; sie machten ihn trübselig; sie
machten ihm das Hungern entsetzlich schwer; manchmal überwand
er seine Schwäche und sang während dieser Wachzeit, solange er es
nur aushielt, um den Leuten zu zeigen, wie ungerecht sie ihn ver-
dächtigten. Doch half das wenig; sie wunderten sich dann nur über
seine Geschicklichkeit, selbst während des Singens zu essen. Viel
lieber waren ihm die Wächter, welche sich eng zum Gitter setzten,
mit der trüben Nachtbeleuchtung des Saales sich nicht begnügten,
sondern ihn mit den elektrischen Taschenlampen bestrahlten, die
ihnen der Impresario zur Verfügung stellte. Das grelle Licht störte
ihn gar nicht, schlafen konnte er ja überhaupt nicht, und ein wenig
hindämmern konnte er immer, bei jeder Beleuchtung und zu jeder
Stunde, auch im übervollen, lärmenden Saal. Er war sehr gerne
bereit, mit solchen Wächtern die Nacht gänzlich ohne Schlaf zu verbringen; er war bereit, mit ihnen zu scherzen, ihnen Geschichten aus
seinem Wanderleben zu erzählen, dann wieder ihre Erzählungen
anzuhören, alles nur, um sie wachzuhalten, um ihnen immer wieder
zeigen zu können, daß er nichts Eßbares im Käfig hatte und daß er
hungerte, wie keiner von ihnen es könnte. Am glücklichsten aber war
er, wenn dann der Morgen kam und ihnen auf seine Rechnung ein

was, but then became altogether self-immersed again, cared
about nobody, not even about the chiming of the clock (the sole
furnishing in his cage), which was so important to him, but
merely gazed in front of him with nearly closed eyes, from time
to time sipping water from a tiny glass to moisten his lips.

Besides the spectators who'd come and go, there were also
constant guards present, chosen by the audience; oddly enough,
these were usually butchers, always three at a time, whose duty
it was to observe the hunger artist day and night, so that he
didn't actually take nourishment in some secret way. But that
was merely a formality introduced to appease the masses, because the initiates were well aware that, in his periods of fasting,
the hunger artist wouldn't have eaten the slightest thing—ever,
under any circumstances, even under compulsion—the honor of
his art forbade it. Of course, not every guard could comprehend
this; at times there were groups of guards at night who performed their guard duty with great laxity, intentionally sitting together in a remote corner and burying themselves in a card
game there, with the obvious purpose of granting the hunger
artist a little refreshment, which, as they supposed, he could take
out of some hidden supply or other. Nothing tortured the
hunger artist more than that kind of guard; they made him
melancholy; they made his fasting terribly hard on him; at times
he overcame his weakness and sang during this guard stint, as
long as he could keep it up, to show the people how unjust their
suspicion of him was. But that didn't do much good; at such
times they were merely surprised at his ability to eat even while
singing. He much preferred the guards who sat down close to
the cage and weren't satisfied with the dim night lights in the auditorium, but played their flashlights over him (they had been
provided by the impresario). The glaring light didn't disturb
him, in any case he was unable to sleep, and he could always
doze a little, in any kind of light and at any time, even when the
auditorium was packed and noisy. He was quite willing to spend
the whole night without sleeping in the company of such guards;
he was ready to joke with them, to tell them anecdotes from his
nomadic life, then listen to their stories in turn, everything just
to keep them awake, so that he could show them again and again
that he had nothing edible in his cage and that he was able to fast
better than any of them could. But he was happiest when morning finally came and they were brought a copious breakfast at his

überreiches Frühstück gebracht wurde, auf das sie sich warfen mit
dem Appetit gesunder Männer nach einer mühevoll durchwachten
Nacht. Es gab zwar sogar Leute, die in diesem Frühstück eine unge-
bührliche Beeinflussung der Wächter sehen wollten, aber das ging
doch zu weit, und wenn man sie fragte, ob etwa sie nur um der Sache
willen ohne Frühstück die Nachtwache übernehmen wollten, verzo-
gen sie sich, aber bei ihren Verdächtigungen blieben sie dennoch.

Dieses allerdings gehörte schon zu den vom Hungern überhaupt
nicht zu trennenden Verdächtigungen. Niemand war ja imstande, alle
die Tage und Nächte beim Hungerkünstler ununterbrochen als
Wächter zu verbringen, niemand also konnte aus eigener Anschauung
wissen, ob wirklich ununterbrochen, fehlerlos gehungert worden war;
nur der Hungerkünstler selbst konnte das wissen, nur er also gleichzeitig der von seinem Hungern vollkommen befriedigte Zuschauer
sein. Er aber war wieder aus einem andern Grunde niemals befriedigt; vielleicht war er gar nicht vom Hungern so sehr abgemagert,
daß manche zu ihrem Bedauern den Vorführungen fernbleiben
mußten, weil sie seinen Anblick nicht ertrugen, sondern er war nur so
abgemagert aus Unzufriedenheit mit sich selbst. Er allein nämlich
wußte, auch kein Eingeweihter sonst wußte das, wie leicht das Hungern war. Es war die leichteste Sache von der Welt. Er verschwieg es
auch nicht, aber man glaubte ihm nicht, hielt ihn günstigenfalls für
bescheiden, meist aber für reklamesüchtig oder gar für einen
Schwindler, dem das Hungern allerdings leicht war, weil er es sich
leicht zu machen verstand, und der auch noch die Stirn hatte, es halb
zu gestehn. Das alles mußte er hinnehmen, hatte sich auch im Laufe
der Jahre daran gewöhnt, aber innerlich nagte diese Unbefriedigtheit
immer an ihm, und noch niemals, nach keiner Hungerperiode –
dieses Zeugnis mußte man ihm ausstellen – hatte er freiwillig den
Käfig verlassen. Als Höchstzeit für das Hungern hatte der Impresario
vierzig Tage festgesetzt, darüber hinaus ließ er niemals hungern, auch
in den Weltstädten nicht, und zwar aus gutem Grund. Vierzig Tage
etwa konnte man erfahrungsgemäß durch allmählich sich steigernde
Reklame das Interesse einer Stadt immer mehr aufstacheln, dann
aber versagte das Publikum, eine wesentliche Abnahme des
Zuspruchs war festzustellen; es bestanden natürlich in dieser Hinsicht
kleine Unterschiede zwischen den Städten und Ländern, als Regel
aber galt, daß vierzig Tage die Höchstzeit war. Dann also am vierzigsten Tage wurde die Tür des mit Blumen umkränzten Käfigs geöffnet,
eine begeisterte Zuschauerschaft erfüllte das Amphitheater, eine
Militärkapelle spielte, zwei Ärzte betraten den Käfig, um die nötigen

expense, on which they seized with the appetite of healthy men after a night of laborious wakefulness. To be sure, there were even people who considered that breakfast to be an improper influence on the guards, but that was going too far, and when they were asked whether they were willing to take over the nighttime guard duty without breakfast just for the sake of doing it, they took off, though they still harbored their suspicions.

But these were part of the suspicions that can never be absent in matters of fasting. You see, no one was able to spend all those days and nights uninterruptedly guarding the hunger artist, and so no one could know from his own observation whether the fasting had been truly uninterrupted and flawless; only the hunger artist himself could know that, and so, at the same time, only he could be the perfectly satisfied spectator of his fasting. But, for another reason, he himself was never satisfied; perhaps it wasn't from fasting that he was so emaciated that many people regretfully had to stay away from the performances because they couldn't abide the sight of him, but he was so emaciated, instead, out of dissatisfaction with himself. Because he alone knew (and no other initiate knew it) how easy it was to fast. It was the easiest thing in the world. And he didn't conceal the fact, but people didn't believe him; at best they considered him modest, but generally thought of him as publicity-mad or even as a swindler, for whom fasting was surely easy because he knew how to make it easy on himself, and who then, to top it all, had the nerve to admit it partially. He had to submit to all that, in the course of the years he had even grown used to it, but that dissatisfaction always gnawed at him inside, and never yet, after any period of fasting— this testimonial everyone had to grant him—had he left his cage voluntarily. His impresario had established forty days as the maximum extent of his fasting, and never let him fast longer than that, not even in a great metropolis, and naturally for a good reason. Experience showed that for about forty days you could keep on whetting a town's interest by means of increasingly heightened publicity, but then the audience became reluctant and a substantial decrease in demand could be observed; in this regard there were naturally small differences between the cities and countries, but the rule held that forty days was the maximum time. And so then, on the fortieth day, the door of the flower-garlanded cage was opened, an enthusiastic audience filled the amphitheater, a military band played, two doctors entered the cage to study the

Messungen am Hungerkünstler vorzunehmen, durch ein Megaphon wurden die Resultate dem Saale verkündet, und schließlich kamen zwei junge Damen, glücklich darüber, daß gerade sie ausgelost worden waren, und wollten den Hungerkünstler aus dem Käfig ein paar Stufen hinabführen, wo auf einem kleinem Tischchen eine sorgfältig ausgewählte Krankenmahlzeit serviert war. Und in diesem Augenblick wehrte sich der Hungerkünstler immer. Zwar legte er noch freiwillig seine Knochenarme in die hilfsbereit ausgestreckten Hände der zu ihm hinabgebeugten Damen, aber aufstehen wollte er nicht. Warum gerade jetzt nach vierzig Tagen aufhören? Er hätte es noch lange, unbeschränkt lange ausgehalten; warum gerade jetzt aufhören, wo er im besten, ja noch nicht einmal im besten Hungern war? Warum wollte man ihn des Ruhmes berauben, weiter zu hungern, nicht nur der größte Hungerkünstler aller Zeiten zu werden, der er ja wahrscheinlich schon war, aber auch noch sich selbst zu übertreffen bis ins Unbegreifliche, denn für seine Fähigkeit zu hungern fühlte er keine Grenzen. Warum hatte diese Menge, die ihn so sehr zu bewundern vorgab, so wenig Geduld mit ihm; wenn er es aushielt, noch weiter zu hungern, warum wollte sie es nicht aushalten? Auch war er müde, saß gut im Stroh und sollte sich nun hoch und lang aufrichten und zu dem Essen gehn, das ihm schon allein in der Vorstellung Übelkeiten verursachte, deren Äußerung er nur mit Rücksicht auf die Damen mühselig unterdrückte. Und er blickte empor in die Augen der scheinbar so freundlichen, in Wirklichkeit so grausamen Damen und schüttelte den auf dem schwachen Halse überschweren Kopf. Aber dann geschah, was immer geschah. Der Impresario kam, hob stumm – die Musik machte das Reden unmöglich – die Arme über dem Hungerkünstler, so, als lade er den Himmel ein, sich sein Werk hier auf dem Stroh einmal anzusehn, diesen bedauernswerten Märtyrer, welcher der Hungerkünstler allerdings war, nur in ganz anderem Sinn; faßte den Hungerkünstler um die dünne Taille, wobei er durch übertriebene Vorsicht glaubhaft machen wollte, mit einem wie gebrechlichen Ding er es hier zu tun habe; und übergab ihn – nicht ohne ihn im geheimen ein wenig zu schütteln, so daß der Hungerkünstler mit den Beinen und dem Oberkörper unbeherrscht hin und her schwankte – den inzwischen totenbleich gewordenen Damen. Nun duldete der Hungerkünstler alles; der Kopf lag auf der Brust, es war, als sei er hingerollt und halte sich dort unerklärlich; der Leib war ausgehöhlt; die Beine drückten sich im Selbsterhaltungstrieb fest in den Knien aneinander, scharrten aber doch den Boden, so, als sei es nicht der wirkliche, den wirklichen suchten sie erst; und die ganze,

necessary life signs of the hunger artist, the results were announced to the auditorium through a megaphone, and finally two young ladies, glad that they and no others had been chosen by lot, came and tried to lead the hunger artist down the couple of steps from his cage to where a carefully selected convalescent's meal had been served on a small table. And at that moment the hunger artist always resisted. To be sure, he voluntarily placed his bony arms in the helpfully extended hands of the ladies who were bending over him, but he refused to stand up. Why stop just now after forty days? He could have kept it up longer, for an unlimitedly longer time; why stop just now, when he was at the peak—no, not yet even the peak—of his ability to fast? Why did they want to rob him of his glory in continuing to fast, in becoming not only the greatest hunger artist of all time, which he probably was already, but even surpassing himself to an incomprehensible degree, since he felt no limits to his ability to fast? Why did this crowd, which claimed to admire him so, have so little patience with him? If he could endure further fasting, why didn't they want to endure it? Besides, he was tired, he was comfortable sitting on the straw, and now had to stand up straight and tall and go over to the food, the very thought of which gave him nausea, the outer signs of which he painfully repressed merely out of consideration for the ladies. And he looked up into the eyes of those ladies, apparently so friendly but actually so cruel, and shook his head, which was too heavy for his feeble neck. But then what always happened, happened. His impresario came; in silence (the music made it impossible to speak) he lifted his arms over the hunger artist, as if he were inviting heaven to look down upon its handiwork here on the straw, this pitiable martyr, which the hunger artist was, to be sure, but in a very different sense; he grasped the hunger artist around his thin waist, whereby his exaggerated caution was intended to convince people that he was handling something immensely fragile; and, not without shaking him surreptitiously so that the hunger artist's legs and torso swayed uncontrolledly to and fro, he handed him over to the ladies, who meanwhile had turned deathly pale. Now the hunger artist put up with everything; his head was on his chest, as if it had rolled there and was remaining there in some inexplicable way; his body was hollowed out; his legs, in his urge for self-preservation, were tightly pressed together at the knees, but were scraping the ground as if it weren't the real one but they were still seek-

allerdings sehr kleine Last des Körpers lag auf einer der Damen, welche hilfesuchend, mit fliegendem Atem – so hatte sie sich dieses Ehrenamt nicht vorgestellt – zuerst den Hals möglichst streckte, um wenigstens das Gesicht vor der Berührung mit dem Hungerkünstler zu bewahren, dann aber, da ihr dies nicht gelang und ihre glücklichere Gefährtin ihr nicht zu Hilfe kam, sondern sich damit begnügte, zitternd die Hand des Hungerkünstlers, dieses kleine Knochenbündel, vor sich herzutragen, unter dem entzückten Gelächter des Saales in Weinen ausbrach und von einem längst bereitgestellten Diener abgelöst werden mußte. Dann kam das Essen, von dem der Impresario dem Hungerkünstler während eines ohnmachtähnlichen Halbschlafes ein wenig einflößte, unter lustigem Plaudern, das die Aufmerksamkeit vom Zustand des Hungerkünstlers ablenken sollte; dann wurde noch ein Trinkspruch auf das Publikum ausgebracht, welcher dem Impresario angeblich vom Hungerkünstler zugeflüstert worden war; das Orchester bekräftigte alles durch einen großen Tusch, man ging auseinander, und niemand hatte das Recht, mit dem Gesehenen unzufrieden zu sein, niemand, nur der Hungerkünstler, immer nur er.

So lebte er mit regelmäßigen kleinen Ruhepausen viele Jahre, in scheinbarem Glanz, von der Welt geehrt, bei alledem aber meist in trüber Laune, die immer noch trüber wurde dadurch, daß niemand sie ernst zu nehmen verstand. Womit sollte man ihn auch trösten? Was blieb ihm zu wünschen übrig? Und wenn sich einmal ein Gutmütiger fand, der ihn bedauerte und ihm erklären wollte, daß seine Traurigkeit wahrscheinlich von dem Hungern käme, konnte es, besonders bei vorgeschrittener Hungerzeit, geschehn, daß der Hungerkünstler mit einem Wutausbruch antwortete und zum Schrecken aller wie ein Tier an dem Gitter zu rütteln begann. Doch hatte für solche Zustände der Impresario ein Strafmittel, das er gern anwandte. Er entschuldigte den Hungerkünstler vor versammeltem Publikum, gab zu, daß nur die durch das Hungern hervorgerufene, für satte Menschen nicht ohne weiteres begreifliche Reizbarkeit das Benehmen des Hungerkünstler verzeihlich machen könne; kam dann im Zusammenhang damit auch auf die ebenso zu erklärende Behauptung des Hungerkünstlers zu sprechen, er könnte noch viel länger hungern, als er hungere; lobte das hohe Streben, den guten Willen, die große Selbstverleugnung, die gewiß auch in dieser Behauptung enthalten seien; suchte dann aber die Behauptung einfach genug durch Vorzeigen von Photographien, die gleichzeitig verkauft wurden, zu widerlegen, denn auf den Bildern sah man den

ing the real one; and the entire, of course very slight, weight of his body fell onto one of the ladies, who, imploring some aid, her breath coming in gasps (she hadn't envisioned her honorary office in this fashion), first stretched out her neck as far as she could to keep at least her face from touching the hunger artist, but then, when she was unsuccessful in this (and her more fortunate companion failed to come to her aid but was satisfied tremblingly to hold the hunger artist's hand, that little heap of bones, in front of her as they proceeded), she burst into tears, to the audience's delighted laughter, and had to be replaced by an attendant who had long been in readiness. Then came the food, a little of which the impresario shoveled into the hunger artist while he drowsed as if he were unconscious, with cheerful conversation intended to distract attention from the hunger artist's condition; then a toast to the audience was proposed, which had allegedly been whispered to the impresario by the hunger artist; the band confirmed all of this with a mighty flourish, the people dispersed, and no one had any right to be dissatisfied with what they had seen, no one except the hunger artist, always he alone.

And in that way he lived many years, with regularly spaced brief rest periods, in apparent glory, honored by the world, but despite all that usually in a sad mood which was made even sadder all the time because no one thought to take it seriously. With what was he to be consoled, anyway? What did he have left to wish for? And whenever some good-natured person showed up who pitied him and tried to make him see that his sadness was probably a result of his fasting, it sometimes occurred, especially when the fasting had been going on for some time, that the hunger artist responded with a fit of rage and, to everyone's horror, began to rattle the bars like a wild animal. But for such conditions his impresario had a means of punishment that he liked to apply. He apologized to the assembled audience for the hunger artist's behavior, admitting that only the irritability caused by hunger, not easily understood by well-fed people, could excuse it; then, in that connection, he would change the subject to the similarly explainable assertion by the hunger artist that he could fast much longer than he did; he would praise the lofty endeavor, good will, and great self-denial which were certainly also contained in that assertion; but then he would attempt to refute the assertion by the simple enough means of showing photographs, which were sold at the same time, because in the pictures could be seen the hunger

Hungerkünstler an einem vierzigsten Hungertag, im Bett, fast ver-
löscht vor Entkräftung. Diese dem Hungerkünstler zwar wohlbe-
kannte, immer aber von neuem ihn entnervende Verdrehung der
Wahrheit war ihm zu viel. Was die Folge der vorzeitigen Beendigung
des Hungerns war, stellte man hier als die Ursache dar! Gegen diesen
Unverstand, gegen diese Welt des Unverstandes zu kämpfen, war unmöglich. Noch hatte er immer wieder im gutem Glauben begierig
am Gitter dem Impresario zugehört, beim Erscheinen der
Photographien aber ließ er das Gitter jedesmal los, sank mit Seufzen
ins Stroh zurück, und das beruhigte Publikum konnte wieder herankommen und ihn besichtigen.

Wenn die Zeugen solcher Szenen ein paar Jahre später daran
zurückdachten, wurden sie sich oft selbst unverständlich. Denn inzwischen war jener erwähnte Umschwung eingetreten; fast plötzlich
war das geschehen; es mochte tiefere Gründe haben, aber wem lag
daran, sie aufzufinden; jedenfalls sah sich eines Tages der verwöhn-
te Hungerkünstler von der vergnügungssüchtigen Menge verlassen,
die lieber zu anderen Schaustellungen strömte. Noch einmal jagte
der Impresario mit ihm durch halb Europa, um zu sehn, ob sich
nicht noch hie und da das alte Interesse wiederfände; alles vergeblich; wie in einem geheimen Einverständnis hatte sich überall geradezu eine Abneigung gegen das Schauhungern ausgebildet.
Natürlich hatte das in Wirklichkeit nicht plötzlich so kommen können, und man erinnerte sich jetzt nachträglich an manche zu ihrer
Zeit im Rausch der Erfolge nicht genügend beachtete, nicht genügend unterdrückte Vorboten, aber jetzt etwas dagegen zu unternehmen, war zu spät. Zwar war es sicher, daß einmal auch für das
Hungern wieder die Zeit kommen werde, aber für die Lebenden
war das kein Trost. Was sollte nun der Hungerkünstler tun? Der,
welchen Tausende umjubelt hatten, konnte sich nicht in
Schaubuden auf kleinen Jahrmärkten zeigen, und um einen andern
Beruf zu ergreifen, war der Hungerkünstler nicht nur zu alt, sondern vor allem dem Hungern allzu fanatisch ergeben. So verabschiedete er denn den Impresario, den Genossen einer Laufbahn
ohnegleichen, und ließ sich von einem großen Zirkus engagieren;
um seine Empfindlichkeit zu schonen, sah er die Vertrags-
bedingungen gar nicht an.

Ein großer Zirkus mit seiner Unzahl von einander immer wieder
ausgleichenden und ergänzenden Menschen und Tieren und Ap-
paraten kann jeden und zu jeder Zeit gebrauchen, auch einen
Hungerkünstler, bei entsprechend bescheidenen Ansprüchen natür-

artist on one of his fortieth days of fasting, in bed, almost wiped out by loss of strength. This distortion of the truth, which of course the hunger artist was quite familiar with but which never failed to get on his nerves, was too much for him. That which was the result of the premature breaking of his fast was here presented as its cause! To combat this foolishness this world of foolishness, was impossible. Time and again he had still listened to his impresario eagerly, in good faith, holding onto the bars of his cage, but when the photographs appeared, he let go of the bars each time, falling back onto the straw with a sigh, and the audience, calmed down again, could once more approach and look at him.

When the witnesses to such scenes thought back on them a few years later, they frequently couldn't understand themselves. Because in the interim that above-mentioned shift in taste had occurred; it had happened almost in a flash; there may have been deeper-lying reasons for it, but who cared about unearthing them? At any rate, one day the spoiled hunger artist found himself abandoned by the pleasure-crazed crowd, which preferred to frequent other kinds of performances. Once more his impresario raced with him through half of Europe to see whether the old interest might still be rediscovered here or there; all in vain; as if by some secret accord an actual dislike for professional starving had taken shape everywhere. Naturally that couldn't really have come about all that suddenly, and now belatedly people remembered many omens which in the intoxication of success at the time had been insufficiently noticed and insufficiently countered; but it was now too late to undertake some campaign to combat the dislike. Of course, it was a certainty that the time even for fasting would come again, but that was no consolation for those now alive. What was the hunger artist to do now? He, who had been cheered by thousands, couldn't exhibit himself in booths at small fairs, and the hunger artist was not only too old to engage in another calling: above all, he was too fanatically devoted to fasting. And so he dismissed his impresario, the companion of an incomparable career, and signed on with a big circus; to spare his sensibilities, he didn't even look at the clauses in the contract.

A big circus, with its huge number of people, animals, and equipment, constantly supplementing and compensating for one another, can use anyone at any time, even a hunger artist, naturally one who made such modest demands, and, besides, in this

lich, und außerdem war es ja in diesem besonderen Fall nicht nur der Hungerkünstler selbst, der engagiert wurde, sondern auch sein alter berühmter Name, ja man konnte bei der Eigenart dieser im zunehmenden Alter nicht abnehmenden Kunst nicht einmal sagen, daß ein ausgedienter, nicht mehr auf der Höhe seines Könnens stehender Künstler sich in einen ruhigen Zirkusposten flüchten wolle, im Gegenteil, der Hungerkünstler versicherte, daß er, was durchaus glaubwürdig war, ebensogut hungere wie früher, ja er behauptete sogar, er werde, wenn man ihm seinen Willen lasse, und dies versprach man ihm ohne weiteres, eigentlich erst jetzt die Welt in berechtigtes Erstaunen setzen, eine Behauptung allerdings, die mit Rücksicht auf die Zeitstimmung, welche der Hungerkünstler im Eifer leicht vergaß, bei den Fachleuten nur ein Lächeln hervorrief.

Im Grunde aber verlor auch der Hungerkünstler den Blick für die wirklichen Verhältnisse nicht und nahm es als selbstverständlich hin, daß man ihn mit seinem Käfig nicht etwa als Glanznummer mitten in die Manege stellte, sondern draußen an einem im übrigen recht gut zugänglichen Ort in der Nähe der Stallungen unterbrachte. Große, bunt gemalte Aufschriften umrahmten den Käfig und verkündeten, was dort zu sehen war. Wenn das Publikum in den Pausen der Vorstellung zu den Ställen drängte, um die Tiere zu besichtigen, war es fast unvermeidlich, daß es beim Hungerkünstler vorüberkam und ein wenig dort haltmachte, man wäre vielleicht länger bei ihm geblieben, wenn nicht in dem schmalen Gang die Nachdrängenden, welche diesen Aufenthalt auf dem Weg zu den ersehnten Ställen nicht verstanden, eine längere ruhige Betrachtung unmöglich gemacht hätten. Dies war auch der Grund, warum der Hungerkünstler vor diesen Besuchszeiten, die er als seinen Lebenszweck natürlich herbeiwünschte, doch auch wieder zitterte. In der ersten Zeit hatte er die Vorstellungspausen kaum erwarten können; entzückt hatte er der sich heranwälzenden Menge entgegengesehn, bis er sich nur zu bald – auch die hartnäckigste, fast bewußte Selbsttäuschung hielt den Erfahrungen nicht stand – davon überzeugte, daß es zumeist der Absicht nach, immer wieder, ausnahmslos, lauter Stallbesucher waren. Und dieser Anblick von der Ferne blieb noch immer der schönste. Denn wenn sie bis zu ihm herangekommen waren, umtobte ihn sofort Geschrei und Schimpfen der ununterbrochen neu sich bildenden Parteien, jener, welche – sie wurde dem Hungerkünstler bald die peinlichere – ihn bequem ansehen wollte, nicht etwa aus Verständnis, sondern aus Laune und Trotz, und jener zweiten, die zunächst nur nach den

particular instance, it wasn't merely the hunger artist himself who was hired, but also his former great reputation; in fact, given the special nature of this art, which doesn't diminish with increasing age, people couldn't even say that a superannuated artist, no longer at the peak of his powers, wished to take refuge in a quiet position in the circus; on the contrary, the hunger artist gave assurances (and this was altogether believable) that he could fast just as well as before; in fact, he claimed that, if allowed to do as he liked (and he was immediately given that promise), he would now really astonish the world legitimately for the first time—an assertion, however, which, with regard to the atmosphere of the moment (which the hunger artist, in his enthusiasm, readily forgot), elicited only a smile in professional quarters.

But, basically, even the hunger artist didn't lose his eye for actual circumstances, and he accepted it as something natural that he and his cage weren't placed in the center of the arena like some star attraction, but were stationed at a place (which was quite accessible, all the same) in the vicinity of the menagerie. Large, multicolored signs framed the cage, announcing what was to be seen there. When the spectators pushed their way to the cages during intermissions in the show, to look at the animals, it was nearly unavoidable for them to pass by the hunger artist and linger there a while; they might have stayed with him longer, had not a longer, relaxed viewing been made impossible by the people who were shoving their way through the narrow passage and didn't understand this delay on the way to the desirable animal cages. This was also the reason why the hunger artist always trembled at these visiting times, which he naturally longed for as being his aim in life. At first he had hardly been able to wait for the intermissions; he had looked forward with delight to the crowd that came surging up, until, all too soon (even the most obstinate, almost conscious self-deception couldn't withstand his experiences), he became convinced that, time and again, they were most often, without exception, intending only to visit the menagerie. And the sight of them from a distance was always the most pleasurable. Because when they had arrived near him, he was immediately deafened by the yells and curses of the uninterruptedly reforming factions: those who wished to view the hunger artist in comfort, not because they understood him but out of caprice and defiance (this group was soon the one that made him suffer more), and the second group, who wanted nothing but to reach

Ställen verlangte. War der große Haufe vorüber, dann kamen die Nachzügler, und diese allerdings, denen es nicht mehr verwehrt war, stehenzubleiben, solange sie nur Lust hatten, eilten mit langen Schritten, fast ohne Seitenblick, vorüber, um rechtzeitig zu den Tieren zu kommen. Und es war kein allzu häufiger Glücksfall, daß ein Familienvater mit seinen Kindern kam, mit dem Finger auf den Hungerkünstler zeigte, ausführlich erklärte, um was es sich hier handelte, von früheren Jahren erzählte, wo er bei ähnlichen, aber unvergleichlich großartigeren Vorführungen gewesen war, und dann die Kinder, wegen ihrer ungenügenden Vorbereitung von Schule und Leben her, zwar immer noch verständnislos blieben – was war ihnen Hungern? – aber doch in dem Glanz ihrer forschenden Augen etwas von neuen, kommenden, gnädigeren Zeiten verrieten. Vielleicht, so sagte sich der Hungerkünstler dann manchmal, würde alles doch ein wenig besser werden, wenn sein Standort nicht gar so nahe bei den Ställen wäre. Den Leuten wurde dadurch die Wahl zu leicht gemacht, nicht zu reden davon, daß ihn die Ausdünstungen der Ställe, die Unruhe der Tiere in der Nacht, das Vorübertragen der rohen Fleischstücke für die Raubtiere, die Schreie bei der Fütterung sehr verletzten und dauernd bedrückten. Aber bei der Direktion vorstellig zu werden, wagte er nicht; immerhin verdankte er ja den Tieren die Menge der Besucher, unter denen sich hie und da auch ein für ihn Bestimmter finden konnte, und wer wußte, wohin man ihn verstecken würde, wenn er an seine Existenz erinnern wollte und damit auch daran, daß er, genau genommen, nur ein Hindernis auf dem Weg zu den Ställen war.

Ein kleines Hindernis allerdings, ein immer kleiner werdendes Hindernis. Man gewöhnte sich an die Sonderbarkeit, in den heutigen Zeiten Aufmerksamkeit für einen Hungerkünstler beanspruchen zu wollen, und mit dieser Gewöhnung war das Urteil über ihn gesprochen. Er mochte so gut hungern, als er nur konnte, und er tat es, aber nichts konnte ihn mehr retten, man ging an ihm vorüber. Versuche, jemandem die Hungerkunst zu erklären! Wer es nicht fühlt, dem kann man es nicht begreiflich machen. Die schönen Aufschriften wurden schmutzig und unleserlich, man riß sie herunter, niemandem fiel es ein, sie zu ersetzen; das Täfelchen mit der Ziffer der abgeleisteten Hungertage, das in der ersten Zeit sorgfältig täglich erneuert worden war, blieb schon längst immer das gleiche, denn nach den ersten Wochen war das Personal selbst dieser kleinen Arbeit überdrüssig geworden; und so hungerte zwar der Hungerkünstler weiter, wie er es früher einmal erträumt hatte, und es gelang ihm ohne Mühe ganz so,

the animals. Once the main throng had passed by, the stragglers arrived, but they, for whom there was no longer any obstacle to remaining as long as they wished, hastened by with great strides, practically without looking to either side, in order to reach the animals in time. And it wasn't a very frequent piece of luck when a father came with his children, pointed to the hunger artist with his finger, explained in detail what it was all about, and told about earlier years when he had attended similar shows, but on an incomparably larger scale, and then the children, because of their inadequate preparation at school and in life, always still remained uncomprehending, to be sure (what did fasting mean to them?), but nevertheless, in the gleam of their examining eyes, revealed something of new, more gratifying times to come. Perhaps, the hunger artist sometimes told himself on such occasions, everything would get a little better anyway, if only his spot weren't so very close to the menagerie. As it was, people's choice was made too easy for them, not to mention that he was very unnerved and constantly depressed by the stench from the cages, the animals' restlessness at night, the carrying by of the hunks of raw meat for the predators, and their cries while being fed. But he didn't dare complain to the management; anyway, he *was* under obligation to the animals for the large number of visitors, among whom now and then there might even be one who was glad to see *him*, and who knew where they would stick him if he tried to remind them of his existence and of the fact that, strictly speaking, he was only an obstacle on the way to the animals?

A small obstacle, though, an obstacle that was becoming smaller and smaller. People grew accustomed to the peculiarity of wishing to claim attention for a hunger artist in that day and age, and as they grew accustomed, his sentence was pronounced. He might fast as skillfully as he could (and he did so), but nothing could save him any more, people walked right by him. Go and try to explain the art of fasting to anybody! If someone doesn't feel it, you can't make him understand it. The pretty signs became dirty and illegible, they were torn down and it didn't occur to anyone to replace them; the board with the number of days he had fasted, which had at first been carefully kept up to date daily, had for a long time remained unchanged, because after the first few weeks even the staff had grown tired of that little task; and so the hunger artist kept on fasting, as he had once dreamed of doing in the past, and he succeeded effortlessly

wie er es damals vorausgesagt hatte, aber niemand zählte die Tage, niemand, nicht einmal der Hungerkünstler selbst wußte, wie groß die Leistung schon war, und sein Herz wurde schwer. Und wenn einmal in der Zeit ein Müßiggänger stehenblieb, sich über die alte Ziffer lustig machte und von Schwindel sprach, so war das in diesem Sinn die dümmste Lüge, welche Gleichgültigkeit und eingeborene Bösartigkeit erfinden konnten, denn nicht der Hungerkünstler betrog, er arbeitete ehrlich, aber die Welt betrog ihn um seinen Lohn.

Doch vergingen wieder viele Tage, und auch das nahm ein Ende. Einmal fiel einem Aufseher der Käfig auf, und er fragte die Diener, warum man hier diesen gut brauchbaren Käfig mit dem verfaulten Stroh drinnen unbenützt stehenlasse; niemand wußte es, bis sich einer mit Hilfe der Ziffertafel an den Hungerkünstler erinnerte. Man rührte mit Stangen das Stroh auf und fand den Hungerkünstler darin. »Du hungerst noch immer?« fragte der Aufseher, »wann wirst du denn endlich aufhören?« »Verzeiht mir alle«, flüsterte der Hungerkünstler; nur der Aufseher, der das Ohr ans Gitter hielt, verstand ihn. »Gewiß«, sagte der Aufseher und legte den Finger an die Stirn, um damit den Zustand des Hungerkünstlers dem Personal anzudeuten, »wir verzeihen dir.« »Immerfort wollte ich, daß ihr mein Hungern bewundert«, sagte der Hungerkünstler. »Wir bewundern es auch«, sagte der Aufseher entgegenkommend. »Ihr solltet es aber nicht bewundern«, sagte der Hungerkünstler. »Nun, dann bewundern wir es also nicht«, sagte der Aufseher, »warum sollen wir es denn nicht bewundern?« »Weil ich hungern muß, ich kann nicht anders«, sagte der Hungerkünstler. »Da sieh mal einer«, sagte der Aufseher, »warum kannst du denn nicht anders?« »Weil ich«, sagte der Hungerkünstler, hob das Köpfchen ein wenig und sprach mit wie zum Kuß gespitzten Lippen gerade in das Ohr des Aufsehers hinein, damit nichts verloren ginge, »weil ich nicht die Speise finden konnte, die mir schmeckt. Hätte ich sie gefunden, glaube mir, ich hätte kein Aufsehen gemacht und mich vollgegessen wie du und alle.« Das waren die letzten Worte, aber noch in seinen gebrochenen Augen war die feste, wenn auch nicht mehr stolze Überzeugung, daß er weiterhungere.

»Nun macht aber Ordnung!« sagte der Aufseher, und man begrub den Hungerkünstler samt dem Stroh. In den Käfig aber gab man einen jungen Panther. Es war eine selbst dem stumpfsten Sinn fühlbare Erholung, in dem so lange öden Käfig dieses wilde Tier sich herumwerfen zu sehn. Ihm fehlte nichts. Die Nahrung, die ihm schmeckte, brachten ihm ohne langes Nachdenken die Wächter;

just as he had then predicted, but no one counted the days; no one, not even the hunger artist himself, knew how great his achievement already was, and his heart grew heavy. And when once in a while some idler lingered, laughed at the outdated number, and spoke of a swindle, in this sense it was the dumbest lie that indifference and inborn malice could invent, because the hunger artist wasn't doing any cheating, he was working honestly, but the world was cheating him out of his reward.

But many more days went by, and even that came to an end. Once a supervisor noticed the cage, and he asked the attendants why this perfectly useful cage was left there unoccupied with rotting straw inside; no one knew why, until one of them, with the help of the board with figures, remembered the hunger artist. They poked through the straw with poles and found the hunger artist in it. "You're still fasting?" asked the supervisor. "When will you finally give up?" "Forgive me, everybody," the hunger artist whispered; only the supervisor, whose ear was to the bars, understood him. "Of course," said the supervisor, putting one finger to his forehead to show the hunger artist's condition to the staff, "we forgive you." "I always wanted you to admire my fasting," said the hunger artist. "And we do admire it," said the supervisor obligingly. "But you shouldn't admire it," said the hunger artist. "All right, then we don't admire it," said the supervisor, "but why shouldn't we admire it?" "Because I have to fast, I can't help it," said the hunger artist. "Well, what do you know!" said the supervisor. "Why can't you help it?" "Because," the hunger artist said, raising his head a little and speaking right into the supervisor's ear, his lips puckered as if for a kiss, so that no word would be lost, "because I could never find a dish I liked. If I had found one, believe me, I would have made no fuss and I would have filled my belly like you and everyone else." Those were his last words, but in his glazed eyes there was still the firm, if no longer proud, conviction that he was continuing to fast.

"Now clear everything away!" said the supervisor, and they buried the hunger artist along with the straw. But into the cage they put a young panther. It was visibly refreshing to even the dullest intellect to see that wild beast thrashing about in the cage that had been dreary so long. He lacked nothing. The keepers brought him the food he liked without stopping long to think it

nicht einmal die Freiheit schien er zu vermissen; dieser edle, mit allem Nötigen bis knapp zum Zerreißen ausgestattete Körper schien auch die Freiheit mit sich herumzutragen; irgendwo im Gebiß schien sie zu stecken; und die Freude am Leben kam mit derart starker Glut aus seinem Rachen, daß es für die Zuschauer nicht leicht war, ihr standzuhalten. Aber sie überwanden sich, umdrängten den Käfig und wollten sich gar nicht fortrühren.

over; he didn't even seem to miss his freedom; his noble body, furnished with everything needful until it was nearly bursting, seemed to carry even freedom around in it; that freedom seemed to be located somewhere in his teeth; and joy in life emanated from his maw with such great heat that it wasn't easy for the spectators to withstand it. But they mastered themselves, crowded around the cage, and refused to move away again.

RILKE: ERZÄHLUNGEN

Die Weise von Liebe und Tod
des Cornets Christoph Rilke

». . . den 24. November 1663 wurde Otto von Rilke / auf Langenau / Gränitz und Ziegra / zu Linda mit seines in Ungarn gefallenen Bruders Christoph hinterlassenem Antheile am Gute Linda beliehen; doch mußte er einen Revers ausstellen / nach welchem die Lehensreichung null und nichtig sein sollte / im Falle sein Bruder Christoph (der nach beigebrachtem Totenschein als Cornet in der Compagnie des Freiherrn von Pirovano des kaiserl. oesterr. Heysterschen Regiments zu Roß . . . verstorben war) zurückkehrt . . .«

Reiten, reiten, reiten, durch den Tag, durch die Nacht, durch den Tag.
Reiten, reiten, reiten.
Und der Mut ist so müde geworden und die Sehnsucht so groß. Es gibt keine Berge mehr, kaum einen Baum. Nichts wagt aufzustehen. Fremde Hütten hocken durstig an versumpften Brunnen. Nirgends ein Turm. Und immer das gleiche Bild. Man hat zwei Augen zuviel. Nur in der Nacht manchmal glaubt man den Weg zu kennen. Vielleicht kehren wir nächtens immer wieder das Stück zurück, das wir in der fremden Sonne mühsam gewonnen haben? Es kann sein. Die Sonne ist schwer, wie bei uns tief im Sommer. Aber wir haben im Sommer Abschied genommen. Die Kleider der Frauen leuchteten lang aus dem Grün. Und nun reiten wir lang. Es muß also Herbst sein. Wenigstens dort, wo traurige Frauen von uns wissen.

✿   ✿   ✿

RILKE: STORIES

The Ballad of Love and Death
of Cornet[3] Christoph Rilke

"*. . . on November 24, 1663, Otto von Rilke / lord of Langenau / Gränitz, and Ziegra / was invested at Linda with the share in the Linda estate left behind by his brother Christoph, who was killed in action in Hungary; but he had to give written assurances / according to which the enfeoffment would be null and void / in case his brother (who, according to the death certificate furnished, had died as cornet in the company of Baron von Pirovano of the Imperial Austrian Heyster Cavalry Regiment) should return. . . .*"

Riding, riding, riding, through the day, through the night, through the day.

Riding, riding, riding.

And my spirits have grown so weary and my longing so great. There are no mountains anymore, scarcely a tree. Nothing dares to stand erect. Unfamiliar cottages squat thirstily by boggy springs. Nowhere a tower. And the same view always. One's two eyes are superfluous. Only at times in the night you think you know the route. Perhaps at night we constantly retrace the piece of ground that we laboriously gained during the unfamiliar sunshine? That may be. The sun is heavy, as it is at home far into the summer. But we said good-bye in summer. The women's dresses shone out of the greenery for a long time. And now we've been riding for a long time. So it must be autumn. At least there, where sad women know we exist.

✿　　✿　　✿

---

3. Standard-bearer in a cavalry troop; a low-ranking commissioned officer.

Der von Langenau rückt im Sattel und sagt: »Herr Marquis . . .«
Sein Nachbar, der kleine feine Franzose, hat erst drei Tage lang
gesprochen und gelacht. Jetzt weiß er nichts mehr. Er ist wie ein
Kind, das schlafen möchte. Staub bleibt auf seinem feinen weißen
Spitzenkragen liegen; er merkt es nicht. Er wird langsam welk in
seinem samtenen Sattel.
Aber der von Langenau lächelt und sagt: »Ihr habt seltsame Augen,
Herr Marquis. Gewiß seht Ihr Eurer Mutter ähnlich —«
Da blüht der Kleine noch einmal auf und stäubt seinen Kragen ab
und ist wie neu.

Jemand erzählt von seiner Mutter. Ein Deutscher offenbar. Laut
und langsam setzt er seine Worte. Wie ein Mädchen, das Blumen
bindet, nachdenklich Blume um Blume probt und noch nicht weiß,
was aus dem Ganzen wird —: so fügt er seine Worte. Zu Lust? Zu
Leide? Alle lauschen. Sogar das Spucken hört auf. Denn es sind lauter
Herren, die wissen, was sich gehört. Und wer das Deutsche nicht
kann in dem Haufen, der versteht es auf einmal, fühlt einzelne Worte:
»Abends« . . . »Klein war . . .«

Da sind sie alle einander nah, diese Herren, die aus Frankreich
kommen und aus Burgund, aus den Niederlanden, aus Kärntens
Tälern, von den böhmischen Burgen und vom Kaiser Leopold. Denn
was der Eine erzählt, das haben auch sie erfahren und gerade so. Als
ob es nur *eine* Mutter gäbe . . .

So reitet man in den Abend hinein, in irgend einen Abend. Man
schweigt wieder, aber man hat die lichten Worte mit. Da hebt der
Marquis den Helm ab. Seine dunklen Haare sind weich und, wie er
das Haupt senkt, dehnen sie sich frauenhaft auf seinem Nacken. Jetzt
erkennt auch der von Langenau: Fern ragt etwas in den Glanz hinein,
etwas Schlankes, Dunkles. Eine einsame Säule, halbverfallen. Und
wie sie lange vorüber sind, später, fällt ihm ein, daß das eine Madonna
war.

Wachtfeuer. Man sitzt rundumher und wartet. Wartet, daß einer
singt. Aber man ist so müd. Das rote Licht ist schwer. Es liegt auf den
staubigen Schuhn. Es kriecht bis an die Kniee, es schaut in die gefalteten Hände hinein. Es hat keine Flügel. Die Gesichter sind dunkel.
Dennoch leuchten eine Weile die Augen des kleinen Franzosen mit
eigenem Licht. Er hat eine kleine Rose geküßt, und nun darf sie

The nobleman from Langenau shifts on his saddle and says: "Marquis . . ."

His neighbor, the small, delicate Frenchman, spoke and laughed for three days at first. Now he has no more to say. He's like a child that wants to sleep. Dust stays put on his elegant white lace collar; he doesn't notice it. Slowly he fades away on his velvet saddle.

But he of Langenau smiles and says: "You have odd eyes, marquis. You must surely resemble your mother—"

Then the little man blossoms out again, dusts off his collar, and is like new.

Someone is telling about his mother. Obviously a German. He utters one word after another loudly and slowly. Like a girl making a garland, thoughtfully trying out one flower after another and still not knowing how the whole thing will turn out: that's how he joins his words together. In pleasure? In sorrow? Everyone listens. Even the spitting ceases. Because everyone here is a gentleman who knows what's proper. And anyone in the group who doesn't know German suddenly understands it, senses individual words: "In the evening," "Small was . . ."

Then they're all close to one another, these gentlemen who come from France and Burgundy, from the Low Countries, from the valleys of Carinthia, from the hill castles of Bohemia, and from Emperor Leopold. Because what one of them tells, the others have also experienced, and in just the same way. As if there were only one mother in the world. . . .

And so we ride into the evening, into some evening or other. We are silent again, but we carry those bright words with us. Then the marquis removes his helmet. His dark hair is soft and, when he lowers his head, his hair spreads over the back of his neck like a woman's. Now he of Langenau recognizes it, too: in the distance something looms up into the bright light, something slender, dark. A solitary column, half-decayed. And long after they have passed it, he realizes it was a Madonna.

A watch fire. Men sit around it, waiting. Waiting for someone to sing. But they're so tired. The red light is heavy. It lies on their dusty shoes. It creeps up to their very knees, it looks into their clasped hands. It has no wings. Their faces are dark. And yet for a while the little Frenchman's eyes shine with a light of their own. He has just kissed a small rose, and now it may go on fading on his bosom. He of

weiterwelken an seiner Brust. Der von Langenau hat es gesehen, weil er nicht schlafen kann. Er denkt: Ich habe keine Rose, keine.

Dann singt er. Und das ist ein altes trauriges Lied, das zu Hause die Mädchen auf den Feldern singen, im Herbst, wenn die Ernten zu Ende gehen.

Sagt der kleine Marquis: »Ihr seid sehr jung, Herr?«
Und der von Langenau, in Trauer halb und halb im Trotz: »Achtzehn.« Dann schweigen sie.

Später fragt der Franzose: »Habt Ihr auch eine Braut daheim, Herr Junker?«
»Ihr?« gibt der von Langenau zurück.
»Sie ist blond wie Ihr.«

Und sie schweigen wieder, bis der Deutsche ruft: »Aber zum Teufel, warum sitzt Ihr denn dann im Sattel und reitet durch dieses giftige Land den türkischen Hunden entgegen?«
Der Marquis lächelt. »Um wiederzukehren.«

Und der von Langenau wird traurig. Er denkt an ein blondes Mädchen, mit dem er spielte. Wilde Spiele. Und er möchte nach Hause, für einen Augenblick nur, nur für so lange, als es braucht, um die Worte zu sagen: »Magdalena, – daß ich immer *so war*, verzeih!«
Wie – war? denkt der junge Herr. – Und sie sind weit.

Einmal, am Morgen, ist ein Reiter da, und dann ein zweiter, vier, zehn. Ganz in Eisen, groß. Dann tausend dahinter: Das Heer.
Man muß sich trennen.
»Kehrt glücklich heim, Herr Marquis. –«
»Die Maria schützt Euch, Herr Junker.«
Und sie können nicht voneinander. Sie sind Freunde auf einmal, Brüder. Haben einander mehr zu vertrauen; denn sie wissen schon so viel Einer vom Andern. Sie zögern. Und ist Hast und Hufschlag um sie. Da streift der Marquis den großen rechten Handschuh ab. Er holt die kleine Rose hervor, nimmt ihr ein Blatt. Als ob man eine Hostie bricht.
»Das wird Euch beschirmen. Lebt wohl.«
Der von Langenau staunt. Lange schaut er dem Franzosen nach. Dann schiebt er das fremde Blatt unter den Waffenrock. Und es treibt auf und ab auf den Wellen seines Herzens. Hornruf. Er reitet zum Heer, der Junker. Er lächelt traurig: ihn schützt eine fremde Frau.

✿   ✿   ✿

Langenau has seen this, because he can't sleep. He thinks to himself: "I have no rose, none."

Then he sings. And it's an old, sad song, which the girls back home sing in the fields, in autumn, when the harvest is nearly over.

The little marquis says: "You're very young, sir?"

And he of Langenau, half in sadness and half in defiance: "Eighteen." Then they are silent.

Later the Frenchman asks: "Do you, too, have a fiancée at home, my young lord?"

"Do you?" he of Langenau counters.

"She's blonde, like you."

And again they are silent until the German cries: "What the hell, then why are you sitting in the saddle and riding through this poisonous country to meet the Turkish dogs?"

The marquis smiles. "In order to return."

And he of Langenau becomes sad. He is thinking about a blonde girl he used to play with. Reckless games. And he'd like to be home, if only for a moment, for just as long as it takes to say the words: "Magdalena, forgive me for having always been *like that!*"

"Been like what?" the young lord thinks.—And they are far away.

One morning a cavalryman appeared, and then a second, four, ten. All in iron, tall. Then a thousand behind them: the army.

It's necessary to separate.

"Get home safely, marquis!"—

"The Virgin protects you, young lord."

And they're unable to part. Suddenly they're friends, brothers. They have more to confide in each other; because they already know so much about each other. They hesitate. And all around them is haste and hoofbeats. Then the marquis pulls off his large right glove. He takes out the little rose and removes one petal from it. As if a consecrated wafer were being broken.

"This will guard you. Farewell!"

He of Langenau is amazed. For a long time he gazes after the Frenchman. Then he puts the other man's petal beneath his tunic. And it is tossed to and fro on the waves of his heart. Bugle call. He rides toward the army, the young lord does. He smiles sadly: an unknown woman is protecting him.

✿   ✿   ✿

Ein Tag durch den Troß. Flüche, Farben, Lachen –: davon blendet das Land. Kommen bunte Buben gelaufen. Raufen und Rufen. Kommen Dirnen mit purpurnen Hüten im flutenden Haar. Winken. Kommen Knechte, schwarzeisern wie wandernde Nacht. Packen die Dirnen heiß, daß ihnen die Kleider zerreißen. Drücken sie an den Trommelrand. Und von der wilderen Gegenwehr hastiger Hände werden die Trommeln wach, wie im Traum poltern sie, poltern –. Und Abends halten sie ihm Laternen her, seltsame: Wein, leuchtend in eisernen Hauben. Wein? Oder Blut? – Wer kann's unterscheiden?

Endlich vor Spork. Neben seinem Schimmel ragt der Graf. Sein langes Haar hat den Glanz des Eisens.

Der von Langenau hat nicht gefragt. Er erkennt den General, schwingt sich vom Roß und verneigt sich in einer Wolke Staub. Er bringt ein Schreiben mit, das ihn empfehlen soll beim Grafen. Der aber befiehlt: »Lies mir den Wisch.« Und seine Lippen haben sich nicht bewegt. Er braucht sie nicht dazu; sind zum Fluchen gerade gut genug. Was drüber hinaus ist, redet die Rechte. Punktum. Und man sieht es ihr an. Der junge Herr ist längst zu Ende. Er weiß nicht mehr, wo er steht. Der Spork ist vor Allem. Sogar der Himmel ist fort. Da sagt Spork, der große General:

»Cornet.«

Und das ist viel.

Die Kompagnie liegt jenseits der Raab. Der von Langenau reitet hin, allein. Ebene. Abend. Der Beschlag vorn am Sattel glänzt durch den Staub. Und dann steigt der Mond. Er sieht es an seinen Händen.

Er träumt.

Aber da schreit es ihn an.

Schreit, schreit,

zerreißt ihm den Traum.

Das ist keine Eule. Barmherzigkeit:

der einzige Baum

schreit ihn an:

Mann!

Und er schaut: es bäumt sich. Es bäumt sich ein Leib

den Baum entlang, und ein junges Weib,

A day riding through the baggage train. Curses, colors, laughter—
the countryside dazzles with it. Boys in motley garb come running.
Tussling and shouting. Harlots come, with purple hats on their flow-
ing hair. Beckoning. Troopers come in black iron, as if the night were
walking. They seize the harlots so ardently that their dresses rip. They
press them against the rims of the drums. And the wilder resistance of
hasty hands awakens the drums, which rumble, rumble, as if in
dreams.—And in the evening they hold out lanterns to him, peculiar
ones: wine, gleaming in iron helmets. Wine? Or blood?—Who can tell
the difference?

Finally in the presence of Sporck. The count looms up alongside his
dapple gray. His long hair has the sheen of iron.

He of Langenau has asked no questions. He recognizes the general,
he leaps off his horse, and bows low in a cloud of dust. He has with
him a letter of recommendation addressed to the count. But the count
orders: "Read me that scrap!" And his lips didn't move. He doesn't use
them for that; cursing is quite enough for them. Anything beyond that
is stated by his right arm. Period. And you can tell by looking at that
arm. The young lord has finished reading long since. He no longer
knows where he is. Sporck comes before everything else. Even the sky
has departed. Then Sporck, the great general, says:

"Cornet."

And that's a lot.

The company is located across the Raab.[4] He of Langenau rides
over to it, alone. The plain. Evening. The metal fittings on the front of
his saddle gleam through the dust. And then the moon rises. He sees
it when he looks at his hands.

He daydreams.

But then someone screams at him.

Screams, screams,

rending his dream.

It isn't an owl. "Mercy!"

the solitary tree

screams at him:

"You there!"

And he looks: it rears up. A body rears up

against the tree trunk, and a young woman,

---

4. A river that rises in Austria and flows into the Danube in Hungary.

blutig und bloß,
fällt ihn an: Mach mich los!

Und er springt hinab in das schwarze Grün
und durchhaut die heißen Stricke;
und er sieht ihre Blicke glühn
und ihre Zähne beißen.

Lacht sie?

Ihn graust.
Und er sitzt schon zu Roß
und jagt in die Nacht. Blutige Schnüre fest in der Faust.

Der von Langenau schreibt einen Brief, ganz in Gedanken.
Langsam malt er mit großen, ernsten, aufrechten Lettern:

>>*Meine gute Mutter,*
>>*seid stolz: Ich trage die Fahne,*
>>*seid ohne Sorge: Ich trage die Fahne,*
>>*habt mich lieb: Ich trage die Fahne —«*

Dann steckt er den Brief zu sich in den Waffenrock, an die heim-
lichste Stelle, neben das Rosenblatt. Und denkt: er wird bald duften
davon. Und denkt: vielleicht findet ihn einmal Einer . . . Und
denkt: . . . ; denn der Feind ist nah.

Sie reiten über einen erschlagenen Bauer. Er hat die Augen weit
offen und Etwas spiegelt sich drin; kein Himmel. Später heulen
Hunde. Es kommt also ein Dorf, endlich. Und über den Hütten steigt
steinern ein Schloß. Breit hält sich ihnen die Brücke hin. Groß wird
das Tor. Noch willkommt das Horn. Horch: Poltern, Klirren und
Hundegebell! Wiehern im Hof, Hufschlag und Ruf.

Rast! Gast sein einmal. Nicht immer selbst seine Wünsche be-
wirten mit kärglicher Kost. Nicht immer feindlich nach allem
fassen; einmal sich alles geschehen lassen und wissen: was
geschieht, ist gut. Auch der Mut muß einmal sich strecken und sich
am Saume seidener Decken in sich selber überschlagen. Nicht
immer Soldat sein. Einmal die Locken offen tragen und den weiten
offenen Kragen und in seidenen Sesseln sitzen und bis in die
Fingerspitzen so: nach dem Bad sein. Und wieder erst lernen, was
Frauen sind. Und wie die weißen tun und wie die blauen sind; was

bloodstained and naked,
assails him: "Cut me loose!"

And he jumps down into the black greenery
and cuts through the hot ropes;
and he sees her gaze glow
and her teeth bite.

Is she laughing?

He shudders.
And at once he's back on his horse
and dashing into the night. Bloodstained cords tight in his fist.

He of Langenau is writing a letter, lost in thought. Slowly he paints
with large, earnest, upright letters:

> "*My good mother,*
> *be proud: I bear the standard;*
> *be without care: I bear the standard;*
> *love me: I bear the standard—*"

Then he places the letter inside his tunic, in the most secret place,
next to the rose petal. And he thinks: "The letter will soon take on its
fragrance." And he thinks: "Perhaps someday someone will find it . . ."
And he thinks: ". . . ." Because the enemy is near.

They ride over a slain peasant. His eyes are wide open and something is reflected in them; not the sky. Later, dogs howl. And so they're
reaching a village, finally. And above the cottages a mansion rises
stonily. The bridge offers them a wide passage. The gateway becomes
large. The horn welcomes them loudly. Listen! Rattling, clattering,
and barking! Neighing in the courtyard, hoofbeats and calls.

Repose! To be someone's guest for a change. Not always to entertain
one's own wishes with frugal fare. Not always to grab for everything
like an enemy; for once to take everything as it comes and to know:
everything that's coming is good. Even one's mind must sometimes
stretch itself lazily and, holding onto the borders of silken blankets,
tumble over into its proper nature. Not always to be a soldier. For once
to have one's tresses uncovered and free, to wear a wide, open collar,
to sit on silk-covered chairs, and to feel to one's very fingertips as if one
were just out of the bath. And to begin to learn again what women are.

für Hände sie haben, wie sie ihr Lachen singen, wenn blonde
Knaben die schönen Schalen bringen, von saftigen Früchten
schwer.

Als Mahl begann's. Und ist ein Fest geworden, kaum weiß man wie.
Die hohen Flammen flackten, die Stimmen schwirrten, wirre Lieder
klirrten aus Glas und Glanz, und endlich aus den reifgewordnen
Takten: entsprang der Tanz. Und alle riß er hin. Das war ein
Wellenschlagen in den Sälen, ein Sich-Begegnen und ein Sich-
Erwählen, ein Abschiednehmen und ein Wiederfinden, ein Glanz-
genießen und ein Lichterblinden und ein Sich-Wiegen in den
Sommerwinden, die in den Kleidern warmer Frauen sind.
Aus dunklem Wein und tausend Rosen rinnt die Stunde rauschend
in den Traum der Nacht.

Und Einer steht und staunt in diese Pracht. Und er ist so geartet,
daß er wartet, ob er erwacht. Denn nur im Schlafe schaut man
solchen Staat und solche Feste solcher Frauen: ihre kleinste Geste ist
eine Falte, fallend in Brokat. Sie bauen Stunden auf aus silbernen
Gesprächen, und manchmal heben sie die Hände so –, und du mußt
meinen, daß sie irgendwo, wo du nicht hinreichst, sanfte Rosen
brächen, die du nicht siehst. Und da träumst du: Geschmückt sein mit
ihnen und anders beglückt sein und dir eine Krone verdienen für
deine Stirne, die leer ist.

Einer, der weiße Seide trägt, erkennt, daß er nicht erwachen kann;
denn er ist wach und verwirrt von Wirklichkeit. So flieht er bange in
den Traum und steht im Park, einsam im schwarzen Park. Und das
Fest ist fern. Und das Licht lügt. Und die Nacht ist nahe um ihn und
kühl. Und er fragt eine Frau, die sich zu ihm neigt:
»Bist Du die Nacht?«
Sie lächelt.
Und da schämt er sich für sein weißes Kleid.
Und möchte weit und allein und in Waffen sein.
Ganz in Waffen.

Hast Du vergessen, daß Du mein Page bist für diesen Tag?
Verlässest Du mich? Wo gehst Du hin? Dein weißes Kleid gibt mir
Dein Recht –.«

»Sehnt es Dich nach Deinem rauhen Rock?«

And how the ones in white behave, and what the ones in blue are like; what sort of hands they have, how they sing their laughter when blonde pages bring the beautiful bowls laden with juicy fruit.

It began as a meal. And it became a banquet, somehow or other. The tall flames flickered, the voices buzzed, confused songs clinked from the glass and the gleam, and finally, from the measures which had reached maturity, the dance arose. And carried everyone away. It was a beating of waves in the halls, a meeting and choosing of partners, a leavetaking and a reunion, an enjoyment of the brightness and a blinding by the light and a rocking to and fro in the summer breezes that are contained in the dresses of congenial women.
From dark wine and a thousand roses the hours trickle away noisily into the dream of night.

And a man stands gazing in wonder at that splendor. And his nature is such that he waits to see whether he will awaken. Because only in sleep does one behold such pomp and such feasts given by such women: their slightest gesture is a fold made in brocade. They construct hours out of silvery conversations, and at times they raise their hands like this—and you've got to believe that somewhere where you can't reach they're plucking soft roses which you can't see. And then you dream: to be adorned with them and to be made happy in another way and to earn a crown for your brow, which is empty.

A man dressed in white silk realizes that he cannot awaken: because he's already awake and confused by reality. And so he timidly retreats into dreams and stands in the park, alone in the black park. And the festivities are far away. And the light is deceptive. And night is close around him and cool. And he asks a woman who leans over to him:
"Are you the night?"
She smiles.
And then he's ashamed of his white outfit.
And would like to be far away and alone and in armor.
Completely in armor.

"Have you forgotten that you're my page for today? Are you deserting me? Where are you off to? Your white outfit gives me a claim on you—."

"Do you long for your rough cavalry tunic?"

»Frierst Du? – Hast Du Heimweh?«
Die Gräfin lächelt.
Nein. Aber das ist nur, weil das Kindsein ihm von den Schultern
gefallen ist, dieses sanfte dunkle Kleid. Wer hat es fortgenommen?
»Du?« fragt er mit einer Stimme, die er noch nicht gehört hat. »Du!«
Und nun ist nichts an ihm. Und er ist nackt wie ein Heiliger. Hell
und schlank.

Langsam lischt das Schloß aus. Alle sind schwer: müde oder verliebt
oder trunken. Nach so vielen leeren, langen Feldnächten: Betten.
Breite eichene Betten. Da betet sichs anders als in der lumpigen
Furche unterwegs, die, wenn man einschlafen will, wie ein Grab wird.
»Herrgott, wie Du willst!«
Kürzer sind die Gebete im Bett.
Aber inniger.

Die Turmstube ist dunkel.
Aber sie leuchten sich ins Gesicht mit ihrem Lächeln. Sie tasten vor
sich her wie Blinde und finden den Andern wie eine Tür. Fast wie
Kinder, die sich vor der Nacht ängstigen, drängen sie sich in einander
ein. Und doch fürchten sie sich nicht. Da ist nichts, was gegen sie
wäre: kein Gestern, kein Morgen; denn die Zeit ist eingestürzt. Und
sie blühen aus ihren Trümmern.
Er fragt nicht: »Dein Gemahl?«
Sie fragt nicht: »Dein Namen?«
Sie haben sich ja gefunden, um einander ein neues Geschlecht zu sein.
Sie werden sich hundert neue Namen geben und einander alle
wieder abnehmen, leise, wie man einen Ohrring abnimmt.

Im Vorsaal über einem Sessel hängt der Waffenrock, das Bandelier
und der Mantel von dem von Langenau. Seine Handschuhe liegen auf
dem Fußboden. Seine Fahne steht steil, gelehnt an das Fensterkreuz.
Sie ist schwarz und schlank. Draußen jagt ein Sturm über den
Himmel hin und macht Stücke aus der Nacht, weiße und schwarze.
Der Mondschein geht wie ein langer Blitz vorbei, und die reglose
Fahne hat unruhige Schatten. Sie träumt.

War ein Fenster offen? Ist der Sturm im Haus? Wer schlägt die
Türen zu? Wer geht durch die Zimmer? – Laß. Wer es auch sei. Ins
Turmgemach findet er nicht. Wie hinter hundert Türen ist dieser
große Schlaf, den zwei Menschen gemeinsam haben; so gemeinsam
wie *eine* Mutter oder *einen* Tod.

"Are you cold? Are you homesick?"

The countess smiles.

No. But this is only because his childhood has slipped from his shoulders, that soft, dark garment. Who has taken it away? "You?" he asks with a tone of voice he has never yet heard. "You!"

And now there is nothing on him. And he is as naked as a saint. Bright and slim.

Slowly the lights in the mansion go out. Everyone is heavy: tired or in love or drunk. After so many long, empty nights in the field: beds. Wide oak beds. Praying there is different than in a shabby furrow along the way, which, when you try to fall asleep, becomes like a grave.

"Lord God, Thy will be done!"

Prayers in bed are briefer.

But more heartfelt.

The tower room is dark.

But they illuminate each other's faces with their smiles. They grope in front of them as if blind, each finding the other, like a door. Almost like children afraid of the night, they press against each other. And yet they have no fear. Nothing there can be against them: no yesterday, no tomorrow; because time has collapsed. And they are blossoming from its ruins.

He doesn't ask: "Your husband?"

She doesn't ask: "Your name?"

They have indeed found each other, to be a new race for each other.

They will give each other a hundred new names and take them all away again, quietly, as one takes off an earring.

Over a chair in the anteroom are draped the uniform, bandoleer, and cape of the man of Langenau. His gloves lie on the floor. His standard leans stiffly against the window cross. It is black and slender. Outdoors a storm chases across the sky, tearing the night into pieces, white and black. The moonlight passes by like a long lightning flash, and the immobile standard casts restless shadows. It is dreaming.

Was a window open? Is the storm in the house? Who is slamming the doors? Who is walking through the rooms?—Let it go! Whoever it is, he won't find his way into the tower room. As if sheltered by a hundred doors is this deep sleep which two people possess in common; just as much in common as one mother or one death.

❈   ❈   ❈

Ist das der Morgen? Welche Sonne geht auf? Wie groß ist die
Sonne. Sind das Vögel? Ihre Stimmen sind überall.
Alles ist hell, aber es ist kein Tag.
Alles ist laut, aber es sind nicht Vogelstimmen.
Das sind die Balken, die leuchten. Das sind die Fenster, die
schrein. Und sie schrein, rot, in die Feinde hinein, die draußen stehn
im flackernden Land, schrein: Brand.
Und mit zerrissenem Schlaf im Gesicht drängen sich alle, halb
Eisen, halb nackt, von Zimmer zu Zimmer, von Trakt zu Trakt und
suchen die Treppe.
Und mit veschlagenem Atem stammeln Hörner im Hof:
Sammeln, sammeln!
Und bebende Trommeln.

Aber die Fahne ist nicht dabei.
Rufe: Cornet!
Rasende Pferde, Gebete, Geschrei,
Flüche: Cornet!
Eisen an Eisen, Befehl und Signal;
Stille: Cornet!
Und noch ein Mal: Cornet!
Und heraus mit der brausenden Reiterei.

Aber die Fahne ist nicht dabei.

Er läuft um die Wette mit brennenden Gängen, durch Türen, die
ihn glühend umdrängen, über Treppen, die ihn versengen, bricht er
aus aus dem rasenden Bau. Auf seinen Armen trägt er die Fahne wie
eine weiße, bewußtlose Frau. Und er findet ein Pferd, und es ist wie
ein Schrei: über alles dahin und an allem vorbei, auch an den Seinen.
Und da kommt auch die Fahne wieder zu sich und niemals war sie so
königlich; und jetzt sehn sie sie alle, fern voran, und erkennen den
hellen, helmlosen Mann und erkennen die Fahne . . .
Aber da fängt sie zu scheinen an, wirft sich hinaus und wird groß
und rot . . .

Da brennt ihre Fahne mitten im Feind, und sie jagen ihr nach.

Der von Langenau ist tief im Feind, aber ganz allein. Der
Schrecken hat um ihn einen runden Raum gemacht, und er hält, mitten drin, unter seiner langsam verlodernden Fahne.

❋   ❋   ❋

Is this morning? What sun rises? How big the sun is! Are those birds? Their voices are everywhere.
Everything is bright, but it isn't day.
Everything is loud, but those aren't birds' voices.
It's the beams gleaming. It's the windows shouting. And they shout redly at the enemy, who are standing outside in the flickering countryside; they shout: "Fire!"
And with their curtailed sleep on their faces, all of them, half in armor, half undressed, push their way from room to room, from wing to wing, seeking the front steps.
And with impeded breath bugles in the courtyard stammer: "Assembly! Assembly!"
And quivering drums.

But the standard isn't there.
Cries: "Cornet!"
Frenzied horses, prayers, shouting,
curses: "Cornet!"
Iron against iron, orders and signals;
silence: "Cornet!"
And once again: "Cornet!"
And the noisy cavalry departs.

But the standard isn't there.

He races in competition with burning corridors; through glowing doors that surround him closely, down stairways that scorch him, he breaks out of the frenzied building. In his arms he carries the standard like a white, unconscious woman. And he finds a horse, and it is like a shout: away over everything and past everything, including his own people. And then the standard regains consciousness, too, and never was it so regal; and now they all see it, far in front, and they recognize the bright, helmetless man and they recognize the standard. . . .
But then it begins to shine, it spreads out and becomes big and red. . . .

Then their standard breaks into the midst of the enemy, and they hurtle after it.

He of Langenau is deep within enemy lines, but all alone. Terror has created a round space all about him and, in the center of it, he makes a stand below his standard, which is being slowly extinguished.

Langsam, fast nachdenklich, schaut er um sich. Es ist viel Fremdes, Buntes vor ihm. Gärten – denkt er und lächelt. Aber da fühlt er, daß Augen ihn halten und erkennt Männer und weiß, daß es die heidnischen Hunde sind –: und wirft sein Pferd mitten hinein.

Aber, als es jetzt hinter ihm zusammenschlägt, sind es doch wieder Gärten, und die sechzehn runden Säbel, die auf ihn zuspringen, Strahl um Strahl, sind ein Fest.

Eine lachende Wasserkunst.

Der Waffenrock ist im Schlosse verbrannt, der Brief und das Rosenblatt einer fremden Frau. –

Im nächsten Frühjahr (es kam traurig und kalt) ritt ein Kurier des Freiherrn von Pirovano langsam in Langenau ein. Dort hat er eine alte Frau weinen sehen.

Die Turnstunde

In der Militärschule zu Sankt Severin. Turnsaal. Der Jahrgang steht in den hellen Zwillichblusen, in zwei Reihen geordnet, unter den großen Gaskronen. Der Turnlehrer, ein junger Offizier mit hartem braunen Gesicht und höhnischen Augen, hat Freiübungen kommandiert und verteilt nun die Riegen. »Erste Riege Reck, zweite Riege Barren, dritte Riege Bock, vierte Riege Klettern! Abtreten!« Und rasch, auf den leichten, mit Kolophonium isolierten Schuhen, zerstreuen sich die Knaben. Einige bleiben mitten im Saale stehen, zögernd, gleichsam unwillig. Es ist die vierte Riege, die schlechten Turner, die keine Freude haben an der Bewegung bei den Geräten und schon müde sind von den zwanzig Kniebeugen und ein wenig verwirrt und atemlos.

Nur Einer, der sonst der Allerletzte blieb bei solchen Anlässen, Karl Gruber, steht schon an den Kletterstangen, die in einer etwas dämmerigen Ecke des Saales, hart vor den Nischen, in denen die abgelegten Uniformröcke hängen, angebracht sind. Er hat die nächste Stange erfaßt und zieht sie mit ungewöhnlicher Kraft nach vorn, so daß sie frei an dem zur Übung geeigneten Platze schwankt. Gruber läßt nicht einmal die Hände von ihr, er springt auf und bleibt, ziemlich hoch, die Beine ganz unwillkürlich im Kletterschluß verschränkt, den er sonst niemals begreifen konnte, an der Stange hängen. So erwartet er die Riege und betrachtet – wie es scheint – mit besonderem Vergnügen den erstaunten Ärger des kleinen polnischen Unteroffiziers,

Slowly, almost contemplatively, he looks around. There is a great deal that is strange and confused in front of him. "Gardens," he thinks, and he smiles. But then he senses that eyes are holding him fast; he recognizes men and he knows they are the heathen dogs—and he spurs his horse into their midst.

But, as they now close around him, they are gardens again, and the sixteen curved sabers that leap at him, beam after beam of light, are a festivity.

A laughing ornamental fountain.

His tunic was burnt in the mansion, along with his letter and the unknown woman's rose petal.

The following spring (which was sad and cold) a courier from the Baron of Pirovano rode slowly into Langenau. There he saw an old woman weeping.

The Gym Class

In the military school at Sankt Severin. Gymnasium. The age-group, in their bright blouses of drill, are arranged in two rows, standing under the large gas chandeliers. The gym instructor, a young officer with a hard, brown face and mocking eyes, has given the order for gymnastics and is now distributing the squads. "First squad, horizontal bar; second squad, parallel bars; third squad, the buck; fourth squad, climbing! Fall out!" And swiftly, in their light, rosin-rubbed shoes, the boys disperse. Some remain in the middle of the room, hesitantly, as if reluctant. They are the fourth squad, the poor gymnasts, who take no joy in exercising on the apparatus and are already tired from the twenty knee bends, and a little confused and out of breath.

Only one of them, who has usually been the very last one remaining on such occasions, Karl Gruber, is already standing by the climbing poles, which are located in a rather shady corner of the gym, just in front of the niches where the uniforms the boys have taken off are hanging. He has grasped the nearest pole, and he pulls it forward with unusual strength, so that it sways freely on the spot designated for the exercise. Gruber doesn't even take his hands off it, he leaps up and remains clinging to the pole, fairly high up, his legs quite involuntarily locked in the foot grip which he has never before been able to understand. In that position he awaits his squad and observes—with particular pleasure, it would seem—the astonished vexation of the little

der ihm zuruft, abzuspringen. Aber Gruber ist diesmal sogar ungehor-
sam und Jastersky, der blonde Unteroffizier, schreit endlich: »Also, entweder Sie kommen herunter oder Sie klettern hinauf, Gruber! Sonst
melde ich dem Herrn Oberlieutenant . . .« Und da beginnt Gruber, zu
klettern, erst heftig mit Überstürzung, die Beine wenig aufziehend und
die Blicke aufwärts gerichtet, mit einer gewissen Angst das unermeßliche Stück Stange abschätzend, das noch bevorsteht. Dann ver-
langsamt sich seine Bewegung; und als ob er jeden Griff genösse, wie
etwas Neues, Angenehmes, zieht er sich höher, als man gewöhnlich zu
klettern pflegt. Er beachtet nicht die Aufregung des ohnehin gereizten
Unteroffiziers, klettert und klettert, die Blicke immerfort aufwärts
gerichtet, als hätte er einen Ausweg in der Decke des Saales entdeckt
und strebte danach, ihn zu erreichen. Die ganze Riege folgt ihm mit
den Augen. Und auch aus den anderen Riegen richtet man schon da
und dort die Aufmerksamkeit auf den Kletterer, der sonst kaum das
erste Dritteil der Stange keuchend, mit rotem Gesicht und bösen
Augen erklomm. »Bravo, Gruber!« ruft jemand aus der ersten Riege
herüber. Da wenden viele ihre Blicke aufwärts, und es wird eine Weile
still im Saal, – aber gerade in diesem Augenblick, da alle Blicke an der
Gestalt Grubers hängen, macht er noch oben unter der Decke eine
Bewegung, als wollte er sie abschütteln; und da ihm Das offenbar nicht
gelingt, bindet er alle diese Blicke oben an den nackten eisernen Haken
und saust die glatte Stange herunter, so daß alle immer noch hinaufse-
hen, als er schon längst, schwindelnd und heiß, unten steht und mit
seltsam glanzlosen Augen in seine glühenden Handflächen schaut. Da
fragt ihn der eine oder der andere der ihm zunächst stehenden
Kameraden, was denn heute in ihn gefahren sei. »Willst wohl in die
erste Riege kommen?« Gruber lacht und scheint etwas antworten zu
wollen, aber er überlegt es sich und senkt schnell die Augen. Und dann,
als das Geräusch und Getöse wieder seinen Fortgang hat, zieht er sich
leise in die Nische zurück, setzt sich nieder, schaut ängstlich um sich
und holt Atem, zweimal rasch, und lacht wieder und will was sagen . . .
aber schon achtet niemand mehr seiner. Nur Jerome, der auch in der
vierten Riege ist, sieht, daß er wieder seine Hände betrachtet, ganz
darüber gebückt wie einer, der bei wenig Licht einen Brief entziffern
will. Und er tritt nach einer Weile zu ihm hin und fragt: »Hast du dir
weh getan?« Gruber erschrickt. »Was?« macht er mit seiner gewöhnlichen, in Speichel watenden Stimme. »Zeig mal!« Jerome nimmt die
eine Hand Grubers und neigt sie gegen das Licht. Sie ist am Ballen ein
wenig abgeschürft. »Weißt du, ich habe etwas dafür,« sagt Jerome, der
immer Englisches Pflaster von zu Hause geschickt bekommt, »komm

Polish noncom who is shouting to him to jump down. But this time Gruber is actually disobedient, and Jastersky, the blonde noncom, finally yells: "All right, either you come down or you climb up, Gruber! Or else I'll report you to the first lieutenant. . . ." and then Gruber begins to climb, at first with a lot of force and too hurriedly, drawing up his legs only a little and directing his gaze upward, gauging with some fear the immeasurable length of pole still ahead of him. Then his motions slow down; and as if he were enjoying every handhold like something new and pleasant, he pulls himself higher up than the boys normally climb. He doesn't observe the excitement of the already irritable noncom, he climbs and climbs, his gaze steadily directed upward, as if he had discovered a way out in the ceiling of the gym and were striving to reach it. The whole squad watches him climb. And even in the other squads, some attention is paid here and there to the climber, who has formerly scarcely clambered up the first third of the pole, gasping, his face red and his eyes with a mean look in them. "Bravo, Gruber!" someone from the first squad yells over. Then a number of boys look upward, and for a while it's quiet in the gym— but right at this moment, when all gazes are glued to Gruber's figure, high up below the ceiling he makes a gesture as if he wanted to shake them off; and since he obviously doesn't succeed in this, he ties all those gazes to the bare iron hook up there and he whizzes down the smooth pole so fast that everyone is still looking upward after he has been standing down below for some time, dizzy and hot, looking at his burning palms with oddly dulled eyes. Then one or another of the classmates standing nearest him asks him what has gotten into him today. "Are you trying to get into the first squad?" Gruber laughs and seems about to make some reply, but he has second thoughts and he lowers his eyes quickly. And then, when the noise and the hubbub resume, he withdraws quietly into the niche, sits down, looks around in fear, and takes two breaths in close succession, laughs again and starts to say something . . . but by this time no one is paying any more attention to him. Only Jerome, who is also in the fourth squad, sees that he's looking at his hands again, completely stooped over them like someone trying to decipher a letter in insufficient light. And after a while he steps over to him and asks: "Did you hurt yourself?" Gruber gets frightened. "What?" he says, in his usual, saliva-clogged voice. "Let me see!" Jerome takes one of Gruber's hands and inclines it toward the light. It's a little skinned on the palm. "You know what? I've got something for that," says Jerome, who always receives packages of medicinal plaster from home; "come see me later." But Gruber seems

dann nachher zu mir.« Aber es ist, als hätte Gruber nicht gehört; er
schaut geradeaus in den Saal hinein, aber so, als sähe er etwas
Unbestimmtes, vielleicht nicht im Saal, draußen vielleicht, vor den
Fenstern, obwohl es dunkel ist, spät und Herbst.

In diesem Augenblick schreit der Unteroffizier in seiner hoch-
fahrenden Art:»Gruber!« Gruber bleibt unverändert, nur seine Füße,
die vor ihm ausgestreckt sind, gleiten, steif und ungeschickt, ein wenig
auf dem glatten Parkett vorwärts. »Gruber!« brüllt der Unteroffizier
und die Stimme schlägt ihm über. Dann wartet er eine Weile und sagt
rasch und heiser, ohne den Gerufenen anzusehen:»Sie melden sich
nach der Stunde. Ich werde Ihnen schon . . .« Und die Stunde geht
weiter.»Gruber,« sagt Jerome und neigt sich zu dem Kameraden, der
sich immer tiefer in die Nische zurücklehnt, »es war schon wieder an
dir, zu klettern, auf dem Strick, geh mal, versuchs, sonst macht dir der
Jastersky irgend eine Geschichte, weißt du . . .« Gruber nickt. Aber
statt aufzustehen, schließt er plötzlich die Augen und gleitet unter
den Worten Jeromes durch, als ob eine Welle ihn trüge, fort, gleitet
langsam und lautlos tiefer, tiefer, gleitet vom Sitz, und Jerome weiß
erst, was geschieht, als er hört, wie der Kopf Grubers hart an das Holz
des Sitzes prallt und dann vornüberfällt . . .»Gruber!« ruft er heiser.
Erst merkt es niemand. Und Jerome steht ratlos mit hängenden
Händen und ruft:»Gruber, Gruber!« Es fällt ihm nicht ein, den anderen aufzurichten. Da erhält er einen Stoß, jemand sagt ihm:
»Schaf«, ein anderer schiebt ihn fort, und er sieht, wie sie den
Reglosen aufheben. Sie tragen ihn vorbei, irgend wohin, wahrscheinlich in die Kammer nebenan. Der Oberlieutenant springt herzu. Er
giebt mit harter, lauter Stimme sehr kurze Befehle. Sein Kommando
schneidet das Summen der vielen schwatzenden Knaben scharf ab.
Stille. Man sieht nur da und dort noch Bewegungen, ein Ausschwingen
am Gerät, einen leisen Absprung, ein verspätetes Lachen von einem,
der nicht weiß, um was es sich handelt. Dann hastige Fragen:»Was?
Was? Wer? Der Gruber? Wo?« Und immer mehr Fragen. Dann sagt
jemand laut:»Ohnmächtig.« Und der Zugführer Jastersky läuft mit
rotem Kopf hinter dem Oberlieutenant her und schreit mit seiner
boshaften Stimme, zitternd vor Wut:»Ein Simulant, Herr Oberlieutenant, ein Simulant!« Der Oberlieutenant beachtet ihn gar nicht.
Er sieht geradeaus, nagt an seinem Schnurrbart, wodurch das harte
Kinn noch eckiger und energischer vortritt, und giebt von Zeit zu Zeit
eine knappe Weisung. Vier Zöglinge, die Gruber tragen, und der
Oberlieutenant verschwinden in der Kammer. Gleich darauf kommen
die vier Zöglinge zurück. Ein Diener läuft durch den Saal. Die vier

not to have heard; he is looking straight into the gym, but as if he saw something indefinable, perhaps not in the gym, outdoors perhaps, right outside the windows, even though it's dark and late on an autumn day.

At that moment the noncom shouts in his overbearing way: "Gruber!" Gruber remains unchanged; only his feet, which are stretched out in front of him, slide forward a little on the smooth parquet, stiffly and awkwardly. "Gruber!" bellows the noncom, his voice cracking. Then he waits a while and says, swiftly and hoarsely, without looking at the boy he's addressing: "Go on report after class! I'll teach you . . ." And the class continues. "Gruber," Jerome says, bending toward his classmate, who is leaning farther and farther back into the niche, "it was your turn again to climb, on the rope; go, try it, or else Jastersky will have it in for you, you know. . . ." Gruber nods. But instead of standing up, he suddenly shuts his eyes and slips through beneath Jerome's words, carried away as if by a wave; slowly and noiselessly he slips deeper and deeper, slips from his seat, and Jerome doesn't know what's going on until he hears Gruber's head give a resounding knock against the wood of the seat and then sees it fall forward. . . . "Gruber!" he calls hoarsely. At first nobody notices. And Jerome stands there helplessly with dangling hands, calling: "Gruber, Gruber!" It doesn't occur to him to help the other boy up. Then he feels a shove, and someone says to him: "Imbecile!" Someone else pushes him away and he sees them picking up the motionless victim. They carry him past, somewhere or other, probably to the small room adjoining. The first lieutenant runs up to join them. He issues very brief orders in a hard, loud voice. His words of command cut short abruptly the humming sound produced by all those chattering boys. Silence. Only here and there are some movements still to be seen, a final swing on some piece of equipment, a quiet jump off, a belated laugh from someone who doesn't know what's happening. Then, hasty questions: "What? What? Who? Gruber? Where?" And more and more questions. Then someone says loudly: "Unconscious." And platoon leader Jastersky runs after the first lieutenant with his face all red, shouting with his malicious voice, trembling with rage: "A malingerer, lieutenant, a malingerer!" The first lieutenant pays no attention to him. He looks straight ahead, gnaws at his mustache, making his hard chin even pointier and more energetically prominent, and from time to time gives concise instructions. Four students, carrying Gruber, and the first lieutenant vanish into the small room. Immediately afterward, the four

werden groß angeschaut und mit Fragen bedrängt: »Wie sieht er aus?
Was ist mit ihm? Ist er schon zu sich gekommen?« Keiner von ihnen
weiß eigentlich was. Und da ruft auch schon der Oberlieutenant
herein, das Turnen möge weitergehen, und übergiebt dem Feldwebel
Goldstein das Kommando. Also wird wieder geturnt, beim Barren,
beim Reck, und die kleinen dicken Leute der dritten Riege kriechen
mit weitgekretschten Beinen über den hohen Bock. Aber doch sind
alle Bewegungen anders als vorher; als hätte ein Horchen sich über
sie gelegt. Die Schwingungen am Reck brechen so plötzlich ab und
am Barren werden nur lauter kleine Übungen gemacht. Die Stimmen
sind weniger verworren und ihre Summe summt feiner, als ob alle
immer nur ein Wort sagten: »*Ess, Ess, Ess* . . .« Der kleine schlaue
Krix horcht inzwischen an der Kammertür. Der Unteroffizier der
zweiten Riege jagt ihn davon, indem er zu einem Schlage auf seinen
Hintern ausholt. Krix springt zurück, katzenhaft, mit hinterlistig
blitzenden Augen. Er weiß schon genug. Und nach einer Weile, als
ihn niemand betrachtet, giebt er dem Pawlowitsch weiter: »Der
Regimentsarzt ist gekommen.« Nun, man kennt ja den Pawlowitsch;
mit seiner ganzen Frechheit geht er, als hätte ihm irgendwer einen
Befehl gegeben, quer durch den Saal von Riege zu Riege und sagt
ziemlich laut: »Der Regimentsarzt ist drin.« Und es scheint, auch die
Unteroffiziere interessieren sich für diese Nachricht. Immer häufiger
wenden sich die Blicke nach der Tür, immer langsamer werden die
Übungen; und ein Kleiner mit schwarzen Augen ist oben auf dem
Bock hocken geblieben und starrt mit offenem Mund nach der
Kammer. Etwas Lähmendes scheint in der Luft zu liegen. Die Stärk-
sten bei der ersten Riege machen zwar noch einige Anstrengungen,
gehen dagegen an, kreisen mit den Beinen; und Pombert, der kräftige
Tiroler, biegt seinen Arm und betrachtet seine Muskeln, die sich
durch den Zwillich hindurch breit und straff ausprägen. Ja, der kleine,
gelenkige Baum schlägt sogar noch einige Armwellen, – und plötzlich
ist diese heftige Bewegung die einzige im ganzen Saal, ein großer
flimmernder Kreis, der etwas Unheimliches hat inmitten der allgemeinen Ruhe. Und mit einem Ruck bringt sich der kleine Mensch
zum Stehen, läßt sich einfach unwillig in die Knie fallen und macht
ein Gesicht, als ob er alle verachte. Aber auch seine kleinen stumpfen
Augen bleiben schließlich an der Kammertür hängen.

Jetzt hört man das Singen der Gasflammen und das Gehen der
Wanduhr. Und dann schnarrt die Glocke, die das Stundenzeichen
giebt. Fremd und eigentümlich ist heute ihr Ton; sie hört auch ganz un-
vermittelt auf, unterbricht sich mitten im Wort. Feldwebel Goldstein

students return. An attendant runs through the gym. The four boys are goggled at and assailed with questions: ""How does he look? What's wrong with him? Has he come to yet?" None of them really knows anything. And then the first lieutenant already calls into the gym, saying that the gymnastics are to continue, and he places Sergeant Goldstein in charge. And so the exercises resume, on the parallel bars, on the horizontal bar, and the short, fat boys in the third squad crawl over the tall buck with widely spread legs. But nevertheless all the activities are different from before, as if overlaid by a need to keep listening. And so the swings on the horizontal bar are suddenly broken off, and only small exercises are performed on the parallel bars. The boys' voices are less confused and their humming has a more delicate sound, as if they were all constantly saying only: "Sss, sss, sss. . . ." Sly little Krix, meanwhile, is eavesdropping at the door to the small room. The second-squad noncom chases him away, hauling back to aim a slap at his behind. Krix jumps back like a cat, his eyes flashing with cunning. He already knows enough. And after a while, when no one is watching him, he passes the word to Pawlowitsch: "The regimental doctor has arrived." Now, Pawlowitsch is well known; with all his impudence, as if someone had given him orders, he crosses the gym from squad to squad, saying fairly loudly: "The regimental doctor is in there." And even the noncoms seem interested in that news. With increasing frequency the boys' glances are directed toward that door, and the exercises slow down more and more; and a little boy with dark eyes has remained squatting up on the buck, staring openmouthed at the room. Something numbing seems to be in the air. To be sure, the strongest boys, in the first squad, still make a few efforts, tackle the apparatus, make circles with their legs; and Pombert, the powerful Tyrolean, bends his arm and observes his muscles, which stand out, wide and firm, through the drill cloth. Yes, small, supple Baum even goes on doing a few arm rotations—and suddenly that violent activity is the only one in the entire gym, a large, glimmering circle that is slightly uncanny amid the general repose. And with a jerk the little fellow comes to a halt, simply drops to his knees indignantly, and makes a face expressive of contempt for everybody. But even his dull little eyes are finally glued to the door to the small room.

Now they can hear the hissing of the gas flames and the ticking of the wall clock. And then comes the drone of the bell that marks the end of the hour. Its sound is strange and singular today; and, indeed, it stops quite suddenly, breaking off in the middle of its utterance. But

aber kennt seine Pflicht. Er ruft: »Antreten!« Kein Mensch hört ihn. Keiner kann sich erinnern, welchen Sinn dieses Wort besaß, – vorher. Wann vorher? »Antreten!« krächzt der Feldwebel böse und gleich schreien jetzt die anderen Unteroffiziere ihm nach: »Antreten!« Und auch mancher von den Zöglingen sagt wie zu sich selbst, wie im Schlaf: »Antreten! Antreten!« Aber im Grunde wissen alle, daß sie noch etwas abwarten müssen. Und da geht auch schon die Kammertür auf; eine Weile nichts; dann tritt Oberlieutenant Wehl heraus und seine Augen sind groß und zornig und seine Schritte fest. Er marschiert wie beim Defilieren und sagt heiser: »Antreten!« Mit unbeschreiblicher Geschwindigkeit findet sich alles in Reihe und Glied. Keiner rührt sich. Als wenn ein Feldzeugmeister da wäre. Und jetzt das Kommando: »Achtung!« Pause und dann, trocken und hart: »Euer Kamerad Gruber ist soeben gestorben. Herzschlag. Abmarsch!« Pause.

Und erst nach einer Weile die Stimme des diensttuenden Zöglings, klein und leise: »Links um! Marschieren: Compagnie, Marsch!« Ohne Schritt und langsam wendet sich der Jahrgang zur Tür. Jerome als der letzte. Keiner sieht sich um. Die Luft aus dem Gang kommt, kalt und dumpfig, den Knaben entgegen. Einer meint, es rieche nach Karbol. Pombert macht laut einen gemeinen Witz in Bezug auf den Gestank. Niemand lacht. Jerome fühlt sich plötzlich am Arm gefaßt, so angesprungen. Krix hängt daran. Seine Augen glänzen und seine Zähne schimmern, als ob er beißen wollte. »Ich hab ihn gesehen«, flüstert er atemlos und preßt Jeromes Arm und ein Lachen ist innen in ihm und rüttelt ihn hin und her. Er kann kaum weiter: »Ganz nackt ist er und eingefallen und ganz lang. Und an den Fußsohlen ist er versiegelt . . .«

Und dann kichert er, spitz und kitzlich, kichert und beißt sich in den Ärmel Jeromes hinein.

Geschichten vom lieben Gott

Das Märchen von den Händen Gottes

Neulich, am Morgen, begegnete mir die Frau Nachbarin. Wir begrüßten uns.

»Was für ein Herbst!« sagte sie nach einer Pause und blickte nach dem Himmel auf. Ich tat desgleichen. Der Morgen war allerdings sehr klar und köstlich für Oktober. Plötzlich fiel mir etwas ein: »Was für ein Herbst!« rief ich und schwenkte ein wenig mit den Händen. Und die Frau Nachbarin nickte beifällig. Ich sah ihr so einen Augenblick zu. Ihr gutes gesundes

Sergeant Goldstein knows his duty. He calls: "Fall in!" No one hears him. No one can remember what that call used to mean—in the past. When in the past? "Fall in!" the sergeant groans angrily, and at once the other noncoms are now repeating his cry: "Fall in!" And some of the students, too, say, as if to themselves, as if asleep: "Fall in! Fall in!" But basically they all know that they still have to await some result. And now, indeed, the door to that room opens; for a moment, nothing else happens; then First Lieutenant Wehl walks out, and his eyes are large and wrathful, and his steps are firm. He marches as if on parade, and says hoarsely: "Fall in!" With indescribable speed everyone is in proper rank and file. No one stirs. As if a general were present. And now the command: "Attention!" A pause, and then, dry and hard: "Your schoolmate Gruber has just died. Heart attack. Forward march!" A pause.

And only after a while, the voice of the student on duty, small and quiet: "To the left, march! Company, march!" Slowly, out of step, the age-group turns toward the door. Jerome is the last. No one looks around. The air from the corridor greets the boys, cold and stuffy. One boy says it smells of carbolic acid. Loudly Pombert makes a vulgar joke about the stench. Nobody laughs. Jerome suddenly feels someone grabbing his arm, as if leaping onto him. It's Krix clinging to it. His eyes are shining and his teeth are glimmering as if he was about to take a bite. "I've seen him," he whispers breathlessly, squeezing Jerome's arm, and there's laughter inside him which shakes him back and forth. He can hardly continue: "He's all naked and caved in and very long. And there are wax seals on the soles of his feet. . . ."

And then he gives a short, high giggle, as if being tickled; he giggles and bites into Jerome's sleeve.

Stories About the Good Lord

The Tale of God's Hands

One morning recently, I was met by the lady who's my neighbor. We said hello.

"What an autumn!" she said after a pause, and she looked up at the sky. I did the same. It happened to be a very clear and delightful morning for October. Suddenly I had an idea. "What an autumn!" I cried, with a slight wave of my hands. And my neighbor nodded approvingly. I looked at her for a moment. Her kindly,

Gesicht ging so lieb auf und nieder. Es war recht hell, nur um die Lippen und an den Schläfen waren kleine schattige Falten. Woher sie das haben mag? Und da fragte ich ganz unversehens: »Und Ihre kleinen Mädchen?« Die Falten in ihrem Gesicht verschwanden eine Sekunde, zogen sich aber gleich, noch dunkler, zusammen. »Gesund sind sie, gottseidank, aber –« die Frau Nachbarin setzte sich in Bewegung, und ich schritt jetzt an ihrer Linken, wie es sich gehört. »Wissen Sie, sie sind jetzt beide in dem Alter, die Kinder, wo sie den ganzen Tag *fragen*. Was, den ganzen Tag, bis in die gerechte Nacht hinein.« »Ja,« murmelte ich, – »es giebt eine Zeit . . .« Sie aber ließ sich nicht stören: »Und nicht etwa: Wohin geht diese Pferdebahn? Wie viel Sterne giebt es? Und ist zehntausend mehr als viel? Noch ganz andere Sachen! Zum Beispiel: Spricht der liebe Gott auch chinesisch? und: Wie sieht der liebe Gott aus? Immer alles vom lieben Gott! Darüber weiß man doch nicht Bescheid –.« »Nein, allerdings,« stimmte ich bei, »man hat da gewisse Vermutungen . . .« »Oder von den Händen vom lieben Gott, was soll man da –.«

Ich schaute der Nachbarin in die Augen: »Erlauben Sie,« sagte ich recht höflich, »Sie sagten zuletzt die Hände vom lieben Gott – nichtwahr?« Die Nachbarin nickte. Ich glaube, sie war ein wenig erstaunt. »Ja« – beeilte ich mich anzufügen, – »von den Händen ist mir allerdings einiges bekannt. Zufällig –« bemerkte ich rasch, als ich ihre Augen rund werden sah, – »ganz zufällig – ich habe – – – nun« schloß ich mit ziemlicher Entschiedenheit, »ich will Ihnen erzählen, was ich weiß. Wenn Sie einen Augenblick Zeit haben, ich begleite Sie bis zu Ihrem Hause, das wird gerade reichen.«

»Gerne,« sagte sie, als ich sie endlich zu Worte kommen ließ, immer noch erstaunt, »aber wollen Sie nicht vielleicht den Kindern selbst? . . .«

»Ich den Kindern selbst erzählen? Nein, liebe Frau, das geht nicht, das geht auf keinen Fall. Sehen Sie, ich werde gleich verlegen, wenn ich mit den Kinder sprechen muß. Das ist an sich nicht schlimm. Aber die Kinder könnten meine Verwirrung dahin deuten, daß ich mich lügen fühle . . . Und da mir sehr viel an der Wahrhaftigkeit meiner Geschichte liegt – Sie können es den Kindern ja wiedererzählen; Sie treffen es ja gewiß auch viel besser. Sie werden es verknüpfen und ausschmücken, ich werde nur die einfachen Tatsachen in der kürzesten Form berichten. Ja?« »Gut, gut«, machte die Nachbarin zerstreut.

Ich dachte nach: »Im Anfang . . .« aber ich unterbrach mich sofort. »Ich kann bei Ihnen, Frau Nachbarin, ja manches als bekannt voraussetzen, was ich den Kindern erst erzählen müßte. Zum Beispiel die Schöpfung . . .« Es entstand eine ziemliche Pause. Dann: »Ja – – und

healthy face was bobbing up and down. It was really bright, except for small shadowy wrinkles around her lips and at her temples. Where could she have gotten that? Then I asked, quite unexpectedly: "And your little girls?" The wrinkles in her face disappeared for a second, but re-formed immediately, and were even darker. "They're well, thank God, but—" My neighbor started walking, and now I was proceeding at her left, as courtesy demands. "You know, the children are both now at the age when they *ask questions* all day long. What am I saying, all day long? All the way into the night!" "Yes," I murmured, "there's a time . . ." But she wouldn't be interrupted: "And not questions like 'Where does this horsecar go?' or 'How many stars are there?' or 'Is ten thousand more than a lot?' Quite different things, besides! For example: 'Does God speak Chinese, too?' or 'What does God look like?' It's always all about the Good Lord! After all, no one really has the facts about it—." "Of course not," I agreed, "though we have certain assumptions. . . ." "Or about God's hands, what is one to say about that?"

I looked my neighbor in the eye. "Permit me," I said most politely, "you just mentioned God's hands, didn't you?" My neighbor nodded. I think she was a little surprised. "Yes," I hastened to add, "I do happen to know a little about his hands. By accident," I remarked quickly, upon seeing her eyes grow round, "quite by accident—I have—well, now," I concluded with a fair amount of determination, "I'll tell you what I know. If you have a few minutes' time, I'll accompany you home, it will take only that long."

"Gladly," she said, when I finally let her get a word in, though she was still surprised, "but wouldn't you perhaps want to see the children . . ."

"And tell it to the children myself? No, my dear lady, that won't do, that won't do at all. You see, I get embarrassed immediately when I have to talk with children. In itself that isn't a bad thing. But the children might take my confusion to mean that I was aware I was lying. . . . And since the truthfulness of my story is very important to me— you can repeat it to the children, can't you? I'm sure you'll even do a much better job of it. You'll add connections and ornamentations, I'll merely report the simple facts in their most concise form. All right?" "Fine, fine," said my neighbor distractedly.

I stopped to think: "In the beginning . . . ," but I broke off at once. "In your case, dear neighbor, I can surely presuppose that you already know a great deal of what I'd have to tell the children first. For example, the Creation. . . ." A considerable pause ensued. Then: "Yes—

am siebenten Tage . . .«, die Stimme der guten Frau war hoch und spitzig. »Halt!« machte ich, »wir wollen doch auch der früheren Tage gedenken; denn gerade um diese handelt es sich. Also der liebe Gott begann, wie bekannt, seine Arbeit, indem er die Erde machte, diese vom Wasser unterschied und Licht befahl. Dann formte er in bewundernswerter Geschwindigkeit die Dinge, ich meine die großen wirklichen Dinge, als da sind: Felsen, Gebirge, einen Baum und nach diesem Muster viele Bäume.« Ich hörte hier schon eine Weile lang Schritte hinter uns, die uns nicht überholten und auch nicht zurückblieben. Das störte mich, und ich verwickelte mich in der Schöpfungsgeschichte, als ich folgendermaßen fortfuhr: »Man kann sich diese schnelle und erfolgreiche Tätigkeit nur begreiflich machen, wenn man annimmt, daß eben nach langem, tiefem Nachdenken alles in seinem Kopfe ganz fertig war, ehe er . . .« Da endlich waren die Schritte neben uns, und eine nicht gerade angenehme Stimme klebte an uns: »O, Sie sprechen wohl von Herrn Schmidt, verzeihen Sie . . .« Ich sah ärgerlich nach der Hinzugekommenen, die Frau Nachbarin aber geriet in große Verlegenheit: »Hm,« hustete sie, »nein – das heißt – ja, – wir sprachen gerade, gewissermaßen –«. »Was für ein Herbst«, sagte auf einmal die andere Frau, als ob nichts geschehen wäre, und ihr rotes, kleines Gesicht glänzte. »Ja« – hörte ich meine Nachbarin antworten: »Sie haben recht, Frau Hüpfer, ein selten schöner Herbst!« Dann trennten sich die Frauen. Frau Hüpfer kicherte noch: »Und grüßen sie mir die Kinderchen.« Meine gute Nachbarin achtete nicht mehr darauf; sie war doch neugierig, meine Geschichte zu erfahren. Ich aber behauptete mit unbegreiflicher Härte: »Ja *jetzt* weiß ich nicht mehr, wo wir stehen geblieben sind.« »Sie sagten eben etwas von seinem Kopfe, das heißt –«, die Frau Nachbarin wurde ganz rot.

Sie tat mir aufrichtig leid, und so erzählte ich schnell: »Ja sehen Sie also, so lange nur die *Dinge* gemacht waren, hatte der liebe Gott nicht notwendig, beständig auf die Erde herunterzuschauen. Es konnte sich ja nichts dort begeben. Der Wind ging allerdings schon über die Berge, welche den Wolken, die er schon seit lange kannte, so ähnlich waren, aber den Wipfeln der Bäume wich er noch mit einem gewissen Mißtrauen aus. Und das war dem lieben Gott sehr recht. Die Dinge hat er sozusagen im Schlafe gemacht, allein schon bei den Tieren fing die Arbeit an, ihm interessant zu werden; er neigte sich darüber und zog nur selten die breiten Brauen hoch, um einen Blick auf die Erde zu werfen. Er vergaß sie vollends, als er den Menschen formte. Ich weiß nicht bei welchem komplizierten Teil des Körpers er gerade angelangt war, als es um ihn rauschte von Flügeln. Ein Engel eilte vorüber und sang: ›Der Du alles siehst . . .‹

and on the seventh day . . . ," said the good lady in a high, sharp voice. "Stop!" I interposed; "we've got to think about the previous days, too, don't we? Because the story is precisely about them. So then, as everyone knows, the Good Lord began his work by making the earth, separating it from the water, and commanding light to appear. Then, with admirable speed, he formed the things, I mean the large-scale, real-and-true things, such as cliffs, mountains, a tree, and many more trees on the same pattern." At this point I had for some time already been hearing footsteps behind us which neither caught up with us nor lagged far behind. That disturbed me, and I became enveloped in the story of Creation, continuing as follows: "It's only possible to make this rapid and successful activity understandable by assuming that everything was fully prepared in his head after a long period of deep contemplation, before he . . ." Now the footsteps were finally alongside us, and a voice that was not exactly pleasant pasted itself on us: "Oh, you must be talking about Mr. Schmidt, excuse me. . . ." I looked with annoyance at the woman who had joined us, but my neighbor became very embarrassed: "Hm," she coughed, "no—that is—yes—we were just speaking, in a way—." "What an autumn!" the other woman suddenly said, as if nothing had happened; her little red face was shining. "Yes," I heard my neighbor reply, "you're right, Mrs. Hüpfer, an unusually beautiful autumn!" Then the women separated. Mrs. Hüpfer continued with a giggle: "And say hello for me to your little children!" My kind neighbor was no longer paying attention to that; after all, she was curious to learn my story. But I asserted with inexplicable severity: "Well, *now* I no longer recall where we left off." "You were just saying something about his head; I mean—"; my neighbor turned quite red.

I was truly sorry for her, and so I resumed my narrative quickly: "Well, then, you see, as long as only *things* were being made, the Good Lord had no need to keep looking down at the earth. After all, nothing could occur there. To be sure, the wind was already blowing over the mountains, which so much resembled the clouds that it had long been familiar with, but it was still avoiding the treetops with a certain amount of distrust. And that suited the Good Lord very well. He had made the things in his sleep, so to speak, but with the animals his work already began to interest him; he concentrated on it, and only rarely did he raise his broad eyebrows in order to cast a glance at the earth. He forgot about it altogether when he was forming man. I don't know which complicated part of the body he had just gotten to, when there was a rustling of wings around him. An angel hastened past, singing: 'Thou that seest everything. . . .'

Der liebe Gott erschrak. Er hatte den Engel in Sünde gebracht, denn
eben hatte dieser eine Lüge gesungen. Rasch schaute Gottvater hinunter. Und freilich, da hatte sich schon irgend etwas ereignet, was kaum
gutzumachen war. Ein kleiner Vogel irrte, als ob er Angst hätte, über
die Erde hin und her, und der liebe Gott war nicht imstande, ihm
heimzuhelfen, denn er hatte nicht gesehen, aus *welchem* Walde das
arme Tier gekommen war. Er wurde ganz ärgerlich und sagte: ›Die
Vögel haben sitzen zu bleiben, wo ich sie hingesetzt habe.‹ Aber er erinnerte sich, daß er ihnen auf Fürbitte der Engel Flügel verliehen hatte,
damit es auch auf Erden so etwas wie Engel gebe, und dieser Umstand
machte ihn nur noch verdrießlicher. Nun ist gegen solche Zustände des
Gemütes nichts so heilsam wie Arbeit. Und mit dem Bau des
Menschen beschäftigt, wurde Gott auch rasch wieder froh. Er hatte die
Augen der Engel wie Spiegel vor sich, maß darin seine eigenen Züge
und bildete langsam und vorsichtig an einer Kugel auf seinem Schooße
das erste Gesicht. Die Stirne war ihm gelungen. Viel schwerer wurde es
ihm, die beiden Nasenlöcher symmetrisch zu machen. Er bückte sich
immer mehr darüber, bis es wieder wehte über ihm; er schaute auf.
Derselbe Engel umkreiste ihn; man hörte diesmal keine Hymne, denn
in seiner Lüge war dem Knaben die Stimme erloschen, aber an seinem
Mund erkannte Gott, daß er immer noch sang: ›Der Du alles siehst.‹
Zugleich trat der heilige Nikolaus, der bei Gott in besonderer Achtung
steht, an ihn heran und sagte durch seinen großen Bart hindurch:
›Deine Löwen sitzen ruhig, sie sind recht hochmütige Geschöpfe, das
muß ich sagen! Aber ein kleiner Hund läuft ganz am Rande der Erde
herum, ein Terrier, siehst Du, er wird gleich hinunterfallen.‹ Und wirklich merkte der liebe Gott etwas Heiteres, Weißes, wie ein kleines Licht
hin und her tanzen in der Gegend von Skandinavien, wo es schon so
furchtbar rund ist. Und er wurde recht bös und warf dem heiligen
Nikolaus vor, wenn ihm seine Löwen nicht recht seien, so solle er versuchen, auch welche zu machen. Worauf der heilige Nikolaus aus dem
Himmel ging und die Türe zuschlug, daß ein Stern herunterfiel, gerade
dem Terrier auf den Kopf. Jetzt war das Unglück vollständig, und der
liebe Gott mußte sich eingestehen, daß er ganz allein an allem schuld
sei, und beschloß, nicht mehr den Blick von der Erde zu rühren. Und
so geschah's. Er überließ seinen Händen, welche ja auch weise sind, die
Arbeit, und obwohl er recht neugierig war zu erfahren, wie der Mensch
wohl aussehen mochte, starrte er unablässig auf die Erde hinab, auf
welcher sich jetzt, wie zum Trotz, nicht ein Blättchen regen wollte. Um
doch wenigstens eine kleine Freude zu haben nach aller Plage, hatte er
seinen Händen befohlen, ihm den Menschen erst zu zeigen, ehe sie ihn

"The Good Lord was alarmed. He had led the angel into sin, because the angel had just sung a lie. God the Father quickly looked down. And, what do you know, there had already been an occurrence which could scarcely be rectified. A little bird was straying to and fro over the earth, as if in fear, and the Good Lord was unable to help it reach home because he hadn't seen from *which* forest the poor creature had come. He became quite vexed and said: 'The birds must stay put where I placed them!' But he remembered that, at the angels' intercession, he had lent them wings, so that there might be something like angels on the earth, too; and that circumstance made him even more peevish. Now, there's nothing as beneficial as work to combat similar mental states. And, occupied with the construction of man, God did indeed quickly cheer up again. He had the eyes of the angels for mirrors in front of him; in them he measured his own features, and on a sphere in his lap he slowly and carefully modeled the first face. He had done a good job with the forehead. He found it much harder to make the two nostrils symmetrical. He was stooping over his work, lower all the time, until there was another air current above him, and he looked up. The same angel was circling him; this time no hymn could be heard, because when the lad had lied, his voice had been extinguished, but from his lips God could tell that he was still singing: 'Thou that seest everything.' At the same time Saint Nicholas, whom God holds in particular esteem, came up to him and said through his big beard: 'Your lions are sitting calmly; they're really arrogant creatures, I must say! But a little dog, is running around right at the edge of the earth, a terrier, you see, and he'll soon fall off.' And, indeed, the Good Lord noticed something merry and white dancing to and fro like a small light in the vicinity of Scandinavia, where the globe is already so terribly curved. And he became really angry and said reproachfully to Saint Nicholas that, if he was unhappy with his lions, he should try to make some of his own. Whereupon Saint Nicholas left heaven, slamming the door so hard that a star fell, right on the terrier's head. Now the disaster was total; the Good Lord had to admit that he alone was to blame for the whole thing, and he resolved never again to take his eyes off the earth. And he kept his resolve. He entrusted the work to his hands, which are also wise, you know, and, although he was very curious to learn what man actually looked like, he stared down incessantly at the earth, on which, as if for spite, not even a little leaf would now budge. But, in order to have at least some small satisfaction after all that trouble, he had ordered his hands to show him man before they delivered him over to life. He asked repeatedly, like children

dem Leben ausliefern würden. Wiederholt fragte er, wie Kinder, wenn
sie Verstecken spielen: ›Schon?‹ Aber er hörte als Antwort das Kneten
seiner Hände und wartete. Es erschien ihm sehr lange. Da auf einmal
sah er etwas durch den Raum fallen, dunkel und in der Richtung, als ob
es aus seiner Nähe käme. Von einer bösen Ahnung erfüllt, rief er seine
Hände. Sie erschienen ganz von Lehm befleckt, heiß und zitternd. ›Wo
ist der Mensch?‹ schrie er sie an. Da fuhr die Rechte auf die Linke los:
›Du hast ihn losgelassen!‹ ›Bitte,‹ sagte die Linke gereizt, ›du wolltest ja
alles allein machen, *mich* ließest du ja überhaupt gar nicht mitreden.‹
›Du hättest ihn eben halten müssen!‹ Und die Rechte holte aus. Dann
aber besann sie sich, und beide Hände sagten einander überholend: ›Er
war so ungeduldig, der Mensch. Er wollte immer schon leben. Wir können beide nichts dafür, gewiß, wir sind beide unschuldig.‹

Der liebe Gott aber war ernstlich böse. Er drängte beide Hände
fort; denn sie verstellten ihm die Aussicht über die Erde: ›Ich
kenne euch nicht mehr, macht was ihr wollt.‹ Das versuchten die
Hände auch seither, aber sie können nur *beginnen,* was sie auch
tun. Ohne Gott giebt es keine Vollendung. Und da sind sie es
endlich müde geworden. Jetzt knien sie den ganzen Tag und tun
Buße, so erzählt man wenigstens. Uns aber erscheint es, als ob Gott
ruhte, weil er auf seine Hände böse ist. Es ist immer noch siebben-
ter Tag.«

Ich schwieg einen Augenblick. Das benützte die Frau Nachbarin
sehr vernünftig: »Und Sie glauben, daß nie wieder eine Versöhnung
zu stande kommt?« »O doch,« sagte ich, »ich hoffe es wenigstens.«

»Und wann sollte das sein?«

»Nun, bis Gott wissen wird, wie der Mensch, den die Hände gegen
seinen Willen losgelassen haben, aussieht.«

Die Frau Nachbarin dachte nach, dann lachte sie: »Aber dazu hätte
er doch bloß heruntersehen müssen . . .«

»Verzeihen Sie,« sagte ich artig, »Ihre Bemerkung zeugt von Scharf-
sinn, aber meine Geschichte ist noch nicht zu Ende. Also, als die Hände
beiseite getreten waren und Gott die Erde wieder überschaute, da war
eben wieder eine Minute, oder sagen wir ein Jahrtausend, was ja
bekanntlich dasselbe ist, vergangen. Statt *eines* Menschen gab es schon
eine Million. Aber sie waren alle schon in Kleidern. Und da die Mode
damals gerade sehr häßlich war und auch die Gesichter arg entstellte, so
bekam Gott einen ganz falschen und (ich will es nicht verhehlen) sehr
schlechten Begriff von den Menschen.« »Hm«, machte die Nachbarin
und wollte etwas bemerken. Ich beachtete es nicht, sondern schloß mit
starker Betonung: »Und darum ist es dringend notwendig, daß Gott er-

playing hide-and-seek: 'Now?' But the answer he heard was the kneading of his hands, and he waited. It seemed like a very long wait to him. Then all at once he saw something falling through space, something dark and heading as if it were coming from somewhere close to him. Filled with an evil premonition, he called to his hands. They came up, stained all over with clay, hot and trembling. 'Where is man?' he yelled at them. Then the right hand lashed out at the left: 'You let go of him!' 'Pardon me,' said the left hand in irritation, 'you wanted to do everything yourself; in fact you wouldn't let *me* have a word in the matter at all.' 'But you should have been holding onto him!' And the right hand hauled back for a punch. But then it had second thoughts, and the two hands said, racing to be first: 'Man was so impatient. He kept wanting to start living. Neither of us could help it, surely, we're both innocent.'

"But the Good Lord was really angry. He shoved away both hands, because they were obstructing his view of the earth. 'I disown you henceforth; do whatever you like.' And afterwards the hands tried to do just that, but they can merely make a *beginning* of whatever they do. Without God there's no completion. And so they finally got tired of it. Now they kneel all day long and do penance; at least that's the story. But to us it seems as if God were resting because he's angry at his hands. We're still always in the seventh day."

I was silent for a moment, which my neighbor made very sensible use of. "And you believe that there will never again be a reconciliation?" "Oh, I do," I said; "at least I hope so."

"And when might that be?"

"Well, at the time when God knows what man, whom the hands released against his wishes, looks like."

My neighbor thought this over, then laughed: "But to see that, all he'd have to do is look down. . . ."

"Excuse me," I said politely; "your remark testifies to your acumen, but my story isn't over yet. Well, then, after the hands had stepped aside and God was once again surveying the earth, another minute, or let's say a millennium, which, as you know, is the same thing, had just elapsed. Instead of one human being there were already a million. But all of them were already clothed. And since the fashions at that time happened to be very ugly and they even badly disfigured people's faces, God received an altogether incorrect and (I won't conceal it) very bad impression of mankind." "Hm," my neighbor said, and she wanted to add some remark. I paid no attention, but concluded with strong emphasis: "And therefore it's urgently necessary for God to

fährt, wie der Mensch wirklich ist. Freuen wir uns, daß es solche giebt,
die es ihm sagen . . .« Die Frau Nachbarin freute sich noch nicht: »Und
wer sollte das sein, bitte?« »Einfach die Kinder und dann und wann auch
diejenigen Leute, welche malen, Gedichte schreiben, bauen . . .« »Was
denn bauen, Kirchen?« »Ja, und auch sonst, überhaupt . . .«

    Die Frau Nachbarin schüttelte langsam den Kopf. Manches erschien
ihr doch recht verwunderlich. Wir waren schon über ihr Haus hinausge-
gangen und kehrten jetzt langsam um. Plötzlich wurde sie sehr lustig und
lachte: »Aber, was für ein Unsinn, Gott ist doch auch allwissend. Er hätte
ja genau wissen müssen, woher zum Beispiel der kleine Vogel gekommen
ist.« Sie sah mich triumphierend an. Ich war ein bißchen verwirrt, ich muß
gestehen. Aber als ich mich gefaßt hatte, gelang es mir ein überaus ernstes
Gesicht zu machen: »Liebe Frau,« belehrte ich sie, »das ist eigentlich eine
Geschichte für sich. Damit Sie aber nicht glauben, das sei nur eine
Ausrede von mir (sie verwahrte sich nun natürlich heftig dagegen), will ich
Ihnen in Kürze sagen: Gott hat *alle* Eigenschaften, natürlich. Aber ehe er
in die Lage kam, sie auf die Welt – gleichsam – anzuwenden, erschienen
sie ihm alle wie eine einzige große Kraft. Ich weiß nicht, ob ich mich deut-
lich ausdrücke. Aber angesichts der Dinge spezialisierten sich seine Fähig-
keiten und wurden bis zu einem gewissen Grade: Pflichten. Er hatte
Mühe, sich alle zu merken. Es giebt eben Konflikte. (Nebenbei: das alles
sage ich nur Ihnen, und Sie müssen es den Kindern keineswegs wiedererzählen.)« »Wo denken Sie hin«, beteuerte meine Zuhörerin.

    »Sehen Sie, wäre ein Engel vorübergeflogen, singend: ›Der Du
alles *weißt*‹, so wäre alles gut geworden . . .«

    »Und diese Geschichte wäre überflüssig?«

    »Gewiß«, bestätigte ich. Und ich wollt mich verabschieden. »Aber
wissen Sie das alles auch ganz bestimmt?« »Ich weiß es ganz bestimmt«, erwiderte ich fast feierlich. »Da werde ich den Kindern
heute zu erzählen haben!« »Ich würde es gerne anhören dürfen.
Leben Sie wohl.« »Leben Sie wohl«, antwortete sie.

    Dann kehrte sie nochmals zurück: »Aber weshalb ist gerade dieser
Engel . . .« »Frau Nachbarin,« sagte ich, indem ich sie unterbrach,
»ich merke jetzt, daß Ihre beiden lieben Mädchen gar nicht deshalb
soviel fragen, weil sie Kinder sind –« »Sondern?« fragte meine Nachbarin neugierig. »Nun, die Ärzte sagen, es giebt gewisse Vererbungen
. . .« Meine Frau Nachbarin drohte mir mit dem Finger. Aber wir
schieden dennoch als gute Freunde.

    Als ich meiner lieben Nachbarin später (übrigens nach ziemlich langer
Pause) wieder einmal begegnete, war sie nicht allein, und ich konnte

find out what man is really like. Let's be glad that there are some people who tell him. . . ." My neighbor was not yet glad: "And who might they be, please?" "Simply the children and, from time to time, also those people who paint, write poems, build . . ." "Build what? Churches?" "Yes, or just build, in general. . . ."

My neighbor shook her head slowly. After all, some of what I had said seemed quite astonishing to her. We had already walked past her house, and we were now slowly turning back. Suddenly she became very merry and said laughingly: "But what nonsense! After all, God is omniscient, as well. For instance, he must have known exactly where the little bird came from." She gave me a look of triumph. I was a little confused, I must confess. But after pulling myself together, I managed to put on a thoroughly grave expression: "My dear lady," I instructed her, "actually that's another story. But so you won't think I'm just making an excuse," (now she naturally protested violently against that notion) "I'll tell you briefly: of course, God possesses every capacity. But before he was in a position to apply those capacities to the world, as it were, they all seemed to him to be a single great force. I don't know whether I'm expressing myself clearly. But, in view of the things he created, his faculties became specialized and to a certain extent became duties. He had a hard time remembering them all. You see, conflicts arise. (Incidentally: I'm telling all this to you alone, and you must refrain by all means from repeating it to the children.)" "I should say not!" my listener asseverated.

"You see, if an angel had flown by singing 'Thou that *knowest* everything,' everything would have turned out all right. . . ."

"And this story wouldn't have been necessary?"

"Exactly," I said in confirmation. And I wanted to take my leave. "But do you know all this for a certainty?" "I know it for a certainty," I replied almost solemnly. "Then I'll have a story for the children today!" "I wouldn't mind being permitted to listen. Good-bye!" "Good-bye!" she replied.

Then she turned back again: "But why did just that angel . . ." "Dear neighbor," I said, interrupting her, "I now see that, if your two sweet girls ask so many questions, it's not at all because they're children." "Why else?" my neighbor asked with curiosity. "Well, doctors say that there are certain hereditary traits. . . ." My neighbor shook a menacing finger at me. But all the same we parted as good friends.

When I happened to meet my dear neighbor again some time afterward (after quite a long interval, incidentally), she wasn't alone, and

nicht erfahren, ob sie ihren Mädchen meine Geschichte berichtet hätte und mit welchem Erfolg. Über diesen Zweifel klärte mich ein Brief auf, welchen ich kurz darauf empfing. Da ich von dem Absender desselben nicht die Erlaubnis erhalten habe, ihn zu veröffentlichen, so muß ich mich darauf beschränken, zu erzählen, wie er endete, woraus man ohne weiteres erkennen wird, von wem er stammte. Er schloß mit den Worten: »Ich und noch fünf andere Kinder, nämlich, weil ich mit dabei bin.«

Ich antwortete, gleich nach Empfang, folgendes: »Liebe Kinder, daß euch das Märchen von den Händen vom lieben Gott gefallen hat, glaube ich gern; mir gefällt es auch. Aber ich kann trotzdem nicht zu euch kommen. Seid nicht böse deshalb. Wer weiß, ob ich euch gefiele. Ich habe keine schöne Nase, und wenn sie, was bisweilen vorkommt, auch noch ein rotes Pickelchen an der Spitze hat, so würdet ihr die ganze Zeit dieses Pünktchen anschauen und anstaunen und gar nicht hören, was ich ein Stückchen tiefer unten sage. Auch würdet ihr wahrscheinlich von diesem Pickelchen träumen. Das alles wäre mir gar nicht recht. Ich schlage darum einen anderen Ausweg vor. Wir haben (auch außer der Mutter) eine große Anzahl gemeinsamer Freunde und Bekannte, die *nicht* Kinder sind. Ihr werdet schon erfahren, welche. Diesen werde ich von Zeit zu Zeit eine Geschichte erzählen, und ihr werdet sie von diesen Vermittlern immer noch schöner empfangen, als ich sie zu gestalten vermöchte. Denn es sind gar große Dichter unter diesen unseren Freunden. Ich werde euch nicht verraten, wovon meine Geschichten handeln werden. Aber, weil euch nichts so sehr beschäftigt und am Herzen liegt, wie der liebe Gott, so werde ich an jeder passenden Gelegenheit einfügen, was ich von ihm weiß. Sollte etwas davon nicht richtig sein, so schreibt mir wieder einen schönen Brief, oder laßt es mir durch die Mutter sagen. Denn es ist möglich, daß ich mich an mancher Stelle irre, weil es schon so lange ist, seit ich die schönsten Geschichten erfahren habe, und weil ich seither mir viele habe merken müssen, die nicht so schön sind. Das kommt im Leben so mit. Trotzdem ist das Leben etwas ganz Prächtiges: auch *davon* wird des öfteren in meinen Geschichten die Rede sein. Damit grüßt euch – Ich, aber auch nur deshalb Einer, weil ich mit dabei bin.«

Der fremde Mann

Ein fremder Mann hat mir einen Brief geschrieben. Nicht von Europa schrieb mir der fremde Mann, nicht von Moses, weder von den großen, noch von den kleinen Propheten, nicht vom Kaiser von Rußland oder dem Zaren Iwan, dem Grausen, seinem fürchterlichen

I was unable to learn whether she had told my story to her girls, and with what results. This doubt was dispelled by a letter I received shortly afterward. Since I haven't received the sender's permission to make it public, I must confine myself to a report of how it ended, from which it will immediately be clear from whom it came. It closed with the words: "I and five other children—because I'm including myself in, you see."

I replied, right after receiving it, as follows: "Dear children, I gladly believe that you liked the tale of the Good Lord's hands; I like it, too. But, all the same, I can't visit you. Don't be angry over that. Who knows whether you'd like me? My nose isn't beautiful and when, in addition, it has a little red pimple on its tip (this happens occasionally), you'd be staring in amazement at that little dot the whole time, and you wouldn't hear what I'm going to say a little bit later in this letter. Also, you'd probably have dreams about that pimple. All of that would displease me. Therefore I suggest a different solution. Besides your mother, we have a large number of friends and acquaintances in common who are *not* children. You will soon learn whom I mean. From time to time I'll tell *them* a story, and you'll hear them from these go-betweens told much more beautifully than I could shape them. Because there are very great poets among these friends of ours. I won't reveal the subjects of my stories to you. But, since nothing occupies your minds or is closer to your hearts than the Good Lord, I'll insert what I know about him on every suitable occasion. If some of this should be incorrect, write me another lovely letter, or let me know by way of your mother. Because it's possible for me to make a mistake sometimes, for it's been so long since I learned the prettiest stories and in the meanwhile I've had to remember many that aren't as beautiful. That's one of the things that happen in life. All the same, life is something quite splendid; *that* subject, too, will come up frequently in my stories. And with that, I say good-bye—I, who only count because I'm 'including myself in.'"

The Stranger

A stranger has written me a letter. The stranger wrote to me not about Europe, not about Moses, neither about the major prophets nor the minor ones, not about the Emperor of Russia or about Tsar Ivan the Terrible, his fearful predecessor. Not about the mayor or

Vorfahren. Nicht vom Bürgermeister oder vom Nachbar Flick-
schuster, nicht von der nahen Stadt, nicht von den fernen Städten;
und auch der Wald mit den vielen Rehen, darin ich jeden Morgen
mich verliere, kommt in seinem Briefe nicht vor. Er erzählt mir auch
nichts von seinem Mütterchen oder von seinen Schwestern, die gewiß
längst verheiratet sind. Vielleicht ist auch sein Mütterchen tot; wie
könnte es sonst sein, daß ich sie in einem vierseitigen Briefe nirgends
erwähnt finde! Er erweist mir ein viel, viel größeres Vertrauen, er
macht mich zu seinem Bruder, er spricht mir von seiner Not.

Am Abend kommt der fremde Mann zu mir. Ich zünde keine Lampe
an, helfe ihm den Mantel ablegen und bitte ihn, mit mir Tee zu trinken,
weil das gerade die Stunde ist, in welcher ich täglich meinen Tee trinke.
Und bei so nahen Besuchen muß man sich keinen Zwang auferlegen.
Als wir uns schon an den Tisch setzen wollen, bemerke ich, daß mein
Gast unruhig ist; sein Gesicht ist voll Angst und seine Hände zittern.
»Richtig,« sage ich, »hier ist ein Brief für Sie.« Und dann bin ich dabei
den Tee einzugießen. »Nehmen Sie Zucker und vielleicht Zitrone? Ich
habe in Rußland gelernt den Tee mit Zitrone zu trinken. Wollen Sie
versuchen?« Dann zünde ich eine Lampe an und stelle sie in eine entfernte Ecke, etwas hoch, so daß eigentlich Dämmerung bleibt im
Zimmer, nur eine etwas wärmere als früher, eine rötliche. Und da
scheint auch das Gesicht meines Gastes sicherer, wärmer und um vieles
bekannter zu sein. Ich begrüße ihn noch einmal mit den Worten:
»Wissen Sie, ich habe Sie lange erwartet.« Und ehe der Fremde Zeit
hat zu staunen, erkläre ich ihm. »Ich weiß eine Geschichte, welche ich
niemandem erzählen mag als Ihnen; fragen Sie mich nicht warum,
sagen Sie mir nur, ob Sie bequem sitzen, ob der Tee genug süß ist und
ob Sie die Geschichte hören wollen.« Mein Gast mußte lächeln. Dann
antwortete er einfach: »Ja.« »Auf alles drei: Ja?« »Auf alles drei.«

Wir lehnten uns beide zugleich in unseren Stühlen zurück, so daß
unsere Gesichter schattig wurden. Ich stellte mein Teeglas nieder,
freute mich daran, wie goldig der Tee glänzte, vergaß diese Freude
langsam wieder und fragte plötzlich: »Erinnern Sie sich noch an den
lieben Gott?«

Der Fremde dachte nach. Seine Augen vertieften sich ins Dunkel,
und mit den kleinen Lichtpunkten in den Pupillen glichen sie zwei
langen Laubengängen in einem Parke, über welchem leuchtend und
breit Sommer und Sonne liegt. Auch diese beginnen so, mit runder
Dämmerung, dehnen sich in immer engerer Finsternis bis zu einem
fernen, schimmernden Punkt: dem jenseitigen Ausgang in einen
vielleicht noch viel helleren Tag. Während ich das erkannte, sagte er

his neighbor the cobbler, not about the nearby city, not about the distant cities; and even the forest with its many roe deer, in which I lose myself every morning, isn't mentioned in his letter. Nor does he tell me anything about his dear mother or his sisters, who have surely long been married. Perhaps his mother is even dead; what other reason could there be for not finding her mentioned anywhere in a letter four pages long? He displays a much, much greater confidence in me, he makes me his brother, he tells me of his distress.

In the evening the stranger comes to me. I don't light a lamp; I help him take off his coat and I ask him to drink tea with me, because it's just the time when I drink my daily tea. And when our visitors are so close to us, we mustn't adhere to ceremony. When we are finally about to sit down at the table, I notice that my guest is nervous; his face is full of anxiety and his hands are trembling. "Right," I say, "here is a letter for you." And then I make ready to pour the tea. "Do you take sugar and perhaps lemon? In Russia I learned to drink tea with lemon. Do you want to try?" Then I light a lamp and place it in a distant corner, a little high up, so that the room actually remains in twilight, but one that is a little warmer than before, a reddish one. And then even my guest's face seems more secure, warmer, and much more familiar. I greet him again with the words: "You know, I've been waiting for you a long time." And before the stranger has time to be surprised, I explain it to him. "I know a story which I don't want to tell to anyone but you; don't ask me why, just tell me whether your chair is comfortable, whether the tea is sweet enough, and whether you want to hear the story." My guest was compelled to smile. Then he answered simply: "Yes." "Yes to all three questions?" "To all three."

The two of us leaned back in our chairs at the same time, so that our faces were in shadow. I put down my glass of tea, happy that the tea had such a golden glow, slowly forgot about that happiness again, and suddenly asked: "Do you still remember the Good Lord?"

The stranger stopped to think. His eyes sank deeper into the darkness, and the small dots of light in their pupils made them resemble two long paths through tall shrubbery in the park of some mansion, over which summer and sunshine lie, broadly gleaming. These paths also begin that way, with a circle of half-light, then extend into ever more narrowly enclosing darkness until one sees a distant, glimmering point: the exit, opposite, into sunshine perhaps much brighter still.

zögernd und als ob er sich nur ungern seiner Stimme bediente: »Ja,
ich erinnere mich noch an Gott.« »Gut,« dankte ich ihm, »denn gerade von ihm handelt meine Geschichte. Doch zuerst sagen Sie mir
noch: Sprechen Sie bisweilen mit Kindern?« »Es kommt wohl vor, so
im Vorübergehen, wenigstens –« »Vielleicht ist es Ihnen bekannt, daß
Gott infolge eines häßlichen Ungehorsams seiner Hände nicht weiß,
wie der fertige Mensch eigentlich aussieht?« »Das habe ich einmal irgendwo gehört, ich weiß indessen nicht von wem« – entgegnete mein
Gast, und ich sah unbestimmte Erinnerungen über seine Stirn jagen.
»Gleichviel,« störte ich ihn, »hören Sie weiter. Lange Zeit ertrug Gott
diese Ungewißheit. Denn seine Geduld ist wie seine Stärke groß.
Einmal aber, als dichte Wolken zwischen ihm und der Erde standen
viele Tage lang, so daß er kaum mehr wußte, ob er alles: Welt und
Menschen und Zeit nicht nur geträumt hatte, rief er seine rechte
Hand, die so lange von seinem Angesicht verbannt und verborgen
gewesen war in kleinen unwichtigen Werken. Sie eilte bereitwillig
herbei; denn sie glaubte, Gott wolle ihr endlich verzeihen. Als Gott
sie so vor sich sah in ihrer Schönheit, Jugend und Kraft, war er schon
geneigt, ihr zu vergeben. Aber rechtzeitig besann er sich und gebot,
ohne hinzusehen: ›Du gehst hinunter auf die Erde. Du nimmst die
Gestalt an, die du bei den Menschen siehst, und stellst dich, nackt, auf
einen Berg, so daß ich dich genau betrachten kann. Sobald du unten
ankommst, geh zu einer jungen Frau und sag ihr, aber ganz leise: Ich
möchte leben. Es wird zuerst ein kleines Dunkel um dich sein und
dann ein großes Dunkel, welches Kindheit heißt, und dann wirst du
ein Mann sein und auf den Berg steigen, wie ich es dir befohlen habe.
Das alles dauert ja nur einen Augenblick. Leb wohl.‹
    Die Rechte nahm von der Linken Abschied, gab ihr viele freundliche
Namen, ja es wurde sogar behauptet, sie habe sich plötzlich vor ihr
verneigt und gesagt: ›Du, heiliger Geist.‹ Aber schon trat der heilige
Paulus herzu, hieb dem lieben Gott die rechte Hand ab, und ein
Erzengel fing sie auf und trug sie unter seinem weiten Gewand davon.
Gott aber hielt sich mit der Linken die Wunde zu, damit sein Blut nicht
über die Sterne ströme und von da in traurigen Tropfen herunterfiele auf
die Erde. Eine kurze Zeit später bemerkte Gott, der aufmerksam alle
Vorgänge unten betrachtete, daß die Menschen in den eisernen Kleidern
sich um einen Berg mehr zu schaffen machten, als um alle anderen
Berge. Und er erwartete, dort seine Hand hinaufsteigen zu sehen. Aber
es kam nur ein Mensch in einem, wie es schien, roten Mantel, welcher
etwas schwarzes Schwankendes aufwärts schleppte. In demselben
Augenblicke begann Gottes linke Hand, die vor seinem offenen Blute

While I realized this, he was saying hesitantly, as if using his voice only unwillingly: "Yes, I still remember God." "Good," I said, thanking him, "because my story is precisely about him. But first tell me one thing more: do you occasionally talk with children?" "It can happen, at least when I walk past them—" "You may perhaps be aware that, as a result of the nasty disobedience of his hands, God doesn't know exactly what completed man looks like." "I heard that somewhere once, right now I don't recall from whom," my guest replied, and I saw uncertain recollections racing across his brow. "It doesn't matter," I said, disturbing him, "hear me out. For a long time God endured this uncertainty. For his patience is as great as his might. But once, after dense clouds had hung between him and the earth for many days, so that he scarcely knew any more whether he hadn't merely dreamed it all—world and mankind and time—he summoned his right hand, which had been exiled from his sight for so long and had been doing small, unimportant tasks in concealment. It hastened over willingly, because it thought God was about to pardon it at last. When God saw it before him in its beauty, youth, and strength, he was already inclined to forgive it. But he changed his mind in time and, without looking at it, ordered: 'You are to go down to earth. You shall assume the shape that you see human beings have, and you shall place yourself naked on a mountain, so I can observe you closely. As soon as you arrive down there, go to a young woman and say to her, but very softly: "I want to live." At first there will be a small darkness around you, and then a great darkness, which is called childhood, and then you'll be a man and you'll climb the mountain, as I've ordered you. After all, the whole thing will only last a moment. Farewell!'

"The right hand took leave of the left hand, calling it many friendly names; in fact, some people assert that it suddenly bowed in front of the left hand, saying: 'Thou, Holy Spirit.' But by then Saint Paul had come up; he hacked off the Good Lord's right hand, and an archangel caught it and carried it away beneath his wide robe. But God held the wound closed with his left hand, so his blood wouldn't gush over the stars and fall on the earth from there in sorrowful drops. Shortly thereafter God, who was observing all earthly events attentively, noticed that the people in the iron garments were busying themselves around one mountain more than any other. And he expected to see his hand climb up it. But there came only a human being, in a cloak that seemed to be red, who was dragging upward something black that was swaying. At the same moment God's left hand, which was placed right next to his bleed-

lag, unruhig zu werden, und mit einem Mal verließ sie, ehe Gott es verhindern konnte, ihren Platz und irrte wie wahnsinnig zwischen den
Sternen umher und schrie: ›Oh, die arme rechte Hand, und ich kann ihr
nicht helfen.‹ Dabei zerrte sie an Gottes linkem Arm, an dessen äußer-
stem Ende sie hing, und bemühte sich loszukommen. Die ganze Erde
aber war rot vom Blute Gottes, und man konnte nicht erkennen, was
darunter geschah. Damals wäre Gott fast gestorben. Mit letzter Anstrengung rief er seine Rechte zurück; sie kam blaß und bebend und legte sich
an ihren Platz, wie ein krankes Tier. Aber auch die Linke, die doch schon
manches wußte, da sie die rechte Hand Gottes damals unten auf der
Erde erkannt hatte, als diese in einem roten Mantel den Berg erstieg,
konnte von ihr nicht erfahren, was sich weiter auf diesem Berge begeben
hat. Es muß etwas sehr Schreckliches gewesen sein. Denn Gottes Rechte
hat sich noch nicht davon erholt, und sie leidet unter ihrer Erinnerung
nicht weniger, als unter dem alten Zorne Gottes, der ja seinen Händen
immer noch nicht verziehen hat.«

Meine Stimme ruhte ein wenig aus. Der Fremde hatte sein Gesicht
mit den Händen verhüllt. Lange blieb alles so. Dann sagte der fremde
Mann mit einer Stimme, die ich längst kannte: »Und warum haben
Sie *mir* diese Geschichte erzählt?«

»Wer hätte mich sonst verstanden? Sie kommen zu mir ohne Rang,
ohne Amt, ohne irgend eine zeitliche Würde, fast ohne Namen. Es
war dunkel, als Sie eintraten, allein ich bemerkte in Ihren Zügen eine
Ähnlichkeit –« Der fremde Mann blickte fragend auf. »Ja,« erwiderte
ich seinem stillen Blick, »ich denke oft, vielleicht ist Gottes Hand
wieder unterwegs . . .«

Die Kinder haben diese Geschichte erfahren, und offenbar wurde
sie ihnen so erzählt, daß sie alles verstehen konnten; denn sie haben
diese Geschichte lieb.

Warum der liebe Gott will, daß es arme Leute giebt

Die vorangehende Geschichte hat sich so verbreitet, daß der Herr
Lehrer mit sehr gekränktem Gesicht auf der Gasse herumgeht. Ich
kann das begreifen. Es ist immer schlimm für einen Lehrer, wenn die
Kinder plötzlich etwas wissen, was er ihnen nicht erzählt hat. Der
Lehrer muß sozusagen das einzige Loch in der Planke sein, durch
welches man in den Obstgarten sieht; sind noch andere Löcher da, so
drängen sich die Kinder jeden Tag vor einem anderen und werden
bald des Ausblicks überhaupt müde. Ich hätte diesen Vergleich nicht

ing open wound, began to get restless, and all at once it left its place before God could prevent it, and roamed among the stars as if insane, crying: 'Oh, that poor right hand, and I can't help it!' At the same time it tugged at God's left arm, to which it was attached at the very end, and struggled to get free. But the whole earth was red with God's blood, and it was impossible to make out what was happening below. At that time God nearly died. In a final effort he summoned back his right hand; it came, pale and shuddering, and lay down in its place, like a sick animal. But even the left hand, which already knew a great deal because it had recognized God's right hand down on earth when it was climbing the mountain in a red cloak, couldn't learn from it the rest of the occurrences on that mountain. It must have been something very terrifying. Because God's right hand still hasn't recovered from it, and the memory of it makes it suffer no less than that old anger of God does, for he still hasn't pardoned his hands."

I rested my voice a little. The stranger had buried his face in his hands. Things remained that way for some time. Then the stranger said, in a voice long familiar to me: "And why did you tell this story to *me?*"

"Who else would have understood me? You come to see me without mentioning your rank or official title, or any other mark of secular dignity, practically without a name. It was dark when you came in, but in your features I noticed a resemblance—" The stranger looked up questioningly. "Yes," I replied to his quiet glance, "I often think that God's hand may be resuming its travels. . . ."

The children got to hear this story, and obviously it was told to them in such a way that they could understand all of it; because they love this story.

Why the Good Lord Wants Poor People to Exist

The foregoing story was spread abroad so far and wide that our schoolteacher goes around the street with a very grieved expression. I can understand that. It's always hard on a teacher when the children suddenly know something that he hasn't told them. The teacher, so to speak, has to be the only hole in the fence which offers a view into the orchard; if there are other holes, the children crowd around a different one every day and soon become tired of the view altogether. I wouldn't have set down this comparison here,

hier aufgezeichnet, denn nicht jeder Lehrer ist vielleicht damit einverstanden, ein Loch zu sein; aber der Lehrer, von dem ich rede,
mein Nachbar, hat den Vergleich zuerst von mir vernommen und ihn
sogar als äußerst treffend bezeichnet. Und sollte auch jemand anderer
Meinung sein, die Autorität meines Nachbars ist mir maßgebend.

Er stand vor mir, rückte beständig an seiner Brille und sagte:»Ich
weiß nicht, wer den Kindern diese Geschichte erzählt hat, aber es ist jedenfalls unrecht, ihre Phantasie mit solchen ungewöhnlichen
Vorstellungen zu überladen und anzuspannen. Es handelt sich um eine
Art Märchen –«»Ich habe es zufällig erzählen hören«, unterbrach ich
ihn. (Dabei log ich nicht, denn seit jenem Abend ist es mir wirklich
schon von meiner Frau Nachbarin wiederberichtet worden.) »So«,
machte der Lehrer; er fand das leicht erklärlich.»Nun, was sagen Sie
dazu?« Ich zögerte, auch fuhr er sehr schnell fort: »Zunächst finde ich
es unrecht, religiöse, besonders biblische Stoffe frei und eigenmächtig
zu gebrauchen. Es ist das alles im Katechismus jedenfalls so ausgedrückt, daß es besser nicht gesagt werden kann . . .« Ich wollte etwas
bemerken, erinnerte mich aber im letzten Augenblick, daß der Herr
Lehrer »zunächst« gebraucht hatte, daß also jetzt nach der Grammatik
und um der Gesundheit des Satzes willen ein »dann« und vielleicht
sogar ein »und endlich« folgen mußte, ehe ich mir erlauben durfte,
etwas anzufügen. So geschah es auch. Ich will, da der Herr Lehrer
diesen selben Satz, dessen tadelloser Bau jedem Kenner Freude berei-
ten wird, auch anderen übermittelt hat, die ihn ebensowenig wie ich
vergessen dürften, hier nur noch das aufzeichnen, was hinter dem schönen, vorbereitenden Worte: »Und endlich« wie das Finale einer
Ouvertüre kam. »Und endlich . . . (die sehr phantastische Auffassung
hingehen lassend) erscheint mir der Stoff gar nicht einmal genügend
durchdrungen und nach allen Seiten hin berücksichtigt zu sein. Wenn
ich Zeit hätte, Geschichten zu schreiben –«»Sie vermissen etwas in der
bewußten Erzählung?« konnte ich mich nicht enthalten ihn zu unter-
brechen. »Ja, ich vermisse manches. Vom literarisch-kritischen
Standpunkt gewissermaßen. Wenn ich zu Ihnen als Kollege sprechen
darf –« Ich verstand nicht, was er meinte, und sagte bescheiden: »Sie
sind zu gütig, aber ich habe nie eine Lehrertätigkeit . . .« Plötzlich fiel
mir etwas ein, ich brach ab, und er fuhr etwas kühl fort: »Um nur eins
zu nennen: es ist nicht anzunehmen, daß Gott (wenn man schon auf
den Sinn der Geschichte soweit eingehen will), daß Gott, also – sage ich
– daß Gott keinen weiteren Versuch gemacht haben sollte, einen
Menschen zu sehen, wie er ist, ich meine –« Jetzt glaubte ich den Herrn
Lehrer wieder versöhnen zu müssen. Ich verneigte mich ein wenig und

because not every teacher may consent to being considered a hole; but the teacher I'm talking about, my neighbor, heard that comparison from me first and even called it extremely accurate. And even if someone else has a different opinion, my neighbor's judgment is authoritative to me.

He was standing in front of me, constantly tugging at his glasses, and saying: "I don't know who told the children that story, but in any case it's wrong to overload and overexcite their imagination with such unusual ideas. It's a kind of fairy tale—" "I heard it told by accident," I said, interrupting him. (That wasn't a lie on my part, because since that evening it has already actually been repeated to me by my neighbor lady.) "So!" said the teacher; he found that easy to explain. "Now, what do you say about it?" I hesitated, and he continued very quickly: "In the first place, I find it improper to make free and arbitrary use of religious subjects, especially from the Bible. All of that is so well expressed in the Catechism, anyway, that it can't be stated any better. . . ." I wanted to make some remark, but at the last moment I recalled that the teacher had used the term "in the first place," and that therefore, grammatically and for the sake of the sentence's good health, a "second place" and perhaps even an "and finally" had to follow before I could take the liberty of adding anything. And so it turned out. Since the teacher has communicated the same sentence, the faultless construction of which will give joy to every connoisseur, to others as well, who are as little likely as I am to forget it, I shall here merely set down the part that followed the beautiful preparatory phrase "and finally" like the finale to an overture. "And finally . . . (setting aside the very fantastic conception) the subject matter seems to me not to have been sufficiently grasped and regarded from all sides. If I had time to write stories—" "You find something lacking in the story under discussion?" I couldn't help asking, though I was interrupting. "Yes, I find a great deal lacking. From the literary-critical standpoint, in a manner of speaking. If I may address you as a colleague—" I didn't understand what he meant, and I said modestly: "You're too kind, but I've never done any teaching. . . ." Suddenly I thought of something, I broke off, and he resumed, somewhat coolly: "To mention just one thing: it's impossible to accept the fact that God (assuming that one wants to go along that far with the sense of the story), that God, I say, should have made no further attempt to see a human being, as he is, I mean—" Now I thought I ought to make things right with the teacher again. I made a slight bow and began: "It's common knowl-

begann: »Es ist allgemein bekannt, daß Sie sich eingehend (und, wenn
man so sagen darf, nicht ohne Gegenliebe zu finden) der sozialen Frage
genähert haben.« Der Herr Lehrer lächelte. »Nun, dann darf ich annehmen, daß was ich Ihnen im folgenden mitzuteilen gedenke, Ihrem
Interesse nicht ganz ferne steht, zumal ich ja auch an Ihre letzte, sehr
scharfsinnige Bemerkung anknüpfen kann.« Er sah mich erstaunt an:
»Sollte Gott etwa . . .« »In der Tat,« bestätigte ich, »Gott ist eben dabei,
einen neuen Versuch zu machen.« »Wirklich?,« fuhr mich der Lehrer
an, »ist das an maßgebender Stelle bekannt geworden?« »Darüber kann
ich Ihnen nichts Genaues sagen –« bedauerte ich – »ich bin nicht in
Beziehung mit jenen Kreisen, aber wenn Sie dennoch meine kleine
Geschichte hören wollen?« »Sie würden mir einen großen Gefallen erweisen.« Der Lehrer nahm seine Brille ab und putzte sorgfältig die
Gläser, während seine nackten Augen sich schämten.

Ich begann: »Einmal sah der liebe Gott in eine große Stadt. Als ihm
von dem vielen Durcheinander die Augen ermüdeten (dazu trugen die
Netze mit den elektrischen Drähten nicht wenig bei), beschloß er, seine
Blicke auf ein einziges hohes Mietshaus für eine Weile zu beschränken,
weil dieses weit weniger anstrengend war. Gleichzeitig erinnerte er sich
seines alten Wunsches, einmal einen lebenden Menschen zu sehen, und
zu diesem Zwecke tauchten seine Blicke ansteigend in die Fenster der
einzelnen Stockwerke. Die Leute im ersten Stockwerke (es war ein rei-
cher Kaufmann mit Familie) waren fast nur Kleider. Nicht nur, daß alle
Teile ihres Körpers mit kostbaren Stoffen bedeckt waren, die äußeren
Umrisse dieser Kleidung zeigten an vielen Stellen eine solche Form, daß
man sah, es konnte kein Körper mehr darunter sein. Im zweiten Stock
war es nicht viel besser. Die Leute, welche drei Treppen wohnten, hatten zwar schon bedeutend weniger an, waren aber so schmutzig, daß der
liebe Gott nur graue Furchen erkannte und in seiner Güte schon bereit
war, zu befehlen, sie möchten fruchtbar werden. Endlich unter dem
Dach, in einem schrägen Kämmerchen, fand der liebe Gott einen Mann
in einem schlechten Rock, der sich damit beschäftigte, Lehm zu kneten.
›Oho, woher hast du das?‹ rief er ihn an. Der Mann nahm seine Pfeife
gar nicht aus dem Munde und brummte: ›Der Teufel weiß woher. Ich
wollte, ich wär Schuster geworden. Da sitzt man und plagt sich . . .‹ Und
was der liebe Gott auch fragen mochte, der Mann war schlechter Laune
und gab keine Antwort mehr. – Bis er eines Tages einen großen Brief
vom Bürgermeister dieser Stadt bekam. Da erzählte er dem lieben Gott,
ungefragt, alles. Er hatte so lange keinen Auftrag bekommen. Jetzt,
plötzlich, sollte er eine Statue für den Stadtpark machen, und sie sollte
heißen: die Wahrheit. Der Künstler arbeitete Tag und Nacht in einem

edge that you have studied social problems thoroughly (and, if I may say so, not without meeting a friendly response)." The teacher smiled. "Now, in that case I may assume that what I intend to communicate to you next doesn't lie far outside your interests, especially because I can also pick up the thread of your last, very intelligent observation." He looked at me in surprise: "Should God by some chance. . . ." "Indeed," I assured him, "God is on the very point of making a new attempt." "Really?" the teacher said aggressively. "Has that been made known to the authorities?" "About that, I can't tell you anything precise," I said regretfully; "I'm not in contact with those circles, but if you nevertheless wish to hear my little story?" "You'd be doing me a great favor." The teacher took off his glasses and carefully cleaned the lenses, while his eyes looked ashamed of their nakedness.

I began: "Once, the Good Lord looked down into a big city. When his eyes grew tired of all the confusion (the networks of electric wires were no small contributing factor), he resolved to confine his glances to a single tall apartment building for a while, because that was much less of a strain. At the same time he recalled his old desire to see a living person at last, and for that purpose his eyes moved upward from one story to another, as he looked into the windows. The people one story up (a rich merchant and his family) were practically nothing but clothes. Not only was every part of their body covered with expensive fabrics; in many places the outer contours of that clothing showed such a form that obviously there could no longer be any body beneath them. On the second story up, it wasn't much better. The people who lived three flights up had significantly less on, it's true, but were so dirty that the Good Lord made out only gray furrows and in his kindness was already prepared to command them to be fruitful. Finally, below the roof, in a tiny room with a slanted ceiling, the Good Lord found a man in a shabby jacket busy kneading clay. 'Oh, ho, where did you learn that?' he called to him. The man, who didn't even take his pipe out of his mouth, grumbled: 'The devil knows where. I wish I had become a shoemaker. Here I sit and sweat it out. . . .' And no matter what the Good Lord asked him, the man stayed in a bad mood and refused to give any more answers.—Until, one day, he got a long letter from the mayor of that city. Then he told the Good Lord everything without being asked. For such a long time he hadn't received any commissions. Now, suddenly, he was to make a statue for the municipal park, and it was to be called Truth. The artist worked

entfernten Atelier, und dem lieben Gott kamen verschiedene alte
Erinnerungen, wie er das so sah. Wenn er seinen Händen nicht immer
noch böse gewesen wäre, er hätte wohl auch wieder irgendwas begonnen. – Als aber der Tag kam, da die Bildsäule, welche die Wahrheit
hieß, hinausgetragen werden sollte, auf ihren Platz in den Garten, wo
auch Gott sie hätte sehen können in ihrer Vollendung, da entstand ein
großer Skandal, denn eine Kommission von Stadtvätern, Lehrern und
anderen einflußreichen Persönlichkeiten hatte verlangt, die Figur müsse
erst teilweise bekleidet werden, ehe das Publikum sie zu Gesicht
bekäme. Der liebe Gott verstand nicht weshalb, so laut fluchte der
Künstler. Stadtväter, Lehrer und die anderen haben ihn in diese Sünde
gebracht, und der liebe Gott wird gewiß an denen – Aber Sie husten ja
fürchterlich!« »Es geht schon vorüber –« sagte mein Lehrer mit vollkommen klarer Stimme. »Nun, ich habe nur noch ein weniges zu
berichten. Der liebe Gott ließ das Mietshaus und den Stadtpark los und
wollte seinen Blick schon ganz zurückziehen, wie man eine Angelrute
aus dem Wasser zieht, mit einem Schwung, um zu sehen, ob nicht etwas
angebissen hat. In diesem Falle hing wirklich etwas daran. Ein ganz
kleines Häuschen mit mehreren Menschen drinnen, die alle sehr wenig
anhatten, denn sie waren sehr arm. ›Das also ist es –‹ dachte der liebe
Gott, ›arm müssen die Menschen sein. Diese hier sind, glaub ich, schon
recht arm, aber ich will sie so arm machen, daß sie nicht einmal ein
Hemd zum Anziehen haben.‹ So nahm sich der liebe Gott vor.«

Hier machte ich beim Sprechen einen Punkt, um anzudeuten, daß ich
am Ende sei. Der Herr Lehrer war damit nicht zufrieden; er fand diese
Geschichte ebensowenig abgeschlossen und gerundet, wie die vorherge-
hende. »Ja« – entschuldigte ich mich – »da müßte eben ein Dichter kommen, der zu dieser Geschichte irgend einen phantastischen Schluß
erfindet, denn tatsächlich hat sie noch kein Ende.« »Wieso?« machte der
Herr Lehrer und schaute mich gespannt an. »Aber, lieber Herr Lehrer,«
erinnerte ich, »wie vergeßlich Sie sind! Sie sind doch selbst im Vorstand
des hiesigen Armenvereins . . .« »Ja, seit etwa zehn Jahren bin ich das und
–?« »Das ist es eben; Sie und Ihr Verein verhindern den lieben Gott die
längste Zeit, sein Ziel zu erreichen. Sie kleiden die Leute –« »Aber ich
bitte Sie,« sagte der Lehrer bescheiden, »das ist einfach Nächstenliebe.
Das ist doch Gott im höchsten Grade wohlgefällig.« »Ach, davon ist man
maßgebenden Orts wohl überzeugt?« fragte ich arglos. »Natürlich ist
man das. Ich habe gerade in meiner Eigenschaft als Vorstandsmitglied
des Armenvereins manches Lobende zu hören bekommen. Vertraulich
gesagt, man will auch bei der nächsten Beförderung meine Tätigkeit in
dieser Weise – – – Sie verstehen?« Der Herr Lehrer errötete schamhaft.

day and night in a remote studio, and the Good Lord had various recollections of old days when he beheld that. If he hadn't still been so angry at his hands, he might have started something again, too.— But when the day came on which the statue called Truth was to be moved out to its spot in the park, where God, too, could have seen it in its finished state, a great scandal arose, because a committee of city fathers, teachers, and other influential personalities had demanded that the figure first be partially draped, before the public got to see it. The Good Lord didn't understand why, because the artist was cursing so loudly. City fathers, teachers, and the rest, he said, had led him into this sin, and the Good Lord would surely take it out on them— But you're coughing something awful!" "It will pass right away," said the teacher in a perfectly clear voice. "Well, I have only a little more to tell. The Good Lord drew away from the apartment house and the municipal park, and wanted to withdraw his gaze entirely, the way you draw your fishing line out of the water, with a strong pull, to see if some fish hasn't bitten. In this case, there was really something on the hook. A very tiny house with several people in it, all dressed very scantily because they were very poor. 'That's it, then,' the Good Lord thought; 'people have to be poor. These here are already pretty poor, I think, but I'll make them so poor that they don't even have a shirt to put on.' That's what the Good Lord resolved."

Here I expressed a verbal period to indicate that I was done. The teacher wasn't satisfied with that; he found this story just as incomplete and inconclusive as the preceding one. "Yes," I said in excuse, "then a poet would have to come and invent some kind of imaginary ending for this story, because in actuality it still has no ending." "How so?" said the teacher, looking at me in suspense. "But, my dear teacher," I reminded him, "how forgetful you are! After all, you yourself are on the committee of the local welfare organization. . . ." "Yes, I have been for about ten years; so?" "That's just it; you and your organization have been preventing the Good Lord for the longest time from attaining his goal. You put clothes on people." "But please recall," said the teacher modestly, "that's simple Christian charity. Surely it's pleasing to God in the highest degree." "Ah, are the authorities really convinced of that?" I asked innocently. "Of course they are. Precisely in my capacity as committee member of the welfare association I've received quite a bit of praise. Speaking confidentially, at the next promotion my activity in this area will also be— —You understand?" The teacher blushed modestly. "I wish you all

»Ich wünsche Ihnen das Beste«, entgegnete ich. Wir reichten uns die Hände, und der Herr Lehrer ging mit so stolzen, gemessenen Schritten fort, daß ich überzeugt bin: er ist zu spät in die Schule gekommen.

Wie ich später vernahm, ist ein Teil dieser Geschichte (soweit sie für Kinder paßt) den Kindern doch bekannt geworden. Sollte der Herr Lehrer sie zu Ende gedichtet haben?

Wie der Verrat nach Rußland kam

Ich habe noch einen Freund hier in der Nachbarschaft. Das ist ein blonder, lahmer Mann, der seinen Stuhl, winters wie sommers, hart am Fenster hat. Er kann sehr jung aussehen, ja in seinem lauschenden Gesicht ist manchmal etwas Knabenhaftes. Aber es giebt auch Tage, da er altert, die Minuten gehen wie Jahre über ihn, und plötzlich ist er ein Greis, dessen matte Augen das Leben fast schon losgelassen haben. Wir kennen uns lang. Erst haben wir uns immer angesehen, später lächelten wir unwillkürlich, ein Jahr lang grüßten wir einander, und seit Gott weiß wann erzählen wir uns das Eine und das Andere, wahllos, wie es eben passiert. »Guten Tag,« rief er, als ich vorüberkam und sein Fenster war noch offen in den reichen und stillen Herbst hinaus. »Ich habe Sie lange nicht gesehen.«

»Guten Tag, Ewald –.« Ich trat an sein Fenster, wie ich immer zu tun pflegte, im Vorübergehen. »Ich war verreist.« »Wo waren Sie?« fragte er mit ungeduldigen Augen. »In Rußland.« »Oh so weit –« er lehnte sich zurück, und dann: »Was ist das für ein Land, Rußland? Ein sehr großes, nicht wahr?« »Ja,« sagte ich, »groß ist es und außerdem –« »Habe ich dumm gefragt?«lächelte Ewald und wurde rot. »Nein, Ewald, im Gegenteil. Da Sie fragen: was ist das für ein Land? wird mir verschiedenes klar. Zum Beispiel woran Rußland grenzt.« »Im Osten?« warf mein Freund ein. Ich dachte nach: »Nein.« »Im Norden?« forschte der Lahme. »Sehen Sie,« fiel mir ein, »das Ablesen von der Landkarte hat die Leute verdorben. Dort ist alles plan und eben, und wenn sie die vier Weltgegenden bezeichnet haben, scheint ihnen alles getan. Ein Land ist doch aber kein Atlas. Es hat Berge und Abgründe. Es muß doch auch oben und unten an etwas stoßen.« »Hm –« überlegte mein Freund, »Sie haben recht. Woran könnte Rußland an diesen beiden Seiten grenzen?« Plötzlich sah der Kranke wie ein Knabe aus. »Sie wissen es,« rief ich. »Vielleicht an Gott?« »Ja,« bestätigte ich, »an Gott.« »So« – nickte mein Freund ganz verständnisvoll. Erst dann kamen ihm einzelne Zweifel: »Ist denn Gott ein

the best," I replied. We shook hands, and the teacher departed with such proud, measured steps that I'm convinced that he got to school late.

As I heard afterward, a part of this story (to the extent that it's suitable for children) nevertheless became known to the children. Could the teacher have composed an ending for it?

How Treachery Arrived in Russia

I have yet another friend here in the neighborhood. He's a blond, paralyzed man, whose chair is placed right next to the window, winter and summer. He can have a very young appearance; indeed, there's often something boyish in his face when he listens to you. But there are also days when he grows old, when the minutes pass over him like years, and he's suddenly an old man whose dull eyes have already almost lost their hold on life. We're known each other a long time. At first we always looked at each other, later on we'd smile involuntarily, for a whole year we said hello, and since God knows when we've been telling each other this and that, at random, as things occur. "Good day!" he called as I walked by; his window was still open to the rich, quiet autumn. "I haven't seen you for some time."

"Good day, Ewald." I walked up to his window, as I always used to do when passing by. "I was on a trip." "Where were you?" he asked with impatience in his eyes. "In Russia." "Oh, that far—" He leaned back, then said: "What kind of country is Russia? A very big one, isn't it?" "Yes," I said, "it *is* big, and besides that—" "Was it a stupid question?" Ewald asked with a smile, blushing. "No, Ewald, just the opposite. Now that you ask what sort of country it is, various things become clear to me. For example, Russia's borders." "To the east?" my friend interjected. I thought that over: "No." "To the north?" the paralyzed man inquired. "Look," it occurred to me to say, "map reading has ruined people. There, everything is flat and smooth, and after they've drawn in the four corners of the world, they think that's the end of it. But a country isn't an atlas. It has mountains and abysses. After all it has to border on something above and below, as well." "Hm—," said my friend, considering this; "you're right. On what might Russia border in those two directions?" Suddenly the invalid looked like a boy. "You know the answer," I cried. "Perhaps on God?" "Yes," I said in confirmation, "on God." "So," my friend said with a nod of full understanding. Only then did some doubts assail him: "Is God a country,

Land?« »Ich glaube nicht,« erwiderte ich, »aber in den primitiven
Sprachen haben viele Dinge denselben Namen. Es ist da wohl ein
Reich, das heißt Gott, und der es beherrscht, heißt auch Gott.
Einfache Völker können ihr Land und ihren Kaiser oft nicht unter-
scheiden; beide sind groß und gütig, furchtbar und groß.«

»Ich verstehe«, sagte langsam der Mann am Fenster. »Und merkt
man in Rußland diese Nachbarschaft?« »Man merkt sie bei allen
Gelegenheiten. Der Einfluß Gottes ist sehr mächtig. Wie viel man
auch aus Europa bringen mag, die Dinge aus dem Westen sind
Steine, sobald sie über die Grenze sind. Mitunter kostbare Steine,
aber eben nur für die Reichen, die sogenannten ›Gebildeten‹,
während von drüben aus dem anderen Reich das Brot kommt, wovon
das Volk lebt.« »Das hat das Volk wohl in Überfluß?« Ich zögerte:
»Nein, das ist nicht der Fall, die Einfuhr aus Gott ist durch gewisse
Umstände erschwert —« Ich suchte ihn von diesem Gedanken
abzubringen. »Aber man hat vieles aus den Gebräuchen jener breiten
Nachbarschaft angenommen. Das ganze Zeremoniell beispielsweise.
Man spricht zu dem Zaren ähnlich wie zu Gott.« »So, man sagt also
nicht: Majestät?« »Nein, man nennt beide Väterchen.« »Und man
kniet vor beiden?« »Man wirft sich vor beiden nieder, fühlt mit der
Stirn den Boden und weint und sagt: ›Ich bin sündig, verzeih mir,
Väterchen.‹ Die Deutschen, welche das sehen, behaupten: eine ganz
unwürdige Sklaverei. Ich denke anders darüber. Was soll das Knien
bedeuten? Es hat den Sinn zu erklären: Ich habe Ehrfurcht. Dazu
genügt es auch, das Haupt zu entblößen, meint der Deutsche. Nun ja,
der Gruß, die Verbeugung, gewissermaßen sind auch sie Ausdrücke
dafür, Abkürzungen die entstanden sind in den Ländern, wo nicht soviel Raum war, daß jeder sich hätte niederlegen können auf der Erde.
Aber Abkürzungen gebraucht man bald mechanisch und ohne sich
ihres Sinnes mehr bewußt zu werden. Deshalb ist es gut, wo noch
Raum und Zeit dafür ist, die Gebärde auszuschreiben, das ganze
schöne und wichtige Wort: Ehrfurcht.«

»Ja, wenn ich könnte, würde ich auch niederknien —«, träumte der
Lahme. »Aber es kommt« – fuhr ich nach einer Pause fort – »in
Rußland auch vieles andere von Gott. Man hat das Gefühl, jedes Neue
wird von ihm eingeführt, jedes Kleid, jede Speise, jede Tugend und
sogar jede Sünde muß erst von ihm bewilligt werden, ehe sie in
Gebrauch kommt.« Der Kranke sah mich fast erschrocken an. »Es ist
nur ein Märchen, auf welches ich mich berufe,« eilte ich ihn zu beruhi-

then?" "I don't think so," I replied, "but in primitive languages many things have the same name. There is probably a kingdom called God, and its ruler is also called God. Simple peoples often fail to make a distinction between their country and their emperor; both are great and kind, fearsome and great."

"I understand," the man at the window said slowly. "And are people in Russia aware of that neighbor?" "They're aware of him on all occasions. God's influence is very powerful. No matter how much is brought from Europe, the things from the West are stones as soon as they cross the border. Sometimes precious stones, but only for the rich, the so-called educated class, whereas from that other direction, that other kingdom, comes the bread that the masses live on." "I suppose the people have an abundance of it?" I hesitated: "No, that isn't the case; importation from God is made difficult by certain circumstances—" I tried to get him off that topic. "But they've taken over many of the customs of that wide neighboring land. For instance, their entire ceremonial. The tsar is addressed just like God." "So they don't say 'Your Majesty'?" "No, both are called Little Father." "And they kneel to both?" "They prostrate themselves before both; they feel the ground with their forehead and weep and say: 'I'm a poor sinner; forgive me, Little Father!' The Germans who see that claim it's a most undignified form of slavery. My opinion of it is different. What does kneeling mean? It expresses the idea: I show respect. 'For that it's enough to bare one's head,' a German believes. Well, yes, the salutation and the bow are also expressions of that to some extent, abbreviations which arose in countries where there wasn't enough room for everyone to be able to stretch out on the ground. But soon people start using abbreviations mechanically, no longer conscious of what they stand for. Therefore it's a good thing, where there's still enough space and time to do so, to spell out the entire gesture, the entire beautiful and significant word 'respect.'"

"Yes, if I could, I'd kneel down, too—," the paralyzed man said dreamily. "But in Russia," I resumed after a pause, "many other things come from God, as well. You have the feeling that everything new is imported from him; that every garment, every foodstuff, every virtue, and even every sin must be approved by him before it becomes part of daily life." The invalid looked at me almost in alarm. "It's only a folktale I'm referring to," I hastened to calm him, "a so-called *bylina*,[5]

---

5. A *bylina* is a narrative poem, often about mythical folk heroes.

gen, »eine sogenannte Bylina, ein Gewesenes zu deutsch. Ich will
Ihnen kurz den Inhalt erzählen. Der Titel ist: ›Wie der Verrat nach
Rußland kam‹.« Ich lehnte mich ans Fenster, und der Gelähmte schloß
die Augen, wie er gerne tat, wenn irgendwo eine Geschichte begann.

»Der schreckliche Zar Iwan wollte den benachbarten Fürsten Tribut
auferlegen und drohte ihnen mit einem großen Krieg, falls sie nicht
Gold nach Moskau, in die weiße Stadt, schicken würden. Die Fürsten
sagten, nachdem sie Rat gepflogen hatten, wie ein Mann: ›Wir geben
dir drei Rätselfragen auf. Komm an dem Tage, den wir dir bestimmen,
in den Orient, zu dem weißen Stein, wo wir versammelt sein werden,
und sage uns die drei Lösungen. Sobald sie richtig sind, geben wir dir
die zwölf Tonnen Goldes, die du von uns verlangst. Zuerst dachte der
Zar Iwan Wassiljewitsch nach, aber es störten ihn die vielen Glocken
seiner weißen Stadt Moskau. Da rief er seine Gelehrten und Räte vor
sich, und jeden, der die Fragen nicht beantworten konnte, ließ er auf
den großen, roten Platz führen, wo gerade die Kirche für Wassilij, den
Nackten, gebaut wurde, und einfach köpfen. Bei einer solchen
Beschäftigung verging ihm die Zeit so rasch, daß er sich plötzlich auf
der Reise fand nach dem Orient, zu dem weißen Stein, bei welchem die
Fürsten warteten. Er wußte auf keine der drei Fragen etwas zu er-
widern, aber der Ritt war lang, und es war immer noch die Möglichkeit,
einem Weisen zu begegnen; denn damals waren viele Weise unterwegs
auf der Flucht, da alle Könige die Gewohnheit hatten, ihnen den Kopf
abschneiden zu lassen, wenn sie ihnen nicht weise genug schienen. Ein
solcher kam ihm nun allerdings nicht zu Gesicht, aber an einem
Morgen sah er einen alten, bärtigen Bauer, welcher an einer Kirche
baute. Er war schon dabei angelangt, den Dachstuhl zu zimmern und
die kleinen Latten darüberzulegen. Da war es nun recht verwunderlich,
daß der alte Bauer immer wieder von der Kirche herunterstieg, um von
den schmalen Latten, welche unten aufgeschichtet waren, jede einzeln
zu holen, statt viele auf einmal in seinem langen Kaftan mitzunehmen.
Er mußte so beständig auf- und niederklettern, und es war garnicht
abzusehen, daß er auf diese Weise überhaupt jemals alle vielhundert
Latten an ihren Ort bringen würde. Der Zar wurde deshalb ungeduldig: ›Dummkopf,‹ schrie er (so nennt man in Rußland meistens die
Bauern), ›du solltest dich tüchtig beladen mit deinem Holz und dann
auf die Kirche kriechen, das wäre bei weitem einfacher.‹ Der Bauer, der

in German 'a bygone thing.' I'll narrate the plot to you briefly. The title is 'How Treachery Arrived in Russia.'" I leaned against the window, and the paralyzed man shut his eyes, as he usually did when some story began.

"Tsar Ivan the Terrible[6] wished to impose tribute on the neighboring princes, and threatened them with a great war if they refused to send gold to Moscow, the white city. After the princes had taken counsel, they replied as one man: 'We set you three riddles. On the day we establish, come to the East, to the white stone where we will be assembled, and tell us the three solutions. If they're correct, we'll give you the twelve casks of gold that you demand of us. At first Tsar Ivan Vasilievich thought this over, but he was disturbed by the many bells of his white city of Moscow. Then he summoned his scholars and advisers, and anyone who couldn't answer the questions was led to the great red square, where the church was being built for Vasily the naked,[7] and was unceremoniously beheaded. While he was occupied in this manner, he found time going by so fast that he suddenly found himself on his journey to the East, to the white stone where the princes were waiting. He had no answer to any of the three questions, but the ride was long, and there was still the possibility of meeting some sage; because at that time many sages were refugees along the roads, since all the kings followed the custom of having them beheaded if they didn't consider them wise enough. As it happened, he didn't catch sight of any such wise man, but one morning he saw an old, bearded peasant building a church. He had already reached the point of carpentering the roof frame and placing the small laths over it. Now, it was truly astonishing that, time and again, the old peasant climbed down from the church to fetch individually each of the narrow laths that were piled up on the ground, instead of taking along several at a time in his long caftan. And so he had to keep climbing up and down, and there was no prospect of his ever getting all those hundreds of laths in place that way. And so the tsar became impatient: 'Imbecile!' he shouted (that's what the peasants are generally called in Russia); 'you ought to pick up a proper load of wood and then crawl up to the church; that would be much simpler.' The peasant, who was on the ground just then, came to a halt,

---

6. Ivan IV (reigned 1547–1584).   7. Vasily (1489–1552) was a "holy fool," a simple-minded holy man who drew great crowds as he traveled the roads of Russia in tatters ("naked"). After his death, Ivan IV had the famous St. Basil's Cathedral in Red Square built in his honor (construction lasted from 1555 to 1560).

gerade unten war, blieb stehen, hielt die Hand über die Augen und antwortete: ›Das mußt du schon mir überlassen, Zar Iwan Wassiljewitsch, jeder versteht sein Handwerk am besten; indessen, weil du schon hier vorüberreitest, will ich dir die Lösung der drei Rätsel sagen, welche du am weißen Stein im Orient, gar nicht weit von hier, wirst wissen müssen.‹ Und er schärfte ihm die drei Antworten der Reihe nach ein. Der Zar konnte vor Erstaunen kaum dazu kommen, zu danken. ›Was soll ich dir geben zum Lohne?‹ fragte er endlich. ›Nichts‹, machte der Bauer, holte eine Latte und wollte auf die Leiter steigen. ›Halt,‹ befahl der Zar, ›das geht nicht an, du mußt dir etwas wünschen.‹ ›Nun, Väterchen, wenn du befiehlst, gieb mir eine von den zwölf Tonnen Goldes, welche du von den Fürsten im Orient erhalten wirst.‹ ›Gut –,‹ nickte der Zar. ›Ich gebe dir eine Tonne Goldes.‹ Dann ritt er eilends davon, um die Lösungen nicht wieder zu vergessen.

Später, als der Zar mit den zwölf Tonnen zurückgekommen war aus dem Orient, schloß er sich in Moskau in seinen Palast, mitten im fünftorigen Kreml ein und schüttete eine Tonne nach der anderen auf die glänzenden Dielen des Saales aus, so daß ein wahrer Berg aus Gold entstand, der einen großen schwarzen Schatten über den Boden warf. In Vergeßlichkeit hatte der Zar auch die zwölfte Tonne ausgeleert. Er wollte sie wieder füllen, aber es tat ihm leid, soviel Gold von dem herrlichen Haufen wieder fortnehmen zu müssen. In der Nacht ging er in den Hof hinunter, schöpfte feinen Sand in die Tonne, bis sie zu drei Vierteilen voll war, kehrte leise in seinen Palast zurück, legte Gold über den Sand und schickte die Tonne mit dem nächsten Morgen durch einen Boten in die Gegend des weiten Rußland, wo der alte Bauer seine Kirche baute. Als dieser den Boten kommen sah, stieg er von dem Dach, welches noch lange nicht fertig war, und rief: ›Du mußt nicht näher kommen, mein Freund, reise zurück samt deiner Tonne, welche drei Vierteile Sand und ein knappes Viertel Gold enthält; ich brauche sie nicht. Sage deinem Herrn, bisher hat es keinen Verrat in Rußland gegeben. Er aber ist selbst daran schuld, wenn er bemerken sollte, daß er sich auf keinen Menschen verlassen kann; denn er hat nunmehr gezeigt, wie man verrät, und von Jahrhundert zu Jahrhundert wird sein Beispiel in ganz Rußland viele Nachahmer finden. Ich brauche nicht das Gold, ich kann ohne Gold leben. Ich erwartete nicht Gold von ihm, sondern Wahrheit und Rechtlichkeit. Er aber hat mich getäuscht. Sage das deinem Herrn, dem schrecklichen Zaren Iwan Wassiljewitsch, der in seiner weißen Stadt Moskau sitzt mit seinem bösen Gewissen und in einem goldenen Kleid.‹

Nach einer Weile Reitens wandte sich der Bote nochmals um: der

shaded his eyes with one hand, and replied: 'You've got to leave that to me, Tsar Ivan Vasilievich; everyone understands his own trade best; meanwhile, since you're already riding by here, I'll tell you the solutions to the three riddles that you will need to know at the white stone in the East, which isn't far from here.' And, one by one, he drilled the three answers into him. The tsar was so amazed that he could scarcely think of thanking him. 'What shall I give you as a reward?' he finally asked. 'Nothing,' said the peasant, who fetched a lath and began climbing the ladder. 'Stop!' the tsar ordered; 'that won't do; you must request something.' 'Well, Little Father, if you command it, give me one of the twelve casks of gold that you'll receive from the princes in the East.' 'Agreed,' said the tsar with a nod. 'I'll give you a cask of gold.' Then he rode away speedily, so he wouldn't forget the solutions.

Afterward, when the tsar had returned from the East with the twelve casks, he shut himself away in his palace in Moscow, in the center of the five-towered Kremlin, and poured out one cask after another onto the gleaming floorboards of the great hall, so that a real mountain of gold was heaped up, casting a large black shadow across the floor. Out of forgetfulness the tsar had emptied the twelfth cask, too. He was about to fill it again, but he felt bad about removing all that gold from the splendid pile. At night he went down into the courtyard, ladled fine sand into the cask until it was three-quarters filled, returned quietly to his palace, placed gold over the sand, and, on the next morning, sent the cask by messenger to the region of broad Russia where the old peasant was building his church. When the peasant saw the messenger coming, he climbed down from the roof, which was still far from being completed, and called: 'You mustn't come any closer, my friend; journey back along with your cask, which is three-quarters filled with sand and a scanty one quarter of gold; I don't need it. Tell your master that up to now there has never been any treachery in Russia. But he himself is to blame if he should observe that he can't rely on anyone; because he has now showed people how to commit treachery, and from century to century his example will find many imitators all over Russia. I don't need the gold, I can live without gold. I wasn't expecting gold from him, but truth and equity. But he deceived me. Tell that to your master, Ivan Vasilievich the Terrible, who sits in his white city of Moscow with his bad conscience and in his golden robes.'

After riding for a way, the messenger turned around again: the

Bauer und seine Kirche waren verschwunden. Und auch die aufgeschichteten Latten lagen nicht mehr da, es war alles leeres, flaches Land. Da jagte der Mann entsetzt zurück nach Moskau, stand atemlos vor dem Zaren und erzählte ihm ziemlich unverständlich, was sich begeben hatte, und daß der vermeintliche Bauer niemand anderes gewesen sei, als Gott selbst.«

»Ob er wohl recht gehabt hat damit?« meinte mein Freund leise, nachdem meine Geschichte verklungen war.

»Vielleicht –,« entgegnete ich, »aber, wissen Sie, das Volk ist – abergläubisch – indessen, ich muß jetzt gehen, Ewald.« »Schade,« sagte der Lahme aufrichtig. »Wollen Sie mir nicht bald wieder eine Geschichte erzählen?« »Gerne –, aber unter einer Bedingung.« Ich trat noch einmal ans Fenster heran. »Nämlich?« staunte Ewald. »Sie müssen alles gelegentlich den Kindern in der Nachbarschaft weitererzählen«, bat ich. »Oh, die Kinder kommen jetzt so selten zu mir.« Ich vertröstete ihn: »Sie werden schon kommen. Offenbar haben Sie in der letzten Zeit nicht Lust gehabt, ihnen etwas zu erzählen, und vielleicht auch keinen Stoff, oder zu viel Stoffe. Aber wenn einer eine wirkliche Geschichte weiß, glauben Sie, das kann verborgen bleiben? Bewahre, das spricht sich herum, besonders unter den Kindern!« »Auf Wiedersehen.« Damit ging ich.

Und die Kinder haben die Geschichte noch an demselben Tage gehört.

Wie der alte Timofei singend starb

Was für eine Freude ist es doch, einem lahmen Menschen zu erzählen. Die gesunden Leute sind so ungewiß; sie sehen die Dinge bald von der, bald von jener Seite an, und wenn man mit ihnen eine Stunde lang so gegangen ist, daß sie zur Rechten waren, kann es geschehen, daß sie plötzlich von links antworten, nur, weil es ihnen einfällt, daß das höflicher sei und von feinerer Bildung zeuge. Beim Lahmen hat man das nicht zu befürchten. Seine Unbeweglichkeit macht ihn den Dingen ähnlich, mit denen er auch wirklich viele herzliche Beziehungen pflegt, macht ihn, sozusagen, zu einem den anderen sehr überlegenen Ding, zu einem Ding, das nicht nur lauscht mit seiner Schweigsamkeit, sondern auch mit seinen seltenen leisen Worten und mit seinen sanften, ehrfürchtigen Gefühlen.

Ich mag am liebsten meinem Freund Ewald erzählen. Und ich war sehr froh, als er mir von seinem täglichen Fenster aus zurief: »Ich muß Sie etwas fragen.«

peasant and his church had disappeared. Nor were the piled-up laths lying there any longer; it was all empty, flat land. Then the man raced back to Moscow in horror, stood before the tsar breathlessly, and told him in a rather incomprehensible way what had happened, and that the supposed peasant had been none other than God himself."

"Was he right about that, I wonder?" said my friend softly, after the tones of my story had faded away.

"Perhaps," I replied, "but you know, the people are—superstitious. In the meantime, I must go now, Ewald." "Too bad," the paralyzed man said in honest tones. "Won't you come soon and tell me another story?" "Gladly, but on one condition." I walked over to the window again. "Which is?" Ewald asked in surprise. "From time to time you must repeat all the stories to the children in the neighborhood," I requested. "Oh, the children come to see me so seldom now." I consoled him: "They'll come! Obviously you haven't been in the mood recently to tell them stories, and perhaps you haven't had a subject, or you had too many subjects. But when someone knows a real story, do you think it can remain concealed? Not in the least! People get to hear of it, especially the children!" "See you soon." Then I left.

And the children heard the story that very same day.

How Old Timofei Died with a Song

What a real joy it is to tell stories to a paralyzed person! Healthy people are so unreliable; they look at things, now from one viewpoint, now from another, and after you've been walking with them for an hour and they've always been to the right of you, they sometimes answer you from the left all of a sudden, merely because it occurs to them that it's more polite and shows better breeding. With a paralyzed man one need have no fear of that. His immobility makes him resemble inanimate objects, with which he actually has many cordial relationships; it makes him, so to speak, an object far superior to all the rest, an object that not only listens with its taciturnity, but also with its very few, quiet phrases and with its gentle, respectful feelings.

I like best of all to tell stories to my friend Ewald. And I was very happy when he called to me from his daily window: "I must ask you something."

Rasch trat ich zu ihm und begrüßte ihn. »Woher stammt die Geschichte, die Sie mir neulich erzählt haben?« bat er endlich. »Aus einem Buch?« »Ja« – entgegnete ich traurig, »die Gelehrten haben sie darin begraben, seit sie tot ist; das ist garnicht lange her. Noch vor hundert Jahren lebte sie, gewiß sehr sorglos, auf vielen Lippen. Aber die Worte, welche die Menschen jetzt gebrauchen, diese schweren, nicht sangbaren Worte, waren ihr feind und nahmen ihr einen Mund nach dem anderen weg, so daß sie zuletzt, nur sehr eingezogen und ärmlich, auf ein paar trockenen Lippen, wie auf einem schlechten Witwengut, lebte. Dort verstarb sie auch, ohne Nachkommen zu hinterlassen, und wurde, wie schon erwähnt, mit allen Ehren in einem Buche bestattet, wo schon andere aus ihrem Geschlechte lagen.« »Und sie war sehr alt, als sie starb?« fragte mein Freund, in meinen Ton eingehend. »400 bis 500 Jahre,« berichtete ich der Wahrheit gemäß, »verschiedene von ihren Verwandten haben noch ein ungleich höheres Alter erreicht.« »Wie, ohne jemals in einem Buche zu ruhen?« staunte Ewald. Ich erklärte: »Soviel ich weiß, waren sie die ganze Zeit von Lippe zu Lippe unterwegs.« »Und haben nie geschlafen?« »Doch, von dem Munde des Sängers steigend, blieben sie wohl dann und wann in einem Herzen, darin es warm und dunkel war.« »Waren denn die Menschen so still, daß Lieder schlafen konnten in ihren Herzen?« Ewald schien mir recht ungläubig. »Es muß wohl so gewesen sein. Man behauptet, sie sprachen weniger, tanzten langsam anwachsende Tänze, die etwas Wiegendes hatten, und vor allem: sie lachten nicht laut, wie man es heute trotz der allgemeinen hohen Kultur nicht selten vernehmen kann.«

Ewald schickte sich an, noch etwas zu fragen, aber er unterdrückte es und lächelte: »Ich frage und frage, – aber Sie haben vielleicht eine Geschichte vor?« Er sah mich erwartungsvoll an.

»Eine Geschichte? Ich weiß nicht. Ich wollte nur sagen: Diese Gesänge waren das Erbgut in gewissen Familien. Man hatte es übernommen und man gab es weiter, nicht ganz unbenützt, mit den Spuren eines täglichen Gebrauchs, aber doch unbeschädigt, wie etwa eine alte Bibel von Vätern zu Enkeln geht. Der Enterbte unterschied sich von den in ihre Rechte eingesetzten Geschwistern dadurch, daß er nicht singen konnte, oder er wußte wenigstens nur einen kleinen Teil der Lieder seines Vaters und Großvaters und verlor mit den übrigen Gesängen das große Stück Erleben, das alle diese Bylinen und Skaski dem Volke bedeuten. So hatte zum Beispiel Jegor Timofejewitsch gegen den Willen seines Vaters, des alten Timofei, ein junges, schönes

I walked over to him quickly and said hello. "What is the source of the story you told me recently?" he finally asked. "Did it come from a book?" "Yes," I replied sadly, "the scholars have buried it in one ever since it died, which isn't very long ago. A hundred years ago it was still alive, and certainly quite carefree, on many lips. But the words that people now use, these heavy words that are hard to sing to, were hostile to it and stole one mouth after another from it, so that finally it lived on, but very withdrawn and impoverished, only on a few dry lips, as if on a poor widow's farm. There it also died, without leaving any descendants, and, as I mentioned, was buried with all honors in a book, where others of its lineage already lay." "And was it very old when it died?" my friend asked, picking up my metaphor. "Four or five hundred years old," I reported truthfully; "several of its relatives have attained an immeasurably greater age." "What, without ever reposing in a book?" Ewald asked in surprise. I explained: "As far as I know, they were journeying from mouth to mouth the whole time." "And they never slept?" "Oh, yes; arising from the lips of the singer, they surely remained occasionally in someone's heart, where it was warm and dark." "Then, were people so tranquil that songs could sleep in their hearts?" Ewald seemed quite incredulous to me. "It must have been that way. It's claimed that they spoke less, performed slowly accelerating dances that had a cradling motion, and above all, didn't laugh loudly the way you can often hear people do today despite our universally loftier social graces."

Ewald prepared himself to ask another question, but he repressed it and said with a smile: "I keep on asking things—but perhaps you have a story in mind?" He looked at me expectantly.

"A story? I don't know. I merely wanted to say: Those songs were the heirlooms in certain families. That inherited property had been received and handed down again, not quite as good as new, showing the traces of daily use, but nevertheless undamaged, just as an old Bible, let's say, goes from forefather to grandchild. The man without inheritance differed from his siblings who had received their rightful due in that he couldn't sing, or else at least he knew only a small part of his father's and grandfather's songs, and, losing the rest of the songs, he lost that large segment of experience which all those *byliny* and *skazki*[8] mean to the people. And so, for example, Yegor Timofeievich had married a young, beautiful woman

8. Folktales (*märchen*).

Weib geheiratet und war mit ihr nach Kiew gegangen, in die heilige
Stadt, bei welcher sich die Gräber der größten Märtyrer der heiligen,
rechtgläubigen Kirche versammelt haben. Der Vater Timofei, der als
der kundigste Sänger auf zehn Tagereisen im Umkreis galt, verfluchte
seinen Sohn, und erzählte seinen Nachbarn, daß er oft überzeugt sei,
niemals einen solchen gehabt zu haben. Dennoch verstummte er in
Gram und Traurigkeit. Und er wies alle die jungen Leute zurück, die
sich in seine Hütte drängten, um die Erben der vielen Gesänge zu werden, welche in dem Alten eingeschlossen waren, wie in einer ver-
staubten Geige. ›Vater, du unser Väterchen, gieb uns nur eines oder das
andere Lied. Siehst du, wir wollen es in die Dörfer tragen, und du sollst
es hören aus allen Höfen, sobald der Abend kommt und das Vieh in den
Ställen ruhig geworden ist.‹ Der Alte, der beständig auf dem Ofen saß,
schüttelte den ganzen Tag den Kopf. Er hörte nicht mehr gut, und da
er nicht wußte, ob nicht einer von den Burschen, die jetzt fortwährend
sein Haus umhorchten, eben wieder gefragt hatte, machte er mit
seinem weißen Kopf zitternd: Nein, nein, nein, bis er einschlief und
auch dann noch eine Weile – im Schlaf. Er hätte den Burschen gerne
ihren Willen getan; es war ihm selber leid, daß sein stummer, verstor-
bener Staub über diesen Liedern liegen sollte, vielleicht schon ganz
bald. Aber hätte er versucht, einen von ihnen etwas zu lehren, gewiß
hätte er sich dabei seines Jegoruschka erinnern müssen und dann – wer
weiß – was dann geschehen wäre. Denn nur, weil er überhaupt schwieg,
hatte ihn niemand weinen sehen. Hinter jedem Wort stand es ihm, das
Schluchzen, und er mußte immer sehr schnell und vorsichtig den
Mund schließen, sonst wäre es einmal doch mitgekommen.

Der alte Timofei hatte seinen einzigen Sohn Jegor von ganz früh an
einzelne Lieder gelehrt, und als fünfzehnjähriger Knabe wußte dieser
schon mehr und richtiger zu singen als alle erwachsenen Burschen im
Dorfe und in der Nachbarschaft. Gleichwohl pflegte der Alte meistens am Feiertag, wenn er etwas trunken war, dem Burschen zu
sagen: ›Jegoruschka, mein Täubchen, ich habe dich schon viele Lieder
singen gelehrt, viele Bylinen und auch die Legenden von Heiligen,
fast für jeden Tag eine. Aber ich bin, wie du weißt, der Kundigste im
ganzen Gouvernement, und mein Vater kannte sozusagen alle Lieder
von ganz Rußland und auch noch tatarische Geschichten dazu. Du
bist noch sehr jung, und deshalb habe ich dir die schönsten Bylinen,
darin die Worte wie Ikone sind und gar nicht zu vergleichen mit den
gewöhnlichen Worten, noch nicht erzählt und du hast noch nicht ge-

against the wishes of his father, old Timofei, and had moved with her to Kiev, the holy city, in which the tombs of the great martyrs of the holy orthodox church have gathered. His father Timofei, who was reputed to be the most knowledgeable singer in a radius of ten days' journey, cursed his son and told his neighbors that he was often convinced that he had never had one. All the same, he grew mute in his grief and sorrow. And he rejected all the young men who crowded into his hut in order to fall heir to the many songs that were shut away in the old man, as in a dust-covered violin. 'Father, little father of ours, just give us one song or another. You see, we'll take it to the villages, and you'll hear it from every courtyard as soon as evening comes and the cattle have become quiet in their stables.' The old man, who constantly sat on the heated platform, shook his head all day long. His hearing was no longer good, and since he didn't know whether one of the lads who were now forever listening around his house had just made another request, he would signal no, no, no with his trembling white head until he fell asleep, and even kept doing it for a while in his sleep. He would gladly have done what the lads wanted; he himself was sorry that his mute, dead dust would lie upon these songs, perhaps very soon now. But if he had tried to teach one of them anything, it would surely have reminded him of his Yegorushka, and then, who knows what might have happened? Because it was only his perpetual silence that kept anyone from seeing him cry. Behind each word of his lay a sob, and he always had to shut his mouth very quickly and carefully to keep it from escaping at the same time.

"From early on, old Timofei had taught his only son, Yegor, a few songs, and when a boy of fifteen he was already able to sing more songs more correctly than any of the fully grown lads in the village or in its vicinity. All the same, the old man used to say to the lad, generally on holidays, when he was slightly drunk: 'Yegorushka, my little dove, I've already taught you to sing many songs, many *byliny*, and also the legends of the saints, one for nearly every day. But, as you know, I'm the most knowledgeable in the whole *gouvernement*,[9] and my father knew every song in Russia, so to speak, and Tatar stories, besides. You're still very young, and so I have not yet told you the best *byliny*, in which the words are like icons and can't be compared with everyday words, and you have not yet learned how to sing those melodies which no one yet, be he a Cossack or a peasant, has ever

---

9. French for the sort of large administrative district called in Russian *guberniya*.

lernt, jene Weisen zu singen, die noch keiner, er mochte ein Kosak
sein oder ein Bauer, hat anhören können ohne zu weinen.‹ Dieses
wiederholte Timofei seinem Sohne an jedem Sonntag und an allen
vielen Feiertagen des russischen Jahres, also ziemlich oft. Bis dieser
nach einem heftigen Auftritt mit dem Alten, zugleich mit der schönen
Ustjènka, der Tochter eines armen Bauern, verschwunden war.

Im dritten Jahre nach diesem Vorfall erkrankte Timofei, zur selben Zeit,
als einer jener vielen Pilgerzüge, die aus allen Teilen des weiten Reiches
beständig nach Kiew ziehen, aufbrechen wollte. Da trat Ossip, der
Nachbar, bei dem Kranken ein: ›Ich gehe mit den Pilgern, Timofei
Iwanitsch, erlaube mir, dich noch einmal zu umarmen.‹ Ossip war nicht
befreundet mit dem Alten, aber nun, da er diese weite Reise begann, fand
er es für notwendig, von ihm, wie von einem Vater, Abschied zu nehmen.
›Ich habe dich manchmal gekränkt,‹ schluchzte er, ›verzeih mir, mein
Herzchen, es ist im Trunke geschehen und da kann man nichts dafür, wie
du weißt. Nun, ich will für dich beten und eine Kerze anstecken für dich;
leb wohl, Timofei Iwanitsch, mein Väterchen, vielleicht wirst du wieder
gesund, wenn Gott es will, dann singst du uns wieder etwas. Ja, ja, das ist
lange her, seit du gesungen hast. Was waren das für Lieder. Das von Djuk
Stepanowitsch zum Beispiel, glaubst du, ich habe das vergessen? Wie
dumm du bist! Ich weiß es noch ganz genau. Freilich, so wie du, – *du* hast
es eben gekonnt, das muß man sagen. Gott hat dir *das* gegeben, einem
anderen giebt er etwas *anderes*. Mir zum Beispiel –‹

Der Alte, der auf dem Ofen lag, drehte sich ächzend um und
machte eine Bewegung, als ob er etwas sagen wollte. Es war als hörte
man ganz leise den Namen Jegors. Vielleicht wollte er ihm eine
Nachricht schicken. Aber als der Nachbar, von der Türe her, fragte:
›Sagst du etwas, Timofei Iwanitsch?‹ lag er schon wieder ganz ruhig da
und schüttelte nur leise seinen weißen Kopf. Trotzdem, weiß Gott wie
es geschah, kaum ein Jahr nachdem Ossip fortgegangen war, kehrte
Jegor ganz unvermutet zurück. Der Alte erkannte ihn nicht gleich,
denn es war dunkel in der Hütte, und die greisen Augen nahmen nur
ungern eine neue fremde Gestalt auf. Aber als Timofei die Stimme des
Fremden gehört hatte, erschrak er und sprang vom Ofen herab, auf
seine alten, schwankenden Beine. Jegor fing ihn auf, und sie hielten
sich in den Armen. Timofei weinte. Der junge Mensch fragte in einem
fort: ›Bist du schon lange krank, Vater?‹ Als sich der Alte ein wenig
beruhigt hatte, kroch er auf seinen Ofen zurück und erkundigte sich in
einem anderen strengen Ton: ›Und dein Weib?‹ Pause. Jegor spuckte

been able to hear without weeping.' Timofei would repeat this to his
son on every Sunday and all the many feast days in the Russian calen-
dar; that is, fairly often. Until, after a violent scene with the old man,
the boy had vanished together with the beautiful Ustyonka, the
daughter of a poor peasant.

"In the third year after that incident, Timofei fell ill, just at the
time when one of those numerous bands of pilgrims which constantly converge on Kiev from all sections of the extensive empire
was about to set out. Then the sick man's neighbor Osip came to see
him: 'I'm leaving with the pilgrims, Timofei Ivanich; permit me to
embrace you once again.' Osip wasn't friendly with the old man, but
now that he was undertaking that distant journey, he felt it needful
to take leave of him, as if of a father. 'I've hurt your feelings at
times,' he sobbed; 'forgive me, dear heart, it happened while I was
drunk and no one can help that, as you know. Now, I'll pray for you
and light a candle for you; farewell, Timofei Ivanich, little father;
perhaps you'll get well again, if God wishes, then you'll sing to us
again. Yes, yes, it's been a long time since you've sung. What songs
those were! The one about Dyuk Stepanovich,[10] for instance: do
you think I've forgotten it? How foolish you are! I still know it all by
heart. Of course, not like you; *you* really and truly knew it, I've got
to say! God gave you *that*, to another man he gives other gifts. To
me, for example—'

"The old man, who was lying on the heated platform, turned
around with a groan and made a gesture as if he wanted to say something. It was as if the name of Yegor could be faintly heard. Perhaps
he wanted to send him some news. But when his neighbor, already at
the door, asked: 'Did you say something, Timofei Ivanich?' he was already lying there perfectly still and merely shaking his white head
gently. Nevertheless, God knows how it happened, scarcely a year
after Osip's departure Yegor returned quite unexpectedly. The old
man didn't recognize him immediately because it was dark in the hut
and his aged eyes didn't easily accept a strange new figure. But after
Timofei heard the stranger's voice, he became alarmed and leaped
off the heated platform onto his shaky old legs. Yegor caught him,
and they hugged each other. Timofei was weeping. The young man
kept on asking: 'Have you been sick long, father?' After the old man
calmed down a bit, he crept back onto his heated platform and inquired, in a different, severe tone: 'And your wife?' A pause. Yegor

---

10. One of the principal *bylina* heroes.

aus: ›Ich hab sie fortgejagt, weißt du, mit dem Kind.‹ Er schwieg eine
Weile. ›Da kommt einmal der Ossip zu mir; Ossip Nikiphorowitsch?
sag ich. Ja, antwortet er, ich bins. Dein Vater ist krank, Jegor. Er kann
nicht mehr singen. Es ist jetzt ganz still im Dorfe, als ob es keine Seele
mehr hätte, unser Dorf. Nichts klopft, nichts rührt sich, es weint niemand mehr, und auch zum Lachen ist kein rechter Grund. Ich denke
nach. Was ist da zu machen? Ich rufe also mein Weib. Ustjênka – sag
ich – ich muß nach Hause, es singt sonst keiner mehr dort, die Reihe
ist an mir. Der Vater ist krank. Gut, sagt Ustjênka. Aber ich kann dich
nicht mitnehmen, – so erklär ich ihr – der Vater, weißt du, will dich
nicht. Und auch zurückkommen werd ich wahrscheinlich nicht zu dir,
wenn ich erst einmal wieder dort bin und singe. Ustjênka versteht
mich: Nun, Gott mit dir! Es sind jetzt viele Pilger hier, da giebt es viel
Almosen. Gott wird schon helfen, Jegor. Und so geh ich also fort. Und
nun, Vater, sag mir alle deine Leider.‹

Es verbreitete sich das Gerücht, daß Jegor zurückgekehrt sei und
daß der alte Timofei wieder singe. Aber in diesem Herbst ging der
Wind so heftig durch das Dorf, daß niemand von den Vorübergehen-
den mit Sicherheit ermitteln konnte, ob in Timofei's Hause wirklich
gesungen werde oder nicht. Und die Tür wurde keinem Pochenden
geöffnet. Die beiden wollten allein sein. Jegor saß am Rande des
Ofens, auf welchem der Vater lag, und kam mit dem Ohr bisweilen
dem Munde des Alten entgegen; denn dieser sang in der Tat. Seine
alte Stimme trug, etwas gebückt und zitternd, alle die schönsten
Lieder zu Jegor hin, und dieser wiegte manchmal den Kopf oder bewegte die herabhängenden Beine, ganz, als ob er schon selber sänge.
Das ging so viele Tage lang fort. Timofei fand immer noch ein
schöneres Lied in seiner Erinnerung; oft, nachts, weckte er den Sohn,
und indem er mit den welken, zuckenden Händen ungewisse Bewegungen machte, sang er ein kleines Lied und noch eines und noch
eines – bis der träge Morgen sich zu rühren begann. Bald nach dem
schönsten starb er. Er hatte sich in den letzten Tagen oft arg beklagt,
daß er noch eine Unmenge Lieder in sich trüge und nicht mehr Zeit
habe, sie seinem Sohne mitzuteilen. Er lag da mit gefurchter Stirne,
in angestrengtem, ängstlichen Nachdenken, und seine Lippen zitterten vor Erwartung. Von Zeit zu Zeit setzte er sich auf, wiegte eine
Weile den Kopf, bewegte den Mund, und endlich kam irgend ein
leises Lied hinzu; aber jetzt sang er meistens immer dieselben
Strophen von Djuk Stepanowitsch, die er besonders liebte, und sein
Sohn mußte erstaunt sein und tun, als vernähme er sie zum erstenmal, um ihn nicht zu erzürnen.

spat out the words: 'I've chased her away, you know, along with the child.' He was silent for a while. 'Osip came to see me once. "Osip Nikiforovich?" I said. "Yes," he answered, "it's me. Your father is sick, Yegor. he can't sing any more. It's completely quiet in the village now, as if it had no more soul, our village. No one knocks, no one budges, no one cries any more, and there's no real reason for laughing, either." I thought about it. What was to be done? So I called over my wife. "Ustyonka," I said, "I must go home, no one else sings there any more, it's up to me. My father is sick." "All right," said Ustyonka. "But I can't take you along," I explained to her, "as you know, my father doesn't want you. And I probably won't come back to you, either, once I'm back there singing." Ustyonka understood me: "Well, then, God go with you! There are many pilgrims here now, so people give lots of alms. God will help me, Yegor." And so I left. And now, father, tell me all your songs!'

"Word got around that Yegor had returned and that old Timofei was singing again. But that autumn the wind blew so violently through the village that no passerby could ascertain with any assurance whether there was really singing in Timofei's house or not. And the door wasn't opened to anyone who knocked. The two men wanted to be alone. Yegor sat on the edge of the heated platform on which his father lay, and at times brought his ear right up to the old man's lips; for he was indeed singing. His old voice, somewhat stooped and trembling, carried all the best songs over to Yegor, who often waved his head or moved his dangling feet, exactly as if he were already singing them himself. Things went on that way for many days. Timofei kept finding some even lovelier song in his memory; often he'd awaken his son at night and, while making indistinct gestures with his withered, twitching hands, he'd sing a short song and then another and yet another, until the lazy morning began to stir. Soon after the most beautiful one he died. In the last days he had frequently lamented that he still had a vast number of songs inside him and had no more time to impart them to his son. He lay there with furrowed brow, in strained, anxious thought, and his lips trembled with expectancy. From time to time he sat up, waved his head to and fro for a while, and moved his lips, and finally some quiet song was added to the sum; but now he generally kept repeating the same stanzas about Dyuk Stepanovich that were his special favorites, and his son had to act amazed, as if he were hearing them for the first time, to avoid getting him angry.

Als der alte Timofei Iwanitsch gestorben war, blieb das Haus, welches Jegor jetzt allein bewohnte, noch eine Zeit lang verschlossen. Dann, im ersten Frühjahr, trat Jegor Timofejewitsch, der jetzt einen ziemlich langen Bart hatte, aus seiner Tür, begann im Dorfe hin und her zu gehen und zu singen. Später kam er auch in die benachbarten Dörfer, und die Bauern erzählten sich schon, daß Jegor ein mindestens ebenso kundiger Sänger geworden sei, wie sein Vater Timofei; denn er wußte eine große Anzahl ernster und heldenhafter Gesänge und alle jene Weisen, die keiner, er mochte ein Kosak sein oder ein Bauer, anhören konnte, ohne zu weinen. Dabei soll er noch so einen sanften und traurigen Ton gehabt haben, wie man ihn noch von keinem Sänger vernommen hat. Und dieser Ton fand sich immer, ganz unerwartet, im Kehrreim vor, wodurch er besonders rührend wirkte. So habe ich wenigstens erzählen hören.«

»Diesen Ton hat er also nicht von seinem Vater gelernt?« sagte mein Freund Ewald nach einer Weile. »Nein,« erwiderte ich, »man weiß nicht, woher der ihm kam.« Als ich vom Fenster schon fortgetreten war, machte der Lahme noch eine Bewegung und rief mir nach: »Er hat vielleicht an sein Weib und sein Kind gedacht. Übrigens, hat er sie nie kommen lassen, da ja sein Vater nun tot war?« »Nein, ich glaube nicht. Wenigstens ist er später allein gestorben.«

Das Lied von der Gerechtigkeit

Als ich das nächste Mal an Ewalds Fenster vorüberkam, winkte er mir und lächelte: »Haben Sie den Kindern etwas Bestimmtes versprochen?« »Wieso?« staunte ich. »Nun, als ich ihnen die Geschichte von Jegor erzählt hatte, beklagten sie sich, daß Gott in derselben nicht vorkäme.« Ich erschrak: »Was, eine Geschichte ohne Gott, aber wie ist denn das möglich?« Dann besann ich mich: »In der Tat, es ist wahr, von Gott sagt die Geschichte, wie ich sie mir jetzt überdenke, nichts. Ich begreife nicht, wie das geschehen konnte; hätte jemand von mir eine solche verlangt, ich glaube ich hätte mein ganzes Leben nachgedacht, ohne Erfolg . . .«

Mein Freund lächelte über diesen Eifer: »Sie müssen sich deshalb nicht erregen,« unterbrach er mich mit einer gewissen Güte, »ich denke mir, man kann ja nie wissen, ob Gott in einer Geschichte ist, ehe man sie auch ganz beendet hat. Denn wenn auch nur noch zwei Worte fehlen sollten, ja selbst, wenn nur noch die Pause hinter dem letzten Worte der Erzählung aussteht: Er kann immer noch kommen.« Ich nickte, und der Lahme sagte in anderem Ton: »Wissen Sie nicht noch etwas von diesen russischen Sängern?«

"After old Timofei Ivanich died, the house, in which Yegor now lived alone, still remained locked for a time. Then, in early spring, Yegor Timofeievich, who now had a fairly long beard, stepped out of his door and began to wander through the village singing. Afterward he visited the neighboring villages, too, and the peasants were already telling one another that Yegor had become a singer at least as knowledgeable as his father Timofei, for he knew a large number of religious and heroic songs and all those melodies which no one, be he a Cossack or a peasant, could hear without weeping. In addition, he was said to have a soft, sad tone that no other singer had yet possessed. And this tone was always to be heard, quite unexpectedly, in the refrains, which made him particularly effective emotionally. At least, that's what I heard tell."

"So he didn't learn that tone from his father?" my friend Ewald asked after a while. "No," I replied, "no one knows where he got it from." After I had already stepped away from the window, the paralyzed man made another gesture and called after me: "Perhaps he was thinking about his wife and child. Besides, did he never send for them, seeing that his father was now dead?" "No, I don't think so. At any rate, when he died afterward he was alone."

The Song of Justice

The next time I passed by Ewald's window, he beckoned to me and said with a smile: "Have you made the children any definite promise?" "What do you mean?" I said in surprise. "Well, after I told them the story of Yegor, they complained that God didn't appear in it." I became alarmed: "What, a story without God? But how is that possible?" Then I collected my thoughts: "In fact, it's true that the story, as I think through it now, says nothing about God. I don't understand how that could have happened; if someone had asked me for such a story, I believe I would have racked my brains for it my whole life, unsuccessfully. . . ."

My friend smiled at that enthusiasm: "You mustn't get upset over it," he interrupted me with a certain kindness, "I imagine that no one can ever know whether God is in a story until it's completely finished. Because, even if only two words are still missing, yes, even if the storyteller has not yet paused after the last word of the story, he can still arrive." I nodded, and the paralyzed man said, in a different tone of voice: "Don't you know anything more about those Russian singers?"

Ich zögerte: »Ja, wollen wir nicht lieber von Gott reden, Ewald?«
Er schüttelte den Kopf: »Ich wünsche mir so, mehr von diesen eigentümlichen Männern zu vernehmen. Ich weiß nicht wie es kommt, ich
denke mir immer, wenn so einer hier bei mir einträte –« und er
wandte den Kopf ins Zimmer, nach der Türe zu. Aber seine Augen
kehrten schnell, und nicht ohne Verlegenheit, zu mir zurück – »Doch,
das ist ja wohl nicht möglich«, verbesserte er eilig. »Warum sollte das
nicht möglich sein, Ewald? Ihnen kann manches begegnen, was den
Menschen, die ihre Beine brauchen können, verwehrt bleibt, weil sie
an so vielem vorübergehen und vor so manchem davonlaufen. Gott
hat Sie, Ewald, dazu bestimmt, ein ruhiger Punkt zu sein mitten in
aller Hast. Fühlen Sie nicht, wie alles sich um Sie bewegt? Die anderen jagen den Tagen nach, und wenn sie mal einen erreicht haben,
sind sie so atemlos, daß sie gar nicht mit ihm sprechen können. Sie
aber, mein Freund, sitzen einfach an Ihrem Fenster und warten; und
den Wartenden geschieht immer etwas. Sie haben ein ganz besonderes Los. Denken Sie, sogar die iberische Madonna in Moskau muß
aus ihrem Kapellchen heraus und fährt in einem schwarzen Wagen
mit vier Pferden zu denen, die irgend etwas feiern, sei es die Taufe
oder den Tod. Zu Ihnen aber muß *alles* kommen –«
»Ja,« sagte Ewald mit einem fremden Lächeln, »ich kann sogar dem
Tod nicht entgegengehen. Viele Menschen finden ihn unterwegs. Er
scheut sich, ihre Häuser zu betreten, und ruft sie hinaus in die Fremde, in
den Krieg, auf einen steilen Turm, auf eine schwankende Brücke, in eine
Wildnis oder in den Wahnsinn. Die meisten holen ihn wenigstens draußen
irgendwo ab und tragen ihn dann auf ihren Schultern nach Hause, ohne
es zu merken. Denn der Tod ist träge; wenn die Menschen ihn nicht
fortwährend stören würden, wer weiß, er schliefe vielleicht ein.« Der
Kranke dachte eine Weile nach und fuhr dann mit einem gewissen Stolz
fort: »Aber zu mir wird er kommen müssen, wenn er mich will. Hier in
meine kleine helle Stube, in der die Blumen sich so lange halten, über
diesen alten Teppich, an diesem Schrank vorbei, zwischen Tisch und
Bettende durch (es ist gar nicht leicht vorüber zu kommen) bis her an
meinen breiten, lieben, alten Stuhl, der dann wahrscheinlich mit mir sterben wird, weil er, sozusagen, mit mir gelebt hat. Und er wird dies alles tun
müssen in der üblichen Art, ohne Lärm, ohne etwas umzuwerfen, ohne
etwas Ungewöhnliches zu beginnen, wie ein Besuch. Dieser Umstand

I hesitated: "Shouldn't we rather talk about God, Ewald?" He shook his head: "I want so much to hear more about those singular men. I don't know how it is, but I keep on thinking: if one of them should come here to see me—" and he looked back into the room, at the door. But his eyes returned to me quickly, not without some embarrassment: "But that's surely not possible," he hastily corrected himself. "Why isn't it possible, Ewald? Many things can happen to you which are out of the question for people who can use their legs, because they walk right by so many things and run away from so many. Ewald, God has destined you to be a focus of calm amid all that haste. Don't you feel that everything is moving around you? The others chase after the days, and whenever they catch up with one, they're so out of breath that they can't even speak to it. But you, my friend, simply sit by your window and wait; and something always happens to those who wait. You have a very special lot in life. Imagine, even the Iverian[11] Madonna in Moscow sometimes has to leave her little chapel and ride in a black carriage with four horses to those who are celebrating something, whether it's a christening or a funeral. But to you *everyone else* must come—."

"Yes," said Ewald with a strange smile, "I can't even go out to meet death. Many people find it while walking outdoors. It avoids entering their houses and calls them out into foreign lands, into battle, onto a steep tower, onto a shaky bridge, into a wilderness, or into madness. At any rate, most people fetch it somewhere outside and then carry it home on their shoulders, without noticing. Because death is lazy; if people didn't constantly disturb it, who knows? Maybe it would go to sleep." The invalid thought for a while, then resumed with a certain pride: "But it will have to come to me if it wants me. Here, into my little bright room, in which flowers last so long, across this old carpet, past this wardrobe, between the table and the foot of the bed (it's not at all easy to get by them), all the way here to my dear old wide chair, which will then probably die along with me, because it has lived with me, so to speak. And death will have to do all this in the usual way, noiselessly, without knocking anything over, without undertaking anything out of the ordinary, like a visitor. That circumstance brings my

---

11. Iverian = from Iberia = from Georgia (in the Caucasus). The original miraculous icon was housed in the Georgian monastery of the international monastic complex on Mount Athos in Greece. In 1648 a copy was sent to Moscow and placed in a chapel in the Resurrection Gate on Red Square.

bringt mir meine Stube merkwürdig nah. Es wird sich alles hier abspielen
auf dieser engen Szene, und darum wird auch dieser letzte Vorgang sich
nicht sehr von allen anderen Ereignissen unterscheiden, welche sich hier
begeben haben und noch bevorstehen. Es hat mir immer schon, als Kind,
seltsam geschienen, daß die Menschen vom Tode anders sprechen, als von
allen anderen Begebenheiten, und das nur deshalb, weil jeder von dem,
was ihm nachher geschieht, nichts mehr verrät. Wodurch aber unter-
scheidet sich denn ein Toter von einem Menschen, welcher ernst wird, auf
die Zeit verzichtet und sich einschließt, um über etwas ruhig nachzudenken, dessen Lösung ihn lange schon quält? Unter den Leuten kann
man sich doch nicht einmal des Vaterunsers erinnern, wie denn erst irgend eines anderen dunkleren Zusammenhanges, der vielleicht nicht in
Worten, sondern in Ereignissen besteht. Man muß abseits gehen in irgend
eine unzugängliche Stille, und vielleicht sind die Toten solche, die sich
zurückgezogen haben, um über das Leben nachzudenken.«

Es entstand eine kleine Schweigsamkeit, die ich mit folgenden
Worten begrenzte: »Ich muß dabei an ein junges Mädchen denken.
Man kann sagen, daß sie in den ersten siebzehn Jahren ihres heiteren
Lebens nur *geschaut* hat. Ihre Augen waren so groß und so selb-
ständig, daß sie alles, was sie empfingen, selbst verbrauchten, und das
Leben in dem ganzen Körper des jungen Geschöpfes ging, unab-
hängig davon, von schlichten, inneren Geräuschen genährt, vor sich.
Am Ende dieser Zeit aber störte irgend ein zu heftiges Ereignis dieses
doppelte, kaum sich berührende Leben, die Augen brachen gleichsam nach innen durch, und die ganze Schwere des Äußeren fiel durch
sie in das dunkle Herz hinein, und jeder Tag stürzte mit solcher
Wucht in die tiefen, steilen Blicke, daß er in der engen Brust zer-
sprang wie ein Glas. Da wurde das junge Mädchen blaß, begann zu
kränkeln, einsam zu werden, nachzudenken, und endlich suchte es
selbst jene Stille auf, darin die Gedanken wahrscheinlich nicht mehr
gestört werden.«

»Wie ist sie gestorben?« fragte mein Freund leise, mit etwas hei-
serer Stimme. »Sie ist ertrunken. In einem tiefen, stillen Teich, und
an der Oberfläche desselben entstanden viele Ringe, die langsam weit
wurden und unter den weißen Wasserrosen hin wuchsen, so daß alle
diese badenden Blüten sich bewegten.«

»Ist das auch eine Geschichte?« sagte Ewald, um die Stille hinter
meinen Worten nicht mächtig werden zu lassen. »Nein,« entgegnete
ich, »das ist ein Gefühl.« »Aber könnte man es nicht auch den
Kindern übermitteln – dieses Gefühl?« Ich überlegte. »Vielleicht –.«
»Und wodurch?« »Durch eine andere Geschichte.« Und ich erzählte:

room strangely close to me. Everything will take place here on this narrow stage, and thus this final scene, too, won't differ substantially from all the other events that have occurred here and will still occur. Always before now, even as a child, I found it odd that people speak in a different way about death than about all other events, and only because none of them ever again reveals what happens to him afterward. But how does a dead man differ from one who becomes earnest, renounces time, and shuts himself in so he can calmly think over some problem the solution to which has long been tormenting him? In the company of people you can't even remember the Lord's Prayer, let alone some other, more obscure chain of ideas which may perhaps consist not of words, but of occurrences. You have to retreat into some inaccessible silence, and perhaps the dead are those who have withdrawn in order to think about life."

A brief period of silence ensued, which I brought to an end with the following words: "In that connection, I have to think of a young girl. You might say that, for the first seventeen years of her cheerful life, all she did was *look*. Her eyes were so big and so self-sufficient that they themselves consumed everything they took in, and the life in the rest of the body of that young being just went on independently, nourished by simple inner sounds. But at the end of that period, some all-too-violent occurrence upset those twin lives that were hardly in contact with each other; it was as if her eyes collapsed inwardly and the entire weight of the outside world fell through them into her shaded heart; and every day plunged with such force into her profound, rigid gazes that it shattered like a glass within her narrow bosom. Then the girl became pale, started to feel ill, to become lonely, to be lost in thought; and finally she herself sought and found that silence in which one's thoughts are probably no longer disturbed."

"How did she die?" my friend asked softly in a somewhat hoarse voice. "She drowned. In a deep, calm pond, and on its surface many ripples formed, gradually getting wider and growing outward beneath the white water lilies, setting all those floating blossoms in motion."

"Is that a story, too?" asked Ewald, to prevent the silence that followed my words from taking over. "No," I replied, "it's an emotion." "But couldn't that emotion be communicated to the children, as well?" I considered that. "Maybe." "And how?" "By means of another story." And I narrated:

»Es war zur Zeit, als man im südlichen Rußland um die Freiheit kämpfte.«

»Verzeihen Sie,« sagte Ewald, »wie ist das zu verstehen – wollte sich das Volk etwa vom Zaren losmachen? Das würde nicht zu dem passen, was ich mir von Rußland denke, und auch mit Ihren früheren Erzählungen in Widerspruch stehen. In diesem Falle würde ich vorziehen, Ihre Geschichte nicht zu hören. Denn ich liebe das Bild, welches ich mir von den Dingen dort gemacht habe, und will es unbeschädigt behalten.«

Ich mußte lächeln und beruhigte ihn: »Die polnischen Pans (ich hätte das vorausschicken müssen) waren Herren im südlichen Rußland und in jenen stillen, einsamen Steppen, welche man mit dem Namen Ukraine bezeichnet. Sie waren harte Herren. Ihre Bedrückung und die Habgier der Juden, welche sogar den Kirchenschlüssel in Händen hatten, den sie nur gegen Bezahlung den Rechtgläubigen auslieferten, hatte das jugendliche Volk um Kiew herum und den ganzen Dnjepr aufwärts müde und nachdenklich gemacht. Die Stadt selbst, Kiew, das Heilige, der Ort, wo Rußland zuerst mit vierhundert Kirchenkuppeln von sich erzählte, versank immer mehr in sich selbst und verzehrte sich in Bränden wie in plötzlichen, irren Gedanken, hinter denen die Nacht nur immer uferloser wird. Das Volk in der Steppe wußte nicht recht, was geschah. Aber, von seltsamer Unruhe erfaßt, traten die Greise nachts aus den Hütten und betrachteten schweigend den hohen, ewig windlosen Himmel, und am Tage konnte man Gestalten auf dem Rücken der Kurgane auftauchen sehen, die sich wartend vor der flachen Ferne erhoben. Diese Kurgane sind Grabstätten vergangener Geschlechter, die die ganze Heide wie ein erstarrter, schlafender Wellenschlag durchziehen. Und in diesem Land, in welchem die Gräber die Berge sind, sind die Menschen die Abgründe. Tief, dunkel, schweigsam ist die Bevölkerung, und ihre Worte sind nur schwache, schwankende Brücken über ihrem wirklichen Sein. – Manchmal heben sich dunkle Vögel von den Kurganen. Manchmal stürzen wilde Lieder in die dämmernden Menschen hinein und verschwinden in ihnen tief, während die Vögel im Himmel verloren gehen. Nach allen Richtungen hin scheint alles grenzenlos. Die Häuser selbst können nicht beschützen vor dieser Unermeßlichkeit; ihre kleinen

"It was in the days when people were fighting for their freedom in the south of Russia."

"Excuse me," said Ewald, "how am I to understand that? Did the people possibly want to break away from the tsar? That wouldn't correspond to my conception of Russia, and it would also contradict your previous narratives. In that case, I'd prefer not to hear your story. Because I love the image I have formulated of matters there, and I want to preserve it intact."

I had to laugh, and I placated him: "The Polish pans,[12] as I should have told you in advance, were then lords of southern Russia, in those quiet, lonely steppes called by the name of Ukraine. They were rigorous lords. Their oppression, and the greed of the Jews, who even had possession of the keys to the churches and would only hand them over to the Orthodox for money,[13] had made the young people around Kiev and upstream along the entire Dnieper weary and contemplative. The city itself, Kiev the holy, the spot where Russia first proclaimed herself with four hundred church domes, was subsiding into itself more and more, and was consuming itself in conflagrations and in sudden wild ideas, behind which night only becomes increasingly shoreless. The people on the steppe weren't really aware of what was going on. But, gripped by a strange unrest, the old men would step out of their huts at night and silently study the lofty, eternally windless sky, and by day one could see figures appearing on top of the kurgans that rose expectantly in front of the level distance. These kurgans are the burial places of bygone peoples, which dot the entire plain like the aftermath of an ocean wave that is now rigid and sleeping. And in that land, where the graves are the mountains, people are the abysses. The population is deep, dark, taciturn, and their words are merely weak, shaky bridges across their true being.—At times dark birds arise from the kurgans. At times wild songs plunge into the drowsing people and disappear deep inside them, while the birds become lost in the sky. In every direction everything seems to lack boundaries. The houses themselves are no protection against this measurelessness; their small windows are filled with it. Only, in the darkening corners of

---

12. Noblemen, landowners. The Ukrainian revolts against Poland took place in the late sixteenth and seventeenth centuries.   13. The landowners employed the Jews as rent and tax collectors and in other odious occupations. If any Jews did willingly exploit the Ukrainian peasants, their coreligionists paid the price many times over in the horrendous pogroms attendant on the wars of liberation from Poland. Rilke is fairer to Jews in the next section of *Stories About the Good Lord.*

Fenster sind voll davon. Nur in den dunkelnden Ecken der Stuben stehen die alten Ikone, wie Meilensteine Gottes, und der Glanz von einem kleinen Licht geht durch ihre Rahmen, wie ein verirrtes Kind durch die Sternennacht. Diese Ikone sind der einzige Halt, das einzige zuverlässige Zeichen am Wege, und kein Haus kann ohne sie bestehen. Immer wieder werden welche notwendig; wenn eines zerbricht vor Alter und Wurm, wenn jemand heiratet und sich eine Hütte zimmert, oder wenn einer, wie zum Beispiel der alte Abraham, stirbt, mit dem Wunsch, den heiligen Nikolaus, den Wundertäter, in den gefalteten Händen mitzunehmen, wahrscheinlich, um die Heiligen im Himmel mit diesem Bilde zu vergleichen und den besonders Verehrten vor allen anderen zu erkennen.

So kommt es, daß Peter Akimowitsch, eigentlich Schuster von Beruf, auch Ikone malt. Wenn er von der einen Arbeit müde ist, geht er, nachdem er sich dreimal bekreuzt hat, zu der anderen über, und über seinem Nähen und Hämmern, wie über seinem Malen, waltet die gleiche Frömmigkeit. Jetzt ist er schon ein alter Mann, aber doch ziemlich rüstig. Den Rücken, den er über die Stiefel biegt, richtet er vor den Bildern wieder gerade, und so hat er sich eine gute Haltung bewahrt und ein gewisses Gleichgewicht in den Schultern und im Kreuz. Den größten Teil seines Lebens hat er ganz allein verbracht, sich garnicht hineinmischend in die Unruhe, die dadurch entstand, daß sein Weib Akulina ihm Kinder gebar und daß diese verstarben oder sich verheirateten. Erst in seinem siebzigsten Jahre hatte Peter sich mit denen in Verbindung gesetzt, die in seinem Hause verblieben waren und die er nun erst als wirklich vorhanden betrachtete. Das waren: Akulina, sein Weib, eine stille, demütige Person, die sich fast ganz in den Kindern fortgegeben hatte, eine alternde, häßliche Tochter und Aljoscha, ein Sohn, welcher, unverhältnismäßig spät geboren, erst siebzehn Jahre zählte. Diesen wollte Peter für die Malerei heranbilden; denn er sah ein, daß er bald nicht allen Bestellungen würde entsprechen können. Aber er gab den Unterricht bald auf. Aljoscha hatte die allerheiligste Jungfrau gemalt, aber das strenge und richtige Vorbild so wenig erreicht, daß sein Machwerk aussah, wie ein Bild der Mariana, der Tochter des Kosaken Golokopytenko, also wie etwas durchaus Sündiges, und der alte Peter beeilte sich, nachdem er sich oft bekreuzt hatte, das beleidigte Brett mit einem heiligen Dmitrij zu übermalen, welchen er aus einem unbekannten Grunde über alle anderen Heiligen stellte.

Aljoscha versuchte auch nie mehr ein Bild zu beginnen. Wenn ihm der Vater nicht befahl, einen Nimbus zu vergolden, war er meistens draußen in der Steppe, kein Mensch wußte wo. Niemand hielt ihn zu Hause. Die Mutter wunderte sich über ihn und hatte eine Scheu, mit ihm zu reden, als ob er ein Fremder wäre oder ein Beamter. Die

the main rooms the old icons stand, like God's milestones, and the glow of a little candle penetrates their frames, like a lost child on a starry night. These icons are the only stopping place, the only reliable sign along the road, and no house can exist without them. New ones become necessary again and again: when one of them crumbles from old age and termites, when someone gets married and builds himself a hut, or when someone, like old Avraam, for example, dies with the wish to take along Saint Nicholas the Wonder Worker in his clasped hands, probably so he can compare the picture with the saints in heaven and single out the one he reveres most from all the others.

"And so it is that Pyotr Akimovich, actually a shoemaker by trade, also paints icons. When he's tired of one job, he goes to the other, after crossing himself three times, and the same piety presides over his stitching and hammering as over his painting. By now he's an old man, but fairly sturdy. He bends his back over boots, but straightens it up again in front of the images, and so he has maintained a good posture and a certain balance in his shoulders and the small of his back. He has spent the greater part of his life all alone, without any participation in the flurry caused by his wife Akulina's bearing him children or by their death or marriage. Not until his seventieth year did Pyotr establish contact with those who had remained in his house, and begin to regard them as really present. They were: Akulina his wife, a quiet, humble person, who had given practically her all to her children; an ugly daughter who was getting on in years; and a son, Alyosha, who, an uncommonly late child, was only seventeen. Pyotr wanted to train him as a painter, because he realized that soon he'd be unable to undertake all the commissions alone. But he soon gave up the instruction. Alyosha had painted the most holy Virgin, but had fallen so far short of his correct, severe model that his daub resembled a picture of Mariana, the daughter of the Cossack Golokopytenko—that is, something thoroughly sinful—and old Pyotr, after crossing himself over and over again, hastened to paint over the insulted panel with a Saint Dimitri, whom for reasons unknown he placed above all other saints.

Nor did Alyosha ever again try to undertake an image. Whenever his father didn't order him to gild some halo, he was generally out on the steppe, no one knew where. Nobody kept him home. His mother was puzzled over him and was wary of talking to him, as if he were a stranger or an official. His sister had beaten him all the time he was a

Schwester hatte ihn geschlagen, solang er ein Kind war, und jetzt, seit Aljoscha erwachsen war, begann sie ihn zu verachten dafür, daß *er* sie nicht schlug. Aber auch im Dorfe war niemand, der sich um den Burschen kümmerte. Mariana, die Kosakentochter, hatte ihn ausgelacht, als er ihr erklärte, er wolle sie heiraten, und die anderen Mädchen hatte Aljoscha nicht danach gefragt, ob sie ihn als Bräutigam annehmen möchten. In die Ssetsch, zu den Zaporogern, hatte ihn keiner mitnehmen wollen, weil er allen zu schwächlich schien und vielleicht auch noch etwas zu jung. Einmal war er schon davongelaufen bis zum nächsten Kloster, aber die Mönche nahmen ihn nicht auf – und so blieb nur die Heide für ihn, die weite, wogende Heide. Ein Jäger hatte ihm einmal ein altes Gewehr geschenkt, das weiß Gott womit geladen war. Das schleppte Aljoscha immer mit, schoß es aber niemals ab, erstens, weil er den Schuß sparen wollte, und dann, weil er nicht wußte wofür.

An einem lauen, stillen Abend, zu Anfang des Sommers, saßen alle beisammen an dem groben Tisch, auf welchem eine Schüssel mit Grütze stand. Peter aß; und die anderen schauten ihm zu und warteten auf das, was er übrig lassen würde. Plötzlich ließ der Alte den Löffel in der Luft stehen und streckte den breiten welken Kopf in den Lichtstreifen, der von der Tür kam und quer über den Tisch in die Dämmerung lief. Alle horchten. Es war außen an den Wänden der Hütte ein Geräusch, wie wenn ein Nachtvogel mit seinen Flügeln sachte die Balken streifte; aber die Sonne war kaum untergegangen, und die nächtlichen Vögel kamen ja überhaupt selten bis ins Dorf. Und da war es wieder als tappe irgend ein anderes großes Tier ums Haus und als wäre, von allen Wänden zugleich, sein suchender Schritt vernehmbar. Aljoscha erhob sich leise von seiner Bank, in demselben Augenblick verdunkelte sich die Tür von etwas Hohem, Schwarzem; es verdrängte den ganzen Abend, brachte Nacht in die Hütte und bewegte sich in seiner Größe nur unsicher vorwärts. ›Der Ostap!‹ sagte die Häßliche mit ihrer bösen Stimme. Und jetzt erkannten ihn alle. Es war einer von den blinden Kobzars, ein Greis, der mit einer zwölfsaitigen Bandura durch die Dörfer ging und von dem großen Ruhm

child, and now, since Alyosha had grown up, she began to hold him in contempt for not hitting her in turn. Nor was there anyone in the village who showed any concern about the lad. Mariana, the Cossack's daughter, had laughed him to scorn when he declared his wish to marry her, and Alyosha hadn't asked any other girl whether she would accept him as a bridegroom. No one had been willing to make him a member of the Zaporozhe Sech,[14] because everyone thought him too weak and perhaps still a little too young. He had already run away once to the nearest monastery, but the monks refused to accept him— and so all that was left for him was the steppe, the broad, billowing steppe. Once a hunter had made him a present of an old gun (God knows what it was loaded with). Alyosha dragged it along all the time but never fired it, first of all because he wanted to save the shot, and secondly because he didn't know why.

"One warm, quiet evening at the beginning of summer, they were all sitting together at the rough table, on which stood a bowl of porridge. Pyotr was eating, while the others watched him, waiting for whatever he'd leave over. Suddenly the old man let his spoon pause in the air and stretched his wide, withered head into the ray of light that came from the door and ran across the table into the semidarkness. Everyone listened. Outside, along the walls of the hut, there was a noise as if a night bird were softly brushing the logs with its wings; but the sun had scarcely gone down, and, as it was, night birds seldom came all the way into the village. And then, there it was again, as if some other large animal were groping its way around the house and its tentative steps could be heard from every wall at once. Alyosha quietly rose from his bench; at that very moment the doorway was darkened by something tall and black; it eclipsed the entire evening, brought night into the hut, and, in its great size, moved forward only in a gingerly fashion. 'Ostap!' said the ugly daughter in her nasty voice. And now they all recognized him. He was one of the blind kobzars,[15] an old man who wandered through the villages with a twelve-stringed bandura, singing of the great fame of the Cossacks,

14. The celebrated band (*sech*) of Cossacks whose headquarters were beyond the rapids (*za porogami*) of the river Dnieper. Rilke uses the German spelling *Ssetsch* to show that the initial consonant is pronounced like English *s*, not like English *z* (as in *sagen*, for instance). 15. Traditional bards, who originally accompanied their songs on the kobza, a kind of lute. Rilke is said to have based this character on a historical bard of the previous generation, whose first name was Ostap; the song given later on is probably based on a Ukrainian source.

der Kosaken, von ihrer Tapferkeit und Treue, von ihren Hetmans Kirdjaga, Kukubenko, Bulba und anderen Helden sang, so daß alle es gerne hörten. Ostap verneigte sich dreimal tief in der Richtung, in der er das Heiligenbild vermutete (und es war die Znamenskaja, zu der er sich so, unbewußt, wandte), setzte sich dann an den Ofen und fragte mit leiser Stimme: ›Bei wem bin ich eigentlich?‹ ›Bei uns, Väterchen, bei Peter Akimowitsch, dem Schuster‹, erwiderte Peter freundlich. Er war ein Freund des Gesanges und freute sich dieses unerwarteten Besuches. ›Ah, bei Peter Akimowitsch, dem, der die Bilder malt‹, sagte der Blinde, um auch eine Freundlichkeit zu erweisen. Dann wurde es still. In den langen sechs Saiten der Bandura begann ein Klang, wuchs und kam kurz und gleichsam erschöpft von den sechs kurzen Saiten zurück, und diese Wirkung wiederholte sich in immer rascheren Takten, so daß man endlich die Augen schließen mußte, in Angst, den Ton von der in rasendem Lauf erstiegenen Melodie irgendwo hinabstürzen zu sehen; da brach das Lied ab und gab der schönen, schweren Stimme des Kobzars Raum, welche bald das ganze Haus erfüllte und auch aus den benachbarten Hütten die Leute rief, die sich vor der Türe und unter den Fenstern versammelten. Aber nicht von Helden ging diesmal das Lied. Schon ganz sicher schien Bulbas und Ostranitzas und Naliwaikos Ruhm. Für alle Zeiten fest schien die Treue der Kosaken. Nicht von ihren Taten ging heute das Lied. Tiefer zu schlafen schien in allen, welche es vernahmen, der Tanz; denn keiner rührte die Beine oder hob die Hände empor. Wie Ostaps Kopf, so waren auch die anderen Köpfe gesenkt und wurden schwer von dem traurigen Lied:

›Es ist keine Gerechtigkeit mehr in der Welt. Die Gerechtigkeit, wer kann sie finden? Es ist keine Gerechtigkeit mehr in der Welt: denn alle Gerechtigkeit ist den Gesetzen der Ungerechtigkeit unterstellt.

›Heut ist die Gerechtigkeit elend in Fesseln. Und das Unrecht lacht über sie, wir sahns, und sitzt mit den Pans in den goldenen Sesseln und sitzt in dem goldenen Saal mit den Pans.

›Die Gerechtigkeit liegt an der Schwelle und fleht; bei den Pans ist das Unrecht, das Schlechte, zu Gast, und sie laden es lachend in ihren Palast und sie schenken dem Unrecht den Becher voll Met.

their bravery and loyalty, of their hetmans[16] Kirdiaga, Kukubenko, Bul'ba,[17] and other heroes, and everyone enjoyed listening. Ostap made three low bows in the direction of the corner where he assumed the icon was located (and it was the Znamenskaya[18] to which he unconsciously turned), then sat down by the stove and asked in a quiet voice: 'In whose house am I, actually?' 'In ours, little father, the house of Pyotr Akimovich the shoemaker,' Pyotr replied amiably. He was a lover of singing and was delighted by this unexpected visit. 'Ah, the house of Pyotr Akimovich, who paints images,' said the blind man, in order to be amiable in turn. Then everyone was silent. In the six long strings of the bandura a sound arose, swelled, and reechoed curtly, and as if exhausted, from the six short strings, and this effect was repeated in constantly accelerating measures, so that finally one had to close one's eyes in fear of seeing the tone plunge down somewhere from the melody that had climbed so high in its frenzied course; then the song broke off and made way for the beautiful, heavy voice of the kobzar, which soon filled the entire house and even summoned the people from the neighboring huts, who gathered outside the door and below the windows. But this time the song was not about heroes. The fame of Bul'ba, Ostranitza, and Nalivaiko[19] seemed already quite secure. The loyalty of the Cossacks seemed established for all time. Today's song was not about their exploits. In all who heard it, the dance seemed to slumber more profoundly, for no one jiggled his feet or raised his hands. As Ostap's head, so were all the other heads bowed, and they were made heavy by the sorrowful song:

"There is no more justice in the world. Who can find justice? There is no more justice in the world, because all justice is subordinated to the laws of injustice.

Today justice is a miserable prisoner in chains. And injustice mocks it, we've seen this, and sits with the Polish lords on their golden chairs and sits in the golden hall with the Polish lords.

Justice lies on the threshold and implores; in the home of the lords injustice and evil are guests whom they laughingly invite to their palaces, where they pour goblets full of mead for injustice.

---

16. Or "atamans": chieftains.   17. Characters in Gogol's 1835 story *Taras Bul'ba*. 18. Not a specific painted object, but an iconographic *type* of Blessed Virgin (half-length, facing front, hands raised); the name means "of the sign" or "of the apparition." 19. Ostranitza is another character in *Taras Bul'ba*. Severin Nalivaiko was executed in 1597 as a rebel against the government.

›*Oh, Gerechtigkeit, Mütterchen, Mütterchen mein, mit dem Fittich,
der jenem des Adlers gleicht, es kommt vielleicht noch ein Mann, der
gerecht, der gerecht will sein, dann helfe ihm Gott, Er vermag es allein
und macht dem Gerechten die Tage leicht.*‹

Und die Köpfe hoben sich nur mühsam, und auf allen Stirnen stand
Schweigsamkeit; das erkannten auch die, welche reden wollten. Und
nach einer kleinen, ernsten Stille begann wieder das Spiel auf der
Bandura, diesmal schon besser verstanden von der immer wach-
senden Menge. Dreimal sang Ostap sein Lied von der Gerechtigkeit.
Und es war jedesmal ein anderes. War es zum erstenmal Klage, so erschien es bei der Wiederholung Vorwurf, und endlich, da der Kobzar
es zum drittenmal mit hocherhobener Stirne wie eine Kette kurzer
Befehle rief, da brach ein wilder Zorn aus den zitternden Worten und
erfaßte alle und riß sie hin in eine breite und zugleich bange
Begeisterung.

›Wo sammeln sich die Männer?‹ fragte ein junger Bauer, als der
Sänger sich erhob. Der Alte, der von allen Bewegungen der Kosaken
unterrichtet war, nannte einen nahen Ort. Schnell zerstreuten sich die
Männer, man hörte kurze Rufe, Waffen rührten sich, und vor den
Türen weinten die Weiber. Eine Stunde später zog ein Trupp Bauern,
bewaffnet, aus dem Dorfe gegen Tschernigof zu.

Peter hatte dem Kobzar ein Glas Most angeboten, in der Hoffnung
mehr von ihm zu erfahren. Der Alte saß, trank, gab aber nur kurze
Antworten auf die vielen Fragen des Schusters. Dann dankte er und
ging. Aljoscha führte den Blinden über die Schwelle. Als sie draußen
waren in der Nacht und allein, bat Aljoscha: ›Und dürfen alle mitge-
hen in den Krieg?‹ ›Alle‹, sagte der Alte und verschwand rascher aus-
schreitend, als ob er sehend würde in der Nacht.

Als alle schliefen, erhob sich Aljoscha vom Ofen, wo er in den
Kleidern gelegen hatte, nahm sein Gewehr und ging hinaus. Draußen
fühlte er sich mit einem Male umarmt und sanft aufs Haar geküßt.
Gleich darauf erkannte er im Mondlicht Akulina, die eilig und trippelnd
auf das Haus zulief. ›Mutter?!‹ staunte er, und es wurde ihm ganz eigen-
tümlich zu Mut. Er zögerte eine Weile. Eine Tür ging irgendwo, und
ein Hund heulte in der Nähe. Da warf Aljoscha sein Gewehr über die
Schulter und schritt stark aus, denn er gedachte die Männer noch vor
Morgen einzuholen. Im Hause aber taten alle, als ob sie Aljoschas
Fehlen nicht bemerkten. Nur, als sie sich wieder zu Tische setzten, und
Peter den leeren Platz gewahrte, stand er noch einmal auf, ging in die

*'O justice, little mother, my little mother, with the wings that are like
the eagle's, perhaps a man will still come who has the will to be just,
just; then, may God help him! He alone has the power, and he will
make the days of the just man easy.'*

"And their heads arose only with difficulty, and silence was written
on every brow; this was realized even by those who wished to speak.
And after a brief, solemn pause the playing on the bandura resumed,
this time better understood by the constantly growing crowd. Three
times Ostap sang his song about justice. And it was different each
time. If, the first time, it had been a lament, it sounded, when repeated, like a reproach, and finally, when the kobzar exclaimed it for
the third time, with high-uplifted brow, like a string of concise orders,
a wild rage broke out of the trembling words and gripped them all,
carrying them away in extensive, but at the same time timorous enthusiasm.

" 'Where are the men gathering?' a young peasant asked when the
singer arose. The old man, who was informed of all the Cossacks'
moves, named a nearby place. Quickly the men dispersed; one could
hear brief shouts, weapons were handled, and outside doors the
women were weeping. An hour later, a troop of armed peasants
marched out of the village toward Chernigov.[20]

"Pyotr had offered the kobzar a glass of must, in hopes of learning
more from him. The old man sat, drank, but replied only briefly to the
shoemaker's many questions. Then he gave thanks and left. Alyosha
guided the blind man across the threshold. When they were outside
in the night, and alone, Alyosha asked: 'And can anyone join the war?'
'Anyone,' said the old man, and he disappeared with more rapid
strides, as if the night restored his sight.

"When everyone was asleep, Alyosha arose from the heated platform, where he had lain fully dressed, took his gun, and went out.
Outside, he suddenly found himself embraced and gently kissed on
his hair. At once he recognized Akulina in the moonlight, hastily running back to the house, with little steps. 'Mother?!' he cried in amazement, and he felt very peculiar. He hesitated a while. Somewhere a
door shut, and a dog howled nearby. Then Alyosha shouldered his gun
and began taking strong strides, because he intended to catch up with
the men before morning. But in the house everyone acted as if un-
aware that Alyosha was missing. It was only when they sat down at the
table once more, and Pyotr noticed the empty place, that he got up

---

20. A city in north-central Ukraine.

Ecke und zündete eine Kerze an vor der Znamenskaja. Eine ganz dünne Kerze. Die Häßliche zuckte mit den Achseln.

Indessen ging Ostap, der blinde Greis, schon durch das nächste Dorf und begann traurig und mit sanfter klagender Stimme den Gesang von der Gerechtigkeit.«

Der Lahme wartete noch eine Weile. Dann sah er mich erstaunt an: »Nun, weshalb schließen Sie nicht? Es ist doch wie in der Geschichte vom Verrat. Dieser Alte war Gott.«

»Oh, und ich habe es nicht gewußt«, sagte ich erschauernd.

Eine Szene aus dem Ghetto von Venedig

Herr Baum, Hausbesitzer, Bezirksobmann, Ehrenoberster der freiwilligen Feuerwehr und noch verschiedenes andere, aber, um es kurz zu sagen: Herr Baum muß eines meiner Gespräche mit Ewald belauscht haben. Es ist kein Wunder; ihm gehört das Haus, darin mein Freund zu ebener Erde wohnt. Herr Baum und ich, wir kennen uns längst vom Sehen. Neulich aber bleibt der Bezirksobmann stehen, hebt ein wenig den Hut, so daß ein kleiner Vogel hätte ausfliegen können, im Falle einer drunter gefangen gewesen wäre. Er lächelt höflich und eröffnet unsere Bekanntschaft: »Sie reisen manchmal?« »Oh ja –,« erwiderte ich, etwas zerstreut, »das kann wohl sein.« Nun fuhr er vertraulich fort: »Ich glaube, wir sind die beiden Einzigen hier, die in Italien waren.« »So–,« ich bemühte mich etwas aufmerksamer zu sein –, »ja, dann ist es allerdings dringend notwendig, daß wir mit einander reden.«

Herr Baum lachte. »Ja, Italien – das ist doch noch etwas. Ich erzähle immer meinen Kindern –. Zum Beispiel nehmen Sie Venedig!« Ich blieb stehen: »Sie erinnern sich noch Venedigs?« »Aber, ich bitte Sie,« stöhnte er, denn er war etwas zu dick, um sich mühelos zu entrüsten, – »wie sollte ich nicht – wer das einmal gesehen hat –. Diese Piazzetta – nicht wahr?« »Ja,« entgegnete ich, »ich erinnere mich besonders gern der Fahrt durch den Kanal, dieses leisen lautlosen Hingleitens am Rande von Vergangenheiten.« »Der Palazzo Franchetti«, fiel ihm ein. »Die Cà Doro«, – gab ich zurück. »Der Fischmarkt –« »Der Palazzo Vendramin –« »Wo Richard Wagner« – fügte er rasch, als ein gebildeter Deutscher, hinzu. Ich nickte: »Den Ponte, wissen Sie?« Er lächelte mit Orientierung: »Selbstverständlich, und das Museum, die Akademie, nicht zu vergessen, wo ein Tizian . . .«

again, went to the corner, and lit a candle in front of the Znamenskaya. A very thin candle. The ugly daughter shrugged her shoulders.

"Meanwhile, Ostap, the blind old man, was already passing through the next village and, sadly and in a gentle, lamenting voice, was beginning his song about justice."

The paralyzed man waited another while. Then he looked at me in surprise: "Well, why don't you finish? After all, it's like in the story about treachery. That old man was God."

"Oh, and I didn't know," I said with a thrill.

A Scene from the Venetian Ghetto

Mr. Baum, homeowner, district commissioner, honorary chief of the volunteer fire department, and various other things—but, in short: Mr. Baum—must have overheard one of my conversations with Ewald. That isn't surprising, since he owns the house in which my friend lives on the ground floor. Mr. Baum and I have long known each other by sight. But recently the district commissioner halted and raised his hat a little, so that a little bird could have flown out, in case one had been trapped under it. He smiled politely and initiated our acquaintance this way: "You travel sometimes?" "Oh, yes," I replied rather distractedly, "that may be." Then he continued, in confidence: "I think we're the only two here who have been to Italy." "So," I said, making an effort to be a little more attentive; "yes, then it's surely urgently necessary for us to converse."

Mr. Baum laughed. "Yes, Italy, that's really something. I always tell my children—. For instance, take Venice!" I halted: "You still remember Venice?" "Come now, I ask you!" he moaned, because he was a little too fat to become indignant without some strain; "how could I help it? Anyone who's ever seen it . . . That Piazzetta . . . right?" "Yes," I replied, "I recall with particular pleasure the ride through the Canal, that soft, soundless gliding past the rim of days gone by." "The Palazzo Franchetti," it came back to him. "The Cà d'Oro," I countered. "The fish market." "The Palazzo Vendramin—" "Where Richard Wagner[21]—" he swiftly added, cultured German that he was. I nodded: "The Ponte, you know?" He smiled with recognition: "Of course, and not forgetting the museum, the Accademia, where a Titian . . ."

---

21. Died, in 1883.

So hat sich Herr Baum einer Art Prüfung unterzogen, die etwas anstrengend war. Ich nahm mir vor, ihn durch eine Geschichte zu entschädigen. Und begann ohne weiteres:

»Wenn man unter dem Ponte di Rialto hindurchfährt, an dem Fondaco de' Turchi und an dem Fischmarkt vorbei, und dem Gondoliere sagt: ›rechts!‹, so sieht er etwas erstaunt aus und fragt wohl gar: ›Dove?‹. Aber man besteht darauf nach rechts zu fahren, und steigt in einem der kleinen schmutzigen Kanäle aus, handelt mit ihm, schimpft und geht durch gedrängte Gassen und schwarze verqualmte Torgänge auf einen leeren freien Platz hinaus. Alles das einfach aus dem Grunde, weil dort meine Geschichte handelt.«

Herr Baum berührte mich sanft am Arm: »Verzeihen Sie, welche Geschichte?« Seine kleinen Augen gingen etwas beängstigt hin und her.

Ich beruhigte ihn: »Irgend eine, verehrter Herr, keine irgendwie nennenswerte. Ich kann Ihnen auch nicht sagen, wann sie geschah. Vielleicht unter dem Dogen Alvise Mocenigo IV., aber es kann auch etwas früher oder später gewesen sein. Die Bilder von Carpaccio, wenn Sie solche gesehen haben sollten, sind wie auf purpurnem Samt gemalt, überall bricht etwas Warmes, gleichsam Waldiges durch, und um die gedämpften Lichter darin drängen sich horchende Schatten. Giorgione hat auf mattem, alterndem Gold, Tizian auf schwarzem Atlas gemalt, aber in der Zeit, von der ich rede, liebte man lichte Bilder, auf einen Grund von weißer Seide gesetzt, und der Name, mit dem man spielte, den schöne Lippen in die Sonne warfen und den reizende Ohren auffingen, wenn er zitternd niederfiel, dieser Name ist Gian Battista Tiepolo.

Aber das alles kommt in meiner Geschichte nicht vor. Es geht nur das wirkliche Venedig an, die Stadt der Paläste, der Abenteuer, der Masken und der blassen Lagunennächte, die, wie keine anderen Nächte sonst, den Ton von heimlichen Romanzen tragen. – In dem Stück Venedig, von dem ich erzähle, sind nur arme tägliche Geräusche, die Tage gehen gleichförmig darüber hin, als ob es nur ein einziger wäre, und die Gesänge, die man dort vernimmt, sind wachsende Klagen, die nicht aufsteigen und wie ein wallender Qualm über den Gassen lagern. Sobald es dämmert, treibt sich viel scheues Gesindel dort herum, unzählige Kinder haben ihre Heimat auf den Plätzen und in den engen kalten Haustüren und spielen mit den Scherben und Abfällen von buntem Glasfluß, demselben, aus dem die Meister die ernsten Mosaiken von San Marco fügten. Ein Adeliger kommt selten in das Ghetto. Höchstens zur Zeit, wenn die Judenmädchen zum Brunnen kommen, kann man manchmal eine

In that way Mr. Baum had submitted to a kind of quiz that was somewhat exhausting. I resolved to make it up to him with a story. And, with no further preamble, I began:

"When you ride under the Ponte di Rialto, past the Fondaco de' Turchi and the fish market, and tell the gondolier 'To the right,' he looks a little surprised and may even ask 'Dove?'[22] But you insist you want to go to the right, and you get out in one of the dirty little canals, haggle with him, curse, and follow narrow lanes and black, sooty gateways till you reach an empty open square. All this simply because that's where my story takes place."

Mr. Baum touched my arm gently: "Excuse me, what story?" His little eyes were shifting to and fro in a sort of alarm.

I calmed him down: "Any old story, my good sir, none that's particularly noteworthy. Nor can I tell you when it occurred. Perhaps in the reign of the doge Alvise Mocenigo IV,[23] but it could also have been somewhat earlier or later. Carpaccio's pictures, if you've ever seen any, are painted as if on purple velvet, everywhere something warm, as if from a forest, breaks through, and listening shadows crowd around the muted highlights. Giorgione painted on dull, ageing gold, Titian on black satin, but at the time I'm speaking of, people liked bright pictures, set against a background of white silk, and the name that people played with, which lovely lips threw into the sunlight and charming ears caught when it fell down again in a tremble, that name is Gian Battista Tiepolo.

"But none of that is part of my story. That applies only to the real Venice, the city of palaces, adventures, masquerades, and pale nights on the lagoon which, like no other nights, have the tone of secret romances.—In the piece of Venice of which I tell, there are only poor, everyday sounds, which the days pass by monotonously as if only one long day, and the songs you hear there are swelling laments which fail to rise and which cover the lanes like billowing smoke. As soon as twilight comes, many criminals who fear the light of day roam around, numberless children live out in the squares and in the narrow, cold doorways of houses, and play with the broken bits and refuse of multicolored glass flux, the very glass with which the masters fitted together the solemn mosaics of San Marco. A nobleman rarely comes to the ghetto. At best, at the time when the Jewish girls come to the fountain you can sometimes notice a dark figure, cloaked and masked. Certain people know from

---

22. "Where?" (in Italian).   23. Reigned 1763–1778.

Gestalt, schwarz, im Mantel und mit Maske bemerken. Gewisse Leute wissen aus Erfahrung, daß diese Gestalt einen Dolch in den Falten verborgen trägt. Jemand will einmal im Mondlicht das Gesicht des Jünglings gesehen haben, und es wird seither behauptet, dieser schwarze schlanke Gast sei Marcantonio Priuli, Sohn des Proveditore Nicolò Priuli und der schönen Catharina Minelli. Man weiß, er wartet unter dem Torweg des Hauses von Isaak Rosso, geht dann, wenn es einsam wird, quer über den Platz und tritt bei dem alten Melchisedech ein, dem reichen Goldschmied, der viele Söhne und sieben Töchter und von den Söhnen und Töchtern viele Enkel hat. Die jüngste Enkelin, Esther, erwartet ihn, an den greisen Großvater geschmiegt, in einem niederen, dunklen Gemach, in welchem vieles glänzt und glüht, und Seide und Samt hängt sanft über den Gefäßen, wie um ihre vollen, goldenen Flammen zu stillen. Hier sitzt Marcantonio auf einem silbergestickten Kissen, dem greisen Juden zu Füßen, und erzählt von Venedig, wie von einem Märchen, das es nirgendwo jemals ganz so gegeben hat. Er erzählt von den Schauspielen, von den Schlachten des venetianischen Heeres, von fremden Gästen, von Bildern und Bildsäulen, von der ›Sensa‹ am Himmelfahrtstage, von dem Karneval und von der Schönheit seiner Mutter Catharina Minelli. Alles das ist für ihn von ähnlichem Sinn, verschiedene Ausdrücke für Macht und Liebe und Leben. Den beiden Zuhörern ist alles fremd; denn die Juden sind streng ausgeschlossen von jedem Verkehr, und auch der reiche Melchisedech betritt niemals das Gebiet des Großen Rates, obwohl er, als Goldschmied, und weil er allgemeine Achtung genoß, es hätte wagen dürfen. In seinem langen Leben hat der Alte seinen Glaubensgenossen, die ihn alle wie einen Vater fühlten, manche Vergünstigung vom Rate verschafft, aber er hatte auch immer wieder den Rückschlag erlebt. So oft ein Unheil über den Staat hereinbrach, rächte man sich an den Juden; die Venezianer selbst waren von viel zu verwandtem Geiste, als daß sie, wie andere Völker, die Juden für den Handel gebraucht hätten, sie quälten sie mit Abgaben, beraubten sie ihrer Güter, und beschränkten immer mehr das Gebiet des Ghetto, so daß die Familien, die sich mitten in aller Not fruchtbar vermehrten, gezwungen waren, ihre Häuser aufwärts, eines auf das Dach des anderen zu bauen. Und ihre Stadt, die nicht am Meere lag, wuchs so langsam in den Himmel hinaus, wie in ein anderes Meer, und um den Platz mit dem Brunnen erhoben sich auf allen Seiten die steilen Gebäude, wie die Wände irgend eines Riesenturms.

experience that this figure conceals a dagger in the folds of his cloak. Someone claims to have seen the young man's face in the moonlight once, and since then it has been asserted that this dark, slender visitor is Marcantonio Priuli, son of the *provveditore*[24] Niccolò Priuli and the beautiful Catarina Minelli. It is known that he waits under the gateway to the house of Isacco Rosso, then, when no one is about, crosses the square and enters the home of old Melchisedec, the wealthy goldsmith, who has many sons and seven daughters and many grandchildren by his sons and daughters. His youngest granddaughter, Ester, snuggling against her aged grandfather, awaits him in a low-ceilinged, dark room, in which many objects shine and glow, and silk and velvet hang softly over the vessels, as if to temper their strong golden flames. Here Marcantonio sits on a cushion embroidered with silver, at the foot of the aged Jew, and tells about Venice as if telling a fairy tale that never yet has existed quite the same way anywhere else. He tells of the theatrical performances, the battles of the Venetian army, foreign guests, paintings and statues, the Sensa[25] on Ascension Day, Carnival time, and the beauty of his mother, Catarina Minelli. For him all of that is of one piece, varying expressions for power, love, and life. It's all strange to the two listeners, because Jews are strictly excluded from all such traffic, and even wealthy Melchisedec never enters the precincts of the Council of Ten, though, as a goldsmith, and because he enjoys universal esteem, he might safely do so. During his long life the old man has won from the Council many privileges for his coreligionists, who all look on him as a father, but, each time, he has experienced a negative reaction. Whenever a calamity affected the city, people took it out on the Jews; the Venetians themselves were much too similar in character to make use of the Jews in commerce, as other nations did; they plagued them with taxes, stole their possessions, and constantly narrowed the area of the ghetto, so that its families, which amid all their distress increased fruitfully, were compelled to build their houses upward, one on the roof of the other. And *their* city, which didn't border on the sea, slowly grew in that fashion up to the sky, as if into a different sea, and around the square with the fountain the steep buildings rose on every side, like the walls of some gigantic tower.

---

24. A high official of the Venetian Republic.   25. The famous "marriage of Venice to the sea."

Der reiche Melchisedech, in der Wunderlichkeit des hohen Alters, hatte seinen Mitbürgern, Söhnen und Enkeln einen befremdlichen Vorschlag gemacht. Er wollte immer das jeweilig höchste dieser winzigen Häuser, die sich in zahllosen Stockwerken über einander schoben, bewohnen. Man erfüllte ihm diesen seltsamen Wunsch gerne, denn man traute ohnehin nicht mehr der Tragkraft der unteren Mauern und setzte oben so leichte Steine auf, daß der Wind die Wände gar nicht zu bemerken schien. So siedelte der Greis zwei bis dreimal im Jahre um und Esther, die ihn nicht verlassen wollte, immer mit ihm. Schließlich waren sie so hoch, daß, wenn sie aus der Enge ihres Gemachs auf das flache Dach traten, in der Höhe ihrer Stirnen schon ein anderes Land begann, von dessen Gebräuchen der Alte in dunklen Worten, halb psalmend, sprach. Es war jetzt sehr weit zu ihnen hinauf; durch viele fremde Leben hindurch, über steile und glitschige Stufen, an scheltenden Weibern vorüber und über die Überfälle hungernder Kinder hinaus ging der Weg, und seine vielen Hindernisse beschränkten jeden Verkehr. Auch Marcantonio kam nicht mehr zu Besuch, und Esther vermißte ihn kaum. Sie hatte ihn in den Stunden, da sie mit ihm allein gewesen war, so groß und lange angeschaut, daß ihr schien, er wäre damals tief in ihre dunklen Augen gestürzt und gestorben, und jetzt begänne, in ihr selbst, sein neues, ewiges Leben, an das er als Christ doch geglaubt hatte. Mit diesem neuen Gefühl in ihrem jungen Leib, stand sie tagelang auf dem Dache und suchte das Meer. Aber, so hoch die Behausung auch war, man erkannte zuerst nur den Giebel des Palazzo Foscari, irgend einen Turm, die Kuppel einer Kirche, eine fernere Kuppel, wie frierend im Licht, und dann ein Gitter von Masten, Balken, Stangen vor dem Rand des feuchten, zitternden Himmels.

Gegen Ende dieses Sommers zog der Alte, obwohl ihm das Steigen schon schwer fiel, allen Widerreden zum Trotz, dennoch um; denn man hatte eine neue Hütte, hoch über allen, gebaut. Als er nach so langer Zeit wieder über den Platz ging, von Esther gestützt, da drängten sich viele um ihn und neigten sich über seine tastenden Hände und baten ihn um seinen Rat in vielen Dingen; denn er war ihnen wie ein Toter, der aus seinem Grabe steigt, weil irgend eine Zeit sich erfüllt hat. Und so schien es auch. Die Männer erzählten ihm, daß in Venedig ein Aufstand sei, der Adel sei in Gefahr, und über ein kurzes würden die Grenzen des Ghetto fallen und alle würden sich der gleichen Freiheit erfreuen. Der Alte antwortete nichts und nickte nur, als sei ihm dieses alles längst bekannt und noch vieles mehr. Er trat in das Haus des Isaak Rosso, auf dessen Gipfel seine neue Wohnung lag, und stieg, einen halben Tag lang, hinauf. Oben bekam

"Wealthy Melchisedec, in the eccentricity of old age, had made a puzzling suggestion to his fellow citizens, sons, and grandsons. He wanted always to live in the highest of those tiny houses which piled on top of one another in numberless stories. They were glad to grant him that odd wish, because, as it was, they no longer trusted the bearing power of the lower building walls, and placed such light stones on upper floors that the wind didn't seem to notice the room walls. And so the old man moved two or three times a year, and Ester, who wouldn't forsake him, always came along. Finally they were so high up that, when they stepped out of their confining room onto the flat roof, at the level of their foreheads a new country already began, one about whose customs the old man spoke in obscure words, half in psalmody. Now it was a very long walk up to their place; the way led through many lives of other people, up steep and slippery stairs, past scolding women and the assaults of starving children, and its many obstacles limited their social intercourse. Even Marcantonio no longer came visiting, and Ester scarcely missed him. In the hours when she had been alone with him, she had looked at him so long and hard that she felt as if he had then dived deep into her dark eyes and died, and that his new, eternal life, which as a Christian he had after all believed in, was now just beginning, inside her. With this new feeling in her young body, she stood on the roof for days on end, seeking the sea. But, high as her dwelling was, at first one could only make out the gable of the Palazzo Foscari, some tower or other, the dome of a church, a more distant dome that seemed to be freezing in the light, and then a latticework of masts, beams, and poles against the rim of the damp, trembling sky.

"Toward the end of that summer the old man moved again, even though it was already hard for him to climb stairs and everyone tried to talk him out of it; because a new hut had been built high above all the rest. When, after such a long time, he was once again walking across the square, leaning on Ester, many people crowded around him, bowing over his groping hands and asking his advice on many matters; for to them he was like a dead man rising from his grave because a certain era has come to an end. And so it did seem. The men told him that there was a rebellion in Venice, the nobility was in peril, and before long the walls of the ghetto would fall and everyone would enjoy the same freedom. The old man made no reply, but merely nodded, as if he had known all of that, and much more, for a long time. He entered Isacco Rosso's house, on the summit of which his new home was situated, and, taking

Esther ein blondes, zartes Kind. Nachdem sie sich erholt hatte, trug
sie es auf den Armen hinaus auf das Dach und legte zum erstenmal
den ganzen goldenen Himmel in seine offenen Augen. Es war ein
Herbstmorgen von unbeschreiblicher Klarheit. Die Dinge dunkelten,
fast ohne Glanz, nur einzelne fliegende Lichter ließen sich, wie auf
große Blumen, auf sie nieder, ruhten eine Weile und schwebten dann
über die goldlinigen Konturen hinaus in den Himmel. Und dort, wo
sie verschwanden, erblickte man von dieser höchsten Stelle, was noch
keiner vom Ghetto aus je gesehen hatte, – ein stilles, silbernes Licht:
das Meer. Und erst jetzt, da Esthers Augen sich an die Herrlichkeit
gewöhnt hatten, bemerkte sie am Rande des Daches, ganz vorn,
Melchisedech. Er erhob sich mit ausgebreiteten Armen und zwang
seine matten Augen in den Tag zu schauen, der sich langsam entfal-
tete. Seine Arme blieben hoch, seine Stirne trug einen strahlenden
Gedanken; es war, als ob er opferte. Dann ließ er sich immer wieder
vornüberfallen und preßte den alten Kopf an die schlechten kantigen
Steine. Das Volk aber stand unten auf dem Platze versammelt und
blickte herauf. Einzelne Gebärden und Worte erhoben sich aus der
Menge, aber sie reichten nicht bis zu dem einsam betenden Greise.
Und das Volk sah den Ältesten und den Jüngsten wie in den Wolken.
Der Alte aber fuhr fort, sich stolz zu erheben und aufs neue in Demut
zusammenzubrechen, eine ganze Zeit. Und die Menge unten wuchs
und ließ ihn nicht aus den Augen: Hat er das Meer gesehen oder Gott,
den Ewigen, in seiner Glorie?«

Herr Baum bemühte sich, recht schnell etwas zu bemerken. Es
gelang ihm nicht gleich. »Das Meer wahrscheinlich,« – sagte er dann
trocken, »es *ist* ja auch ein Eindruck« – wodurch er sich besonders
aufgeklärt und verständig erwies.

Ich verabschiedete mich eilig, aber ich konnte mich doch nicht enthalten, ihm nachzurufen: »Vergessen Sie nicht, die Begebenheit
Ihren Kindern zu erzählen.« Er besann sich: »Den Kindern? Wissen
Sie, da ist dieser junge Adlige, dieser Antonio, oder wie er heißt, ein
ganz und gar nicht schöner Charakter und dann: das Kind, dieses
Kind! Das dürfte doch – für Kinder –« »Oh,« beruhigte ich ihn, »Sie
haben vergessen, verehrter Herr, daß die Kinder von Gott kommen!
Wie sollten die Kinder zweifeln, daß Esther eines bekam, da sie doch
so nahe am Himmel wohnt!«

Auch *diese* Geschichte haben die Kinder vernommen, und wenn
man sie fragt, wie *sie* darüber denken, was der alte Jude Melchisedech
wohl erblickt haben mag in seiner Verzückung, so sagen sie ohne
nachzusinnen: »Oh, das Meer auch.«

half a day to do it, walked up. Up there Ester gave birth to a delicate blonde child. After recovering, she carried it out onto the roof in her arms and for the first time placed the whole golden sky in its open eyes. It was a fall morning, indescribably clear. The objects were dark, almost with a reflection, with flying patches of light coming to rest on them only here and there, as if on large flowers, reposing a while and then floating out over their golden contours into the sky. And in the place where they vanished, from this loftiest vantage point, one could catch sight of something no one had ever yet seen from the ghetto, a quiet, silvery light: the sea. And only now, when Ester's eyes had grown accustomed to that splendor, did she notice Melchisedec at the edge of the roof, right at the rim. He rose with outstretched arms and forced his dulled eyes to look into the sunlight, which was slowly unfurling. He kept his arms raised; his forehead bore a radiant thought; he looked as if he were sacrificing. Then he let himself fall farther and farther forward, pressing his old head against the rough, pointy stones. But the people were gathered down in the square, looking up. A few individual gestures and words arose from the crowd, but they didn't reach the old man praying in solitude. And the people saw the eldest and the youngest as if in the clouds. But the old man continued to raise himself up proudly and to subside into humility again, for a long time. And the crowd below grew and didn't take their eyes off him: 'Has he seen the sea or God the Eternal in his glory?'"

Mr. Baum strove to make some speedy remark. He didn't succeed right away. "Probably the sea," he then said drily, "that *is* impressive, too"—whereby he proved himself to be particularly enlightened and intelligent.

I took my leave hastily, but all the same I couldn't refrain from calling after him: "Don't forget to tell this event to your children." He thought it over: "To my children? You know, there's that young nobleman, that Antonio or whatever his name was, not at all a fine character, and then, that baby, that baby! After all, for children, that should be—" "Oh," I said, placating him, "you've forgotten, my dear sir, that babies come from God! How can your children doubt that Ester got one, when she was living that close to heaven?"

That story, too, the children got to hear, and when they're asked what *they* think the old Jew Melchisedec may have sighted in his rapture, they say without thinking twice: "Oh, the sea also."

Von Einem, der die Steine belauscht

Ich bin schon wieder bei meinem lahmen Freunde. Er lächelt in seiner eigentümlichen Art: »Und von Italien haben Sie mir noch nie erzählt.« »Das soll heißen, ich möge es sobald als möglich nachholen?«

Ewald nickt und schließt schon die Augen, um zuzuhören. Ich fange also an: »Was wir Frühling fühlen, sieht Gott als ein flüchtiges, kleines Lächeln über die Erde gehen. Sie scheint sich an etwas zu erinnern, im Sommer erzählt sie allen davon, bis sie weiser wird in der großen, herbstlichen Schweigsamkeit, mit welcher sie sich Einsamen vertraut. Alle Frühlinge, welche Sie und ich erlebt haben, zusammengenommen, reichen noch nicht aus, eine Sekunde Gottes zu füllen. Der Frühling, den Gott bemerken soll, darf nicht in Bäumen und auf Wiesen bleiben, er muß irgendwie in den Menschen mächtig werden, denn dann geht er, sozusagen, nicht in der Zeit, vielmehr in der Ewigkeit vor sich und in Gegenwart Gottes.

Als dieses einmal geschah, mußten Gottes Blicke in ihren dunkeln Schwingen über Italien hängen. Das Land unten war hell, die Zeit glänzte wie Gold, aber quer darüber, wie ein dunkler Weg, lag der Schatten eines breiten Mannes, schwer und schwarz, und weit davor der Schatten seiner schaffenden Hände, unruhig, zuckend, bald über Pisa, bald über Neapel, bald zerfließend auf der ungewissen Bewegung des Meeres. Gott konnte seine Augen nicht abwenden von diesen Händen, die ihm zuerst gefaltet schienen, wie betende, – aber das Gebet, welches ihnen entquoll, drängte sie weit auseinander. Es wurde eine Stille in den Himmeln. Alle Heiligen folgten den Blicken Gottes und betrachteten, wie er, den Schatten, der halb Italien verhüllte, und die Hymnen der Engel blieben auf ihren Gesichtern stehen, und die Sterne zitterten, denn sie fürchteten, irgend etwas verschuldet zu haben, und warteten demütig auf Gottes zorniges Wort. Aber nichts dergleichen geschah. Die Himmel hatten sich in ihrer ganzen Breite über Italien aufgetan, so daß Raffael in Rom auf den Knien lag, und der selige Fra Angelico von Fiesole stand in einer Wolke und freute sich über ihn. Viele Gebete waren zu dieser Stunde von der Erde unterwegs. Gott aber erkannte nur eines: die Kraft Michelangelos stieg wie Duft von Weinbergen zu ihm empor. Und er duldete, daß sie seine Gedanken erfüllte. Er neigte sich tiefer, fand den schaffenden Mann, sah über seine Schultern fort auf die am Steine horchenden Hände und erschrak: sollten in den Steinen auch Seelen sein? Warum belauschte dieser Mann die Steine? Und nun erwachten ihm die Hände und wühlten den Stein auf wie ein Grab, darin eine schwache, sterbende Stimme flackert: ›Michelangelo,‹ rief

Of One Who Listens to Stones

Once again I am with my paralyzed friend. He says, smiling in his particular way: "And you have not yet told me about Italy." "Does that mean I must make up for that negligence as soon as possible?"

Ewald nods and already shuts his eyes to listen. So I begin: "What we perceive as springtime, God sees as a small, fleeting smile moving over the earth. The earth seems to be remembering something; in the summertime it tells everyone about it, until it grows wiser in that great taciturnity of autumn with which it confides in lonely people. All the springs that you and I have lived through, taken together, are still insufficient to fill up a second of God's time. The spring that God is to notice mustn't confine itself to trees and meadows, it must somehow become a force within man, because then it occurs not in time, so to speak, but in eternity and the presence of God.

"When this once occurred, God's gaze, with its dark wings, must have been concentrated on Italy. The land below was bright, the weather shone like gold, but athwart it, like an obscure path, lay the shadow of a broad man, heavy and black, and, far in front, the shadow of his creative hands, restless, twitching, now over Pisa, now over Naples, now dissolving onto the uncertain motion of the sea. God couldn't take his eyes off those hands, which at first seemed to him to be clasped, as if in prayer—but the prayer that poured from them forced them wide apart. There was a silence in the heavens. All the saints followed God's gaze and observed, as he did, the shadow which covered half of Italy, and the angels' hymns remained on their faces, and the stars trembled, because they were afraid they had done something wrong, and were humbly awaiting God's wrathful words. But nothing of the sort happened. The heavens had opened to their full extent over Italy, so that Raphael was on his knees in Rome, and the blessed Fra Angelico of Fiesole stood on a cloud and was glad over him. At that hour many prayers were on their way from earth. But God recognized only one: Michelangelo's power arose up to him like the fragrance of vineyards. And he patiently allowed it to complete his thoughts. He stooped lower, found the creative man, looked over his shoulder at his hands listening on the stone, and became alarmed: could there be souls in stones, too? Why was this man listening to the stones? And now his hands awoke and burrowed into the stone as if into a grave in which a weak, dying voice flickers. 'Michelangelo,' God

Gott in Bangigkeit: ›wer ist im Stein?‹ Michelangelo horchte auf; seine
Hände zitterten. Dann antwortete er dumpf: ›Du, mein Gott, wer denn
sonst. Aber ich kann nicht zu dir.‹ Und da fühlte Gott, daß er auch im
Steine sei, und es wurde ihm ängstlich und enge. Der ganze Himmel war
nur ein Stein, und er war mitten drin eingeschlossen und hoffte auf die
Hände Michelangelos, die ihn befreien würden, und er hörte sie kommen, aber noch weit. Der Meister aber war wieder über dem Werke. Er
dachte beständig: Du bist nur ein kleiner Block, und ein anderer könnte
in dir kaum *einen* Menschen finden. Ich aber fühle hier eine Schulter:
es ist die des Josef von Arimathäa, hier neigt sich Maria, ich spüre ihre
zitternden Hände, welche Jesum unseren Herrn halten, der eben am
Kreuze verstarb. Wenn in diesem kleinen Marmor diese drei Raum
haben, wie sollte ich nicht einmal ein schlafendes Geschlecht aus einem
Felsen heben? Und mit breiten Hieben machte er die drei Gestalten
der Pietà frei, aber er löste nicht ganz die steinernen Schleier von ihren
Gesichtern, als fürchtete er, ihre tiefe Traurigkeit könnte sich lähmend
über seine Hände legen. So flüchtete er zu einem anderen Steine. Aber
jedesmal verzagte er, einer Stirne ihre volle Klarheit, einer Schulter ihre
reinste Rundung zu geben, und wenn er ein Weib bildete, so legte er
nicht das letzte Lächeln um ihren Mund, damit ihre Schönheit nicht
ganz verraten sei.

Zu dieser Zeit entwarf er das Grabdenkmal für Julius della Rovere.
Einen Berg wollte er bauen über den eisernen Papst und ein Geschlecht
dazu, welches diesen Berg bevölkerte. Von vielen dunkeln Plänen erfüllt, ging er hinaus nach seinen Marmorbrüchen. Über einem armen
Dorf erhob sich steil der Hang. Umrahmt von Oliven und welkem
Gestein erschienen die frisch gebrochenen Flächen wie ein großes
blasses Gesicht unter alterndem Haar. Lange stand Michelangelo vor
seiner verhüllten Stirne. Plötzlich bemerkte er darunter zwei riesige
Augen aus Stein, welche ihn betrachteten. Und Michelangelo fühlte
seine Gestalt wachsen unter dem Einfluß dieses Blickes. Jetzt ragte auch
er über dem Land, und es war ihm, als ob er von Ewigkeit her diesem
Berg brüderlich gegenüberstände. Das Tal wich unter ihm zurück wie
unter einem Steigenden, die Hütten drängten sich wie Herden aneinander, und näher und verwandter zeigte sich das Felsengesicht unter
seinen weißen steinernen Schleiern. Es hatte einen wartenden
Ausdruck, reglos und doch am Rande der Bewegung. Michelangelo
dachte nach: ›Man kann dich nicht zerschlagen, du bist ja nur Eines‹,
und dann hob er seine Stimme: ›Dich will ich vollenden, du bist mein

called in alarm, 'who is in the stone?' Michelangelo stopped to listen; his hands trembled. Then he replied in muffled tones: 'You, my Lord; who else? But I can't reach you.' And then God sensed that he was also in the *stone,* and he felt anguished and cramped. All of heaven was only a stone, and he was enclosed in the center of it, waiting for Michelangelo's hands to liberate him, and he heard them coming, but still far away. But the master was back at work again. He thought constantly: 'You're only a small block of stone, and another man could scarcely find one human being in you. But here I feel a shoulder, that of Joseph of Arimathaea; here Mary is stooping, I sense her trembling hands holding our Lord Jesus, who has just died on the cross. If those three can fit in this small piece of marble, why shouldn't I at some time raise a sleeping nation out of a large crag?' And with broad strokes he liberated the three figures of the Pietà, but he didn't completely detach the stone veils from their faces, as if he feared that their deep sorrow might cover his hands and paralyze them. And so he took refuge in another stone. But each time he was afraid to give a forehead all its possible clarity, a shoulder its purest curve, and when he formed a woman, he didn't place the ultimate smile on her lips, so that her beauty might not be fully revealed.

At that time he was designing the funerary monument for Giulio della Rovere.[26] He wanted to build a mountain over the iron pope and, with it, a nation to people that mountain. Filled with many obscure plans, he walked out to his marble quarries. The slope rose steeply above an impoverished village. Framed by olive trees and faded rock, the freshly excavated surfaces looked like a large, pale face beneath ageing hair. For a long time Michelangelo stood before its concealed brow. Suddenly he noticed under it two gigantic eyes of stone, looking at him. And Michelangelo felt his form growing under the influence of that gaze. Now he, too, loomed up over the countryside, and he felt as if had been fraternally standing opposite that mountain for all eternity. The valley withdrew below him, as if below a climber, the cottages huddled together like flocks, and the face on the cliff showed itself closer, and more nearly related to him, beneath its white stone veils. It had an expectant expression, motionless and yet on the brink of moving. Michelangelo thought carefully: 'You can't be split apart, you're a unity,' and then he raised his voice: 'I shall complete you, you are my work.' And he turned back to Florence. He saw

---

26. Pope Julius II (reigned 1503–1513).

Werk.‹ Und er wandte sich nach Florenz zurück. Er sah einen Stern und den Turm vom Dom. Und um seine Füße war Abend.

Mit einemmal, an der Porta Romana, zögerte er. Die beiden Häuserreihen streckten sich wie Arme nach ihm aus, und schon hatten sie ihn ergriffen und zogen ihn hinein in die Stadt. Und immer enger und dämmernder wurden die Gassen, und als er sein Haus betrat, da wußte er sich in dunkeln Händen, denen er nicht entgehen konnte. Er flüchtete in den Saal und von da in die niedere, kaum zwei Schritte lange Kammer, darin er zu schreiben pflegte. Ihre Wände legten sich an ihn, und es war, als kämpften sie mit seinen Übermaßen und zwängten ihn zurück in die alte, enge Gestalt. Und er duldete es. Er drückte sich in die Knie und ließ sich formen von ihnen. Er fühlte eine nie gekannte Demut in sich und hatte selbst den Wunsch, irgendwie klein zu sein. Und eine Stimme kam: ›Michelangelo, wer ist in dir?‹ Und der Mann in der schmalen Kammer legte die Stirn schwer in die Hände und sagte leise: ›Du mein Gott, wer denn sonst.‹

Und da wurde es weit um Gott, und er hob sein Gesicht, welches über Italien war, frei empor und schaute um sich: In Mänteln und Mitren standen die Heiligen da, und die Engel gingen mit ihren Gesängen wie mit Krügen voll glänzenden Quells unter den dürstenden Sternen umher, und es war der Himmel kein Ende.«

Mein lahmer Freund hob seine Blicke und duldete, daß die Abendwolken sie mitzogen über den Himmel hin: »Ist Gott denn *dort*?« fragte er. Ich schwieg. Dann neigte ich mich zu ihm: »Ewald,« sind wir denn *hier*?« Und wir hielten uns herzlich die Hände.

Wie der Fingerhut dazu kam, der liebe Gott zu sein

Als ich vom Fenster forttrat, waren die Abendwolken immer noch da. Sie schienen zu warten. Soll ich ihnen auch eine Geschichte erzählen? Ich schlug es ihnen vor. Aber sie hörten mich gar nicht. Um mich verständlich zu machen und die Entfernung zwischen uns zu beschränken, rief ich: »Ich bin auch eine Abendwolke.« Sie blieben stehen, offenbar betrachteten sie mich. Dann streckten sie mir ihre feinen, durchscheinenden rötlichen Flügel entgegen. Das ist die Art, wie Abendwolken sich begrüßen. Sie hatten mich erkannt.

»Wir sind über der Erde,« – erklärten sie – »genauer über Europa, und du?« Ich zögerte: »Es ist da ein Land—« »Wie sieht es aus?« erkundigten sie sich. »Nun,« entgegnete ich – »Dämmerung mit Dingen —« »Das ist Europa auch«, lachte eine junge Wolke.

a star and the campanile of the Duomo. And around his feet was evening.

"All at once, by the Porta Romana, he hesitated. The two rows of houses stretched out toward him like arms, already they had seized him and were drawing him into the city. And the streets became ever narrower and filled with twilight, and when he entered his house, he knew he was in dark hands which he couldn't escape. He fled into the main room and from there into the low-ceilinged room, barely two paces long, in which he used to write. Its walls closed in on him; and seemed to be struggling against his huge dimensions and forcing him back into his old, narrow shape. And he let it happen. He bent his knees and let them form him. He felt a never before known humility within him, and he himself had the wish to be small somehow. And a voice came: 'Michelangelo, who is in you?' And the man in the narrow room placed his heavy brow in his hands and said quietly: 'You, my Lord; who else?'

"And then there was room around God, and he lifted his face, which was over Italy, freely upward and looked around. The saints were standing there in robes and miters, and the angels were walking about among the thirsty stars with their songs, as if with jugs full of gleaming spring water, and there was no end of heavens."

My paralyzed friend raised his eyes and allowed the evening clouds to carry their gaze along across the sky. "Is God *there*, then?" he asked. I was silent. Then I leaned over to him: "Ewald, are we *here*, then?" And we joined hands cordially.

How the Thimble Came to Be the Good Lord

When I walked away from the window, the evening clouds were still there. They seemed to be waiting. Should I tell *them* a story, too? I suggested it to them. But they didn't hear me at all. In order to make myself understood and to decrease the distance between us, I shouted: "I'm an evening cloud, too!" They halted and were obviously looking at me. Then they extended their delicate, translucent, reddish wings toward me. That's the way evening clouds greet one another. They had recognized me.

"We're over the earth," they explained, "over Europe, to be exact. What about you?" I hesitated: "There's a land here—" "What does it look like?" they inquired. "Well," I replied, "twilight with objects . . ." "That's Europe, too," a young cloud said with a laugh. "Maybe," I

»Möglich,« sagte ich, »aber ich habe immer gehört: die Dinge in Europa sind tot.« »Ja, allerdings«, bemerkte eine andere verächtlich. »Was wäre das für ein Unsinn: lebende Dinge?« »Nun,« beharrte ich, »meine leben. Das ist also der Unterschied. Sie können verschiedenes werden, und ein Ding, welches als Bleistift oder als Ofen zur Welt kommt, muß deshalb noch nicht an seinem Fortkommen verzweifeln. Ein Bleistift kann mal ein Stock, wenn es gut geht, ein Mastbaum, ein Ofen aber mindestens ein Stadttor werden.«

»Du scheinst mir eine recht einfältige Abendwolke zu sein«, sagte die junge Wolke, welche sich schon früher so wenig zurückhaltend ausgedrückt hatte. Ein alter Wolkerich fürchtete, sie könnte mich beleidigt haben. »Es giebt ganz verschiedene Länder,« begütigte er, »ich war einmal über ein kleines deutsches Fürstentum geraten, und ich glaube bis heute nicht, daß das zu Europa gehörte.« Ich dankte ihm und sagte: »Wir werden uns schwer einigen können, sehe ich. Erlauben Sie, ich werde Ihnen einfach das erzählen, was ich in der letzten Zeit unter mir erblickte, das wird wohl das beste sein.« »Bitte«, gestattete der weise Wolkerich im Auftrage aller.

Ich begann: »Menschen sind in einer Stube. Ich bin ziemlich hoch, müßt ihr wissen, und so kommt es: sie sehen für mich wie Kinder aus; deshalb will ich auch einfach sagen: Kinder. Also: Kinder sind in einer Stube. Zwei, fünf, sechs, sieben Kinder. Es würde zu lange dauern, sie um ihre Namen zu fragen. Übrigens scheinen die Kinder eifrig etwas zu besprechen; bei dieser Gelegenheit wird sich ja der eine oder der andere Name verraten. Sie stehen wohl schon eine ganze Weile so beisammen, denn der älteste (ich vernehme, daß er Hans gerufen wird) bemerkt gleichsam abschließend: ›Nein, so kann es entschieden nicht bleiben. Ich habe gehört, früher haben die Eltern den Kindern am Abend immer, oder wenigstens an braven Abenden – Geschichten erzählt bis zum Einschlafen. Kommt so etwas heute vor?‹ Eine kleine Pause, dann antwortet Hans selbst: ›Es kommt nicht vor, nirgends. Ich für meinen Teil, auch weil ich schon groß bin gewissermaßen, schenke ihnen ja gern diese paar elenden Drachen, mit denen sie sich quälen würden, aber immerhin, es gehört sich, daß sie uns sagen, es giebt Nixen, Zwerge, Prinzen und Ungeheuer.‹ ›Ich habe eine Tante,‹ bemerkte eine Kleine, ›die erzählt mir manchmal –‹ ›Ach was,‹ schneidet Hans kurz ab, ›Tanten gelten nicht, *die* lügen.‹ Die ganze Gesellschaft war sehr eingeschüchtert angesichts dieser kühnen, aber unwiderlegten

said, "but I've always heard: objects in Europe are dead." "Yes, of course," another observed scornfully. "Wouldn't that be nonsense: living objects?" "Well," I persisted, "mine are alive. That's the difference, then. They can become various things, and an object that comes into the world as a pencil or a stove doesn't need to despair of progressing for that reason. A pencil can turn into a stick some day, into a mast if things go well, and a stove can become a city gate at the very least."

"You seem like a really simpleminded evening cloud to me," said the young cloud that had even earlier expressed itself with so little restraint. An old father-cloud[27] was afraid it might have insulted me. "There are all sorts of different lands," he said appeasingly; "once I found myself over a small German principality, which to this day I can't believe was a part of Europe." I thanked him and said: "I see that it will be hard for us to agree. Permit me to narrate to you briefly something I very recently caught sight of below me; that will probably be best." "Please do," said the father-cloud, giving me permission on behalf of all the rest.

I began: "There are people in a room. I am fairly high up, you must know, and so it happens that they look to me like children; therefore I'll simply call them children. So, then, there are children in a room. Two, five, six, seven children. It would take too long to ask them their names. Besides, the children seem to be having a lively discussion; on that occasion, one name or another will surely be revealed. They've probably been together that way for some time, because the oldest one (I hear him being called Hans) remarks, as if in conclusion: 'No, decidedly things can't remain like this. I've heard that, in the past, parents always told their children stories in the evening (or at least on evenings when they were well behaved) until they fell asleep. Do things like that happen today?' A short pause, then Hans answers his own question: 'They don't happen, not anywhere. For my part, also because I'm fairly grown up already, I gladly spare them that couple of miserable dragons, with which they'd torment themselves, but, all the same, it's only proper for them to tell us that mermaids, dwarfs, princes, and monsters exist.' 'I have an aunt,' a little girl remarked, 'who sometimes tells me—' 'Oh, come now,' Hans cuts her off curtly, 'aunts don't count; they tell lies.' The whole group was quite intimidated by that

---

27. In the German, the word *Wolkerich* is a humorous formation on the word *Wolke* ("cloud"), on the analogy of *Enterich* ("drake") formed from *Ente* ("duck"), for example.

Behauptung. Hans fährt fort: ›Auch handelt es sich hier vor allem um die
Eltern, weil diese gewissermaßen die Verpflichtung haben, uns in dieser
Weise zu unterrichten; bei den anderen ist es mehr Güte. Verlangen
kann man es nicht von ihnen. Aber gebt nur mal acht: was tun unsere
Eltern? Sie gehen mit bösen gekränkten Gesichtern umher, nichts ist
ihnen recht, sie schreien und schelten, aber dabei sind sie doch so
gleichgültig, und wenn die Welt unterginge, sie würden es kaum bemerken. Sie haben etwas, was sie ,Ideale' nennen. Vielleicht ist das auch
so eine Art kleine Kinder, die nicht allein bleiben dürfen und sehr viel
Mühe machen; aber dann hätten sie eben *uns* nicht haben dürfen. Nun,
ich denke so, Kinder: daß die Eltern uns vernachlässigen, ist traurig,
gewiß. Aber wir würden das dennoch ertragen, wenn es nicht ein Beweis
wäre dafür, daß die Großen überhaupt dumm werden, zurückgehen,
wenn man so sagen darf. Wir können ihren Verfall nicht aufhalten; denn
wir können den ganzen Tag keinen Einfluß auf sie ausüben, und kommen wir spät aus der Schule nach Haus, wird kein Mensch verlangen,
daß wir uns hinsetzen und versuchen, sie für etwas Vernünftiges zu
interessieren. Es tut einem auch recht weh, wenn man so unter der
Lampe sitzt und sitzt, und die Mutter begreift nicht einmal den
pythagoräischen Lehrsatz. Nun, es ist einmal nicht anders. So werden
die Großen immer dümmer werden . . . es schadet nichts: was kann uns
dabei verloren gehen? die Bildung? Sie ziehen den Hut vor einander,
und wenn eine Glatze dabei zum Vorschein kommt, so lachen sie. Überhaupt: sie lachen beständig. Wenn wir nicht dann und wann so vernünftig wären, zu weinen, es gäbe durchaus kein Gleichgewicht auch in
diesen Angelegenheiten. Dabei sind sie von einem Hochmut: sie behaupten sogar, der Kaiser sei ein Erwachsener. Ich habe in den Zeitungen gelesen, der König von Spanien sei ein Kind, so ist es mit allen
Königen und Kaisern, – laßt euch nur nichts einreden! Aber neben
allem Überflüssigen haben die Großen doch etwas, was uns durchaus
nicht gleichgültig sein kann: den lieben Gott. Ich habe ihn zwar noch bei
keinem von ihnen gesehen, – aber gerade das ist verdächtig. Es ist mir
eingefallen, sie könnten ihn in ihrer Zerstreutheit, Geschäftigkeit und
Hast irgendwo verloren haben. Nun ist er aber etwas durchaus
Notwendiges. Verschiedenes kann ohne ihn nicht geschehen, die Sonne
kann nicht aufgehen, keine Kinder können kommen, aber auch das Brot
wird aufhören. Wenn es auch beim Bäcker herauskommt, der liebe Gott
sitzt und dreht die großen Mühlen. Es lassen sich leicht viele Gründe
finden, weshalb der liebe Gott etwas Unentbehrliches ist. Aber soviel

bold but unrefuted assertion. Hans continues: 'Also, in this case it's especially a question of our parents, because they have the obligation, so to speak, to instruct us in that manner; with others, it's more a matter of kindness. It can't be demanded of them. But now pay attention: what do our parents do? They go around with angry, grieved faces, they find fault with everything, they yell and scold, but at the same time they're nevertheless so indifferent, and if the world came to an end, they'd hardly notice. They have something they call "ideals." Maybe that's also a sort of little children, who mustn't be left alone, and who give a lot of trouble; but in that case they shouldn't have had *us*. Now, this is what I think, children: that our parents neglect us is a sad thing, certainly. But we'd put up with it, all the same, if it weren't a proof that adults are stupid in general, they're becoming more backward, so to speak. We can't arrest their decline; because all through the day we can't exert any influence on them, and when we come home from school at a late hour, we can't be expected to sit down and try to interest them in something sensible. Also, it's extremely painful when you sit and sit that way under the lamp, and your mother can't even grasp the Pythagorean theorem. Well, that's the way it is. So grownups will get dumber all the time . . . there's no harm in it, what can *we* lose by it? Our upbringing? They take off their hats to one another, and when a bald head is revealed that way, they laugh. In fact, they're constantly laughing. If we weren't occasionally so sensible as to cry, there'd be no equilibrium at all in those matters, either. And, at the same time, they're so arrogant! They even claim that the Emperor is an adult. I've read in the papers that the king of Spain is a child,[28] and it's the same with all kings and emperors—don't let them tell you any different! But, alongside all superfluous things, adults still have something we can by no means remain indifferent to: the Good Lord. To be sure, I've never yet seen him with any of them—but that very fact makes me suspicious. It's occurred to me that, in their absent-mindedness, bustling around, and haste, they may have lost him somewhere. But he's something absolutely necessary. Various things can't happen without him, the sun can't rise, no children can be born, and bread would stop coming, too. Even if the baker still produces it, the Good Lord sits and turns the big mills. It's easy to find many reasons why the Good Lord is something indispensable. But this much is certain: adults don't care about him, so we children

28. The reign of Alfonso XIII began in 1902, when he was sixteen.

steht fest, die Großen kümmern sich nicht um ihn, also müssen wir
Kinder es tun. Hört, was ich mir ausgedacht habe. Wir sind genau sieben
Kinder. Jedes muß den lieben Gott einen Tag tragen, dann ist er die
ganze Woche bei uns, und man weiß immer, wo er sich gerade befindet.‹
    Hier entstand eine große Verlegenheit. Wie sollte das geschehen?
Konnte man denn den lieben Gott in die Hand nehmen oder in die
Tasche stecken? Dazu erzählte ein Kleiner: ›Ich war allein im Zimmer.
Eine kleine Lampe brannte nahe bei mir, und ich saß im Bett und
sagte mein Abendgebet – sehr laut. Es rührte sich etwas in meinen
gefalteten Händen. Es war weich und warm und wie ein kleines
Vögelchen. Ich konnte die Hände nicht auftun, denn das Gebet war
noch nicht aus. Aber ich war sehr neugierig und betete furchtbar
schnell. Dann beim Amen machte ich so (der Kleine streckte die
Hände aus und spreizte die Finger), aber es war nichts da.‹
    Das konnten sich alle vorstellen. Auch Hans wußte keinen Rat. Alle
schauten ihn an. Und auf einmal sagte er: ›Das ist ja dumm. Ein jedes
Ding kann der liebe Gott sein. Man muß es ihm nur sagen.‹ Er
wandte sich an den ihm zunächststehenden, rothaarigen Knaben. ›Ein
Tier kann das nicht. Es läuft davon. Aber ein Ding, siehst du, es steht,
du kommst in die Stube, bei Tag, bei Nacht: es ist immer da, es kann
wohl der liebe Gott sein.‹ Allmählich überzeugten sich die anderen
davon. ›Aber wir brauchen einen kleinen Gegenstand, den man überall mittragen kann, sonst hat es ja keinen Sinn. Leert einmal alle eure
Taschen aus.‹ Da zeigten sich nun sehr seltsame Dinge: Papier-
schnitzel, Federmesser, Radiergummi, Federn, Bindfaden, kleine
Steine, Schrauben, Pfeifen, Holzspänchen und vieles andere, was sich
aus der Ferne gar nicht erkennen läßt, oder wofür der Name mir
fehlt. Und alle diese Dinge lagen in den seichten Händen der Kinder,
wie erschrocken über die plötzliche Möglichkeit, der liebe Gott zu
werden, und welches von ihnen ein bißchen glänzen konnte, glänzte,
um dem Hans zu gefallen. Lange schwankte die Wahl. Endlich fand
sich bei der kleinen Resi ein Fingerhut, den sie ihrer Mutter einmal
weggenommen hatte. Er war licht, wie aus Silber, und um seiner
Schönheit willen wurde er der liebe Gott. Hans selbst steckte ihn ein,
denn er begann die Reihe, und alle Kinder gingen den ganzen Tag
hinter ihm her und waren stolz auf ihn. Nur schwer einigte man sich,
wer ihn morgen haben sollte, und Hans stellte in seiner Umsicht dann
das Programm gleich für die ganze Woche fest, damit kein Streit aus-
bräche.

have to. Listen to the plan I've devised. There are exactly seven of us children. Each one must carry the Good Lord for a day; that way he'll be with us all week long, and we'll always know where he is at any given moment.'

"This gave rise to a major confusion. How was that to be done? Could they take the Good Lord in their hands or put him in their pockets? On that subject, a young boy among them told this story: 'I was alone in the room. A small lamp was burning near me, and I was sitting in bed, saying my evening prayer—very loudly. Something moved inside my clasped hands. It was soft and warm and like a little bird. I couldn't open my hands because the prayer wasn't finished yet. But I was very curious, and I prayed terrifically fast. Then, at the "Amen," I did this' (the little boy held out his hands and spread out his fingers), 'but there was nothing there.'

"They were all able to picture that. Even Hans didn't know what to do. They were all looking at him. Then all at once he said: 'This is really stupid. Any object can be the Good Lord. It just has to be told so.' He turned to the redheaded boy standing nearest him. 'An animal can't do that. It runs away. But an object remains there, you see; you come into the room, by day, by night, and it's always there: it can surely be the Good Lord.' Gradually the others became persuaded of this. 'But we need a small object that we can carry around anywhere, or else it makes no sense. Empty all your pockets!' Now, very unusual things turned up that way: shreds of paper, penknives, erasers, feathers, string, pebbles, screws, whistles, chips of wood, and much more which either can't be made out from a distance or I don't know the name of. And all these things were lying in the children's shallow hands, as if alarmed at the sudden possibility of becoming the Good Lord, and any of them that could shine a little did so to please Hans. The choice was long in the making. Finally a thimble was found in little Resi's[29] possession, one she had once taken away from her mother. It was bright, as if made of silver, and for the sake of its beauty it became the Good Lord. Hans himself put it in his pocket, because he had the first turn, and all the children followed him around all day and were proud of him. It was agreed only with difficulty who was to have it the following day, and then, with his prudence, Hans established the program for the whole week right at the start, to avoid the outbreak of quarrels.

---

29. Short for Therese.

Diese Einrichtung erwies sich im ganzen als überaus zweck-
mäßig. Wer den lieben Gott gerade hatte, konnte man auf den ersten Blick erkennen. Denn der Betreffende ging etwas steifer und
feierlicher und machte ein Gesicht wie am Sonntag. Die ersten drei
Tage sprachen die Kinder von nichts anderem. Jeden Augenblick
verlangte eines den lieben Gott zu sehen, und wenn sich der
Fingerhut unter dem Einfluß seiner großen Würde auch garnicht
verändert hatte, das Fingerhutliche an ihm erschien jetzt nur als
ein bescheidenes Kleid um seine wirkliche Gestalt. Alles ging nach
der Ordnung vor sich. Am Mittwoch hatte ihn Paul, am Donnerstag
die kleine Anna. Der Samstag kam. Die Kinder spielten Fangen
und tollten atemlos durcheinander, als Hans plötzlich rief: ›Wer hat
denn den lieben Gott?‹ Alle standen. Jedes sah das andere an.
Keines erinnerte sich, ihn seit zwei Tagen gesehen zu haben. Hans
zählte ab, wer an der Reihe sei; es kam heraus: die kleine Marie.
Und nun verlangte man ohne weiteres von der kleinen Marie den
lieben Gott. Was war da zu tun? Die Kleine kratzte in ihren
Taschen herum. Jetzt fiel ihr erst ein, daß sie ihn am Morgen erhalten hatte; aber jetzt war er fort, wahrscheinlich hatte sie ihn hier
beim Spielen verloren.

Und als alle Kinder nach Hause gingen, blieb die Kleine auf der
Wiese zurück und suchte. Das Gras war ziemlich hoch. Zweimal
kamen Leute vorüber und fragten, ob sie etwas verloren hätte.
Jedesmal antwortete das Kind: ›Einen Fingerhut‹ – und suchte. Die
Leute taten eine Weile mit, wurden aber bald des Bückens müde,
und einer riet im Fortgehen: ›Geh lieber nach Haus, man kann ja
einen neuen kaufen.‹ Dennoch suchte Mariechen weiter. Die Wiese
wurde immer fremder in der Dämmerung, und das Gras begann naß
zu werden. Da kam wieder ein Mann. Er beugte sich über das Kind:
›Was suchst du?‹ Jetzt antwortete Mariechen, nicht weit vom
Weinen, aber tapfer und trotzig: ›Den lieben Gott.‹ Der Fremde
lächelte, nahm sie einfach bei der Hand, und sie ließ sich führen, als
ob jetzt alles gut wäre. Unterwegs sagte der fremde Manu: ›Und
sieh mal, was ich heute für einen schönen Fingerhut gefunden
habe.‹ –«

Die Abendwolken waren schon längst ungeduldig. Jetzt wandte
sich der weise Wolkerich, welcher indessen dick geworden war, zu
mir: »Verzeihen Sie, dürfte ich nicht den Namen des Landes – über
welchem Sie –« Aber die anderen Wolken liefen lachend in den
Himmel hinein und zogen den Alten mit.

"This arrangement turned out to be thoroughly workable, all in all. A single glance was enough to tell who happened to have the Good Lord on that particular day. Because the child in question walked around a bit more erect and more solemnly, and put on a Sunday face. For the first three days the children spoke of nothing else. Every minute one of them asked to see the Good Lord, and, even though the thimble hadn't changed a bit under the influence of its great dignity, its thimbleness now seemed like merely a modest covering of its true form. Everything happened in an orderly fashion. On Wednesday Paul had it; on Thursday, little Anna. Saturday came. The children were playing tag and crisscrossing one another wildly and breathlessly, when Hans suddenly called: 'Who's got the Good Lord?' They all stood still. Each one looked at the other. None of them remembered having seen him for two days. Hans calculated whose turn it was; it proved to be little Marie. And now, without further ado, little Marie was asked to produce the Good Lord. What could be done in that case? The little girl scratched around in her pockets. Only then did she recall having received him that morning; but now he was gone; she had probably lost him there during the game.

"And when all the children went home, the little girl remained behind in the meadow, searching. The grass was fairly tall. Twice people came by and asked if she had lost anything. Each time the child answered: 'A thimble,' and went on looking. The people joined her for a while, but soon grew tired of bending, and one man suggested as he left: 'You'd do better to go home; you know, a new one can be bought.' But little Marie kept on looking. The meadow became increasingly unfamiliar in the twilight, and the grass started to get damp. Then another man arrived. He stooped over the child: 'What are you looking for?' Now Marie replied, bravely and defiantly, though she was close to tears: 'The Good Lord.' The stranger smiled and simply took her by the hand; she allowed herself to be led as if everything had now been settled. As they walked, the stranger said: 'Just look here at this pretty thimble I found today.'"—

The evening clouds had been impatient for some time. Now the wise father-cloud, who had grown fat in the meantime, turned to me: "Excuse me, might I not inquire the name of the land—over which you—" But the other clouds raced into the sky with a laugh, pulling the old fellow along.

Ein Märchen vom Tod und eine fremde Nachschrift dazu

Ich schaute noch immer hinauf in den langsam verlöschenden Abendhimmel, als jemand sagte: »Sie scheinen sich ja für das Land da oben sehr zu interessieren?«

Mein Blick fiel schnell, wie heruntergeschossen, und ich erkannte: Ich war an die niedere Mauer unseres kleinen Kirchhofs geraten, und vor mir, jenseits derselben, stand der Mann mit dem Spaten und lächelte ernst. »*Ich* interessiere mich wieder für *dieses* Land hier«, ergänzte er und wies nach der schwarzen, feuchten Erde, welche an manchen Stellen hervorsah aus den vielen welken Blättern, die sich rauschend rührten, während ich nicht wußte, daß ein Wind begonnen hatte. Plötzlich sagte ich, von heftigem Abscheu erfaßt: »Warum tun Sie das da?« Der Totengräber lächelte immer noch: »Es ernährt einen auch – und dann, ich bitte Sie, tun nicht die meisten Menschen das gleiche? Sie begraben Gott *dort,* wie ich die Menschen hier.« Er zeigte nach dem Himmel und erklärte mir: »Ja, das ist auch ein großes Grab, im Sommer stehen wilde Vergißmeinnicht drauf –« Ich unterbrach ihn: »Es gab eine Zeit, wo die Menschen Gott im Himmel begruben, das ist wahr –« »Ist das anders geworden?« fragte er seltsam traurig. Ich fuhr fort: »Einmal warf jeder eine Hand Himmel über ihn, ich weiß. Aber da war er eigentlich schon nicht mehr dort, oder doch –« ich zögerte.

»Wissen Sie,« begann ich dann von neuem, »in alten Zeiten beteten die Menschen so.« Ich breitete die Arme aus und fühlte unwillkürlich meine Brust groß werden dabei. »Damals warf sich Gott in alle diese Abgründe voll Demut und Dunkelheit, und nur ungern kehrte er in seine Himmel zurück, die er, unvermerkt, immer näher über die Erde zog. Aber ein neuer Glaube begann. Da dieser den Menschen nicht verständlich machen konnte, worin sein neuer Gott sich von jenem alten unterscheide (sobald er ihn nämlich zu preisen begann, erkannten die Menschen sofort den einen alten Gott auch hier), so veränderte der Verkünder des neuen Gebotes die Art zu beten. Er lehrte das Händefalten und entschied: Seht, unser Gott will *so* gebeten sein, also ist er ein anderer als der, den ihr bisher in euren Armen glaubtet zu empfangen. Die Menschen sahen das ein, und die Gebärde der offenen Arme wurde eine verächtliche und schreckliche, und später heftete man sie ans Kreuz, um sie allen als ein Symbol der Not und des Todes zu zeigen.

Als Gott aber das nächste Mal wieder auf die Erde niederblickte, erschrak er. Neben den vielen gefalteten Händen hatte man viele gotische Kirchen gebaut, und so streckten sich ihm die Hände und die Dächer, gleich steil und scharf, wie feindliche Waffen entgegen. Bei

A Tale of Death, with a Postscript Written by Another

I was still looking up into the slowly fading evening sky when someone said: "You seem quite interested in the land up there?" My gaze fell rapidly, as if shot down, and I realized I had come to the low wall encircling our little churchyard; before me, on the other side of it, stood the man with the spade, smiling earnestly. "As for me, I'm interested in this land here," he went on, pointing to the black, moist earth visible in many places under the numerous withered leaves that stirred with a rustle, whereas I didn't know that a wind had sprung up. Suddenly, gripped by a violent revulsion, I said: "Why do you do that work?" The gravedigger, still smiling: "It's also a way of making a living—and, besides, I ask you, don't most people do the same? They bury God *there* as I bury people here." He pointed to the sky and explained: "Yes, that, too, is a vast grave; in summer there are wild forget-me-nots on it—" I interrupted him: "There was a time when people buried God in heaven, it's true—" "Are things any different?" he asked in unusual sorrow. I continued: "At one time everybody threw a handful of sky over him, I know. But by then he was really no longer there, or maybe he was—" I hesitated.

"You know," I then began afresh, "in olden days people used to pray like this." I opened my arms wide and felt my chest expand involuntarily as I did so. "In those days God used to cast himself into all those abysses filled with humility and shadow, and was reluctant to return to his heavens, which, without anyone noticing, he drew constantly closer to the earth. But a new religion arose. Since it was unable to make people understand in what way its new God differed from the old one (you see, as soon as it began to praise him, people immediately recognized the one old God here, too), the proclaimer of the new law changed the manner of praying. He taught people to clasp their hands, declaring: 'Behold, our God wants to be prayed to like this, and so he's not the same as the one you thought up to now you were receiving in your open arms.' The people grasped this, and the open-arm gesture became a despised and feared one, which was later nailed to the cross, to indicate to everyone that it was a symbol of distress and death.

"But the next time God looked down at the earth again, he was alarmed. Alongside all those clasped hands people had built many Gothic churches, and so the hands and the roofs, equally steep and sharp, were pointed at him like hostile weapons. With God there's a

Gott ist eine *andere* Tapferkeit. Er kehrte in seine Himmel zurück, und als er merkte, daß die Türme und die neuen Gebete hinter ihm her wuchsen, da ging er auf der anderen Seite aus seinen Himmeln hinaus und entzog sich so der Verfolgung. Er war selbst überrascht, jenseits von seiner strahlenden Heimat ein beginnendes Dunkel zu finden, das ihn schweigend empfing, und er ging mit einem seltsamen Gefühl immer weiter in dieser Dämmerung, welche ihn an die Herzen der Menschen erinnerte. Da fiel es ihm zuerst ein, daß die Köpfe der Menschen licht, ihre Herzen aber voll eines ähnlichen Dunkels sind, und eine Sehnsucht überkam ihn, in den Herzen der Menschen zu wohnen und nicht mehr durch das klare, kalte Wachsein ihrer Gedanken zu gehen. Nun, Gott hat seinen Weg fortgesetzt. Immer dichter wird um ihn die Dunkelheit, und die Nacht, durch die er sich drängt, hat etwas von der duftenden Wärme fruchtbarer Schollen. Und nicht lange mehr, so strecken sich ihm die Wurzeln entgegen mit der alten schönen Gebärde des breiten Gebetes. Es giebt nichts Weiseres als den Kreis. Der Gott, der uns in den Himmeln entfloh, aus der Erde wird er uns wiederkommen. Und, wer weiß, vielleicht graben gerade Sie einmal das Tor . . .« Der Mann mit dem Spaten sagte: »Aber das ist ein Märchen.« »In unserer Stimme«, erwiderte ich leise, »wird Alles Märchen, denn es kann sich ja in ihr nie begeben haben.« Der Mann schaute eine Weile vor sich hin. Dann zog er mit heftigen Bewegungen den Rock an und fragte: »Wir können ja wohl zusammengehen?« Ich nickte: »Ich gehe nach Hause. Es wird wohl derselbe Weg sein. Aber wohnen Sie nicht hier?« Er trat aus der kleinen Gittertür, legte sie sanft in ihre klagenden Angeln zurück und entgegnete: »Nein.«

Nach ein paar Schritten wurde er vertraulicher: »Sie haben ganz recht gehabt vorhin. Es ist seltsam, daß sich jemand findet, der das tun mag, das da draußen. Ich habe früher nie daran gedacht. Aber jetzt, seit ich älter werde, kommen mir manchmal Gedanken, eigentümliche Gedanken, wie der mit dem Himmel, und noch andere. Der Tod. Was weiß man davon? Scheinbar alles und vielleicht nichts. Oft stehen die Kinder (ich weiß nicht, wem sie gehören) um mich, wenn ich arbeite. Und mir fällt gerade so etwas ein. Dann grabe ich wie ein Tier, um alle meine Kraft aus dem Kopfe fortzuziehen und sie in den Armen zu verbrauchen. Das Grab wird viel tiefer als die Vorschrift verlangt, und ein Berg Erde wächst daneben auf. Die Kinder aber laufen davon, da sie meine wilden Bewegungen sehen. Sie glauben, daß ich irgendwie zornig bin.« Er dachte nach. »Und es ist ja auch eine Art Zorn. Man wird abgestumpft, man glaubt es überwunden zu haben, und plötzlich . . . Es hilft nichts, der Tod ist etwas Unbegreifliches, Schreckliches.«

different kind of bravery. He returned to his heavens, and when he observed the towers and the new prayers growing upward after him, he departed from his heavens on the other side, thus avoiding that persecution. He himself was surprised to find that, outside his radiant home, there was a nascent darkness that received him in silence, and with an odd feeling he went farther and farther into that twilight, which reminded him of human hearts. Only then did it occur to him that people's heads are bright, but their hearts full of a similar darkness; and a yearning came over him to dwell in the hearts of man and no longer to walk through the clear, cold wakefulness of their thoughts. Well, God continued his journey. The darkness around him grows denser and denser, and the night that he penetrates has something of the fragrant warmth of fertile sods. Before very long, the roots reach out to him with that former beautiful gesture of the open-armed prayer. There's nothing wiser than a circle. The God who escaped us in the heavens will return to us from the earth. And, who knows? Perhaps you are digging the gateway right now. . . ." The man with the spade said: "But that's a fairy tale." "In our voice," I replied softly, "everything becomes a fairy tale, because it can never have taken place there." The man gazed ahead for a while. Then with violent gestures he put on his jacket and asked: "May we walk together?" I nodded: "I'm going home. Our path is probably the same. But don't you live here?" He stepped out of the little barred door, replaced it on its lamenting hinges, and replied: "No."

After a few paces he became more confiding: "What you said before was quite correct. It's strange to find someone willing to do that work back there. Previously I never thought about it. But now that I'm getting older, I sometimes have thoughts, peculiar thoughts, like the one about the sky, and others besides. Death. What do we know about it? Apparently everything, but maybe nothing. Often children stand around me (I don't know whose they are) when I work. And something like that occurs to me. Then I dig like an animal, in order to withdraw all my strength from my head and use it up in my arms. The grave gets much deeper than the regulations require, and a mountain of earth rises beside it. But the children run away when they see my frenzied activity. They think I'm somehow angry." He thought about it. "And it is indeed a sort of anger. You become apathetic, you think you've gotten over it, and suddenly . . . Nothing helps, death is something incomprehensible, terrifying."

Wir gingen eine lange Straße unter schon ganz blätterlosen Obst-
bäumen, und der Wald begann, uns zur Linken, wie eine Nacht, die
jeden Augenblick auch über uns hereinbrechen kann. »Ich will Ihnen
eine kleine Geschichte berichten,« versuchte ich, »sie reicht gerade
bis an den Ort.« Der Mann nickte und zündete sich seine kurze, alte
Pfeife an. Ich erzählte:

»Es waren zwei Menschen, ein Mann und ein Weib, und sie hatten
einander lieb. Liebhaben, das heißt, nichts annehmen, von nirgends,
alles vergessen und von *einem* Menschen alles empfangen wollen, das
was man schon besaß und alles andere. So wünschten es die beiden
Menschen gegenseitig. Aber in der Zeit, im Tage, unter den Vielen,
wo alles kommt und geht, oft ehe man eine wirkliche Beziehung dazu
gewinnt, läßt sich ein solches Liebhaben gar nicht durchführen, die
Ereignisse kommen von allen Seiten, und der Zufall öffnet ihnen jede
Tür.

Deshalb beschlossen die beiden Menschen aus der Zeit in die
Einsamkeit zu gehen, weit fort vom Uhrenschlagen und von den
Geräuschen der Stadt. Und dort erbauten sie sich in einem Garten ein
Haus. Und das Haus hatte zwei Tore, eines an seiner rechten, eines an
seiner linken Seite. Und das rechte Tor war des Mannes Tor, und alles
Seine sollte durch dasselbe in das Haus einziehen. Das linke aber war
das Tor des Weibes, und was ihres Sinnes war, sollte durch seinen Bogen
eintreten. So geschah es. Wer zuerst erwachte am Morgen, stieg hinab
und tat sein Tor auf. Und da kam dann bis spät in die Nacht gar manches
herein, wenn auch das Haus nicht am Rande des Weges lag. Zu denen,
die zu empfangen verstehen, kommt die Landschaft ins Haus und das
Licht und ein Wind mit einem Duft auf den Schultern und viel anderes
mehr. Aber auch Vergangenheiten, Gestalten, Schicksale traten durch
die beiden Tore ein, und allen wurde die gleiche, schlichte Gastlichkeit
zuteil, so daß sie meinten, seit immer in dem Heidehaus gewohnt zu
haben. So ging es eine lange Zeit fort, und die beiden Menschen waren
sehr glücklich dabei. Das linke Tor war etwas häufiger geöffnet, aber
durch das rechte traten buntere Gäste ein. Vor diesem wartete auch
eines Morgens – der Tod. Der Mann schlug seine Tür eilends zu, als er
ihn bemerkte, und hielt sie den ganzen Tag über fest verschlossen. Nach
einiger Zeit tauchte der Tod vor dem linken Eingang auf. Zitternd warf
das Weib das Tor zu und schob den breiten Riegel vor. Sie sprachen
nicht miteinander über dieses Ereignis, aber sie öffneten seltener die
beiden Tore und suchten mit dem auszukommen, was im Hause war. Da
lebten sie nun freilich viel ärmlicher als vorher. Ihre Vorräte wurden
knapp, und es stellten sich Sorgen ein. Sie begannen beide schlecht zu

We walked down a long road under fruit trees that were already completely leafless, and the forest began on our left, like a night that could close over us, too, at any moment. "I'd like to tell you a little story," I said tentatively, "it will last exactly the time it takes us to reach the village." The man nodded and lighted his old short pipe. I narrated:

"There were two people, a man and a woman, who loved each other. To love means not to accept anything from anywhere else, to forget everything and to be willing to receive all things from one person, what you already possessed and all the rest. That was the mutual desire of those two people. But in the course of time, in that day among many on which everything comes and goes, often before you have acquired a true relationship with it, such a love is not allowed to be completed; events come from all sides, and chance opens every door to them.

"Therefore the two people resolved to leave time and enter solitude, very far from the striking of clocks and the noises of the city. And there they built themselves a house in a garden. And the house had two doors, one on its right side, one on its left. And the righthand door was the man's door, and all that was his was to enter the house through it. But the lefthand door was the woman's, and whatever was congenial to her was to come in under its archway. And so it befell. The one who got up first in the morning went downstairs and opened his door. And then, until late at night, many, many things came in, even though the house wasn't on the roadside. For those who know how to receive, the landscape comes into the house, and the light, and a breeze with fragrance on its shoulders, and many things more. But also past events, forms, destinies entered into the two doors, and all received the same simple hospitality, so that they felt they had always been living in that house on the heath. Things went on that way for some time, and the two people were very happy. The lefthand door was opened somewhat more frequently, but more colorful guests arrived through the one on the right. And one morning, in front of it, was waiting—Death. The man slammed his door swiftly when he beheld it, and kept it tightly locked all day long. After a while Death appeared in front of the lefthand entrance. Tremblingly the woman shut the door and shot the heavy bolt to keep it closed. They didn't discuss that event with each other, but they opened the two doors more seldom and tried to make do with what was in the house. Now, to be sure, they were living in poorer conditions than before. Their provisions became short, and worries made their ap-

schlafen, und in einer solchen wachen, langen Nacht vernahmen sie
plötzlich zugleich ein seltsames, schlürfendes und pochendes Geräusch.
Es war hinter der Wand des Hauses, gleich weit entfernt von den beiden Toren, und klang, als ob jemand begänne Steine auszubrechen, um
ein neues Tor mitten in die Mauer zu bauen. Die beiden Menschen
taten in ihrem Schrecken dennoch, als ob sie nichts Besonderes vernäh-
men. Sie begannen zu sprechen, lachten unnatürlich laut, und als sie
müde wurden, war das Wühlen in der Wand verstummt. Seither bleiben
die beiden Tore ganz geschlossen. Die Menschen leben wie Gefangene.
Beide sind kränklich geworden und haben seltsame Einbildungen. Das
Geräusch wiederholt sich von Zeit zu Zeit. Dann lachen sie mit ihren
Lippen, während ihre Herzen fast sterben vor Angst. Und sie wissen
beide, daß das Graben immer lauter und deutlicher wird, und müssen
immer lauter sprechen und lachen mit ihren immer matteren
Stimmen.«

Ich schwieg. »Ja, ja, –« sagte der Mann neben mir, »so ist es, das ist
eine wahre Geschichte.«

»Diese habe ich in einem alten Buche gelesen,« fügte ich hinzu, »und
da ereignete sich etwas sehr Merkwürdiges dabei. Hinter der Zeile,
darin erzählt wird, wie der Tod auch vor dem Tore des Weibes erschien,
war mit alter, verwelkter Tinte ein kleines Sternchen gezeichnet. Es sah
aus den Worten wie aus Wolken hervor, und ich dachte einen
Augenblick, wenn die Zeilen sich verzögen, so könnte offenbar werden,
daß hinter ihnen lauter Sterne stehen, wie es ja wohl manchmal
geschieht, wenn der Frühlingshimmel sich spät am Abend klärt. Dann
vergaß ich des unbedeutenden Umstandes ganz, bis ich hinten im
Einband des Buches dasselbe Sternchen, wie gespiegelt in einem See,
in dem glatten Glanzpapier wiederfand, und nah unter demselben begannen zarte Zeilen, die wie Wellen in der blassen spiegelnden Fläche
verliefen. Die Schrift war an vielen Stellen undeutlich geworden, aber
es gelang mir doch, sie fast ganz zu entziffern. Da stand etwa:

›Ich habe diese Geschichte so oft gelesen, und zwar in allen möglichen
Tagen, daß ich manchmal glaube, ich habe sie selbst, aus der Erinnerung,
aufgezeichnet. Aber bei mir geht es im weiteren Verlaufe so zu, wie ich
es hier niederschreibe. Das Weib hatte den Tod nie gesehen; arglos ließ
es ihn eintreten. Der Tod aber sagte etwas hastig und wie einer, welcher
kein gutes Gewissen hat: ,Gieb das deinem Mann.‘ Und er fügte, als das
Weib ihn fragend anblickte, eilig hinzu: ,Es ist Samen, sehr guter Samen.‘
Dann entfernte er sich ohne zurückzusehen. Das Weib öffnete das
Säckchen, welches er ihr in die Hand gelegt hatte; es fand sich wirklich
eine Art Samen darin, harte, häßliche Körner. Da dachte das Weib: der

pearance. They both began to sleep badly, and on one such long, sleepless night they suddenly heard at the same time a strange noise of slurping and knocking. It was behind the wall of the house, equidistant from the two doors, and sounded as if someone were starting to jimmy out stones in order to build a new doorway in the center of the wall. The two people were frightened, but acted as if they didn't hear anything special. They began to speak, laughed unnaturally loudly, and, when they were tired, the burrowing in the wall was no longer audible. From that time on, the two doors have remained locked. The people live like prisoners. Both have become sickly and have strange hallucinations. The noise returns every so often. Then they laugh with their lips while their hearts are nearly dead with fear. And they both know that the digging is getting louder and more distinct all the time, and they have to speak louder and louder, and laugh with their increasingly duller voices."

I fell silent. "Yes, yes," said the man beside me, "that's how it is, that's a true story."

"I read it in an old book," I added, "and then something very peculiar happened. At the end of the line that told of how Death appeared before the woman's door, as well, a little asterisk had been drawn in in old, faded ink. It looked out from among the words as if out of clouds, and for a moment I thought that, if the lines shifted away, it might become obvious that nothing but stars were behind them, as sometimes does indeed happen when the springtime sky clears up late in the evening. Then I completely forgot about that insignificant circumstance, until, in the binding in back of the book, I rediscovered the same asterisk on the smooth glossy paper, as if reflected in a lake, and close under it began delicate lines of writing, which ran like waves over the pale reflective surface. The hand had become indistinct in many places, but I still managed to make out almost all of it. It read more or less.

"'I've read this story so often, and on all possible days, that I sometimes think I wrote it down myself from my own recollections. But in my case the rest of the plot is as I now set it down. The woman had never seen Death; in her unsuspecting innocence, she let it enter. But Death said, somewhat hastily, like a man with a bad conscience: "Give this to your husband." And when the woman looked at Death questioningly, it hastened to add: "It's seed, very good seed." Then it departed without looking back. The woman opened the little sack that it had placed in her hands. True, a kind of seed was in it, hard, ugly grains. Then the woman thought: "This seed is something unfinished,

Same ist etwas Unfertiges, Zukünftiges. Man kann nicht wissen, was aus ihm wird. Ich will diese unschönen Körner nicht meinem Manne geben, sie sehen gar nicht aus wie ein Geschenk. Ich will sie lieber in das Beet unseres Gartens drücken und warten, was sich aus ihnen erhebt. Dann will ich ihn davorführen und ihm erzählen, wie ich zu dieser Pflanze kam. Also tat das Weib auch. Dann lebten sie dasselbe Leben weiter. Der Mann, der immer daran denken mußte, daß der Tod vor seinem Tore gestanden hatte, war anfangs etwas ängstlich, aber da er das Weib so gastlich und sorglos sah wie immer, tat auch er bald wieder die breiten Flügel seines Tores auf, so daß viel Leben und Licht in das Haus hereinkam. Im nächsten Frühjahr stand mitten im Beete zwischen den schlanken Feuerlilien ein kleiner Strauch. Er hatte schmale, schwärzliche Blätter, etwas spitz, ähnlich denen des Lorbeers, und es lag ein sonderbarer Glanz auf ihrer Dunkelheit. Der Mann nahm sich täglich vor, zu fragen, woher diese Pflanze stamme. Aber er unterließ es täglich. In einem verwandten Gefühl veschwieg auch das Weib von einem Tag zum andern die Aufklärung. Aber die unterdrückte Frage auf der einen, die niegewagte Antwort auf der anderen Seite, führte die beiden Menschen oft bei diesem Strauch zusammen, der sich in seiner grünen Dunkelheit so seltsam von dem Garten unterschied. Als das nächste Frühjahr kam, da beschäftigten sie sich, wie mit den anderen Gewächsen, auch mit dem Strauch, und sie wurden traurig, als er, umringt von lauter steigenden Blüten, unverändert und stumm, wie im ersten Jahr, gegen alle Sonne taub, sich erhob. Damals beschlossen sie, ohne es einander zu verraten, gerade *diesem* im dritten Frühjahr ihre ganze Kraft zu widmen, und als dieses Frühjahr erschien, erfüllten sie leise und Hand in Hand, was sich jeder versprochen hatte. Der Garten umher verwilderte, und die Feuerlilien schienen blasser als sonst zu sein. Aber einmal, als sie nach einer schweren, bedeckten Nacht in den Morgengarten, den stillen, schimmernden traten, da wußten sie: Aus den schwarzen, scharfen Blättern des fremden Strauches war unversehrt eine blasse, blaue Blüte gestiegen, welcher die Knospenschalen schon an allen Seiten enge wurden. Und sie standen davor vereint und schweigend, und jetzt wußten sie sich erst recht nichts zu sagen. Denn sie dachten: Nun blüht der Tod, und neigten sich zugleich, um den Duft der jungen Blüte zu kosten. – Seit diesem Morgen aber ist alles anders geworden in der Welt.‹ So stand es in dem Einband des alten Buches«, schloß ich.

»Und wer das geschrieben hat?« drängte der Mann.

»Eine Frau, nach der Schrift«, antwortete ich. »Aber was hätte es geholfen, nachzuforschen. Die Buchstaben waren sehr verblaßt und etwas altmodisch. Wahrscheinlich war sie schon längst tot.«

for the future. No one can tell what it will turn into. I won't give these unlovely grains to my husband, they don't look like a gift. Instead I'll press them into the flowerbed in our garden, and wait and see what will sprout from them. Then I'll lead him over to it and tell him how I acquired that plant." And so the woman did. Then they continued living the same life. The man, who was unable to stop recalling that Death had stood outside his gate, was somewhat nervous at first, but, seeing his wife as hospitable and carefree as ever, he, too, soon opened the broad wings of his door again, so that much light and life entered the house. The following spring, in the center of the flowerbed, between the slender orange lilies, stood a small bush. It had narrow, blackish leaves, somewhat pointed, like those of the laurel, and an odd glow lay on their darkness. Every day the man resolved to ask where that plant had come from. But every day he failed to do so. Feeling a similar way, the woman, too, failed to enlighten him from one day to the next. But the repressed question on one side, and the never-ventured reply on the other, often brought the two people together at that bush, which differed so oddly from the rest of the garden in its green darkness. When the following spring arrived, they busied themselves with that bush, as with the other plants, and became sad when, encircled by nothing but flowers growing tall, it stood as unchanged and mute as in the first year, unresponsive to all the sunshine. Then they decided, without revealing it to each other, to devote all their strength during the third spring to precisely this plant; and when that spring came, quietly and hand in hand, each of them kept the promise he had made himself. The garden all around went to seed, and the orange lilies seemed paler than usual. But once, after a heavy, overcast night, when they entered the garden in the morning, the silent, glimmering garden, they knew: from the black, sharp leaves of the strange bush there had emerged unscathed a pale blue blossom whose bud scales were already too tight for it all around. And they stood before it united in silence, and now they really had nothing to say to each other. Because they were thinking: "Now Death is blooming," and they bent over at the same time to enjoy the fragrance of the young blossom.—But ever since that morning everything in the world has changed.' That's what was written in the binding of the old book," I said in conclusion.

"And who wrote it?" the man urged.

"A woman, to judge by the writing," I replied. "But what good would it have done to pursue the matter? The letters were very faded and a little old-fashioned. Probably she was already long dead."

Der Mann war ganz in Gedanken. Endlich bekannte er: »Nur eine Geschichte, und doch rührt es einen so an.« »Nun, das ist, wenn man selten Geschichten hört«, begütigte ich. »Meinen Sie?« Er reichte mir seine Hand, und ich hielt sie fest. »Aber ich möchte sie gerne weitersagen. Das darf man doch?« Ich nickte. Plötzlich fiel ihm ein: »Aber ich habe niemanden. Wem sollte ich sie auch erzählen?« »Nun, das ist einfach; den Kindern, die Ihnen manchmal zusehen kommen. Wem sonst?«

Die Kinder haben auch richtig die letzten drei Geschichten gehört. Allerdings, die von den Abendwolken wiederholte, nur teilweise, wenn ich gut unterrichtet bin. Die Kinder sind ja klein und darum von den Abendwolken viel weiter als wir. Doch das ist bei *dieser* Geschichte ganz gut. Trotz der langen, wohlgesetzten Rede des Hans, würden sie erkennen, daß die Sache unter Kindern spielt, und meine Erzählung kritisch, als Sachverständige, betrachten. Aber es ist besser, daß sie nicht erfahren, mit welcher Anstrengung und wie ungeschickt wir die Dinge erleben, die ihnen so ganz mühelos und einfach geschehen.

Ein Verein, aus einem dringenden Bedürfnis heraus

Ich erfahre erst, daß unser Ort auch eine Art Künstlerverein besitzt. Er ist kürzlich aus einem, wie man sich leicht vorstellen kann, sehr dringenden Bedürfnis entstanden, und es geht das Gerücht, daß er »blüht«. Wenn Vereine gar nicht wissen, was sie anfangen sollen, dann blühen sie; sie haben gehört, daß man dies tun muß, um ein richtiger Verein zu sein.

Ich muß nicht sagen, daß Herr Baum Ehrenmitglied, Gründer, Fahnenvater und alles übrige in einer Person ist und Mühe hat, die verschiedenen Würden auseinanderzuhalten. Er sandte mir einen jungen Mann, der mich einladen sollte, an den »Abenden« teilzunehmen. Ich dankte ihm, wie es sich von selbst versteht, sehr höflich und fügte hinzu, daß meine ganze Tätigkeit seit etwa fünf Jahren im Gegenteil bestehe. »Es vergeht, stellen Sie sich vor,« erklärte ich ihm mit dem entsprechenden Ernst, »seit dieser Zeit keine Minute, in welcher ich nicht aus irgend einem Verbande austrete, und doch giebt es noch immer Gesellschaften, welche mich sozusagen enthalten.« Der junge Mann schaute erst erschreckt, dann mit dem Ausdruck respektvollen Bedauerns auf meine Füße. Er mußte ihnen das »Austreten« ansehen, denn er nickte ver-

The man was lost in thought. Finally he admitted: "Only a story, and yet it's so touching." "Well, that's what happens when you don't hear stories often," I said appeasingly. "You think so?" He gave me his hand, which I took firmly. "But I'd like to tell it in my turn. May I?" I nodded. Suddenly it occurred to him: "But I have nobody. To whom shall I tell it?" "Well that's easy: to the children who sometimes come and watch you. To whom else?"

And, indeed, the children have heard the last three stories. To be sure, the one repeated by the evening clouds they heard only in part, if I'm well informed. You see, the children are small and thus much farther away from the evening clouds than we are. But in the case of that story, it's all to the good. In spite of Hans's long, well-expressed speech, they'd recognize that the plot takes place among children, and would study my narrative critically, like experts. But it's better that they don't find out under what strain, and how awkwardly, we experience the things that befall them so effortlessly and naturally.

A Club That Answered a Crying Need

I have just learned that our village also possesses a sort of artists' club. It arose recently from a very urgent need, as is readily understandable, and word is that it's "flourishing." When clubs have no idea what to do with themselves, they flourish; they've heard that they've got to do so if they want to be a real club.

I need not say that Mr. Baum is an honorary member, a founder, the sponsor of the club banner, and everything else all in one, and that he has trouble keeping his various capacities apart. He sent me a young man to invite me to attend their "evenings." I thanked him, as is quite understandable, very politely, adding that for five years I had been busy doing exactly the opposite. "Just imagine," I explained to him with the appropriate gravity, "not a minute has gone by since then in which I haven't walked out[30] of some club or other, and yet there are still societies which include me, so to speak." The young man, at first in alarm, then with an expression of respectful compassion, looked at my feet. He must have seen their tendency to "walk out," because he nodded his head comprehendingly. I

---

30. "Resigned" would be a more normal translation, except for the word play that follows shortly.

ständig mit dem Kopfe. Das gefiel mir gut, und da ich gerade fortgehen mußte, schlug ich ihm vor, mich ein Stückchen zu begleiten. So gingen wir durch den Ort und darüber hinaus, dem Bahnhof zu, denn ich hatte in der Umgebung zu tun. Wir sprachen über mancherlei Dinge; ich erfuhr, daß der junge Mann Musiker sei. Er hatte es mir bescheiden mitgeteilt, ansehen konnte man es ihm nicht. Außer seinen zahlreichen Haaren zeichnete ihn eine große, gleichsam springende Bereitwilligkeit aus. Auf diesem nicht allzulangen Weg hob er mir zwei Handschuhe auf, hielt mir den Schirm, als ich etwas in meinen Taschen suchte, machte mich errötend darauf aufmerksam, daß mir etwas im Barte hinge, daß mir Ruß auf der Nase säße, und dabei wurden ihm die mageren Finger lang, als sehnten sie sich danach, sich meinem Gesichte auf diese Weise hilfreich zu nähern. In seinem Eifer blieb der junge Mensch sogar bisweilen zurück und holte mit sichtlichem Vergnügen die welken Blätter, die im Herabflattern hängen geblieben waren, aus den Ästen der Sträucher. Ich sah ein, daß ich durch diese beständigen Verzögerungen den Zug versäumen würde (der Bahnhof war noch ziemlich weit), und entschloß mich, meinem Begleiter eine Geschichte zu erzählen, um ihn ein wenig an meiner Seite zu halten.

Ich begann ohne weiters: »Mir ist der Verlauf einer derartigen Gründung bekannt, welche auf wirklicher Notwendigkeit beruhte. Sie werden sehen. Es ist nicht sehr lange her, da fanden sich drei Maler durch Zufall in einer alten Stadt zusammen. Die drei Maler sprachen natürlich *nicht* von Kunst. Es schien wenigstens so. Sie verbrachten den Abend in der Hinterstube eines alten Gasthauses damit, sich Reiseabenteuer und Erlebnisse verschiedener Art mitzuteilen, ihre Geschichten wurden immer kürzer und wörtlicher, und endlich blieben noch ein paar Witze übrig, mit denen sie beständig hin und her warfen. Um jedem Mißverständnis vorzubeugen, muß ich übrigens gleich sagen, daß es wirkliche Künstler waren, gewissermaßen von der Natur beabsichtigte, keine zufälligen. Dieser öde Abend in der Hinterstube kann nichts daran ändern; man wird ja auch gleich erfahren, wie er weiter verlief. Es traten andere Leute, profane, in dieses Gasthaus ein, die Maler fühlten sich gestört und brachen auf. Mit dem Augenblick, da sie aus dem Tor traten, waren sie andere Leute. Sie gingen in der Mitte der Gasse, einer vom anderen etwas getrennt. Auf ihren Gesichtern waren noch die Spuren des Lachens, diese merkwürdige Unordnung der Züge, aber die Augen waren bei allen schon ernst und betrachtend. Plötzlich stieß der in der Mitte den Rechten an. Der verstand ihn sofort. Da war vor ihnen eine Gasse, schmal, von feiner, warmer Dämmerung erfüllt. Sie stieg etwas an, so daß sie perspektivisch sehr zur Geltung

liked that very much, and, since I had to go away just then, I suggested that he accompany me a little way. And so we walked
through the village and past it, toward the train station, because I
had business in the vicinity. We spoke about all sorts of things; I
learned that the young man was a musician. He had informed me
of it modestly; you couldn't tell it by looking at him. Besides his
abundant hair, he was characterized by an immense, almost aggres-
sive obligingness. During that not overlong walk, he picked up two
of my gloves, held my umbrella when I was looking for something
in my pockets, and blushingly called my attention to something
stuck in my beard and to soot on my nose, while his skinny fingers
extended as if longing to draw near my face that way in order to as-
sist me. In his eagerness the young man sometimes even hung back
and, with visible pleasure, extracted the withered leaves from the
branches of the bushes in which they had gotten caught when fluttering down. I realized that those constant delays would make me
miss my train (the station was still rather far away), and I determined to tell my accompanier a story in order to keep him alongside me for a while.

Without preamble I began: "I know the whole course of an organization of that sort, which responded to a true need. You'll see. Not
long ago, three painters accidentally met in an old city. Naturally the
three painters did *not* discuss art. At least it seemed so. They spent
the evening in the back room of an old tavern telling each other travel
adventures and experiences of various sorts; their stories became
more and more brief and literal, and finally all that was left was a few
jokes which they constantly tossed back and forth. To preclude any
misunderstanding, incidentally, I must state at once that they were
real artists, so intended by nature, so to speak, and not accidental
ones. That dreary evening in the back room can't alter that fact; indeed, you'll soon hear what happened later on. Other people,
nonartists, entered that tavern; the painters felt that they were being
intruded on, and they left. The moment they stepped out the door,
they were different people. They walked in the middle of the street,
at a little distance from one another. Their faces still bore the traces
of laughter, that peculiar disarrangement of the features, but the eyes
of each one were already serious and observant. Suddenly the one in
the middle poked the one on the right. The latter understood him at
once. There before them was a narrow lane filled with a subtle, warm
half-light. It led upward at a slight angle, so that it was very effective
from the point of view of perspective, and it had an unusually myste-

kam, und hatte etwas ungemein Geheimnisvolles und doch wieder
Vertrautes. Die drei Maler ließen das einen Augenblick auf sich wirken.
Sie sprachen nichts, denn sie wußten: *sagen* kann man das nicht. Sie
waren ja deshalb Maler geworden, weil es manches giebt, was man
nicht sagen kann. Plötzlich erhob sich der Mond irgendwo, zeichnete
den einen Giebel silbern nach, und es stieg ein Lied aus einem Hofe
auf. ›Grobe Effekthascherei —‹, brummte der Mittlere, und sie gingen
weiter. Sie schritten jetzt etwas näher nebeneinander hin, obwohl sie
immer noch die ganze Breite der Gasse brauchten. So gerieten sie unversehens auf einen Platz. Jetzt war es der rechts, welcher die anderen
aufmerksam machte. In dieser breiteren, freieren Szene hatte der
Mond nichts Störendes, im Gegenteil, es war geradezu notwendig, daß
er vorhanden war. Er ließ den Platz größer erscheinen, gab den
Häusern ein überraschendes, lauschendes Leben, und die beleuchtete
Fläche des Pflasters wurde mitten rücksichtslos von einem Brunnen
und seinem schweren Schlagschatten unterbrochen, eine Kühnheit,
welche den Malern ausnehmend imponierte. Sie stellten sich nahe
suzammen und saugten sozusagen an den Brüsten dieser Stimmung.
Aber sie wurden unangenehm unterbrochen. Eilige, leichte Schritte
näherten sich, aus dem Dunkel des Brunnens löste sich eine männliche
Gestalt, empfing jene Schritte, und was sonst zu ihnen gehörte, mit der
üblichen Zärtlichkeit, und der schöne Platz war auf einmal eine er-
bärmliche Illustration geworden, von welcher sich die drei Maler wie
ein Maler abwandten. ›Da ist schon wieder dieses verdammte novellis-
tische Element‹, schrie der rechts, indem er das Liebespaar am
Brunnen mit diesem korrekt technischen Ausdruck begriff. Vereint in
ihrem Groll, wanderten die Maler noch lange planlos in der Stadt
herum, immerfort Motive entdeckend, aber auch jedesmal aufs neue
empört durch die Art, mit welcher irgend ein banaler Umstand die
Stille und Einfachheit jedes Bildes zu nichte machte. Gegen Mitter-
nacht saßen sie im Gasthof, in der Wohnstube des Linken, des Jüngsten, beisammen und dachten nicht ans Schlafengehen. Die nächtliche
Wanderung hatte eine Menge Pläne und Entwürfe in ihnen wach-
gerufen und, da sie zugleich bewiesen hatte, daß sie *eines* Geistes seien
im Grunde, tauschten sie jetzt, im höchsten Maße interessiert, ihre
gegenseitigen Ansichten aus. Man kann nicht behaupten, daß sie tadel-
lose Sätze hervorbrachten, sie schlugen mit ein paar Worten herum, die
kein profaner Mensch begriffen hätte, aber untereinander ver-
ständigten sie sich dadurch so gut, daß sämtliche Zimmernachbarn bis
gegen vier Uhr morgens nicht einschlafen konnten. Das lange
Beisammensitzen hatte aber einen wirklichen, sichtbaren Erfolg. Etwas

rious quality but, at the same time, something familiar about it. The three painters let that operate on them for a moment. They didn't speak because they knew it couldn't be rendered in *words*. They had become painters for the very reason that many things exist which can't be described verbally. Suddenly the moon rose somewhere, tracing the outline of one gable in silver, and a song came from a courtyard. 'Vulgar striving for effect!' the one in the middle grumbled, and they proceeded on. Now they were walking a bit closer to one another, though they were still occupying the full width of the street. In that way they arrived unexpectedly at a square. Now it was the man on the right who called the attention of the others to the view. In this more extensive and open scene the moon had nothing intrusive about it; on the contrary, it was actually necessary for it to be present. It made the square appear larger, it lent the houses a surprising sense of life, as if they were listening, and the illuminated surface of the pavement was ruthlessly interrupted in the center by a fountain and its heavy shadow, a bold stroke that impressed the painters no end. They came close together and, as it were, suckled at the breasts of that atmospheric mood. But they were unpleasantly interrupted. Light, hasty steps approached; from the shadow of the fountain a male figure detached itself, welcomed those steps, and all that went with them, with the customary tenderness; and the beautiful square had suddenly become some pathetic illustration, from which the three painters turned away as one painter. 'There's that damned novelettish element again!' cried the man on the right, designating the pair of lovers at the fountain by that correctly technical expression. United in their vexation, the painters still roamed through the city aimlessly for some time, constantly discovering subjects for pictures, but infuriated each time by the way some banal circumstance destroyed the silence and simplicity of every image. Toward midnight they were sitting together in the hotel, in the parlor of the one on the left, the youngest, and had no thoughts of going to sleep. Their nocturnal jaunt had awakened a number of plans and projects in them, and, since it had also proved that fundamentally they were of one mind, they were now exchanging their mutual views with extreme interest. No one could assert that the sentences they uttered were faultless; they kept batting around a few words that no nonprofessional would have understood, but the meaning of what they said was so clear to one another that no one in neighboring rooms could fall asleep before approximately four in the morning. But that long session had a genuine, visible result. Something resembling a club was formed; that is, it had already begun to exist at

wie ein Verein wurde gebildet; das heißt, er war eigentlich schon da, im Augenblick, als die Absichten und Ziele der drei Künstler sich so verwandt erwiesen, daß man sie nur schwer von einander trennen konnte. Der erste gemeinsame Beschluß des ›Vereins‹ erfüllte sich sofort. Man zog drei Stunden weit ins Land und mietete gemeinsam einen Bauernhof. In der Stadt zu bleiben, hätte zunächst keinen Sinn gehabt. Erst wollte man sich draußen den ›Stil‹ erwerben, die gewisse persönliche Sicherheit, den Blick, die Hand und wie alle die Dinge heißen, ohne welche ein Maler zwar leben, aber nicht malen kann. – Zu allen diesen Tugenden sollte das Zusammenhalten helfen, der ›Verein‹ eben, – besonders aber das Ehrenmitglied dieses Vereins: die Natur. Unter ›Natur‹ stellen sich die Maler alles vor, was der liebe Gott selbst gemacht hat oder doch gemacht haben könnte, unter Umständen. Ein Zaun, ein Haus, ein Brunnen – alle diese Dinge sind ja meistens menschlichen Ursprungs. Aber wenn sie eine Zeit lang in der Landschaft stehen, so daß sie gewisse Eigenschaften von den Bäumen und Büschen und von ihrer anderen Umgebung angenommen haben, so gehen sie gleichsam in den Besitz Gottes über und damit auch in das Eigentum des Malers. Denn Gott und der Künstler haben dasselbe Vermögen und dieselbe Armut, je nachdem. – Nun an der Natur, welche um den gemeinsamen Bauernhof sich erstreckte, glaubte Gott gewiß keinen besonderen Reichtum zu besitzen. Es dauerte indessen nicht lang, so belehrten ihn die Maler eines Besseren. Die Gegend war flach, das ließ sich nicht leugnen. Aber durch die *Tiefe* ihrer Schatten und die Höhe ihrer Lichter waren Abgründe und Gipfel vorhanden, zwischen denen eine Unzahl von Mitteltönen jenen Regionen weiter Wiesen und fruchtbarer Felder entsprach, die den materiellen Wert einer gebirgigen Gegend ausmachen. Es waren nur wenig Bäume vorhanden und fast alle von derselben Art, botanisch betrachtet. Durch die Gefühle indessen, welche sie ausdrückten, durch die Sehnsucht irgend eines Astes oder die sanfte Ehrfurcht des Stammes erschienen sie als eine große Anzahl individueller Wesen, und manche Weide war eine Persönlichkeit, die den Malern durch die Vielseitigkeit und Tiefe ihres Charakters Überraschung um Überraschung bereitete. Die Begeisterung war so groß, man fühlte sich so sehr eins in dieser Arbeit, daß es nichts bedeuten will, daß jeder der drei Maler nach Verlauf eines halben Jahres ein eigenes Haus bezog; das hatte gewiß rein räumliche Gründe. Aber etwas anderes wird man hier doch erwähnen müssen. Die Maler wollten irgendwie das einjährige Bestehen ihres Vereines, aus dem in so kurzer Zeit soviel Gutes gekommen war, feiern, und jeder entschloß sich zu diesem Zweck heimlich die Häuser der anderen zu

the moment when the three artists' aims and goals had proved to be so similar that they could hardly take leave of one another. The first decision taken in common by the 'club' was put into action at once. They went out into the country, three hours' distance from town, and rented a farmhouse together. At the outset, remaining in town would have made no sense. They wanted first to acquire their 'style' on the outside: that certain personal sureness of touch, the eye, the hand, and whatever you call all those things without which a painter *can* live, but can't paint.—They would be aided in attaining all those virtues by sticking together, by their very 'club,' and especially by the honorary member of that club: Nature. By 'Nature' artists understand everything that the Good Lord either created himself or could have created in the proper circumstances. A fence, a house, a well—all of those are, in fact, usually of human origin. But after they've remained in the landscape for a while, and have thus taken on certain characteristics of the trees, bushes, and their other surroundings, they seem to pass over into God's ownership and thereby into the painter's possessions, as well. Because God and the artist share the same riches and the same poverty, as the case may be.—Now, in the nature surrounding the farmhouse they had rented in common, God surely didn't believe he owned any special treasure. But it didn't take long for the painters to show him how wrong he was. The area was flat, that couldn't be denied. But thanks to the *depth* of its shadows and the height of its highlights, it presented abysses and summits, between which a huge number of intermediate tones corresponded to those regions of broad meadow and fertile field which constitute the material value of a hilly district. There were only a few trees, almost all of the same species, botanically speaking. But thanks to the emotions they expressed, thanks to the yearning inherent in some bough or the gentle reverence of some trunk, they seemed to be a large number of individual beings, and many a willow was a personality whose manysidedness and depth of character offered the painters one surprise after another. Their enthusiasm was so great, they felt so much in harmony at their work, that it's quite insignificant that, after six months had gone by, each of the three painters had moved into a separate house; it was certainly purely for reasons of space. Nevertheless, something else must be mentioned here. The painters wished to celebrate in some way the first anniversary of their club, which had produced so many good results in so short a time; and, for that purpose, each of them decided secretly to paint pictures of the others' houses. On the designated day they assembled, each with his

malen. An dem bestimmten Tage kamen sie, jeder mit seinen Bildern, zusammen. Es traf sich, daß sie gerade von ihren jeweiligen Wohnungen, deren Lage, Zweckmäßigkeit usw. sich unterhielten. Sie ereiferten sich ziemlich stark, und es geschah, daß während des Gesprächs jeder seiner mitgebrachten Ölskizzen vergaß und spät nachts mit dem uneröffneten Paket zu Hause ankam. Wie das geschehen konnte, ist schwer begreiflich. Aber sie zeigten sich auch in der nächsten Zeit ihre Bilder nicht, und wenn der eine den andern besuchte (was infolge vieler Arbeit immer seltener geschah), fand er auf der Staffelei des Freundes Skizzen aus jener ersten Zeit, da sie noch gemeinsam denselben Bauernhof bewohnten. Aber einmal entdeckte der Rechte (er *wohnte* jetzt auch zur Rechten, kann also weiter so heißen) bei dem, welchen ich den Jüngsten genannt habe, eines jener genannten, nicht verratenen Jubiläumsbilder. Er betrachtete es eine Weile nachdenklich, trat damit ans Licht und lachte plötzlich: ›Schau, das hab ich gar nicht gewußt, nicht ohne Glück hast du da mein Haus aufgefaßt. Eine wahrhaft geistreiche Karikatur. Mit diesen Übertreibungen in Form und Farbe, mit dieser kühnen Ausgestaltung meines allerdings etwas betonten Giebels, wirklich es liegt etwas darin.‹ Der Jüngste machte keines seiner vorteilhaftesten Gesichter, im Gegenteil; er ging zum Mittleren in seiner Bestürzung, um sich von ihm, dem Besonnensten, beruhigen zu lassen, denn er war nach Vorfällen solcher Art gleich kleinmütig und geneigt, an seiner Begabung zu zweifeln. Er traf den Mittleren nicht zu Haus und stöberte ein wenig im Atelier umher, wobei ihm gleich ein Bild in die Augen fiel, das ihn merkwürdig abstieß. Es war ein Haus, aber ein richtiger Narr mußte darin wohnen. Diese Fassade! Das konnte nur irgendeiner gebaut haben, der von Architektur keine Idee hatte und der seine armseligen, malerischen Ideen anwandte auf ein Gebäude. Plötzlich stellte der Jüngste das Bild fort, als ob es ihm die Finger verbrannt hätte. An dem linken Rande desselben hatte er das Datum jenes ersten Jubiläums gelesen und daneben: ›Das Haus unseres Jüngsten.‹ Er wartete natürlich den Hausherrn nicht ab, sondern kehrte etwas verstimmt nach Hause zurück. Der Jüngste und der rechts waren seither vorsichtig geworden. Sie suchten sich entfernte Motive und dachten selbstverständlich nicht daran, für das Fest des zweijährigen Bestehens ihres so förderlichen Vereins etwas vorzubereiten. Um so eifriger arbeitete der ahnungslose Mittlere daran, ein Motiv, das der Wohnung des Rechten zunächst lag, zu malen. Etwas Unbestimmtes hielt ihn davon ab, dessen Haus selbst zum Vorwand seiner Arbeit zu wählen. – Als er dem Rechtswohnenden das fertige Bild überbrachte, verhielt sich dieser merkwürdig zurück-

pictures. It came about that they were just discussing their individual residences, their siting, their suitability, and the like. They became rather heated, and it befell that, during the discussion each one forgot about the oil sketches he had brought along and got home late at night with the package unopened. How that could happen is hard to understand. But even in the following period they didn't show one another their pictures, and whenever one of them visited another (which happened more and more seldom, they were so busy), he found on his friend's easel sketches from that early period when they were still living in the same farmhouse together. But once, the man on the right (now he even *lived* on the right, so he can still be called that), while visiting the man I've dubbed 'the youngest,' discovered one of those above-mentioned, unrevealed anniversary pictures. He studied it thoughtfully for a while, took it into the light, and suddenly burst out laughing: 'Look! I didn't know about it, you've caught the look of my house here quite felicitously. A truly witty caricature. With those exaggerations of shape and color, with that daring overdevelopment of my gable, which *is* rather prominent, it's really got something.' The youngest man put on an expression which was not among those most becoming to him, on the contrary: he went to see the center man in his dismay in order to be calmed down by him, the most coolheaded among them, because after events like that one he immediately grew fainthearted and inclined to doubt his own talent. The center man wasn't home, and the youngest man rummaged around the studio a bit; as he did so, he immediately caught sight of a picture he found oddly repellent. It was a house, but one in which only a real fool would live. That facade! It could have been built only by someone totally ignorant of architecture, someone who was applying his threadbare painterly ideas to a building. Suddenly the youngest man put away the picture, as if it had burned his fingers. On its left edge he had read the date of that first anniversary, and alongside it: 'Our youngest member's house.' Naturally he didn't await his host's return, but went back home somewhat out of sorts. From that time on, the youngest man and the one on the right had become cautious. They sought out distant subjects for pictures, and of course they had no plans to prepare anything to celebrate the second anniversary of their very beneficial club. The unsuspecting center man was working all the more enthusiastically at painting a subject located right next to the home of the man on the right. An indefinable feeling prevented him from choosing that man's house itself as the pretext for his work.—When he brought the finished picture to the man on the

haltend, schaute es nur flüchtig an und bemerkte etwas Beiläufiges. Dann, nach einer Weile, sagte er: ›Ich habe übrigens gar nicht gewußt, daß du soweit verreist warst in der letzten Zeit?‹ ›Wieso, weit? Verreist?‹ Der Mittlere begriff nicht ein Wort. ›Nun – diese tüchtige Arbeit da,‹ erwiderte der andere, ›offenbar doch irgend ein holländisches Motiv –‹ Der besonnene Mittlere lachte laut auf. ›Köstlich, dieses holländische Motiv befindet sich vor deiner Türe.‹ Und er wollte sich gar nicht beruhigen. Aber der Vereinsgenosse lachte nicht, gar nicht. Er quälte sich ein Lächeln ab und meinte: ›Ein guter Witz.‹ ›Aber ganz und gar nicht, mach mal die Tür auf, ich will dir gleich zeigen –‹ und der Mittlere ging selbst auf die Türe zu. ›Halt,‹ befahl der Hausherr, ›und ich erkläre dir somit, daß ich diese Gegend nie gesehen habe und auch *nie sehen werde,* weil sie für mein Auge überhaupt nicht existenzfähig ist.‹ ›Aber‹, machte der mittlere Maler erstaunt. ›Du bleibst dabei?‹ fuhr der Rechte gereizt fort, ›gut, ich reise heute noch ab. Du zwingst mich fortzugehen, denn ich wünsche nicht in dieser Gegend zu leben. Verstanden?‹ – Damit war die Freundschaft zu Ende, aber nicht der Verein; denn er ist bis heute nicht statutengemäß aufgelöst worden. Niemand hat daran gedacht, und man kann von ihm mit vollstem Rechte sagen, daß er sich über die ganze Erde verbreitet hat.«

»Man sieht,« unterbrach mich der bereitwillige junge Mann, der schon beständig die Lippen spitzte, »wieder einer jener kolossalen Erfolge des Vereinslebens; gewiß sind viele hervorragende Meister aus dieser innigen Verbindung hervorgegangen –«. »Erlauben Sie,« bat ich, und er stäubte mir unversehens den Ärmel ab, »das war eigentlich erst die Einleitung zu meiner Geschichte, obwohl sie komplizierter ist, als die Geschichte selbst. Also, ich sagte, daß der Verein sich über die ganze Erde verbreitet hatte, und dieses ist Tatsache. Seine drei Mitglieder flohen in wahrem Entsetzen von einander. Nirgends war ihnen Ruhe gewährt. Immer fürchtete jeder, der andere könnte noch ein Stück seines Landes erkennen und durch seine ruchlose Darstellung entweihen, und als sie schon an drei entgegengesetzten Punkten der irdischen Peripherie angelangt waren, kam jedem der trostlose Einfall, daß sein Himmel, der Himmel, den er mühsam durch seine wachsende Eigenart erworben hatte, den anderen noch erreichbar sei. In diesem erschütternden Augenblick begannen sie, alle drei zugleich, mit ihren Staffeleien nach rückwärts zu gehen, und noch fünf Schritte und sie wären vom Rande der Erde in die Unendlichkeit gefallen und müßten jetzt in rasender Geschwindigkeit die doppelte Bewegung um diese und um die Sonne vollführen. Aber Gottes Teilnahme und Aufmerksamkeit

right, the latter behaved with an odd reserve, gave only a hasty glance at it, and made some casual remark. Then, after a pause, he said: 'By the way, I didn't know that you had made such a long trip recently.' 'What do you mean, long? What trip?' The center man didn't understand one word. 'Well, this really competent job here,' the other replied, 'is obviously some Dutch subject—' The coolheaded center man gave a loud laugh. 'How funny! This Dutch subject is located right outside your door.' And he refused to calm down. But his fellow club member didn't laugh, not one bit. He forced himself to smile and said: 'A good joke.' 'But not at all; just open your door and I'll show you right away—' and the center man started walking toward the door himself. 'Stop right there!' his host commanded; 'I declare to you herewith that I've never seen that terrain, and *never will see* it, because in my eyes it simply has no chance of really existing.' 'But,' the center painter began in amazement. 'You insist?' the man on the right continued in irritation; 'fine, I'm leaving this place before the day is over. You're forcing me to go, because I don't wish to live in this area. Got it?'—That was the end of the friendship, but not the end of the club; because to this day it hasn't been formally dissolved. No one thought of doing so, and with total justification it can be said that the club has spread all over the world."

Here I was interrupted by the officious young man, who had already been pursing his lips all the time: "This is just one more of those colossal successes of club life; I'm sure that many prominent masters issued from that heartfelt association—" "Excuse me," I requested, and he unexpectedly dusted off my sleeve, "that was actually only the introduction to my story, though it's more complicated than the story itself. So, then, I was saying that the club has spread all over the world, and that's a fact. Its three members fled one another in real horror. They were never allowed any peace. Each one was always afraid that another of them might still recognize a piece of his property and desecrate it with his nefarious depiction of it; and by the time that they had reached three opposite points on the earth's periphery, each of them had the dismaying thought that his sky, the sky he had laboriously won by means of his increasingly individual style, was still attainable by the others. At that shattering moment all three of them, simultaneously, began to step backwards with their easels; five more steps, and they would have fallen off the edge of the earth into infinity, and would have had to execute with furious speed the double motion around the earth and around the sun. But God's sympathy and attentiveness forestalled that cruel fate. God realized the danger, and at

verhütete dieses grausame Schicksal. Gott erkannte die Gefahr und trat im letzten Moment (was hätte er auch sonst tun sollen?) heraus, in die Mitte des Himmels. Die drei Maler erschraken. Sie stellten die Staffelei fest und setzten die Palette auf. Diese Gelegenheit durften sie sich nicht entgehen lassen. Der liebe Gott erscheint nicht alle Tage und auch nicht jedem. Und jeder der Maler meinte natürlich, Gott stünde *nur* vor *ihm*. Im übrigen vertieften sie sich immer mehr in die interessante Arbeit. Und jedesmal, wenn Gott wieder zurück in den Himmel will, bittet der heilige Lukas ihn, noch eine Weile draußen zu bleiben, bis die drei Maler mit ihren Bildern fertig sind.«

»Und die Herren haben diese Bilder ohne Zweifel schon ausgestellt, vielleicht gar verkauft?« fragte der Musiker in den sanftesten Tönen. »Wo denken Sie hin«, wehrte ich ab. »Sie malen immer noch an Gott und werden ihn wohl bis an ihr eigenes Ende malen. Sollten sie aber (was ich für ausgeschlossen halte) noch einmal im Leben zusammenkommen und sich die Bilder, die sie von Gott inzwischen gemalt haben, zeigen, wer weiß: vielleicht würden diese Bilder sich kaum von einander unterscheiden.«

Da war auch schon der Bahnhof. Ich hatte noch fünf Minuten Zeit. Ich dankte dem jungen Mann für seine Begleitung und wünschte ihm alles Glück für den jungen Verein, den er so ausgezeichnet vertrat. Er tippte mit dem rechten Zeigefinger den Staub auf, der die Fensterbretter des kleinen Wartesaals zu bedrücken schien, und war sehr in Gedanken. Ich muß gestehen, ich schmeichelte mir schon, meine kleine Geschichte hätte ihn so nachdenklich gestimmt. Als er mir zum Abschied einen roten Faden aus dem Handschuh zog, riet ich ihm aus Dankbarkeit: »Sie können zurück ja über die Felder gehen, dieser Weg ist bedeutend näher als die Straße.« »Verzeihen Sie,« verneigte sich der bereitwillige junge Mann, »ich werde doch wieder die Straße nehmen. Ich suche mich eben zu besinnen, wo das war. Während Sie die Güte hatten, mir einiges wirklich Bedeutende zu erzählen, glaubte ich eine Vogelscheuche im Acker zu bemerken, in einem alten Rock, und der eine, – mir scheint der linke Ärmel, war hängen geblieben an einem Pfahl, so daß er durchaus nicht wehte. Ich fühle nun gewissermaßen die Verpflichtung, meinen kleinen Tribut an den gemeinsamen Interessen der Menschheit, die mir auch als eine Art Verein erscheint, in welchem jeder etwas zu leisten hat, dadurch zu entrichten, daß ich diesen linken Ärmel seinem eigentlichen Sinne, nämlich: zu wehen, zurückgebe . . .« Der junge Mann entfernte sich mit dem liebenswürdigsten Lächeln. Ich aber hätte beinah meinen Zug versäumt.

the last moment (what else was he to do?) he stepped out into the middle of the sky. The three painters were alarmed. They set up their easels and took up their palettes. They couldn't let such an opportunity slip away. The Good Lord doesn't appear every day, and not to everybody. And each of the painters naturally believed that God was posing just for him. Besides, they became more and more immersed in their interesting task. And every time God wants to return to heaven, Saint Luke[31] asks him to stay outside a little while longer, until the three painters finish their pictures."

"And those gentlemen have doubtless already exhibited those pictures, perhaps even sold them?" the musician asked in the gentlest tones. "What can you be thinking of?" I said, staving him off. "They're still painting God and will probably go on painting him as long as they live. But if they ever meet again in life (which I consider out of the question) and show one another the pictures of God they've painted in the meanwhile, who knows? Maybe those pictures would hardly differ from one another."

Now we were at the station. I still had five minutes' time. I thanked the young man for accompanying me and wished him every success for the new club, of which he was such an outstanding representative. With his right index finger he knocked away the dust that seemed to be weighing down the window sills in the little waiting room, and he was thinking hard. I must confess that I was already flattering myself on having put him in such a thoughtful mood with my little story. When he pulled a red thread out of my glove as we parted, I gratefully advised him: "You know, you can walk back across country, that way is considerably shorter than by the road." "Forgive me," said the officious young man with a bow, "but I'll take the road again, all the same. I've just been trying to remember where that was. While you were kind enough to be narrating some really significant thing, I thought I noticed a scarecrow in a field wearing an old jacket, and one sleeve— the left, I think—had gotten caught on a stake, so that it wasn't waving anymore. Now I feel the obligation to some extent to pay my little tribute to the common interests of mankind, which also seems to me to be a sort of club, in which every member has to do his share, by restoring that left sleeve to its true purpose: to wave. . . ." The young man departed with the most charming smile. But I nearly missed my train.

---

31. Patron saint of artists, because he is said to have painted a portrait of the Blessed Virgin.

Bruchstücke dieser Geschichte wurden von dem jungen Manne an
einem »Abende« des Vereines gesungen. Weiß Gott, wer ihm die
Musik dazu erfunden hat. Herr Baum, der Fahnenvater, hat sie den
Kindern mitgebracht, und die Kinder haben sich einige Melodien
daraus gemerkt.

Der Bettler und das stolze Fräulein

Es traf sich, daß wir – der Herr Lehrer und ich – Zeugen wurden fol-
gender kleinen Begebenheit. Bei uns, am Waldrand, steht bisweilen
ein alter Bettler. Auch heute war er wieder da, ärmer, elender als je,
durch ein mitleidiges Mimikry fast ununterscheidbar von den Latten
des morschen Bretterzauns, an denen er lehnte. Aber da begab es
sich, daß ein ganz kleines Mädchen auf ihn zugelaufen kam, um ihm
eine kleine Münze zu schenken. Das war weiter nicht verwunderlich,
überraschend war nur, wie sie das tat. Sie machte einen schönen
braven Knicks, reichte dem Alten rasch, als ob es niemand merken
sollte, ihre Gabe, knickste wieder, und war schon davon. Diese beiden
Knickse aber waren mindestens eines Kaisers wert. Das ärgerte den
Herrn Lehrer ganz besonders. Er wollte rasch auf den Bettler zuge-
hen, wahrscheinlich, um ihn von seiner Zaunlatte zu verjagen; denn
wie mann weiß, war er im Vorstand des Armenvereins und gegen den
Straßenbettel eingenommen. Ich hielt ihn zurück. »Die Leute werden von uns unterstützt, ja man kann wohl sagen, versorgt«, eiferte er.
»Wenn sie auf der Straße auch noch betteln, so ist das einfach – Über-
mut.« »Verehrter Herr Lehrer –«, suchte ich ihn zu beruhigen, aber
er zog mich immer noch nach dem Waldrand hin. »Verehrter Herr
Lehrer –,« bat ich, »ich muß Ihnen eine Geschichte erzählen.« »So
dringend?« fragte er giftig. Ich nahm es ernst: »Ja eben jetzt. Ehe Sie
vergessen, was wir da gerade zufällig beobachtet haben.« Der Lehrer
mißtraute mir seit meiner letzten Geschichte. Ich las das von seinem
Gesichte und begütigte: »Nicht vom lieben Gott, wirklich nicht. Der
liebe Gott kommt in meiner Geschichte nicht vor. Es ist etwas
Historisches.« Damit hatte ich gewonnen. Man muß nur das Wort
»Historie« sagen, und schon gehen jedem Lehrer die Ohren auf; denn
die Historie ist etwas durchaus Achtbares, Unverfängliches und oft
pädagogisch Verwendbares. Ich sah, daß der Herr Lehrer wieder
seine Brille putzte, ein Zeichen, daß seine Sehkraft sich in die Ohren
geschlagen hatte, und diesen günstigen Moment wußte ich geschickt
zu benutzen. Ich begann:

Fragments of that story were sung by the young man at one of the club's "evenings." God only knows who wrote the music for him. Mr. Baum, the sponsor of the club banner, communicated the story to the children, and the children remembered some of the tunes from it.

The Beggar and the Proud Young Lady

It came about that we—the teacher and I—became witnesses to the following small event. In our village, at the edge of the woods, an old beggar sometimes stands. He was there today again, poorer and more miserable than ever; a sympathetic mimicry made him almost indistinguishable from the pickets of the rotting fence against which he was leaning. But it so befell that a very small girl came running up to him to give him a small coin. There was nothing very peculiar about that; the only surprising thing was the way that she did it. She made a beautiful, polite curtsey, handed the old man her gift quickly, as if to avoid its being noticed by anyone, made another curtsey, and was already gone. But those two curtseys were worthy of an emperor, at least. That annoyed the teacher quite particularly. He wanted to go up to the beggar at once, probably to chase him away from his fence picket; because, as is well known, he was on the committee of the welfare organization and he was prejudiced against begging on the street. I restrained him. "Those people are supported—I may even say, taken care of—by us," he said, bubbling over. "When they also beg on the street, that's simply—wantonness." "My dear schoolmaster," I said, trying to placate him, but he was still drawing me toward the edge of the woods. "My dear schoolmaster," I begged, "I must tell you a story." "Is it that urgent?" he asked venomously. I took it seriously: "Yes, right now. Before you forget what we just happened to observe here by chance." The teacher had mistrusted me ever since my last story. I read that in his face and said appeasingly: "It's not about the Good Lord, honestly it's not. The Good Lord doesn't appear in my story. It's something historical." With that, I had won. You need only utter the word "historical" and at once every teacher's ears prick up; because history is something totally respectable, innocuous, and often applicable pedagogically. I saw the teacher cleaning his glasses again, a sign that his vision had been transferred to his ears, and I was able to make skillful use of that favorable moment. I began:

»Es war in Florenz. Lorenzo de' Medici, jung, noch nicht
Herrscher, hatte gerade sein Gedicht ›Trionfo di Bacco ed Arianna‹ er-
sonnen, und schon wurden alle Gärten davon laut. Damals gab es
lebende Lieder. Aus dem Dunkel des Dichters stiegen sie in die
Stimmen und trieben auf ihnen, wie auf silbernen Kähnen, furchtlos,
ins Unbekannte. Der Dichter begann ein Lied, und alle, die es sangen,
vollendeten es. Im ›Trionfo‹ wird, wie in den meisten Liedern jener
Zeit, das Leben gefeiert, diese Geige mit den lichten, singenden Saiten
und ihrem dunklen Hintergrund: dem Rauschen des Blutes. Die un-
gleichlangen Strophen steigen in eine taumelnde Lustigkeit hinauf,
aber dort, wo diese atemlos wird, setzt jedesmal ein kurzer, einfacher
Kehrreim an, der sich von der schwindelnden Höhe niederneigt und,
vor dem Abgrund bang, die Augen zu schließen scheint. Er lautet:

> *Wie schön ist die Jugend, die uns erfreut,*
> *Doch wer will sie halten? Sie flieht und bereut,*
> *Und wenn einer fröhlich sein will, der sei's heut,*
> *Und für morgen ist keine Gewißheit.*

Ist es wunderlich, daß über die Menschen, welche dieses Gedicht
sangen, eine Hast hereinbrach, ein Bestreben alle Festlichkeit auf
dieses Heute zu türmen, auf den einzigen Fels, auf dem zu bauen sich
verlohnt? Und so kann man sich das Gedränge der Gestalten auf den
Bildern der Florentiner Maler erklären, die sich bemühten, alle ihre
Fürsten und Frauen und Freunde in *einem* Gemälde zu vereinen, denn
man malte langsam, und wer konnte wissen, ob zur Zeit des nächsten
Bildes alle noch so jung und bunt und einig sein würden. Am deutlich-
sten sprach dieser Geist der Ungeduld sich begreiflichermaßen bei den
Jünglingen aus. Die glänzendsten von ihnen saßen nach einem
Gastmahle auf der Terrasse des Palazzo Strozzi beisammen und plauderten von den Spielen, die demnächst vor der Kirche Santa Croce
stattfinden sollten. Etwas abseits in einer Loggia stand Palla degli
Albizzi mit seinem Freunde Tomaso, dem Maler. Sie schienen etwas in
wachsender Erregung zu verhandeln, bis Tomaso plötzlich rief: ›Das
tust du nicht, ich wette, das tust du nicht!‹ Nun wurden die anderen
aufmerksam. ›Was habt ihr?‹ erkundigte sich Gaetano Strozzi und kam
mit einigen Freunden näher. Tomaso erklärte: ›Palla will auf dem Feste
vor Beatrice Altichieri, dieser Hochmütigen, niederknien und sie bitten,

"It was in Florence. Lorenzo de' Medici,[32] young, not yet ruler, had just written his poem 'The Triumph of Bacchus and Ariadne,' and already every garden resounded with it. At that time there were living songs. From the darkness within the poet they rose into people's voices and floated on them, as on silvery boats, fearlessly, into the unknown. The poet began a song and all who sang it completed it. In the 'Trionfo,' as in most songs of that era, life was celebrated, that violin with its bright, singing strings, and its dark background: the loud coursing of the blood. The stanzas, unequal in length, ascend into a reeling merriment, but where that merriment runs out of breath, each time a brief, simple refrain begins, which stoops down from the dizzying heights and, afraid of the abyss, seems to shut its eyes. It runs:

> *How lovely is youth, which gives us pleasure!*
> *But who can hold onto it? It flees and regrets,*
> *so if anyone wants to be happy, let him be so today,*
> *because for tomorrow there's no certainty.*[33]

"Is it any surprise that the people who sang this poem were gripped by a feeling of haste, a striving to heap all festive emotions onto this 'today,' the only rock it pays to build on? And in that way one can understand the crowds of figures in the works of the Florentine painters, who exerted themselves to include all their princes, ladies, and friends in one picture, because they painted slowly, and who could know whether by the time of the next picture they would still all be that young, colorful, and unified in spirit? This mentality of impatience was expressed most clearly among the young men, as is understandable. The most radiant of them were sitting together after a banquet on the terrace of the Palazzo Strozzi, chatting about the games that were soon to be held outside the church of Santa Croce. Standing in a loggia, a little apart, was Palla degli Albizzi with his friend Tommaso the painter. They seemed to be discussing something with growing excitement, until Tommaso suddenly cried: 'You won't do it, I bet you won't do it!' Now the others began to pay attention. 'What's with you?' inquired Gaetano Strozzi, approaching with a few friends. Tommaso explained: 'Palla wants to kneel down before Beatrice Altichieri, that arrogant girl, at the festival and ask her permission to kiss the dusty

---

32. Lived 1449–1492; began to rule in 1469.   33. As befits a true song text for singing by a chorus in procession (at Carnival), the Italian is much briefer, simpler, and airier than Rilke's version. The English translation here is naturally directly from the German.

sie möchte ihm gestatten, den staubigen Saum ihres Kleides zu küssen.‹
Alle lachten, und Lionardo, aus dem Hause Ricardi, bemerkte: ›Palla
wird sich das überlegen; er weiß wohl, daß die schönsten Frauen ein
Lächeln für ihn haben, das man sonst niemals bei ihnen sieht.‹ Und ein
anderer fügte hinzu: ›Und Beatrice ist noch so jung. Ihre Lippen sind
noch zu kinderhaft hart, um zu lächeln. Darum scheint sie so stolz.‹
›Nein –‹, erwiderte Palla degli Albizzi mit übermäßiger Heftigkeit, ›sie
ist stolz, daran ist nicht ihre Jugend schuld. Sie ist stolz wie ein Stein in
den Händen Michelangelos, stolz wie eine Blume an einem
Madonnenbild, stolz wie ein Sonnenstrahl der über Diamanten geht –‹
Gaetano Strozzi unterbrach ihn etwas streng: ›Und du, Palla, bist nicht
auch du stolz? Was du da sagst, das kommt mir vor, als wolltest du dich
unter die Bettler stellen, die um die Vesper im Hofe der S^{ma} Annunziata
warten, bis Beatrice Altichieri ihnen mit abgewendetem Gesicht einen
Soldo schenkt.‹ ›Ich will auch *dieses* tun!‹ rief Palla mit glänzenden
Augen, drängte sich durch die Freunde nach der Treppe durch und verschwand. Tomaso wollte ihm nach. ›Laß‹, hielt Strozzi ihn ab, ›er muß
jetzt allein sein, da wird er am ehesten vernünftig werden.‹ Dann zerstreuten sich die jungen Leute in die Gärten.

Im Vorhofe der Santissima Annunziata warteten auch an diesem
Abend etwa zwanzig Bettler und Bettlerinnen auf die Vesper. Beatrice,
welche sie alle dem Namen nach kannte, und bisweilen auch in ihre
armen Häuser an der Porta San Niccolò zu den Kindern und zu den
Kranken kam, pflegte jeden von ihnen im Vorübergehen mit einem
kleinen Silberstück zu beschenken. Heute schien sie sich etwas zu ver-
späten; die Glocken hatten schon gerufen, und nur Fäden ihres
Klanges hingen noch an den Türmen über der Dämmerung. Es entstand eine Unruhe unter den Armen, auch weil ein neuer unbekannter
Bettler sich in das Dunkel des Kirchentors geschlichen hatte, und
eben wollten sie sich seiner erwehren in ihrem Neid, als ein junges
Mädchen in schwarzem, fast nonnenhaftem Kleide im Vorhofe erschien und, durch ihre Güte gehemmt, von einem zum anderen ging,
während eine der begleitenden Frauen den Beutel offen hielt, aus
welchem sie ihre kleinen Gaben holte. Die Bettler stürzten in die
Knie, schluchzten und suchten ihre welken Finger eine Sekunde lang
an die Schleppe des schlichten Kleides ihrer Wohltäterin zu legen,
oder sie küßten auch den letzten Saum mit ihren nassen, stammelnden
Lippen. Die Reihe war zu Ende; es hatte auch keiner von den Beatrice
wohlbekannten Armen gefehlt. Aber da gewahrte sie unter dem

hem of her gown.' Everyone laughed, and Lionardo, of the house of
Riccardi, remarked: 'Palla is going to think that over; after all, he
knows that the loveliest women have a smile for him that they never
display otherwise." And someone else added: 'And Beatrice is still so
young. Her lips are still too childishly hard for them to smile. That's
why she seems so proud.' 'No,' replied Palla degli Albizzi with excessive force, 'she *is* proud; her youth isn't to blame for that. She's as
proud as a stone in the hands of Michelangelo,[34] proud as a flower on
an image of the Madonna, proud as a sunbeam playing over dia-
monds—' Gaetano Strozzi interrupted him rather severely: 'And you,
Palla, aren't you proud, too? What you're saying here strikes me as if
you intended to mingle with the beggars who await vespers in the
forecourt of the Santissima Annunziata for Beatrice to give them a
soldo with her face averted.' 'I'll do *that*, too!' cried Palla, his eyes
gleaming; he pushed his way through his friends to the staircase and
vanished. Tommaso wanted to follow him. 'Let him be,' said Strozzi,
holding him back; 'he's got to be alone now, then he'll come to his
senses most readily.' Then the young people dispersed into the
gardens.

"In the forecourt of the Santissima Annunziata, that evening,
too, some twenty beggars, men and women, were waiting for vespers. Beatrice, who knew each of them by name, and sometimes
went to their humble houses by the Porta San Niccolò to visit the
children and the sick, used to give each one a little silver coin as
she passed by. Today she seemed to be a little late; the bells had
already called, and only threads of their sound were still caught in
the towers above the twilight. The paupers became restless, also
because a new, unknown beggar had stealthily entered the shadow
of the church portal; and they were just about to keep him at bay
in their envy, when a young girl in black, almost nunlike clothing,
appeared in the forecourt and, hampered by her own kindness,
was walking from one to another, while one of the women escort-
ing her held open the purse from which she drew her small presents. The beggars fell to their knees, sobbed, and tried to place
their withered fingers for a second on the train of their benefac-
tress's simple gown; or else they kissed its lowest hem with their
wet, stammering lips. Their number was at an end; nor had any of
the paupers Beatrice knew so well been missing. But then she noticed in the shadow of the portal another, unknown figure in rags,

---

34. A howling anachronism, really unworthy of Rilke!

Schatten des Tores noch eine fremde Gestalt in Lumpen und erschrak. Sie geriet in Verwirrung. Alle ihre Armen hatte sie schon als Kind gekannt, und sie zu beschenken, war ihr etwas Selbstverständliches geworden, eine Handlung wie etwa die, daß man die Finger in die Marmorschalen voll heiligen Wassers hält, die an den Türen jeder Kirche stehen. Aber es war ihr nie eingefallen, daß es auch *fremde* Bettler geben könnte; wie sollte man das Recht haben, auch diese zu beschenken, da man sich das Vertrauen ihrer Armut nicht verdient hatte durch irgend ein Wissen darum? Wäre es nicht eine unerhörte Überhebung gewesen, einem Unbekannten ein Almosen zu reichen? Und im Widerstreit dieser dunkeln Gefühle ging das Mädchen, als ob es ihn nicht bemerkt hätte, an dem neuen Bettler vorbei und trat rasch in die kühle, hohe Kirche ein. Aber als drinnen die Andacht begann, konnte sie sich keines Gebetes erinnern. Eine Angst überkam sie, daß der arme Mann nach der Vesper nicht mehr am Tore zu finden sein würde und daß sie nichts getan hatte, seine Not zu lindern, während die Nacht so nahe war, darin alle Armut hilfloser und trauriger ist als am Tag. Sie machte derjenigen von ihren Frauen, die den Beutel trug, ein Zeichen und zog sich mit ihr nach dem Eingang zurück. Dort war es indessen leer geworden; aber der Fremde stand immer noch, an eine Säule gelehnt, da und schien dem Gesang zu lauschen, der seltsam fern, wie aus Himmeln, aus der Kirche kam. Sein Gesicht war fast ganz verhüllt, wie es manchmal bei Aussätzigen der Fall ist, die ihre häßlichen Wunden erst entblößen, wenn man nahe vor ihnen steht und sie sicher sind, daß Mitleid und Ekel in gleichem Maße zu ihren Gunsten reden. Beatrice zögerte. Sie hatte den kleinen Beutel selbst in Händen und fühlte nur wenige geringe Münzen darin. Aber mit einem raschen Entschluß trat sie auf den Bettler zu und sagte mit unsicherer, etwas singender Stimme und ohne die flüchtenden Blicke von den eigenen Händen zu heben: ›Nicht um Euch zu kränken, Herr . . . mir ist, erkenn ich Euch recht, ich bin in Eurer Schuld. Euer Vater, ich glaube, hat in unserm Haus das reiche Geländer gemacht, aus getriebenem Eisen, wißt Ihr, welches die Treppe uns ziert. Später einmal – fand sich in der Kammer, – darin er manchmal bei uns zu arbeiten pflegte, – ein Beutel – – ich denke – er hat ihn verloren – gewiß –.‹ Aber die hilflose Lüge ihrer Lippen drückte das Mädchen vor dem Fremden in die Kniee. Sie zwang den Beutel aus Brokat in seine vom Mantel verhüllten Hände und stammelte: ›Verzeiht –.‹

Sie fühlte noch, daß der Bettler zitterte. Dann flüchtete Beatrice mit der erschrockenen Begleiterin zurück in die Kirche. Aus dem eine Weile geöffneten Tor brach ein kurzer Jubel von Stimmen. – Die

and she became alarmed. She got confused. She had already known all her paupers when she was a child, and giving them presents had become a natural action for her, like dipping one's fingers in the marble basins filled with holy water at the entrance to every church. But it had never occurred to her that there could be *unfamiliar* beggars, as well; how was a person to have the right to give gifts to them, as well, not having earned the confidence of their poverty by any knowledge of it? Wouldn't it have been incredibly presumptuous to hand alms to a stranger? And in the conflict of these obscure feelings, the girl walked past the new beggar as if she hadn't noticed him, and stepped quickly into the cool, lofty church. But when the service began inside, she couldn't remember any prayer. A fear came over her that, after vespers, the poor man would no longer be found in the portal, and that she had done nothing to alleviate his want, while it was so close to night, when all poverty is more helpless and sorrowful than by day. She made a sign to that one of her women who carried the purse, and withdrew with her toward the entrance. The portal had emptied out in the meanwhile, but the stranger was still standing there, leaning against a column, seemingly listening to the singing that issued from the church as if from an unusual distance, as if from heaven. His face was almost entirely covered, as is sometimes the case with lepers, who only bare their hideous sores when you're standing right in front of them and they're sure that pity and disgust speak in their favor in equal measure. Beatrice hesitated. She was carrying the little purse herself and could feel only a few small coins in it. But with a swift resolve she walked up to the beggar and said, in an unsure, somewhat singsong tone, without raising her fleeting glances from her own hands: 'Not to hurt your feelings, sir . . . , if I'm not mistaking who you are, I believe I'm in your debt. I think your father built the costly wrought-iron railing in our house, you know: the one that adorns our staircase. Once later on, in the room—in our house where he sometimes used to work—a purse was found—I think— he lost it—surely—.' But that awkward lie from her lips forced the girl onto her knees in front of the stranger. She pressed the brocade purse into his hands, which were covered by his cloak, and stammered: 'Forgive me—.'

"She could still sense that the beggar was trembling. Then Beatrice took refuge again in the church with her frightened chaperone. From the portal, which was opened for a while, there broke a brief sound of

Geschichte ist zu Ende. Messer Palla degli Albizzi blieb in seinen Lumpen. Er verschenkte seine ganze Habe und ging barfuß und arm ins Land. Später soll er in der Nähe von Subiaco gewohnt haben.«

»Zeiten, Zeiten«, sagte der Herr Lehrer. »Was hilft das alles; er war auf dem Wege ein Wüstling zu werden und wurde durch diese Begebenheit ein Landstreicher, ein Sonderling. Heute weiß gewiß kein Mensch mehr von ihm.« »Doch,« – erwiderte ich bescheiden, – »sein Name wird bisweilen bei den großen Litaneien in den katholischen Kirchen unter den Fürbittern genannt; denn er ist ein Heiliger geworden.«

Die Kinder haben auch diese Geschichte vernommen, und sie behaupten, zum Ärger des Herrn Lehrer, auch in *ihr* käme der liebe Gott vor. Ich bin auch ein wenig erstaunt darüber; denn ich habe dem Herrn Lehrer doch versprochen, ihm eine Geschichte ohne den lieben Gott zu erzählen. Aber, freilich: die Kinder müssen es wissen!

Eine Geschichte, dem Dunkel erzählt

Ich wollte den Mantel umnehmen und zu meinem Freunde Ewald gehen. Aber ich hatte mich über einem Buche versäumt, einem *alten* Buche übrigens, und es war Abend geworden, wie es in Rußland Frühling wird. Noch vor einem Augenblick war die Stube bis in die fernsten Ecken klar, und nun taten alle Dinge, als ob sie nie etwas anderes gekannt hätten als Dämmerung; überall gingen große dunkle Blumen auf, und wie auf Libellenflügeln glitt Glanz um ihre samtenen Kelche.

Der Lahme war gewiß nicht mehr am Fenster. Ich blieb also zu Haus. Was hatte ich ihm doch erzählen wollen? Ich wußte es nicht mehr. Aber eine Weile später fühlte ich, daß jemand diese verlorene Geschichte von mir verlangte, irgend ein einsamer Mensch vielleicht, der fern am Fenster seiner finstern Stube stand, oder vielleicht dieses Dunkel selbst, das mich und ihn und die Dinge umgab. So geschah es, daß ich dem Dunkel erzählte. Und es neigte sich immer näher zu mir, so daß ich immer leiser sprechen konnte, ganz, wie es zu meiner Geschichte paßt. Sie handelt übrigens in der Gegenwart und beginnt:

»Nach langer Abwesenheit kehrte Doktor Georg Laßmann in seine enge Heimat zurück. Er hatte nie viel dort besessen, und jetzt lebten ihm nurmehr zwei Schwestern in der Vaterstadt, beide verheiratet, wie

jubilant voices.—The story is over. Messer Palla degli Albizzi remained in his rags. He gave away everything he owned and left town barefoot, in poverty. He is said to have lived in the vicinity of Subiaco[35] later on."

"The times, the times," said the teacher. "What good is it all? He was on the way to becoming a wastrel, and that occurrence made him a tramp, an outsider. Today, surely, no one knows what became of him." "Oh, yes," I said, contradicting him modestly; "his name is sometimes mentioned among the intercessors in the great litanies in Catholic churches; because he became a saint."

The children have heard this story, too, and, to the teacher's vexation, they claim that the Good Lord figures in it, too. I myself am a little amazed at that, because, after all, I had promised the teacher to tell him a story without the Good Lord in it. But, naturally, the children must know!

A Story Told to the Darkness

I was about to put on my coat and visit my friend Ewald. But I had lingered over a book, an *old* book, by the way, and evening had come, the way spring comes in Russia. One minute earlier, the room had still been bright, even in the remotest corners, and now all objects behaved as if they had never known anything but twilight; everywhere large, dark flowers were opening, and, as if on dragonfly wings, light glided around their velvety calyxes.

Surely the paralyzed man was no longer at his window. So I stayed home. What had I intended to tell him, anyway? I no longer remembered. But, a little later, I sensed that someone was demanding that lost story of me, some lonesome person perhaps, who was standing far away at the window of his dark room, or perhaps that very darkness, which was enclosing him, me, and the objects. And so it befell that I told my story to the darkness. And it bent closer to me all the time, so that I was able to speak more and more softly, exactly as suited my story. Incidentally, it takes place at the present day. It begins:

"After a long absence Dr. Georg Lassmann was returning to his confined native region. He had never possessed much there, and now he had only two sisters living in his hometown, both married, and apparently enjoying good marriages; to see them again after

---

35. In Latium; the site of an early Benedictine abbey.

es schien, gut verheiratet; diese nach zwölf Jahren wiederzusehen, war der Grund seine Besuchs. So glaubte er selbst. Aber nachts, während er im überfüllten Zuge nicht schlafen konnte, wurde ihm klar, daß er eigentlich um seiner Kindheit willen kam und hoffte, in den alten Gassen irgend etwas wieder zu finden: ein Tor, einen Turm, einen Brunnen, irgend einen Anlaß zu einer Freude oder zu einer Traurigkeit, an welcher er sich wieder erkennen konnte. Man verliert sich ja so im Leben. Und da fiel ihm verschiedenes ein: Die kleine Wohnung in der Heinrichsgasse mit den glänzenden Türklinken und den dunkelgestrichenen Dielen, die geschonten Möbel und seine Eltern, diese beiden abgenützten Menschen, fast ehrfürchtig neben ihnen; die schnellen gehetzten Wochentage und die Sonntage, die wie ausgeräumte Säle waren, die seltenen Besuche, die man lachend und in Verlegenheit empfing, das verstimmte Klavier, der alte Kanarienvogel, der ererbte Lehnstuhl, auf dem man nicht sitzen durfte, ein Namenstag, ein Onkel, der aus Hamburg kommt, ein Puppentheater, ein Leierkasten, eine Kindergesellschaft und jemand ruft: ›Klara‹. Der Doktor wäre fast eingeschlafen. Man steht in einer Station, Lichter laufen vorüber, und der Hammer geht horchend durch die klingenden Räder. Und das ist wie: Klara, Klara. Klara, überlegt der Doktor, jetzt ganz wach, wer war das doch? Und gleich darauf fühlt er ein Gesicht, ein Kindergesicht mit blondem, glattem Haar. Nicht daß er es schildern könnte, aber er hat die Empfindung von etwas Stillem, Hilflosem, Ergebenem, von ein paar schmalen Kinderschultern, durch ein verwaschenes Kleidchen noch mehr zusammengepreßt, und er dichtet dazu ein Gesicht – aber da weiß er auch schon, er muß es nicht dichten. Es ist da – oder vielmehr es *war* da – damals. So erinnert sich Doktor Laßmann an seine einzige Gespielin Klara, nicht ohne Mühe. Bis zur Zeit, da er in eine Erziehungsanstalt kam, etwa zehn Jahre alt, hat er alles mit ihr geteilt, was ihm begegnete, das Wenige (oder das Viele?). Klara hatte keine Geschwister, und er hatte so gut wie keine; denn seine älteren Schwestern kümmerten sich nicht um ihn. Aber seither hat er niemanden je nach ihr gefragt. Wie war das doch möglich? Er lehnte sich zurück. Sie war ein frommes Kind, erinnerte er sich noch, und dann fragte er sich: Was mag aus ihr geworden sein? Eine Zeitlang ängstigte ihn der Gedanke, sie könnte gestorben sein. Eine unermeßliche Bangigkeit überfiel ihn in dem engen gedrängten Coupé; alles schien diese Annahme zu bestätigen: sie war ein kränkliches Kind, sie hatte es zu Hause nicht besonders gut, sie weinte oft, unzweifelhaft: sie ist tot. Der Doktor ertrug es nicht länger; er störte einzelne Schlafende und schob sich zwischen ihnen durch in den Gang des Waggons. Dort

twelve years was the reason for his visit. That's what he himself thought. But at night, when he was unable to sleep in the over-crowded train, it became clear to him that he was really going there for the sake of his childhood, in hopes of rediscovering something in the old streets: a gate, a tower, a fountain, some occasion for a joy or for a sorrow that would allow him to recognize himself again. Indeed, one loses oneself so in life! And then various things came to his mind: the little dwelling on Heinrichsgasse with the gleaming door handles and the dark-painted wood floors, the well cared-for furniture and his parents, those two worn-out people, almost rever-ent beside that furniture; the swift, frantic weekdays and the Sundays, which were like emptied rooms, the rare visitors who were welcomed with laughter and embarrassment, the out-of-tune piano, the old canary, the heirloom armchair on which you weren't allowed to sit, a name day, an uncle coming from Hamburg, a puppet theater, a hurdygurdy, a group of children, and someone calling: 'Klara.' The doctor had almost fallen asleep. You stop at a station, lanterns rush by, and the hammer passes attentively over the clanking wheels. And that sounds like: Klara, Klara. 'Klara,' the doctor muses; who was she, anyway? And immediately afterward, he senses a face, a child's face with smooth blonde hair. Not that he could describe it, but he has the sensation of something quiet, helpless, devoted, of two nar-row childish shoulders, squeezed even closer together by a little faded dress; and he invents a face to go with all that—but by now he knows that he doesn't need to invent it. It's there—or, rather, it *was* there—then. And so Dr. Lassmann recalls his onetime playmate Klara, not without difficulty. Up to the time when he entered a boarding school, at the age of ten or so, he shared everything with her that happened to him, however little (or much?) it was. Klara had no brothers or sisters, and he had as good as none, because his sisters didn't trouble themselves about him. But, since then, he has-n't asked anyone about her. How was that possible? He leaned back. She was a pious child, he still recalled, and then he asked himself: 'What can have become of her?' For a while he was anguished at the thought that she might have died. An immeasurable alarm came over him in the tightly crowded compartment; everything seemed to confirm that assumption: she was a sickly child, things at home weren't particularly good for her, she often wept; without a doubt, she was dead. The doctor couldn't bear it any longer; he disturbed a few sleepers and pushed his way between them into the corridor of the car. There he opened a window and looked out into the black-

öffnete er ein Fenster und schaute hinaus in das Schwarz mit den tanzenden Funken. Das beruhigte ihn. Und als er später in das Coupé zurückkehrte, schlief er trotz der unbequemen Lage bald ein.

Das Wiedersehen mit den beiden verheirateten Schwestern verlief nicht ohne Verlegenheiten. Die drei Menschen hatten vergessen, wie weit sie einander, trotz ihrer engen Verwandtschaft, doch immer geblieben waren, und versuchten eine Weile, sich wie Geschwister zu benehmen. Indessen kamen sie bald stillschweigend überein, zu dem höflichen Mittelton ihre Zuflucht zu nehmen, den der gesellschaftliche Verkehr für alle Fälle geschaffen hat.

Es war bei der jüngeren Schwester, deren Mann in besonders günstigen Verhältnissen war, Fabrikant mit dem Titel Kaiserlicher Rat, und es war nach dem vierten Gange des Diners, als der Doktor fragte: ›Sag mal, Sophie, was ist denn aus Klara geworden?‹ ›Welcher Klara?‹ ›Ich kann mich ihres Familiennamens nicht erinnern. Der Kleinen, weißt du, der Nachbarstochter, mit der ich als Kind gespielt habe?‹ ›Ach, Klara Söllner meinst du?‹ ›Söllner, richtig, Söllner. Jetzt fällt mir erst ein: Der alte Söllner, das war ja dieser gräßliche Alte – – aber was ist mit Klara?‹ Die Schwester zögerte: ›Sie hat geheiratet – Übrigens lebt sie jetzt ganz zurückgezogen.‹ ›Ja,‹ machte der Herr Rat, und sein Messer glitt kreischend über den Teller, ›ganz zurückgezogen.‹ ›Du kennst sie auch?‹ wandte sich der Doktor an seinen Schwager. ›Ja-a-a – so flüchtig; sie ist ja hier ziemlich bekannt.‹ Die beiden Gatten wechselten einen Blick des Einverständnisses. Der Doktor merkte, daß es ihnen aus irgend einem Grunde unangenehm war, über diese Angelegenheit zu reden, und fragte nicht weiter.

Umsomehr Lust zu diesem Thema bewies der Herr Rat, als die Hausfrau die Herren beim schwarzen Kaffee zurückgelassen hatte. ›Diese Klara‹, fragte er mit listigem Lächeln und betrachtete die Asche, die von seiner Zigarre in den silbernen Becher fiel. ›Sie soll doch ein stilles und überdies häßliches Kind gewesen sein?‹ Der Doktor schwieg. Der Herr Rat rückte vertraulich näher: ›Das war eine Geschichte! – Hast du nie davon gehört?‹ ›Aber ich habe ja mit niemandem gesprochen.‹ ›Was, gesprochen,‹ lächelte der Rat fein, ›man hat es ja in den Zeitungen lesen können.‹ ›Was?‹ fragte der Doktor nervös.

›Also, sie ist ihm durchgegangen‹ – hinter einer Wolke Rauches her schickte der Fabrikant diesen überraschenden Satz und wartete in unendlichem Behagen die Wirkung desselben ab. Aber diese schien ihm nicht zu gefallen. Er nahm eine geschäftliche Miene an, setzte sich gerade und begann in anderem berichtenden Ton, gleichsam gekränkt. ›Hm. Man hatte sie verheiratet an den Baurat Lehr. Du

ness with its dancing sparks. That settled his nerves. And when he later returned to the compartment, he soon fell asleep in spite of his uncomfortable situation.

"The reunion with his two married sisters didn't come off without embarrassing moments. The three people had forgotten how remote they had always remained from one another despite their blood relationship, and for a while they tried to behave like siblings. Meanwhile, they soon tacitly agreed to take refuge in that polite intermediate tone which social intercourse has created for all occasions.

"It was in the home of his younger sister, whose husband was particularly well off, a manufacturer with the title of Imperial Counselor, and it was after the fourth course of dinner, that the doctor asked: 'Tell me, Sophie, what became of Klara?' 'Which Klara?' 'I can't remember her last name. You know, the little one, our neighbor's daughter, with whom I played when I was a child.' 'Oh, you mean Klara Söllner?' "Söllner, that's right, Söllner. Now I suddenly remember: old Söllner was that horrible old man——but what about Klara?' His sister hesitated: 'She married— Anyway she now lives in complete retirement.' 'Yes,' said the counselor, and his knife slid across his plate with a screech, 'complete retirement.' 'You know her, too?' said the doctor, turning to his brother-in-law. 'Ye-e-es, very slightly; she's fairly well known around here.' Husband and wife exchanged a comprehending look. The doctor noticed that for some reason it was unpleasant for them to discuss the matter, and he asked no more questions.

"The counselor displayed all the more pleasure in that subject after the lady of the house had left the gentlemen to their black coffee. 'This Klara,' he asked with a sly smile, studying the ash that fell from his cigar into the silver tray, 'she's said to have been a quiet, and also an ugly child, right?' The doctor was silent. The counselor drew closer, in confidence: 'Was that a story!—You never heard about it?' 'How could I? I've never spoken with anyone.' 'What do you mean, spoken?' said the counselor with a subtle smile, 'after all, anyone could have read about it in the papers.' 'What?' the doctor asked nervously.

"'Yes, she ran away from him.' From behind a cloud of smoke the manufacturer uttered that surprising sentence, then waited in enormous self-satisfaction for it to take effect. But the result didn't seem to please him. He put on a professional air, sat up straight, and changed his tone to that of a narrative, as if his feelings had been hurt: 'Hm. She had been married off to the government architect Lehr. You

wirst ihn nicht mehr gekannt haben. Kein alter Mann, in meinem Alter. Reich, durchaus anständig, weißt du, durchaus anständig. Sie hatte keinen Groschen und war obendrein nicht schön, ohne Erziehung usw. Aber der Baurat wünschte ja auch keine große Dame, eine bescheidene Hausfrau. Aber die Klara – sie wurde überall in der Gesellschaft aufgenommen, man brachte ihr allgemein Wohlwollen entgegen, – wirklich – man benahm sich – also sie hätte sich eine Position schaffen können mit Leichtigkeit, weißt du – aber die Klara, eines Tages – kaum zwei Jahre nach der Hochzeit: fort ist sie. Kannst du dir denken: fort. Wohin? Nach Italien. Eine kleine Vergnügungsreise, natürlich nicht allein. Wir haben sie schon im ganzen letzten Jahr nicht eingeladen gehabt, – als ob wir geahnt hätten! Der Baurat, mein guter Freund, ein Ehrenmann, ein Mann –‹

›Und Klara?‹ unterbrach ihn der Doktor und erhob sich. ›Ach so – ja, na die Strafe des Himmels hat sie erreicht. Also der Betreffende – man sagt ein Künstler, weißt du – ein leichter Vogel, natürlich nur so – Also wie sie aus Italien zurück waren, in München: adieu und ward nicht mehr gesehen. Jetzt sitzt sie mit ihrem Kind!‹

Doktor Laßmann ging erregt auf und nieder: ›In München?‹ ›Ja, in München‹, antwortete der Rat und erhob sich gleichfalls. ›Es soll ihr übrigens recht elend gehen –‹ ›Was heißt elend?‹ –‹ ›Nun,‹ der Rat betrachtete seine Zigarre, ›pekuniär und dann überhaupt – Gott – so eine Existenz – – –‹ Plötzlich legte er seine gepflegte Hand dem Schwager auf die Schulter, seine Stimme gluckste vor Vergnügen: ›weißt du, übrigens erzählte man sich, sie lebe von –‹ Der Doktor drehte sich kurz um und ging aus der Tür. Der Herr Rat, dem die Hand von der Schulter des Schwagers gefallen war, brauchte zehn Minuten, um sich von seinem Staunen zu erholen. Dann ging er zu seiner Frau hinein und sagte ärgerlich: ›Ich hab es immer gesagt, dein Bruder ist ein Sonderling.‹ Und diese, die eben eingenickt war, gähnte träge: ›Ach Gott ja.‹

Vierzehn Tage später reiste der Doktor ab. Er wußte mit einemmal, daß er seine Kindheit anderswo suchen müsse. In München fand er im Adreßbuch: Klara Söllner, Schwabing, Straße und Nummer. Er meldete sich an und fuhr hinaus. Eine schlanke Frau begrüßte ihn in einer Stube voll Licht und Güte.

›Georg, und Sie erinnern sich meiner?‹

Der Doktor staunte. Endlich sagte er: ›Also das sind *Sie*, Klara.‹ Sie hielt ihr stilles Gesicht mit der reinen Stirn ganz ruhig, als wollte sie

probably couldn't have met him before you left. Not an old man: my
age. Wealthy, thoroughly respectable, you know, thoroughly respectable. She didn't have a cent and, on top of that, wasn't pretty, had
no education, etc. But the architect didn't want any grand lady, either;
he wanted a modest housewife. But Klara—she was universally accepted into society and everyone showed her the greatest kindness—
really—people behaved—in short, she might easily have made a position for herself, you know—but Klara, one day—scarcely two years
after they were married: she took off. Can you imagine? She took off.
Where to? To Italy. A short pleasure trip; not alone, of course. That
entire last year, we hadn't been inviting her—as if we had foreseen it!
The architect, a good friend of mine, a man of honor, a man—'

"'And Klara?' the doctor interrupted, standing up. 'Oh, yes—well,
heaven's punishment fell on her. The man in question—an artist, they
say, you know—a bird of passage he had to be— Well, when they were
back from Italy, in Munich: "Good-bye," and he was never seen again.
Now she's left with her child!'

"Dr. Lassmann paced to and fro excitedly: 'In Munich?' 'Yes, in
Munich,' the counselor replied, and he stood up, too. 'By the way,
people say that she's in dire straits—' 'What do you mean by dire
straits?' 'Well,' the counselor said, studying his cigar, 'financially and
in general—God—an existence like that———' Suddenly he placed
his well-tended hand on his brother-in-law's shoulder, his voice cluck-
ing with pleasure: 'You know, people also used to say that she lived
on—' The doctor turned on his heel sharply and went out the door. It
took the counselor, whose hand had fallen from his brother-in-law's
shoulder, ten minutes to get over his amazement. Then he went in to
his wife and said in vexation: 'I've always said your brother was eccentric.' And she, who had just dozed off, yawned lazily: 'Oh God,
yes.'

"Two weeks later the doctor departed. All at once he knew that he
had to seek his childhood elsewhere. In Munich he found in the di-
rectory: Klara Söllner, Schwabing,[36] with the street and house number. He gave word he was coming and rode out there. A slender
woman greeted him in a room full of light and human warmth.

"'Georg, so you still remember me?'

"The doctor was amazed. Finally he said: 'So this is you, Klara.' Her
quiet face, with its pure brow, remained quite calm, as if she wished

---

36. A Munich neighborhood favored by artists and writers, like the Latin Quarter in
Paris, Bloomsbury in London, and Greenwich Village in New York.

ihm Zeit geben, sie zu erkennen. Das dauerte lange. Schließlich
schien der Doktor etwas gefunden zu haben, was ihm bewies, daß
seine alte Spielgefährtin wirklich vor ihm stünde. Er suchte noch einmal ihre Hand und drückte sie; dann ließ er sie langsam los und
schaute in der Stube umher. Diese schien nichts Überflüssiges zu enthalten. Am Fenster ein Schreibtisch mit Schriften und Büchern, an
welchem Klara eben mußte gesessen haben. Der Stuhl war noch
zurückgeschoben. ›Sie haben geschrieben?‹ . . . und der Doktor
fühlte, wie dumm diese Frage war. Aber Klara antwortete unbefan-
gen: ›Ja, ich übersetze.‹ ›Für den Druck?‹ ›Ja,‹ sagte Klara einfach, ›für
einen Verlag.‹ Georg bemerkte an den Wänden einige italienische
Photographien. Darunter das ›Konzert‹ des Giorgione. ›Sie lieben
das?‹ Er trat nahe an das Bild heran. ›Und Sie?‹ ›Ich habe das Original
nie gesehen; es ist in Florenz, nicht wahr?‹ ›Im Pitti. Sie müssen hin-
reisen.‹ ›Zu diesem Zweck?‹ ›Zu diesem Zweck.‹ Eine freie und einfache Heiterkeit war über ihr. Der Doktor sah nachdenklich aus.

›Was haben Sie, Georg. Wollen Sie sich nicht setzen?‹ ›Ich bin traurig‹, zögerte er. ›Ich habe gedacht – aber Sie sind ja gar nicht elend –‹
fuhr es plötzlich heraus. Klara lächelte: ›Sie haben meine Geschichte
gehört?‹ ›Ja, das heißt –‹ ›Oh,‹ unterbrach ihn Klara schnell, als sie
merkte, daß seine Stirn sich verdunkelte, ›es ist nicht die Schuld der
Menschen, daß sie *anders* davon reden. Die Dinge, die wir erleben,
lassen sich oft nicht ausdrücken, und wer sie dennoch erzählt, muß
notwendig Fehler begehen –‹ Pause. Und der Doktor: ›Was hat Sie so
gütig gemacht?‹ ›Alles‹, sagte sie leise und warm. ›Aber warum sagen
Sie: gütig?‹ ›Weil – weil Sie eigentlich hätten hart werden müssen. Sie
waren ein so schwaches, hilfloses Kind; solche Kinder werden später
entweder hart oder –‹ ›Oder sie sterben – wollen Sie sagen. Nun, ich
bin auch gestorben. Oh, ich bin viele Jahre gestorben. Seit ich Sie
zum letztenmal gesehen habe, zu Haus, bis –‹ Sie langte etwas vom
Tische her: ›Sehen Sie, das ist sein Bild. Es ist etwas geschmeichelt.
Sein Gesicht ist nicht so klar, aber – lieber, einfacher. Ich werde Ihnen
dann gleich unser Kind zeigen, es schläft jetzt nebenan. Es ist ein
Bub. Heißt Angelo, wie er. Er ist jetzt fort, auf Reisen, weit.‹

›Und Sie sind ganz allein?‹ fragte der Doktor zerstreut, immer noch
über dem Bilde.

›Ja, ich und das Kind. Ist das nicht genug? Ich will Ihnen erzählen,
wie das kommt. Angelo ist Maler. Sein Name ist wenig bekannt, Sie
werden ihn nie gehört haben. Bis in die letzte Zeit hat er gerungen
mit der Welt, mit seinen Plänen, mit sich und mit mir. Ja, auch mit
mir; denn ich bat ihn seit einem Jahr: du mußt reisen. Ich fühlte, wie

to give him time to recognize her. It took a long while. Finally the doctor seemed to have discovered something that proved to him that his old playmate was really standing there in front of him. Once again he reached for her hand and squeezed it; then he released it slowly and looked around the room. It didn't seem to contain anything superfluous. By the window, a desk with papers and books, at which Klara must have been sitting just before. The chair was still pushed back. 'You were writing?' . . . and the doctor sensed how stupid that question was. But Klara replied without embarrassment: 'Yes, I'm doing a translation.' 'Will it be printed?' 'Yes,' said Klara simply, 'it's for a publisher.' Georg noticed some photos of Italian art on the walls. Among them was Giorgione's *Concert*. 'You like it?' He stepped over to the picture. 'And you?' 'I've never seen the original; it's in Florence, isn't it?' 'In the Pitti. You've got to go there.' 'Just for that purpose?' 'Just for that purpose.' There was an open, simple cheerfulness about her. The doctor looked thoughtful.

"'What's wrong, Georg? Don't you want to sit down?' 'I'm unhappy,' he said hesitantly. 'I thought—but you aren't in dire straits at all,' he suddenly blurted out. Klara smiled: 'You've heard my story?' 'Yes; that is—' 'Oh,' Klara quickly interrupted him, when she noticed his brow growing dark, 'it isn't people's fault if they talk about it *another way*. Often the things we experience can't be expressed, and whoever recounts them in spite of that, must necessarily make mistakes—' A pause. And the doctor: 'What has made you so kindly?' 'Everything,' she said softly and warmly. 'But why do you say "kindly"?' 'Because—because in reality you should have become hard. You were such a weak, helpless child; such children later either become hard or else—' 'Or else they die, you were going to say. Well, I died, too. Oh, I was dead for many years. Since I last saw you, at home, until—' She handed him something from the table: 'Look, this is his picture. It's a little flattering. His face isn't that well-chiseled, but—it's sweeter, simpler. Soon I'll show you our child, who's now sleeping in the next room. It's a boy. Named Angelo, like him. He's away right now, on a trip, far away.'

"'And you're all alone?' the doctor asked absentmindedly, still looking at the picture.

"'Yes, the child and I. Isn't that enough? I'll tell you how it is. Angelo is a painter. His name isn't well known, you've probably never heard it. Until very recently he struggled with the world, with his plans, with himself, and with me. Yes, even with me, because for a year I'd been imploring him: "You've got to travel." I felt how much

sehr ihm das not tat. Einmal sagte er scherzend: ‚Mich oder ein
Kind?' ‚Ein Kind', sagte ich, und dann reiste er.‹

›Und wann wird er zurückkehren?‹

›Bis das Kind seinen Namen sagen kann, so ist es abgemacht.‹ Der
Doktor wollte etwas bemerken. Aber Klara lachte: ›Und da es ein
schwerer Name ist, wird es noch eine Weile dauern. Angelino wird im
Sommer erst zwei Jahre.‹

›Seltsam‹, sagte der Doktor. ›Was, Georg?‹ ›Wie gut Sie das Leben verstehen. Wie groß Sie geworden sind, wie jung. Wo haben Sie Ihre
Kindheit hingetan? – wir waren doch beide so – so hilflose Kinder. Das
läßt sich doch nicht ändern oder ungeschehen machen.‹ ›Sie meinen
also, wir hätten an unserer Kindheit *leiden* müssen, von rechtswegen?‹
›Ja, gerade das meine ich. An diesem schweren Dunkel hinter uns, zu
dem wir so schwache, so ungewisse Beziehungen behalten. Da ist eine
Zeit: wir haben unsere Erstlinge hineingelegt, allen Anfang, alles
Vertrauen, die Keime zu alledem, was vielleicht einmal werden sollte.
Und plötzlich wissen wir: Alles das ist versunken in einem Meer, und wir
wissen nicht einmal genau wann. Wir haben es gar nicht bemerkt. Als ob
jemand sein ganzes Geld zusammensuchte, sich dafür eine Feder kaufte
und sie auf den Hut steckte, hui: der nächste Wind wird sie mitnehmen.
Natürlich kommt er zu Hause ohne Feder an, und ihm bleibt nichts
übrig, als nachzudenken, wann sie wohl könnte davongeflogen sein.‹

›Sie denken daran, Georg?‹

›Schon nicht mehr. Ich habe es aufgegeben. Ich beginne irgendwo
hinter meinem zehnten Jahr, dort, wo ich aufgehört habe zu beten.
Das andere gehört nicht mir.‹

›Und wie kommt es dann, daß Sie sich an *mich* erinnert haben?‹

›Darum komme ich ja zu Ihnen. Sie sind der einzige Zeuge jener
Zeit. Ich glaubte, ich könnte in Ihnen wiederfinden, – was ich in mir
nicht finden kann. Irgend eine Bewegung, ein Wort, einen Namen, an
dem etwas hängt – eine Aufklärung –‹ Der Doktor senkte den Kopf in
seine kalten, unruhigen Hände.

Frau Klara dachte nach: ›Ich erinnere mich an so weniges aus
meiner Kindheit, als wären tausend Leben dazwischen. Aber jetzt,
wie Sie mich so daran mahnen, fällt mir etwas ein. Ein Abend. Sie
kamen zu uns, unerwartet; Ihre Eltern waren ausgegangen, ins
Theater oder so. Bei uns war alles hell. Mein Vater erwartete einen
Gast, einen Verwandten, einen entfernten reichen Verwandten, wenn
ich mich recht entsinne. Er sollte kommen aus, aus – ich weiß nicht
woher, jedenfalls von weit. Bei uns wartet man schon seit zwei
Stunden auf ihn. Die Türen waren offen, die Lampen brannten, die

he needed that. Once he said in a joke: "Me or a child?" "A child," I answered, and then he left.'

"'And when will he be back?'

"'As soon as the child can say his name, that's the agreement we made.' The doctor was about to make a remark. But Klara laughed: 'And since it's a hard name, it will still be some time before he does. Angelino won't be two until next summer.'

"'Strange,' said the doctor. 'What, Georg?' 'How well you understand life. How tall you've become, how young. What did you do to put away your childhood? We were both such—such helpless children. And, after all, that can't be changed or made undone.' 'So you think we should rightly have *suffered* from our childhood?' 'Yes, that's just what I think. Suffered from that heavy darkness behind us, to which we retain such weak, insecure connections. That was a time in which we invested our firstfruits, all our beginnings, all our trust, the seeds of everything that might have followed after. And suddenly we know: all of that is submerged in a sea, and we don't even know exactly when it happened. We didn't notice it. As if someone were to gather together all his money, buy a feather with it, and set it in his cap; whoosh, the next gust of wind will blow it away. Naturally he comes home without the feather, and all he can still do is ponder about when it might have flown away.'

"'You think about that, Georg?'

"'Not any more. I've given it up. My life begins somewhere after I was ten, when I stopped praying. The rest doesn't belong to me.'

"'Then, how is it that you remembered *me?*'

"'But that's why I'm visiting you. You're the only witness to that period. I thought that in you I might rediscover—what I *can't* find in myself. Some activity, a word, a name to which something is attached—an enlightenment—' The doctor buried his head in his cold, restless hands.

"Klara said thoughtfully: 'I remember so little from our childhood, as if a thousand lives had come between then and today. But now that you remind me of it this way, I recall something. One evening. You visited us unexpectedly; your parents had gone out, to the theater or somewhere. In our house everything was bright. My father was expecting a guest, some relation, a distant, wealthy relative, if I recall correctly. He was to come from, from—I don't know where, at any rate, from far away. We had already been waiting two hours for him. Our doors were open, our lamps were lit, my mother occasionally

Mutter ging von Zeit zu Zeit und glättete eine Schutzdecke auf dem
Sofa, der Vater stand am Fenster. Niemand wagte sich zu setzen, um
keinen Stuhl zu verrücken. Da Sie gerade kamen, warteten Sie mit
uns. Wir Kinder horchten an der Tür. Und je später es wurde, einen
desto wunderbarern Gast erwarteten wir. Ja wir zitterten sogar, er
könnte kommen, ehe er jenen letzten Grad von Herrlichkeit erreicht
haben würde, dem er mit jeder Minute seines Ausbleibens näher
kam. Wir fürchteten nicht, er könnte überhaupt nicht erscheinen; wir
wußten bestimmt: er kommt, aber wir wollten ihm Zeit lassen, groß
und mächtig zu werden.‹

Plötzlich hob der Doktor den Kopf und sagte traurig: ›Das also wissen wir beide, daß er *nicht* kam – Ich habe es auch nicht vergessen
gehabt.‹ ›Nein,‹ – bestätigte Klara, ›er kam nicht –‹ Und nach einer
Pause: ›Aber es war doch schön!‹ ›Was?‹ ›Nun so – das Warten, die vielen Lampen, – die Stille – das Feiertägliche.‹

Etwas rührte sich im Nebenzimmer. Frau Klara entschuldigte sich
für einen Augenblick; und als sie hell und heiter zurückkam, sagte sie:
›Wir können dann hineingehen. Er ist jetzt wach und lächelt. – Aber
was wollten Sie eben sagen?‹

›Ich habe mir eben überlegt, was Ihnen könnte geholfen haben zu
– zu sich selbst, zu diesem ruhigen Sichbesitzen. Das Leben hat es
Ihnen doch nicht leicht gemacht. Offenbar half Ihnen etwas, was mir
fehlt?‹ ›Was sollte das sein, Georg?‹ Klara setzte sich neben ihn.

›Es ist seltsam; als ich mich zum erstenmal wieder Ihrer erinnerte,
vor drei Wochen nachts, auf der Reise, da fiel mir ein: sie war ein
frommes Kind. Und jetzt, seit ich Sie gesehen habe, trotzdem Sie so
ganz anders sind, als ich erwartete – trotzdem, ich möchte fast sagen,
nur noch desto sicherer, empfinde ich: was Sie geführt hat, mitten
durch alle Gefahren, war Ihre – Ihre Frömmigkeit.‹

›Was nennen Sie Frömmigkeit?‹

›Nun, Ihr Verhältnis zu Gott, Ihre Liebe zu ihm, Ihr Glauben.‹ –
Frau Klara schloß die Augen: ›Liebe zu Gott? Lassen Sie mich nachdenken.‹ Der Doktor betrachtete sie gespannt. Sie schien ihre Gedanken
langsam auszusprechen, so wie sie ihr kamen: ›Als Kind – Hab ich da Gott
geliebt? Ich glaube nicht. Ja ich habe nicht einmal – es hätte mir wie eine
wahnsinnige Überhebung – das ist nicht das richtige Wort – wie die
größte Sünde geschienen, zu denken: Er ist. Als ob ich ihn damit gezwungen hätte *in mir,* in diesem schwachen Kind mit den lächerlich langen
Armen, zu sein, in unserer armen Wohnung, in der alles unecht und
lügnerisch war, von den Bronzewandtellern aus Papiermaché bis zum
Wein in den Flaschen, die so teure Etiketten trugen. Und später –‹ Frau

went over to smooth a dust cover on the couch, my father was standing at the window. No one dared sit down, so no chair would get moved out of place. Since you happened to come, you were waiting with us. We children listened at the door. And the later it got, the more miraculous the guest we were expecting became. Yes, we even trembled at the thought that he might arrive before he had attained that ultimate degree of splendor which he was steadily approaching with every minute he was still absent. We weren't afraid of his not showing up at all; we knew for a certainty that he was coming, but we wanted to give him enough time to become great and powerful.'

"Suddenly the doctor raised his head and said sadly: 'Well, we both know he *didn't* come. I hadn't forgotten that, either.' 'No,' Klara said in confirmation, 'he didn't come—' And after a pause: 'But it was lovely all the same!' 'What was?' 'You know—the waiting, all those lamps—the silence—the holiday atmosphere.'

"Something stirred in the adjoining room. Klara excused herself for a minute; when she returned, bright and cheerful, she said: 'Now we can go in. Now he's awake and smiling.—But what were you just about to say?'

"'I've just been thinking about what might have helped you to—to become yourself, to be as calmly self-possessed as you are. After all, life didn't make it easy for you. Obviously you were helped by something that I lack.' 'What might that be, Georg?' Klara sat down next to him.

"'It's strange; when I first remembered you again, three weeks ago, at night, while traveling, I recalled: "She was a pious child." And now that I've seen you, even though you're so completely different from my expectations—I could almost say, all the surer of yourself despite that—I feel that the thing that brought you through all those dangers was your—your piety.'

"'What do you call piety?'

"'Well, your relationship to God, your love for him, your faith.'—

"Klara shut her eyes: 'Love for God? Let me think that over.' The doctor observed her in suspense. She seemed to be expressing her thoughts slowly, just as they came to her: 'As a child—did I love God then? I don't think so. In fact, I never even—it would have seemed like insane arrogance—no, that's not the right word—like the greatest sin, to think: "He exists." As if I would thereby have forced him to exist *within me,* in that weak child with the ridiculously long arms, in our humble house, where everything was false and untrue, from the "bronze" decorative wall plates made of papier-mâché to the wine in the bottles that bore such expensive labels. And later on—' Here

Klara machte eine abwehrende Bewegung mit den Händen, und ihre Augen schlossen sich fester, als fürchteten sie, durch die Lider etwas Furchtbares zu sehen – ›ich hätte ihn ja hinausdrängen müssen aus mir, wenn er in mir gewohnt hätte damals. Aber ich wußte nichts von ihm. Ich hatte ihn ganz vergessen. Ich hatte *alles* vergessen. – Erst in Florenz: Als ich zum erstenmal in meinem Leben sah, hörte, fühlte, erkannte und zugleich danken lernte für alles das, da dachte ich wieder an ihn. Überall waren Spuren von ihm. In allen Bildern fand ich Reste von seinem Lächeln, die Glocken lebten noch von seiner Stimme, und an den Statuen erkannte ich Abdrücke seiner Hände.‹

›Und da fanden Sie ihn?‹

Klara schaute den Doktor mit großen, glücklichen Augen an: ›Ich fühlte, daß er *war*, irgendwann einmal *war* . . . warum hätte ich *mehr* empfinden sollen? Das war ja schon Überfluß.‹

Der Doktor stand auf und ging aus Fenster. Man sah ein Stück Feld und die kleine, alte Schwabinger Kirche, darüber Himmel, nicht mehr ganz ohne Abend. Plötzlich fragte Doktor Laßmann, ohne sich umzuwenden: ›Und jetzt?‹ Als keine Antwort kam, kehrte er leise zurück.

›Jetzt –,‹ zögerte Klara, als er gerade vor ihr stand, und hob die Augen voll zu ihm auf: ›jetzt denke ich manchmal: Er wird sein.‹

Der Doktor nahm ihre Hand und behielt sie einen Augenblick. Er schaute so ins Unbestimmte.

›Woran denken Sie, Georg?‹

›Ich denke, daß das wieder wie an jenem Abend ist: *Sie* warten wieder auf den Wunderbaren, auf Gott, und wissen, daß er kommen wird – Und ich komme zufällig dazu –.‹

Frau Klara erhob sich leicht und heiter. Sie sah sehr jung aus. ›Nun, diesmal wollen wirs aber auch abwarten.‹ Sie sagte das so froh und einfach, daß der Doktor lächeln mußte. So führte sie ihn in das andere Zimmer, zu ihrem Kind. –«

In dieser Geschichte ist nichts, was Kinder nicht wissen dürfen. Indessen, die Kinder haben sie *nicht* erfahren. Ich habe sie nur dem Dunkel erzählt, sonst niemandem. Und die Kinder haben Angst vor dem Dunkel, laufen ihm davon, und müssen sie einmal drinnen bleiben, so pressen sie die Augen zusammen und halten sich die Ohren zu. Aber auch für sie wird einmal die Zeit kommen, da sie das Dunkel lieb haben. Sie werden von ihm meine Geschichte empfangen und dann werden sie sie auch besser verstehen.

❀   ❀

❀

Klara made a hand gesture of rebuff, and her eyes closed more tightly, as if in fear of seeing something frightening through their lids— 'I would have had to expel him from me, if he had dwelled in me at that time. But I knew nothing about him. I had completely forgotten about him. I had forgotten about *everything*.—It was only in Florence, when for the first time in my life I saw, heard, felt, realized, and, at the same time, learned how to be grateful for all that, that I thought about him again. There were traces of him everywhere. In old paintings I found remnants of his smile, the bells were still living on his voice, and on the statues I recognized the imprints of his hands.'

"'And then you found him?'"

"Klara looked at the doctor with wide, happy eyes: 'I felt that he existed, just existed at some time . . . why should I have felt *more*? That alone was more than enough.'

"The doctor arose and went to the window. A bit of field was visible, and the small old Schwabing church; above it, sky, no longer completely without evening in it. Suddenly Dr. Lassmann asked, without turning around: 'And now?' Upon receiving no reply, he returned quietly.

"'Now,' said Klara hesitantly, when he was standing right in front of her, and she raised her wide-open eyes toward him. 'Now I sometimes think: "He will exist."'

"The doctor took her hand and held it for a moment. He was gazing into an undefined space.

"'What are you thinking about, Georg?'

"'I'm thinking that it's once again the way it was that evening: once more *you* are waiting for the miraculous guest, for God, knowing that he'll come—and I arrive by chance—.'

"Klara stood up, lightly and cheerfully. She looked very young. 'Well, this time, let's wait for as long as it takes.' She said that so gaily and simply that the doctor had to smile. And so she led him into the adjoining room, to her child.—"

This story contains nothing that children shouldn't know about. Meanwhile, the children have *not* heard it. I've told it only to the darkness, to no one else. And children are afraid of the dark, and run away from it; if they have to remain in it on some occasion, they close their eyes tightly and cover their ears with their hands. But for them, too, the time will come when they love the dark. They will get to hear my story from it, and then they'll also understand the story better.

✧   ✧

✧

A CATALOG OF SELECTED
DOVER BOOKS
IN ALL FIELDS OF INTEREST

A CATALOG OF SELECTED DOVER
BOOKS IN ALL FIELDS OF INTEREST

CONCERNING THE SPIRITUAL IN ART, Wassily Kandinsky. Pioneering work by father of abstract art. Thoughts on color theory, nature of art. Analysis of earlier masters. 12 illustrations. 80pp. of text. 5⅜ x 8½. 0-486-23411-8

CELTIC ART: The Methods of Construction, George Bain. Simple geometric techniques for making Celtic interlacements, spirals, Kells-type initials, animals, humans, etc. Over 500 illustrations. 160pp. 9 x 12. (Available in U.S. only.) 0-486-22923-8

AN ATLAS OF ANATOMY FOR ARTISTS, Fritz Schider. Most thorough reference work on art anatomy in the world. Hundreds of illustrations, including selections from works by Vesalius, Leonardo, Goya, Ingres, Michelangelo, others. 593 illustrations. 192pp. 7⅛ x 10¼. 0-486-20241-0

CELTIC HAND STROKE-BY-STROKE (Irish Half-Uncial from "The Book of Kells"): An Arthur Baker Calligraphy Manual, Arthur Baker. Complete guide to creating each letter of the alphabet in distinctive Celtic manner. Covers hand position, strokes, pens, inks, paper, more. Illustrated. 48pp. 8¼ x 11. 0-486-24336-2

EASY ORIGAMI, John Montroll. Charming collection of 32 projects (hat, cup, pelican, piano, swan, many more) specially designed for the novice origami hobbyist. Clearly illustrated easy-to-follow instructions insure that even beginning papercrafters will achieve successful results. 48pp. 8¼ x 11. 0-486-27298-2

BLOOMINGDALE'S ILLUSTRATED 1886 CATALOG: Fashions, Dry Goods and Housewares, Bloomingdale Brothers. Famed merchants' extremely rare catalog depicting about 1,700 products: clothing, housewares, firearms, dry goods, jewelry, more. Invaluable for dating, identifying vintage items. Also, copyright-free graphics for artists, designers. Co-published with Henry Ford Museum & Greenfield Village. 160pp. 8¼ x 11. 0-486-25780-0

THE ART OF WORLDLY WISDOM, Baltasar Gracian. "Think with the few and speak with the many," "Friends are a second existence," and "Be able to forget" are among this 1637 volume's 300 pithy maxims. A perfect source of mental and spiritual refreshment, it can be opened at random and appreciated either in brief or at length. 128pp. 5⅜ x 8½. 0-486-44034-6

JOHNSON'S DICTIONARY: A Modern Selection, Samuel Johnson (E. L. McAdam and George Milne, eds.). This modern version reduces the original 1755 edition's 2,300 pages of definitions and literary examples to a more manageable length, retaining the verbal pleasure and historical curiosity of the original. 480pp. 5³⁄₁₆ x 8¼. 0-486-44089-3

ADVENTURES OF HUCKLEBERRY FINN, Mark Twain, Illustrated by E. W. Kemble. A work of eternal richness and complexity, a source of ongoing critical debate, and a literary landmark, Twain's 1885 masterpiece about a barefoot boy's journey of self-discovery has enthralled readers around the world. This handsome clothbound reproduction of the first edition features all 174 of the original black-and-white illustrations. 368pp. 5⅜ x 8½. 0-486-44322-1

CATALOG OF DOVER BOOKS

STICKLEY CRAFTSMAN FURNITURE CATALOGS, Gustav Stickley and L. & J. G. Stickley. Beautiful, functional furniture in two authentic catalogs from 1910. 594 illustrations, including 277 photos, show settles, rockers, armchairs, reclining chairs, bookcases, desks, tables. 183pp. 6½ x 9¼.   0-486-23838-5

AMERICAN LOCOMOTIVES IN HISTORIC PHOTOGRAPHS: 1858 to 1949, Ron Ziel (ed.). A rare collection of 126 meticulously detailed official photographs, called "builder portraits," of American locomotives that majestically chronicle the rise of steam locomotive power in America. Introduction. Detailed captions. xi+ 129pp. 9 x 12.   0-486-27393-8

AMERICA'S LIGHTHOUSES: An Illustrated History, Francis Ross Holland, Jr. Delightfully written, profusely illustrated fact-filled survey of over 200 American lighthouses since 1716. History, anecdotes, technological advances, more. 240pp. 8 x 10¾.
0-486-25576-X

TOWARDS A NEW ARCHITECTURE, Le Corbusier. Pioneering manifesto by founder of "International School." Technical and aesthetic theories, views of industry, economics, relation of form to function, "mass-production split" and much more. Profusely illustrated. 320pp. 6⅛ x 9¼. (Available in U.S. only.)   0-486-25023-7

HOW THE OTHER HALF LIVES, Jacob Riis. Famous journalistic record, exposing poverty and degradation of New York slums around 1900, by major social reformer. 100 striking and influential photographs. 233pp. 10 x 7⅞.   0-486-22012-5

FRUIT KEY AND TWIG KEY TO TREES AND SHRUBS, William M. Harlow. One of the handiest and most widely used identification aids. Fruit key covers 120 deciduous and evergreen species; twig key 160 deciduous species. Easily used. Over 300 photographs. 126pp. 5⅜ x 8½.   0-486-20511-8

COMMON BIRD SONGS, Dr. Donald J. Borror. Songs of 60 most common U.S. birds: robins, sparrows, cardinals, bluejays, finches, more–arranged in order of increasing complexity. Up to 9 variations of songs of each species.
Cassette and manual 0-486-99911-4

ORCHIDS AS HOUSE PLANTS, Rebecca Tyson Northen. Grow cattleyas and many other kinds of orchids–in a window, in a case, or under artificial light. 63 illustrations. 148pp. 5⅜ x 8½.   0-486-23261-1

MONSTER MAZES, Dave Phillips. Masterful mazes at four levels of difficulty. Avoid deadly perils and evil creatures to find magical treasures. Solutions for all 32 exciting illustrated puzzles. 48pp. 8¼ x 11.   0-486-26005-4

MOZART'S DON GIOVANNI (DOVER OPERA LIBRETTO SERIES), Wolfgang Amadeus Mozart. Introduced and translated by Ellen H. Bleiler. Standard Italian libretto, with complete English translation. Convenient and thoroughly portable–an ideal companion for reading along with a recording or the performance itself. Introduction. List of characters. Plot summary. 121pp. 5¼ x 8½. 0-486-24944-1

FRANK LLOYD WRIGHT'S DANA HOUSE, Donald Hoffmann. Pictorial essay of residential masterpiece with over 160 interior and exterior photos, plans, elevations, sketches and studies. 128pp. 9¼ x 10¾.   0-486-29120-0

THE CLARINET AND CLARINET PLAYING, David Pino. Lively, comprehensive work features suggestions about technique, musicianship, and musical interpretation, as well as guidelines for teaching, making your own reeds, and preparing for public performance. Includes an intriguing look at clarinet history. "A godsend," *The Clarinet,* Journal of the International Clarinet Society. Appendixes. 7 illus. 320pp. 5⅜ x 8½. 0-486-40270-3

HOLLYWOOD GLAMOR PORTRAITS, John Kobal (ed.). 145 photos from 1926-49. Harlow, Gable, Bogart, Bacall; 94 stars in all. Full background on photographers, technical aspects. 160pp. 8⅜ x 11¼. 0-486-23352-9

THE RAVEN AND OTHER FAVORITE POEMS, Edgar Allan Poe. Over 40 of the author's most memorable poems: "The Bells," "Ulalume," "Israfel," "To Helen," "The Conqueror Worm," "Eldorado," "Annabel Lee," many more. Alphabetic lists of titles and first lines. 64pp. 5$^{3}/_{16}$ x 8¼. 0-486-26685-0

PERSONAL MEMOIRS OF U. S. GRANT, Ulysses Simpson Grant. Intelligent, deeply moving firsthand account of Civil War campaigns, considered by many the finest military memoirs ever written. Includes letters, historic photographs, maps and more. 528pp. 6⅛ x 9¼. 0-486-28587-1

ANCIENT EGYPTIAN MATERIALS AND INDUSTRIES, A. Lucas and J. Harris. Fascinating, comprehensive, thoroughly documented text describes this ancient civilization's vast resources and the processes that incorporated them in daily life, including the use of animal products, building materials, cosmetics, perfumes and incense, fibers, glazed ware, glass and its manufacture, materials used in the mummification process, and much more. 544pp. 6⅛ x 9¼. (Available in U.S. only.) 0-486-40446-3

RUSSIAN STORIES/RUSSKIE RASSKAZY: A Dual-Language Book, edited by Gleb Struve. Twelve tales by such masters as Chekhov, Tolstoy, Dostoevsky, Pushkin, others. Excellent word-for-word English translations on facing pages, plus teaching and study aids, Russian/English vocabulary, biographical/critical introductions, more. 416pp. 5⅜ x 8½. 0-486-26244-8

PHILADELPHIA THEN AND NOW: 60 Sites Photographed in the Past and Present, Kenneth Finkel and Susan Oyama. Rare photographs of City Hall, Logan Square, Independence Hall, Betsy Ross House, other landmarks juxtaposed with contemporary views. Captures changing face of historic city. Introduction. Captions. 128pp. 8¼ x 11. 0-486-25790-8

NORTH AMERICAN INDIAN LIFE: Customs and Traditions of 23 Tribes, Elsie Clews Parsons (ed.). 27 fictionalized essays by noted anthropologists examine religion, customs, government, additional facets of life among the Winnebago, Crow, Zuni, Eskimo, other tribes. 480pp. 6⅛ x 9¼. 0-486-27377-6

TECHNICAL MANUAL AND DICTIONARY OF CLASSICAL BALLET, Gail Grant. Defines, explains, comments on steps, movements, poses and concepts. 15-page pictorial section. Basic book for student, viewer. 127pp. 5⅜ x 8½. 0-486-21843-0

THE MALE AND FEMALE FIGURE IN MOTION: 60 Classic Photographic Sequences, Eadweard Muybridge. 60 true-action photographs of men and women walking, running, climbing, bending, turning, etc., reproduced from rare 19th-century masterpiece. vi + 121pp. 9 x 12. 0-486-24745-7

ANIMALS: 1,419 Copyright-Free Illustrations of Mammals, Birds, Fish, Insects, etc., Jim Harter (ed.). Clear wood engravings present, in extremely lifelike poses, over 1,000 species of animals. One of the most extensive pictorial sourcebooks of its kind. Captions. Index. 284pp. 9 x 12. 0-486-23766-4

1001 QUESTIONS ANSWERED ABOUT THE SEASHORE, N. J. Berrill and Jacquelyn Berrill. Queries answered about dolphins, sea snails, sponges, starfish, fishes, shore birds, many others. Covers appearance, breeding, growth, feeding, much more. 305pp. 5¼ x 8¼. 0-486-23366-9

ATTRACTING BIRDS TO YOUR YARD, William J. Weber. Easy-to-follow guide offers advice on how to attract the greatest diversity of birds: birdhouses, feeders, water and waterers, much more. 96pp. 5³⁄₁₆ x 8¼. 0-486-28927-3

MEDICINAL AND OTHER USES OF NORTH AMERICAN PLANTS: A Historical Survey with Special Reference to the Eastern Indian Tribes, Charlotte Erichsen-Brown. Chronological historical citations document 500 years of usage of plants, trees, shrubs native to eastern Canada, northeastern U.S. Also complete identifying information. 343 illustrations. 544pp. 6½ x 9¼. 0-486-25951-X

STORYBOOK MAZES, Dave Phillips. 23 stories and mazes on two-page spreads: Wizard of Oz, Treasure Island, Robin Hood, etc. Solutions. 64pp. 8¼ x 11. 0-486-23628-5

AMERICAN NEGRO SONGS: 230 Folk Songs and Spirituals, Religious and Secular, John W. Work. This authoritative study traces the African influences of songs sung and played by black Americans at work, in church, and as entertainment. The author discusses the lyric significance of such songs as "Swing Low, Sweet Chariot," "John Henry," and others and offers the words and music for 230 songs. Bibliography. Index of Song Titles. 272pp. 6½ x 9¼. 0-486-40271-1

MOVIE-STAR PORTRAITS OF THE FORTIES, John Kobal (ed.). 163 glamor, studio photos of 106 stars of the 1940s: Rita Hayworth, Ava Gardner, Marlon Brando, Clark Gable, many more. 176pp. 8⅜ x 11¼. 0-486-23546-7

YEKL and THE IMPORTED BRIDEGROOM AND OTHER STORIES OF YIDDISH NEW YORK, Abraham Cahan. Film Hester Street based on *Yekl* (1896). Novel, other stories among first about Jewish immigrants on N.Y.'s East Side. 240pp. 5⅜ x 8½. 0-486-22427-9

SELECTED POEMS, Walt Whitman. Generous sampling from *Leaves of Grass.* Twenty-four poems include "I Hear America Singing," "Song of the Open Road," "I Sing the Body Electric," "When Lilacs Last in the Dooryard Bloom'd," "O Captain! My Captain!"—all reprinted from an authoritative edition. Lists of titles and first lines. 128pp. 5³⁄₁₆ x 8¼. 0-486-26878-0

SONGS OF EXPERIENCE: Facsimile Reproduction with 26 Plates in Full Color, William Blake. 26 full-color plates from a rare 1826 edition. Includes "The Tyger," "London," "Holy Thursday," and other poems. Printed text of poems. 48pp. 5¼ x 7. 0-486-24636-1

THE BEST TALES OF HOFFMANN, E. T. A. Hoffmann. 10 of Hoffmann's most important stories: "Nutcracker and the King of Mice," "The Golden Flowerpot," etc. 458pp. 5⅜ x 8½. 0-486-21793-0

THE BOOK OF TEA, Kakuzo Okakura. Minor classic of the Orient: entertaining, charming explanation, interpretation of traditional Japanese culture in terms of tea ceremony. 94pp. 5⅜ x 8½. 0-486-20070-1

FRENCH STORIES/CONTES FRANÇAIS: A Dual-Language Book, Wallace Fowlie. Ten stories by French masters, Voltaire to Camus: "Micromegas" by Voltaire; "The Atheist's Mass" by Balzac; "Minuet" by de Maupassant; "The Guest" by Camus, six more. Excellent English translations on facing pages. Also French-English vocabulary list, exercises, more. 352pp. 5⅜ x 8½. 0-486-26443-2

CHICAGO AT THE TURN OF THE CENTURY IN PHOTOGRAPHS: 122 Historic Views from the Collections of the Chicago Historical Society, Larry A. Viskochil. Rare large-format prints offer detailed views of City Hall, State Street, the Loop, Hull House, Union Station, many other landmarks, circa 1904-1913. Introduction. Captions. Maps. 144pp. 9⅜ x 12¼. 0-486-24656-6

OLD BROOKLYN IN EARLY PHOTOGRAPHS, 1865-1929, William Lee Younger. Luna Park, Gravesend race track, construction of Grand Army Plaza, moving of Hotel Brighton, etc. 157 previously unpublished photographs. 165pp. 8⅞ x 11¾. 0-486-23587-4

THE MYTHS OF THE NORTH AMERICAN INDIANS, Lewis Spence. Rich anthology of the myths and legends of the Algonquins, Iroquois, Pawnees and Sioux, prefaced by an extensive historical and ethnological commentary. 36 illustrations. 480pp. 5⅜ x 8½. 0-486-25967-6

AN ENCYCLOPEDIA OF BATTLES: Accounts of Over 1,560 Battles from 1479 B.C. to the Present, David Eggenberger. Essential details of every major battle in recorded history from the first battle of Megiddo in 1479 B.C. to Grenada in 1984. List of Battle Maps. New Appendix covering the years 1967-1984. Index. 99 illustrations. 544pp. 6½ x 9¼. 0-486-24913-1

SAILING ALONE AROUND THE WORLD, Captain Joshua Slocum. First man to sail around the world, alone, in small boat. One of great feats of seamanship told in delightful manner. 67 illustrations. 294pp. 5⅜ x 8½. 0-486-20326-3

ANARCHISM AND OTHER ESSAYS, Emma Goldman. Powerful, penetrating, prophetic essays on direct action, role of minorities, prison reform, puritan hypocrisy, violence, etc. 271pp. 5⅜ x 8½. 0-486-22484-8

MYTHS OF THE HINDUS AND BUDDHISTS, Ananda K. Coomaraswamy and Sister Nivedita. Great stories of the epics; deeds of Krishna, Shiva, taken from puranas, Vedas, folk tales; etc. 32 illustrations. 400pp. 5⅜ x 8½. 0-486-21759-0

MY BONDAGE AND MY FREEDOM, Frederick Douglass. Born a slave, Douglass became outspoken force in antislavery movement. The best of Douglass' autobiographies. Graphic description of slave life. 464pp. 5⅜ x 8½. 0-486-22457-0

FOLLOWING THE EQUATOR: A Journey Around the World, Mark Twain. Fascinating humorous account of 1897 voyage to Hawaii, Australia, India, New Zealand, etc. Ironic, bemused reports on peoples, customs, climate, flora and fauna, politics, much more. 197 illustrations. 720pp. 5⅜ x 8½. 0-486-26113-1

THE PEOPLE CALLED SHAKERS, Edward D. Andrews. Definitive study of Shakers: origins, beliefs, practices, dances, social organization, furniture and crafts, etc. 33 illustrations. 351pp. 5⅜ x 8½. 0-486-21081-2

THE MYTHS OF GREECE AND ROME, H. A. Guerber. A classic of mythology, generously illustrated, long prized for its simple, graphic, accurate retelling of the principal myths of Greece and Rome, and for its commentary on their origins and significance. With 64 illustrations by Michelangelo, Raphael, Titian, Rubens, Canova, Bernini and others. 480pp. 5⅜ x 8½. 0-486-27584-1

PSYCHOLOGY OF MUSIC, Carl E. Seashore. Classic work discusses music as a medium from psychological viewpoint. Clear treatment of physical acoustics, auditory apparatus, sound perception, development of musical skills, nature of musical feeling, host of other topics. 88 figures. 408pp. 5⅜ x 8½. 0-486-21851-1

LIFE IN ANCIENT EGYPT, Adolf Erman. Fullest, most thorough, detailed older account with much not in more recent books, domestic life, religion, magic, medicine, commerce, much more. Many illustrations reproduce tomb paintings, carvings, hieroglyphs, etc. 597pp. 5⅜ x 8½. 0-486-22632-8

SUNDIALS, Their Theory and Construction, Albert Waugh. Far and away the best, most thorough coverage of ideas, mathematics concerned, types, construction, adjusting anywhere. Simple, nontechnical treatment allows even children to build several of these dials. Over 100 illustrations. 230pp. 5⅜ x 8½. 0-486-22947-5

THEORETICAL HYDRODYNAMICS, L. M. Milne-Thomson. Classic exposition of the mathematical theory of fluid motion, applicable to both hydrodynamics and aerodynamics. Over 600 exercises. 768pp. 6⅛ x 9¼. 0-486-68970-0

OLD-TIME VIGNETTES IN FULL COLOR, Carol Belanger Grafton (ed.). Over 390 charming, often sentimental illustrations, selected from archives of Victorian graphics–pretty women posing, children playing, food, flowers, kittens and puppies, smiling cherubs, birds and butterflies, much more. All copyright-free. 48pp. 9¼ x 12¼. 0-486-27269-9

PERSPECTIVE FOR ARTISTS, Rex Vicat Cole. Depth, perspective of sky and sea, shadows, much more, not usually covered. 391 diagrams, 81 reproductions of drawings and paintings. 279pp. 5⅜ x 8½. 0-486-22487-2

DRAWING THE LIVING FIGURE, Joseph Sheppard. Innovative approach to artistic anatomy focuses on specifics of surface anatomy, rather than muscles and bones. Over 170 drawings of live models in front, back and side views, and in widely varying poses. Accompanying diagrams. 177 illustrations. Introduction. Index. 144pp. 8⅜ x11¼. 0-486-26723-7

GOTHIC AND OLD ENGLISH ALPHABETS: 100 Complete Fonts, Dan X. Solo. Add power, elegance to posters, signs, other graphics with 100 stunning copyright-free alphabets: Blackstone, Dolbey, Germania, 97 more–including many lower-case, numerals, punctuation marks. 104pp. 8⅛ x 11. 0-486-24695-7

THE BOOK OF WOOD CARVING, Charles Marshall Sayers. Finest book for beginners discusses fundamentals and offers 34 designs. "Absolutely first rate . . . well thought out and well executed."–E. J. Tangerman. 118pp. 7¾ x 10⅝. 0-486-23654-4

ILLUSTRATED CATALOG OF CIVIL WAR MILITARY GOODS: Union Army Weapons, Insignia, Uniform Accessories, and Other Equipment, Schuyler, Hartley, and Graham. Rare, profusely illustrated 1846 catalog includes Union Army uniform and dress regulations, arms and ammunition, coats, insignia, flags, swords, rifles, etc. 226 illustrations. 160pp. 9 x 12. 0-486-24939-5

WOMEN'S FASHIONS OF THE EARLY 1900s: An Unabridged Republication of "New York Fashions, 1909," National Cloak & Suit Co. Rare catalog of mail-order fashions documents women's and children's clothing styles shortly after the turn of the century. Captions offer full descriptions, prices. Invaluable resource for fashion, costume historians. Approximately 725 illustrations. 128pp. 8⅜ x 11¼. 0-486-27276-1

HOW TO DO BEADWORK, Mary White. Fundamental book on craft from simple projects to five-bead chains and woven works. 106 illustrations. 142pp. 5⅜ x 8.
0-486-20697-1

THE 1912 AND 1915 GUSTAV STICKLEY FURNITURE CATALOGS, Gustav Stickley. With over 200 detailed illustrations and descriptions, these two catalogs are essential reading and reference materials and identification guides for Stickley furniture. Captions cite materials, dimensions and prices. 112pp. 6½ x 9¼. 0-486-26676-1

EARLY AMERICAN LOCOMOTIVES, John H. White, Jr. Finest locomotive engravings from early 19th century: historical (1804–74), main-line (after 1870), special, foreign, etc. 147 plates. 142pp. 11⅜ x 8¼. 0-486-22772-3

LITTLE BOOK OF EARLY AMERICAN CRAFTS AND TRADES, Peter Stockham (ed.). 1807 children's book explains crafts and trades: baker, hatter, cooper, potter, and many others. 23 copperplate illustrations. 140pp. 4⅝/8 x 6.
0-486-23336-7

VICTORIAN FASHIONS AND COSTUMES FROM HARPER'S BAZAR, 1867–1898, Stella Blum (ed.). Day costumes, evening wear, sports clothes, shoes, hats, other accessories in over 1,000 detailed engravings. 320pp. 9⅜ x 12¼.
0-486-22990-4

THE LONG ISLAND RAIL ROAD IN EARLY PHOTOGRAPHS, Ron Ziel. Over 220 rare photos, informative text document origin (1844) and development of rail service on Long Island. Vintage views of early trains, locomotives, stations, passengers, crews, much more. Captions. 8⅞ x 11¾. 0-486-26301-0

VOYAGE OF THE LIBERDADE, Joshua Slocum. Great 19th-century mariner's thrilling, first-hand account of the wreck of his ship off South America, the 35-foot boat he built from the wreckage, and its remarkable voyage home. 128pp. 5⅜ x 8½.
0-486-40022-0

TEN BOOKS ON ARCHITECTURE, Vitruvius. The most important book ever written on architecture. Early Roman aesthetics, technology, classical orders, site selection, all other aspects. Morgan translation. 331pp. 5⅜ x 8½. 0-486-20645-9

THE HUMAN FIGURE IN MOTION, Eadweard Muybridge. More than 4,500 stopped-action photos, in action series, showing undraped men, women, children jumping, lying down, throwing, sitting, wrestling, carrying, etc. 390pp. 7⅞ x 10⅝.
0-486-20204-6 Clothbd.

TREES OF THE EASTERN AND CENTRAL UNITED STATES AND CANADA, William M. Harlow. Best one-volume guide to 140 trees. Full descriptions, woodlore, range, etc. Over 600 illustrations. Handy size. 288pp. 4½ x 6⅜. 0-486-20395-6

GROWING AND USING HERBS AND SPICES, Milo Miloradovich. Versatile handbook provides all the information needed for cultivation and use of all the herbs and spices available in North America. 4 illustrations. Index. Glossary. 236pp. 5⅜ x 8½.
0-486-25058-X

BIG BOOK OF MAZES AND LABYRINTHS, Walter Shepherd. 50 mazes and labyrinths in all—classical, solid, ripple, and more—in one great volume. Perfect inexpensive puzzler for clever youngsters. Full solutions. 112pp. 8⅛ x 11. 0-486-22951-3

PIANO TUNING, J. Cree Fischer. Clearest, best book for beginner, amateur. Simple repairs, raising dropped notes, tuning by easy method of flattened fifths. No previous skills needed. 4 illustrations. 201pp. 5⅜ x 8½. 0-486-23267-0

HINTS TO SINGERS, Lillian Nordica. Selecting the right teacher, developing confidence, overcoming stage fright, and many other important skills receive thoughtful discussion in this indispensible guide, written by a world-famous diva of four decades' experience. 96pp. 5⅜ x 8½. 0-486-40094-8

THE COMPLETE NONSENSE OF EDWARD LEAR, Edward Lear. All nonsense limericks, zany alphabets, Owl and Pussycat, songs, nonsense botany, etc., illustrated by Lear. Total of 320pp. 5⅜ x 8½. (Available in U.S. only.) 0-486-20167-8

VICTORIAN PARLOUR POETRY: An Annotated Anthology, Michael R. Turner. 117 gems by Longfellow, Tennyson, Browning, many lesser-known poets. "The Village Blacksmith," "Curfew Must Not Ring Tonight," "Only a Baby Small," dozens more, often difficult to find elsewhere. Index of poets, titles, first lines. xxiii + 325pp. 5⅝ x 8¼. 0-486-27044-0

DUBLINERS, James Joyce. Fifteen stories offer vivid, tightly focused observations of the lives of Dublin's poorer classes. At least one, "The Dead," is considered a masterpiece. Reprinted complete and unabridged from standard edition. 160pp. 5$\frac{3}{16}$ x 8¼. 0-486-26870-5

GREAT WEIRD TALES: 14 Stories by Lovecraft, Blackwood, Machen and Others, S. T. Joshi (ed.). 14 spellbinding tales, including "The Sin Eater," by Fiona McLeod, "The Eye Above the Mantel," by Frank Belknap Long, as well as renowned works by R. H. Barlow, Lord Dunsany, Arthur Machen, W. C. Morrow and eight other masters of the genre. 256pp. 5⅜ x 8½. (Available in U.S. only.) 0-486-40436-6

THE BOOK OF THE SACRED MAGIC OF ABRAMELIN THE MAGE, translated by S. MacGregor Mathers. Medieval manuscript of ceremonial magic. Basic document in Aleister Crowley, Golden Dawn groups. 268pp. 5⅜ x 8½. 0-486-23211-5

THE BATTLES THAT CHANGED HISTORY, Fletcher Pratt. Eminent historian profiles 16 crucial conflicts, ancient to modern, that changed the course of civilization. 352pp. 5⅜ x 8½. 0-486-41129-X

NEW RUSSIAN-ENGLISH AND ENGLISH-RUSSIAN DICTIONARY, M. A. O'Brien. This is a remarkably handy Russian dictionary, containing a surprising amount of information, including over 70,000 entries. 366pp. 4½ x 6⅛. 0-486-20208-9

NEW YORK IN THE FORTIES, Andreas Feininger. 162 brilliant photographs by the well-known photographer, formerly with *Life* magazine. Commuters, shoppers, Times Square at night, much else from city at its peak. Captions by John von Hartz. 181pp. 9¼ x 10¾. 0-486-23585-8

INDIAN SIGN LANGUAGE, William Tomkins. Over 525 signs developed by Sioux and other tribes. Written instructions and diagrams. Also 290 pictographs. 111pp. 6⅛ x 9¼. 0-486-22029-X

ANATOMY: A Complete Guide for Artists, Joseph Sheppard. A master of figure drawing shows artists how to render human anatomy convincingly. Over 460 illustrations. 224pp. 8⅜ x 11¼. 0-486-27279-6

MEDIEVAL CALLIGRAPHY: Its History and Technique, Marc Drogin. Spirited history, comprehensive instruction manual covers 13 styles (ca. 4th century through 15th). Excellent photographs; directions for duplicating medieval techniques with modern tools. 224pp. 8⅜ x 11¼. 0-486-26142-5

DRIED FLOWERS: How to Prepare Them, Sarah Whitlock and Martha Rankin. Complete instructions on how to use silica gel, meal and borax, perlite aggregate, sand and borax, glycerine and water to create attractive permanent flower arrangements. 12 illustrations. 32pp. 5⅜ x 8½.   0-486-21802-3

EASY-TO-MAKE BIRD FEEDERS FOR WOODWORKERS, Scott D. Campbell. Detailed, simple-to-use guide for designing, constructing, caring for and using feeders. Text, illustrations for 12 classic and contemporary designs. 96pp. 5⅜ x 8½.
0-486-25847-5

THE COMPLETE BOOK OF BIRDHOUSE CONSTRUCTION FOR WOOD-WORKERS, Scott D. Campbell. Detailed instructions, illustrations, tables. Also data on bird habitat and instinct patterns. Bibliography. 3 tables. 63 illustrations in 15 figures. 48pp. 5¼ x 8½.   0-486-24407-5

SCOTTISH WONDER TALES FROM MYTH AND LEGEND, Donald A. Mackenzie. 16 lively tales tell of giants rumbling down mountainsides, of a magic wand that turns stone pillars into warriors, of gods and goddesses, evil hags, powerful forces and more. 240pp. 5⅜ x 8½.   0-486-29677-6

THE HISTORY OF UNDERCLOTHES, C. Willett Cunnington and Phyllis Cunnington. Fascinating, well-documented survey covering six centuries of English undergarments, enhanced with over 100 illustrations: 12th-century laced-up bodice, footed long drawers (1795), 19th-century bustles, l9th-century corsets for men, Victorian "bust improvers," much more. 272pp. 5⅜ x 8¼.   0-486-27124-2

ARTS AND CRAFTS FURNITURE: The Complete Brooks Catalog of 1912, Brooks Manufacturing Co. Photos and detailed descriptions of more than 150 now very collectible furniture designs from the Arts and Crafts movement depict davenports, settees, buffets, desks, tables, chairs, bedsteads, dressers and more, all built of solid, quarter-sawed oak. Invaluable for students and enthusiasts of antiques, Americana and the decorative arts. 80pp. 6½ x 9¼.   0-486-27471-3

WILBUR AND ORVILLE: A Biography of the Wright Brothers, Fred Howard. Definitive, crisply written study tells the full story of the brothers' lives and work. A vividly written biography, unparalleled in scope and color, that also captures the spirit of an extraordinary era. 560pp. 6⅛ x 9¼.   0-486-40297-5

THE ARTS OF THE SAILOR: Knotting, Splicing and Ropework, Hervey Garrett Smith. Indispensable shipboard reference covers tools, basic knots and useful hitches; handsewing and canvas work, more. Over 100 illustrations. Delightful reading for sea lovers. 256pp. 5⅜ x 8½.   0-486-26440-8

FRANK LLOYD WRIGHT'S FALLINGWATER: The House and Its History, Second, Revised Edition, Donald Hoffmann. A total revision—both in text and illustrations—of the standard document on Fallingwater, the boldest, most personal architectural statement of Wright's mature years, updated with valuable new material from the recently opened Frank Lloyd Wright Archives. "Fascinating"—*The New York Times*. 116 illustrations. 128pp. 9¼ x 10¾.   0-486-27430-6

PHOTOGRAPHIC SKETCHBOOK OF THE CIVIL WAR, Alexander Gardner. 100 photos taken on field during the Civil War. Famous shots of Manassas Harper's Ferry, Lincoln, Richmond, slave pens, etc. 244pp. 10⅝ x 8¼.   0-486-22731-6

FIVE ACRES AND INDEPENDENCE, Maurice G. Kains. Great back-to-the-land classic explains basics of self-sufficient farming. The one book to get. 95 illustrations. 397pp. 5⅜ x 8½.   0-486-20974-1

A MODERN HERBAL, Margaret Grieve. Much the fullest, most exact, most useful compilation of herbal material. Gigantic alphabetical encyclopedia, from aconite to zedoary, gives botanical information, medical properties, folklore, economic uses, much else. Indispensable to serious reader. 161 illustrations. 888pp. 6½ x 9¼. 2-vol. set. (Available in U.S. only.)   Vol. I: 0-486-22798-7   Vol. II: 0-486-22799-5

HIDDEN TREASURE MAZE BOOK, Dave Phillips. Solve 34 challenging mazes accompanied by heroic tales of adventure. Evil dragons, people-eating plants, blood-thirsty giants, many more dangerous adversaries lurk at every twist and turn. 34 mazes, stories, solutions. 48pp. 8¼ x 11.   0-486-24566-7

LETTERS OF W. A. MOZART, Wolfgang A. Mozart. Remarkable letters show bawdy wit, humor, imagination, musical insights, contemporary musical world; includes some letters from Leopold Mozart. 276pp. 5⅜ x 8½.   0-486-22859-2

BASIC PRINCIPLES OF CLASSICAL BALLET, Agrippina Vaganova. Great Russian theoretician, teacher explains methods for teaching classical ballet. 118 illustrations. 175pp. 5⅜ x 8½.   0-486-22036-2

THE JUMPING FROG, Mark Twain. Revenge edition. The original story of The Celebrated Jumping Frog of Calaveras County, a hapless French translation, and Twain's hilarious "retranslation" from the French. 12 illustrations. 66pp. 5⅜ x 8½.
0-486-22686-7

BEST REMEMBERED POEMS, Martin Gardner (ed.). The 126 poems in this superb collection of 19th- and 20th-century British and American verse range from Shelley's "To a Skylark" to the impassioned "Renascence" of Edna St. Vincent Millay and to Edward Lear's whimsical "The Owl and the Pussycat." 224pp. 5⅜ x 8½.
0-486-27165-X

COMPLETE SONNETS, William Shakespeare. Over 150 exquisite poems deal with love, friendship, the tyranny of time, beauty's evanescence, death and other themes in language of remarkable power, precision and beauty. Glossary of archaic terms. 80pp. 5³⁄₁₆ x 8¼.   0-486-26686-9

HISTORIC HOMES OF THE AMERICAN PRESIDENTS, Second, Revised Edition, Irvin Haas. A traveler's guide to American Presidential homes, most open to the public, depicting and describing homes occupied by every American President from George Washington to George Bush. With visiting hours, admission charges, travel routes. 175 photographs. Index. 160pp. 8¼ x 11.   0-486-26751-2

THE WIT AND HUMOR OF OSCAR WILDE, Alvin Redman (ed.). More than 1,000 ripostes, paradoxes, wisecracks: Work is the curse of the drinking classes; I can resist everything except temptation; etc. 258pp. 5⅜ x 8½.   0-486-20602-5

SHAKESPEARE LEXICON AND QUOTATION DICTIONARY, Alexander Schmidt. Full definitions, locations, shades of meaning in every word in plays and poems. More than 50,000 exact quotations. 1,485pp. 6½ x 9¼. 2-vol. set.
Vol. 1: 0-486-22726-X   Vol. 2: 0-486-22727-8

SELECTED POEMS, Emily Dickinson. Over 100 best-known, best-loved poems by one of America's foremost poets, reprinted from authoritative early editions. No comparable edition at this price. Index of first lines. 64pp. 5³⁄₁₆ x 8¼. 0-486-26466-1

THE INSIDIOUS DR. FU-MANCHU, Sax Rohmer. The first of the popular mystery series introduces a pair of English detectives to their archnemesis, the diabolical Dr. Fu-Manchu. Flavorful atmosphere, fast-paced action, and colorful characters enliven this classic of the genre. 208pp. 5³⁄₁₆ x 8¼.   0-486-29898-1

THE MALLEUS MALEFICARUM OF KRAMER AND SPRENGER, translated by Montague Summers. Full text of most important witchhunter's "bible," used by both Catholics and Protestants. 278pp. 6⅝ x 10. 0-486-22802-9

SPANISH STORIES/CUENTOS ESPAÑOLES: A Dual-Language Book, Angel Flores (ed.). Unique format offers 13 great stories in Spanish by Cervantes, Borges, others. Faithful English translations on facing pages. 352pp. 5⅜ x 8½.
0-486-25399-6

GARDEN CITY, LONG ISLAND, IN EARLY PHOTOGRAPHS, 1869–1919, Mildred H. Smith. Handsome treasury of 118 vintage pictures, accompanied by carefully researched captions, document the Garden City Hotel fire (1899), the Vanderbilt Cup Race (1908), the first airmail flight departing from the Nassau Boulevard Aerodrome (1911), and much more. 96pp. 8⅞ x 11¾. 0-486-40669-5

OLD QUEENS, N.Y., IN EARLY PHOTOGRAPHS, Vincent F. Seyfried and William Asadorian. Over 160 rare photographs of Maspeth, Jamaica, Jackson Heights, and other areas. Vintage views of DeWitt Clinton mansion, 1939 World's Fair and more. Captions. 192pp. 8⅞ x 11. 0-486-26358-4

CAPTURED BY THE INDIANS: 15 Firsthand Accounts, 1750-1870, Frederick Drimmer. Astounding true historical accounts of grisly torture, bloody conflicts, relentless pursuits, miraculous escapes and more, by people who lived to tell the tale. 384pp. 5⅜ x 8½. 0-486-24901-8

THE WORLD'S GREAT SPEECHES (Fourth Enlarged Edition), Lewis Copeland, Lawrence W. Lamm, and Stephen J. McKenna. Nearly 300 speeches provide public speakers with a wealth of updated quotes and inspiration–from Pericles' funeral oration and William Jennings Bryan's "Cross of Gold Speech" to Malcolm X's powerful words on the Black Revolution and Earl of Spenser's tribute to his sister, Diana, Princess of Wales. 944pp. 5⅜ x 8⅜. 0-486-40903-1

THE BOOK OF THE SWORD, Sir Richard F. Burton. Great Victorian scholar/adventurer's eloquent, erudite history of the "queen of weapons"–from prehistory to early Roman Empire. Evolution and development of early swords, variations (sabre, broadsword, cutlass, scimitar, etc.), much more. 336pp. 6⅛ x 9¼.
0-486-25434-8

AUTOBIOGRAPHY: The Story of My Experiments with Truth, Mohandas K. Gandhi. Boyhood, legal studies, purification, the growth of the Satyagraha (nonviolent protest) movement. Critical, inspiring work of the man responsible for the freedom of India. 480pp. 5⅜ x 8½. (Available in U.S. only.) 0-486-24593-4

CELTIC MYTHS AND LEGENDS, T. W. Rolleston. Masterful retelling of Irish and Welsh stories and tales. Cuchulain, King Arthur, Deirdre, the Grail, many more. First paperback edition. 58 full-page illustrations. 512pp. 5⅜ x 8½. 0-486-26507-2

THE PRINCIPLES OF PSYCHOLOGY, William James. Famous long course complete, unabridged. Stream of thought, time perception, memory, experimental methods; great work decades ahead of its time. 94 figures. 1,391pp. 5⅜ x 8½. 2-vol. set.
Vol. I: 0-486-20381-6   Vol. II: 0-486-20382-4

THE WORLD AS WILL AND REPRESENTATION, Arthur Schopenhauer. Definitive English translation of Schopenhauer's life work, correcting more than 1,000 errors, omissions in earlier translations. Translated by E. F. J. Payne. Total of 1,269pp. 5⅜ x 8½. 2-vol. set.   Vol. 1: 0-486-21761-2   Vol. 2: 0-486-21762-0

MAGIC AND MYSTERY IN TIBET, Madame Alexandra David-Neel. Experiences among lamas, magicians, sages, sorcerers, Bonpa wizards. A true psychic discovery. 32 illustrations. 321pp. 5⅜ x 8½. (Available in U.S. only.) 0-486-22682-4

THE EGYPTIAN BOOK OF THE DEAD, E. A. Wallis Budge. Complete reproduction of Ani's papyrus, finest ever found. Full hieroglyphic text, interlinear transliteration, word-for-word translation, smooth translation. 533pp. 6½ x 9¼. 0-486-21866-X

HISTORIC COSTUME IN PICTURES, Braun & Schneider. Over 1,450 costumed figures in clearly detailed engravings–from dawn of civilization to end of 19th century. Captions. Many folk costumes. 256pp. 8⅜ x 11¾. 0-486-23150-X

MATHEMATICS FOR THE NONMATHEMATICIAN, Morris Kline. Detailed, college-level treatment of mathematics in cultural and historical context, with numerous exercises. Recommended Reading Lists. Tables. Numerous figures. 641pp. 5⅜ x 8½. 0-486-24823-2

PROBABILISTIC METHODS IN THE THEORY OF STRUCTURES, Isaac Elishakoff. Well-written introduction covers the elements of the theory of probability from two or more random variables, the reliability of such multivariable structures, the theory of random function, Monte Carlo methods of treating problems incapable of exact solution, and more. Examples. 502pp. 5⅜ x 8½. 0-486-40691-1

THE RIME OF THE ANCIENT MARINER, Gustave Doré, S. T. Coleridge. Doré's finest work; 34 plates capture moods, subtleties of poem. Flawless full-size reproductions printed on facing pages with authoritative text of poem. "Beautiful. Simply beautiful."–*Publisher's Weekly.* 77pp. 9¼ x 12. 0-486-22305-1

SCULPTURE: Principles and Practice, Louis Slobodkin. Step-by-step approach to clay, plaster, metals, stone; classical and modern. 253 drawings, photos. 255pp. 8⅛ x 11. 0-486-22960-2

THE INFLUENCE OF SEA POWER UPON HISTORY, 1660–1783, A. T. Mahan. Influential classic of naval history and tactics still used as text in war colleges. First paperback edition. 4 maps. 24 battle plans. 640pp. 5⅜ x 8½. 0-486-25509-3

THE STORY OF THE TITANIC AS TOLD BY ITS SURVIVORS, Jack Winocour (ed.). What it was really like. Panic, despair, shocking inefficiency, and a little heroism. More thrilling than any fictional account. 26 illustrations. 320pp. 5⅜ x 8½. 0-486-20610-6

ONE TWO THREE . . . INFINITY: Facts and Speculations of Science, George Gamow. Great physicist's fascinating, readable overview of contemporary science: number theory, relativity, fourth dimension, entropy, genes, atomic structure, much more. 128 illustrations. Index. 352pp. 5⅜ x 8½. 0-486-25664-2

DALÍ ON MODERN ART: The Cuckolds of Antiquated Modern Art, Salvador Dalí. Influential painter skewers modern art and its practitioners. Outrageous evaluations of Picasso, Cézanne, Turner, more. 15 renderings of paintings discussed. 44 calligraphic decorations by Dalí. 96pp. 5⅜ x 8½. (Available in U.S. only.) 0-486-29220-7

ANTIQUE PLAYING CARDS: A Pictorial History, Henry René D'Allemagne. Over 900 elaborate, decorative images from rare playing cards (14th–20th centuries): Bacchus, death, dancing dogs, hunting scenes, royal coats of arms, players cheating, much more. 96pp. 9¼ x 12¼. 0-486-29265-7

MAKING FURNITURE MASTERPIECES: 30 Projects with Measured Drawings, Franklin H. Gottshall. Step-by-step instructions, illustrations for constructing handsome, useful pieces, among them a Sheraton desk, Chippendale chair, Spanish desk, Queen Anne table and a William and Mary dressing mirror. 224pp. 8⅛ x 11¼. 0-486-29338-6

NORTH AMERICAN INDIAN DESIGNS FOR ARTISTS AND CRAFTSPEOPLE, Eva Wilson. Over 360 authentic copyright-free designs adapted from Navajo blankets, Hopi pottery, Sioux buffalo hides, more. Geometrics, symbolic figures, plant and animal motifs, etc. 128pp. 8⅜ x 11. (Not for sale in the United Kingdom.) 0-486-25341-4

THE FOSSIL BOOK: A Record of Prehistoric Life, Patricia V. Rich et al. Profusely illustrated definitive guide covers everything from single-celled organisms and dinosaurs to birds and mammals and the interplay between climate and man. Over 1,500 illustrations. 760pp. 7½ x 10⅛. 0-486-29371-8

VICTORIAN ARCHITECTURAL DETAILS: Designs for Over 700 Stairs, Mantels, Doors, Windows, Cornices, Porches, and Other Decorative Elements, A. J. Bicknell & Company. Everything from dormer windows and piazzas to balconies and gable ornaments. Also includes elevations and floor plans for handsome, private residences and commercial structures. 80pp. 9⅜ x 12¼. 0-486-44015-X

WESTERN ISLAMIC ARCHITECTURE: A Concise Introduction, John D. Hoag. Profusely illustrated critical appraisal compares and contrasts Islamic mosques and palaces–from Spain and Egypt to other areas in the Middle East. 139 illustrations. 128pp. 6 x 9. 0-486-43760-4

CHINESE ARCHITECTURE: A Pictorial History, Liang Ssu-ch'eng. More than 240 rare photographs and drawings depict temples, pagodas, tombs, bridges, and imperial palaces comprising much of China's architectural heritage. 152 halftones, 94 diagrams. 232pp. 10¾ x 9⅞. 0-486-43999-2

THE RENAISSANCE: Studies in Art and Poetry, Walter Pater. One of the most talked-about books of the 19th century, *The Renaissance* combines scholarship and philosophy in an innovative work of cultural criticism that examines the achievements of Botticelli, Leonardo, Michelangelo, and other artists. "The holy writ of beauty."–Oscar Wilde. 160pp. 5⅜ x 8½. 0-486-44025-7

A TREATISE ON PAINTING, Leonardo da Vinci. The great Renaissance artist's practical advice on drawing and painting techniques covers anatomy, perspective, composition, light and shadow, and color. A classic of art instruction, it features 48 drawings by Nicholas Poussin and Leon Battista Alberti. 192pp. 5⅜ x 8½. 0-486-44155-5

THE MIND OF LEONARDO DA VINCI, Edward McCurdy. More than just a biography, this classic study by a distinguished historian draws upon Leonardo's extensive writings to offer numerous demonstrations of the Renaissance master's achievements, not only in sculpture and painting, but also in music, engineering, and even experimental aviation. 384pp. 5⅜ x 8½. 0-486-44142-3

WASHINGTON IRVING'S RIP VAN WINKLE, Illustrated by Arthur Rackham. Lovely prints that established artist as a leading illustrator of the time and forever etched into the popular imagination a classic of Catskill lore. 51 full-color plates. 80pp. 8⅜ x 11. 0-486-44242-X

HENSCHE ON PAINTING, John W. Robichaux. Basic painting philosophy and methodology of a great teacher, as expounded in his famous classes and workshops on Cape Cod. 7 illustrations in color on covers. 80pp. 5⅜ x 8½. 0-486-43728-0

CATALOG OF DOVER BOOKS

LIGHT AND SHADE: A Classic Approach to Three-Dimensional Drawing, Mrs. Mary P. Merrifield. Handy reference clearly demonstrates principles of light and shade by revealing effects of common daylight, sunshine, and candle or artificial light on geometrical solids. 13 plates. 64pp. 5⅜ x 8½. 0-486-44143-1

ASTROLOGY AND ASTRONOMY: A Pictorial Archive of Signs and Symbols, Ernst and Johanna Lehner. Treasure trove of stories, lore, and myth, accompanied by more than 300 rare illustrations of planets, the Milky Way, signs of the zodiac, comets, meteors, and other astronomical phenomena. 192pp. 8⅜ x 11. 0-486-43981-X

JEWELRY MAKING: Techniques for Metal, Tim McCreight. Easy-to-follow instructions and carefully executed illustrations describe tools and techniques, use of gems and enamels, wire inlay, casting, and other topics. 72 line illustrations and diagrams. 176pp. 8¼ x 10⅞. 0-486-44043-5

MAKING BIRDHOUSES: Easy and Advanced Projects, Gladstone Califf. Easy-to-follow instructions include diagrams for everything from a one-room house for bluebirds to a forty-two-room structure for purple martins. 56 plates; 4 figures. 80pp. 8¾ x 6⅜. 0-486-44183-0

LITTLE BOOK OF LOG CABINS: How to Build and Furnish Them, William S. Wicks. Handy how-to manual, with instructions and illustrations for building cabins in the Adirondack style, fireplaces, stairways, furniture, beamed ceilings, and more. 102 line drawings. 96pp. 8¾ x 6⅜. 0-486-44259-4

THE SEASONS OF AMERICA PAST, Eric Sloane. From "sugaring time" and strawberry picking to Indian summer and fall harvest, a whole year's activities described in charming prose and enhanced with 79 of the author's own illustrations. 160pp. 8¼ x 11. 0-486-44220-9

THE METROPOLIS OF TOMORROW, Hugh Ferriss. Generous, prophetic vision of the metropolis of the future, as perceived in 1929. Powerful illustrations of towering structures, wide avenues, and rooftop parks–all features in many of today's modern cities. 59 illustrations. 144pp. 8¼ x 11. 0-486-43727-2

THE PATH TO ROME, Hilaire Belloc. This 1902 memoir abounds in lively vignettes from a vanished time, recounting a pilgrimage on foot across the Alps and Apennines in order to "see all Europe which the Christian Faith has saved." 77 of the author's original line drawings complement his sparkling prose. 272pp. 5⅜ x 8½. 0-486-44001-X

THE HISTORY OF RASSELAS: Prince of Abissinia, Samuel Johnson. Distinguished English writer attacks eighteenth-century optimism and man's unrealistic estimates of what life has to offer. 112pp. 5⅜ x 8½. 0-486-44094-X

A VOYAGE TO ARCTURUS, David Lindsay. A brilliant flight of pure fancy, where wild creatures crowd the fantastic landscape and demented torturers dominate victims with their bizarre mental powers. 272pp. 5⅜ x 8½. 0-486-44198-9

Paperbound unless otherwise indicated. Available at your book dealer, online at **www.doverpublications.com**, or by writing to Dept. GI, Dover Publications, Inc., 31 East 2nd Street, Mineola, NY 11501. For current price information or for free catalogs (please indicate field of interest), write to Dover Publications or log on to **www.doverpublications.com** and see every Dover book in print. Dover publishes more than 500 books each year on science, elementary and advanced mathematics, biology, music, art, literary history, social sciences, and other areas.